ABNORMAL
PSYCHOLOGY

ABNORMAL PSYCHOLOGY
Its Experience and Behaviour

PETER McKELLAR

ROUTLEDGE
LONDON AND NEW YORK

First published in 1989 by Routledge
11 New Fetter Lane, London EC4P 4EE
29 West 35th Street, New York, NY 10001

© 1989 Peter McKellar

Typeset by J&L Composition Ltd, Filey, N. Yorkshire
Printed and bound in Great Britain by
Mackays of Chatham PLC, Chatham, Kent

British Library Cataloguing in Publication Data
McKellar, Peter
Abnormal psychology, its experience and
behaviour.
1. Abnormal psychology
I. Title
157

ISBN 0–415–02812–4
0–415–03132–X (pbk)

Library of Congress Cataloging in Publication Data
also available

For Victoria and little James:
her second book, and his first

CONTENTS

CONTENTS

ILLUSTRATIONS

PREFACE

My friend, two different universes walk about under your hat and mine.

Thackeray, quoted by William James

Psychology is defined by William James as 'the science of mental life'. In exploring this subject matter, this book has two points of emphasis. First, it seeks to provide a basis, a frame of reference, to assist understanding of psychological phenomena which are, or seem to be, abnormal. Second, it examines the relation of these to subjective experiences of people we regard as normal. In both tasks I believe we are greatly helped by one of the characteristic features of psychological phenomena: the differences people exhibit from one another. To enter imaginatively into the mental life of a neurotic or psychotic patient may seem difficult: there are many barriers to such empathy. But similar difficulties occur, because of hidden differences individuals also reveal in everyday life. The motives, emotional life, and waking or sleeping imagery of people we know may be surprisingly 'different'. In extending empathy we may be alerted to notice aspects of our own personality: aspects that have led some psychologists to postulate 'unconscious' mental life. Other theorists have preferred an alternative formulation which will much concern us: the notion of sub-systems of the personality and dissociation within it. In wakefulness, the dreamlife of sleep, and in experiences of the drowsy, intervening hypnagogic state we encounter many hidden differences.

Dreams were for Freud not only the 'royal road' to the

unconscious, but also a guide to the understanding of the neuroses. Others like Jung, and many predecessors, viewed the schizophrenic psychoses as an invasion of wakefulness by dreamlike upsurges. Many people in everyday life report the false waking experience; some report lucid dreams, of being aware that they are having a dream while asleep; others experience illusion in pre-sleep states of changes in the shape or size of their bodily self; and some have been aroused from this drowsy state before sleep to answer a purely hallucinatory telephone or doorbell.

What men and women do, their behaviour, becomes more understandable when we know more about their experience: the subjective orientation of their mental life. Psychology is concerned with this two-fold subject matter and the diversity of individual differences it reveals. And what it reveals may be surprising. During her Ph.D. oral examination one postgraduate explained to us how she had come to choose her thesis subject, an investigation of imagery differences. 'My husband is a great visualiser,' she told us, 'but it took me twenty years of marriage before I discovered this.' By contrast with him, she lacked visual imagery in her own subjective equipment for thinking, remembering, and imagining. Darwin's cousin, Sir Francis Galton, found evidence in his early investigation of such differences, a continuum of visual imagery ranging from its virtual absence to vividness of the 'hallucination' kind. In exploring such hidden differences between people we encounter three main types of reaction. Some people wrongly assume that everybody is like themselves. Others become preoccupied with some innocent variant of normal experience, feel isolated and in some way different, and allow it to become a focus of anxiety, even of fears about their sanity. Others again are tempted to resort to supernatural interpretation of such phenomena as false waking illusions, out-of-the-body experiences, and hypnagogic imagery. As Galton stressed in relation to 'visionary' experiences, a culture may encourage supernaturalism. In more recent times the anthropologist Erika Bourguignon found the notion of 'spirit possession' widespread in African countries and some form of 'institutionally encouraged dissociation' in the majority of a wide range of cultures she studied. Issues which interest anthropology and the psychology of the allegedly supernatural will thus concern us.

Along with individual and cross-cultural differences, in attempting a frame of reference to this subject matter, I have taken account of certain neglected ideas from the history of psychology. Moreover, many of the earlier investigators considered have often exhibited imagination and enterprise in their exploratory experiments. Thus Galton in one sought to enter into the mental life of paranoia, and in another into that of an idolater. William James experimented with the effects of nitrous oxide on himself, and from Louis Lewin and Klüver onwards, many have employed hallucinogens in self-experiments. Kleitman and others have investigated hallucinatory effects of severe sleep deprivation. And there have even been those, like Hervey de Saint Denys and Van Eeden, who have conducted experiments on themselves while actually asleep. In his work in New Guinea, Sir Hugh Robson challenged the supernatural beliefs that prevailed by inviting the local practitioners of witchcraft to produce kuru in himself. Silberer's studies of hypnagogic thinking opened up an important, though for a time neglected, new approach to introspective psychology. The study by Rosenhan discussed in Chapter 1 represents the type of experiment which not every investigator would be willing to repeat. There are many stressful and uncomfortable techniques like, for example, sensory deprivation which enterprising pioneers have employed. Thus sometimes they have had to use themselves as their own subjects. Obviously, as a science psychology must build on carefully controlled experiments which – sometimes from the animal laboratory – have contributed valuable information, also therapy techniques in such areas as the psychology of learning. Today this also applies even to subjects like hypnotism. Yet we owe something, as I have tried to show, to preliminary, imaginative, often loosely controlled experiments, especially in the study of altered states of consciousness.

The growing points, as opposed to the dead wood, of a discipline are often to be found on its frontiers. Psychology is too important a human enterprise to be left only to card-carrying professionals. Although as a science it belongs, broadly speaking, with biology, as I will try to show, it has also had things to learn from the arts. In the human imaginings we know as literature, writers have drawn on observations of behaviour and on introspection in creating their characters. Thus while paying attention to principles and generalizations that concern science I have also given some weight to human individuality as portrayed by writers and dramatists.

ACKNOWLEDGEMENTS

I will relate my acknowledgements to areas of psychology given special emphasis in this book. In studying hypnagogic imagery I am indebted to Mrs Lorna Simpson for collaboration in our early questionnaire investigations; in the later period to Messrs Robert Guyton and Philip Scadden, whose intensive studies also provided drawings and paintings; and finally to Dr Andreas Mavromatis for ideas that emerged in discussion of this fascinating topic of mutual interest. In the area of mental imagery more generally I gratefully acknowledge longstanding and stimulating collaboration with Professor David Marks; Dr Akhter Ahsen for valued discussions of eidetic imagery and imagery therapy; and, in an earlier period, Dr Rosemary Gordon. Our experiments with hallucinogens, which I have re-examined, were conducted some years ago at Aberdeen University Medical School. In collaboration on these I am indebted to Dr Stuart Boyd and Dr Max Valentine, and to our subsequent research team: the late Dr Amor Ardis, Professor Elizabeth Fraser, Dr James Drewery, and again Mrs Lorna Simpson. My earliest inquiries into states of hypnosis involved working with Professor John Money, and in the recent period Professor Marks and Mr John Baird.

I was fortunate in being Secretary of one British Psychological Society Committee chaired by the late Professor T. H. Pear, and thus learning from him many things about the unjustifiably neglected psychology of sentiments, with the benefit of his first-hand memories of its relevant pioneers, William McDougall and Alexander Shand. My own Ph.D. research was on sentiments and emotions in the area of human aggression, supervised by the late Professor Sir Cyril Burt, whose kindly, impressive scholarship I remember with great respect. Any university teacher learns much from his students, and in this case they have included, in the area of forensic psychology, classes of police officers and magistrates, from whom I learned, if at times rather ruefully.

Intellectually, as a psychologist I owe much not only to colleagues but also to the recorded work of some of the great figures of the past. In the area of dissociation of the personality these have been William James, Pierre Janet, Morton Prince, and William McDougall, and in recent years the contemporary researches of Ernest Hilgard. Outside psychology intellectual debts have been, in my case, to Schopenhauer, Nietzsche, and – within literature – Coleridge and Dostoevsky. These acknowledgements will help to define the frame of reference to abnormal psychology I have attempted to provide in this book. Its limits of perspective, omissions, and errors I finally acknowledge. They are my own.

Peter McKellar

Chapter One

THE SCIENCE OF EXPERIENCE AND BEHAVIOUR

If to have *feelings or thoughts in their immediacy were enough, babies in the cradle would be psychologists, and infallible ones.*

William James

Psychology deals with *communication* about mental life. This is difficult enough in the realm of the normal. Consider dreams. They are not easy to communicate in words, usually being visual. So also are the mysterious internal displays – like lantern-slides – which some people report in the drowsy state before sleep, known to psychology as hypnagogic images. Many mental events of full wakefulness are similarly pictorial, not verbal, in character. It is not always easy to say what one 'sees when looking into one's mind'. The British psychologist Mace illuminates the point made by William James, his American predecessor. 'This is not because it is difficult to *see* what is there. The difficulty is to *say* what you see – to say it in a clear, correct, and illuminating way' (Mace 1950: 242). Acute frustration is common for many people at discrepancies between what they experience and what they can say. Communication problems, difficult enough in normal mental life, become formidable when we turn to abnormal psychology. First, a brief look at history.

HISTORICAL ORIENTATION

Like the physical sciences, psychology's history extends back more than 2,000 years. Its modern period begins with William James

(1842–1910). Many would still regard him as their ideal psychologist. Consider three things about him. First, he could communicate in vivid, electric prose about subtle and complex mental processes: William James is lucid even on such subjects as mystical states of consciousness. Second, he added living tissue to the dry bones of laboratory experiments by also taking account of psychiatric patients. Hypnotism and dissociation, fugues and somnambulisms, imagery and hallucinations interested him. All found a place in his robust approach to psychology. Third, William James insisted that introspection, as well as external observation, had a legitimate place in the developing science. Within this broad spectrum of interests he maintained a naturalistic standpoint. In this he remained true to a tradition established 2,000 years earlier.

Foundations of psychology as a branch of science were laid by Aristotle (384–322 BC). These were built on the still earlier thought of Socrates and Plato, but for Aristotle 'the soul' was something different. For him it is better labelled as the distinguishing attribute of the organic, the characteristic of the living things he described and classified. Supernatural overtones were absent: Aristotle's approach was fundamentally naturalistic. He studied psychology very much as it is still studied today: 'mind' with reference to its underlying biology. Aristotle treated the functioning of the organism in sleep and dreamlife – no less than the thinking and perception of wakefulness – as legitimate subject matter for naturalistic inquiry. His ideas on logic and ethics have also influenced psychology. In logic he distinguished and classified the different kinds of human thinking. Within ethics he classified virtues and vices as habits; thus he emphasized both the learning process, and the ethical neutrality of the raw materials of human nature. He prepared the way for a value-free development of psychology bereft of supernatural overtones. The doings of the gods and goddesses of Olympus played no part in Aristotle's view of physical nature or human affairs.

Early Greek developments in medicine made a parallel contribution. With Hippocrates (c.460–357 BC) came treatment of both mental and physical illnesses by the methods of a medical orthodoxy that he established. This tradition, along with Aristotle's, survives today in some – certainly not all – parts of the modern world. Supernaturalism still prevails in many areas of culture:

mental illness is diagnosed in such terms as 'spirit possession', with treatment by exorcism. Psychologists interested in cross-cultural studies and the history of ideas, as well as clinicians – medical or psychological – may also have their contribution to provide. Psychiatry is the branch of medicine concerned with diagnosis and treatment of mental illnesses, and today clinical psychologists work closely with their medical colleagues. From the history of conditions they deal with I will take four aspects, each illustrated by a specific contribution.

Basic reform

Within Europe the long struggle with both inhumanity and demonology has been well documented. It is dealt with by Hunter and MacAlpine (1963), who have edited the writings of the major reformers themselves. As illustration take the work of Robert Gardiner Hill, who in the England of the 1880s struggled, but with considerable success, for the total abolition of irons, strait-waistcoats, and other primitive methods of restraint in asylums. His principle was lucid and clear-cut: 'Restraint is never necessary, never justifiable, and always injurious, in all cases of lunacy whatever' (Quoted in Hunter and MacAlpine 1963: 890). Although much has been achieved, much still remains to be done in the modern world on even such basic matters as the principle stated and acted upon by reformers like Hill in England and Pinel in France.

Hypnosis and hypnotism

Mesmer's conception of 'animal magnetism' led him and his disciples into clashes with the rival camp of the exorcists. Eventually there emerged a new orientation. It was a recognition of the importance of human suggestibility, and the uses of hypnotism as a method of therapy. Pierre Janet (1859–1947) was thus led to argue that 'the experimental phenomena created under hypnosis simulate hysterical disabilities, so it is reasonable that the same procedure could remove them' (Janet 1899: 888). We shall be concerned later with the importance of Janet's often neglected contributions to hypnotism, automatisms, and dissociation of the personality.

Psychoanalysis

With Freud and his successors came detailed study and considerable interest in humane treatment of patients as individuals, in the area of neuroses. Freud himself assessed the division of mental life into conscious and unconscious as 'the fundamental premise of psychoanalysis'.

There are many possible interpretations of the notion of 'unconscious', dealt with in the very important historical study by Ellenberger (1970). Outside consciousness there are perhaps several such systems.

Learning and conditioning

From neurology emerged the work of Pavlov on the conditioned reflex, and from psychology the laboratory study of learning. An important derivative was a re-orientation to psychiatric problems as maladaptive learning, and to therapy conceptualized as a re-learning process. In developing such behaviour therapy Eysenck (1952) argued that neurotic behaviour should proceed from our 'knowledge gained in the laboratory of learning and conditioning'.

EXPERIENCE AND BEHAVIOUR

Psychology owes a very great deal to medical science, and not only to psychiatry as one of its specialized branches. In diagnosis, prognosis, and treatment medical practitioners use two kinds of information. These are observable 'signs' on the one hand, and also 'symptoms' reported by patients to them. Psychology recognizes today – though there are exceptions – a parallel two-fold subject matter. On the one hand it deals with behaviour, what people and other organisms can be observed to do; on the other it draws on information about subjective experience, studied by introspection. Introspection is sometimes labelled 'verbal report', though it is not restricted to this kind of communication: drawings and paintings are also used. There are different kinds of introspection: as Boring (1953) indicated in his paper on the history of these methods, instrospecting has functioned under a huge variety of 'aliases'. Both William James and Mace – we have seen – have stressed that introspection involves not only having an experience but in some way communicating it. Elsewhere (1962) I once attempted to distinguish some of the different types and purposes of introspection. To illustrate, different from laboratory situations are occasions when an intelligent and sensitive individual, not necessarily a psychologist, reports on conditions of inhuman hardship he has endured. Dostoevsky's *House of the Dead*, about exile in Siberia, and Bettelheim's diary of his imprisonment in Nazi concentration camps are, among others, outstanding examples. Likewise Koestler (1954) describing extreme hunger, Kleitman (1939) on effects of sleep deprivation, or Weir Mitchell (1896) on altered states of consciousness induced by mescaline, all differ from routine laboratory kinds of introspection. We are wise to take account of them.

The apparent gap between external observation and introspection which troubled early behaviourists like J. B. Watson and E. B. Holt, has narrowed since their time. Very important was a research breakthrough of the 1950s during Kleitman's studies of sleep, namely 'a method of objectively recording incidence and duration of dreaming' (Kleitman 1963: 92). It was in fact a rediscovery, and Kleitman acknowledges both the earlier observations of Ladd (1892) and the somewhat remarkable overlooking of information in this earlier, widely read paper. Kleitman records 'in our own laboratory we literally stumbled on an objective method of studying dreaming while exploring eye motility in adults' (Kleitman op. cit.: 92). Later I will discuss another anticipation in the related introspections of 'Sally' in the Miss Beauchamp multiple personality case that a great deal more dreaming goes on than is often recognized (see Chapter 4). Anyway, by now a scientifically respectable linkage between experience and behaviour has been established, and so we no longer distinguish dreamers from non-dreamers, but rather those who do and those who don't recall and report the often strange events of mental life during sleep. Jerome Singer (1966) was able to report on waking fantasies also in a book sub-titled 'The experimental study of

5

inner experience'. Since the vigorous advances that have occurred in this area, another discovery has been made. Again it relates to sleep experience. An atypical phenomenon is lucid dreams in which the dreamer remains aware that he is asleep and dreaming. In this case also, recordable accompaniments of subjective imagery have been found (Green 1968b; Hearne 1981). Earlier investigators, notably Saint Denys (1867) and Van Eeden (1913), sought ways of communicating while lucid dreaming across the barrier dividing being asleep from being awake. They sought ways of telling others that they were having dreams, and knew they were. Modern researchers have returned to such issues.

In approaching the problems of abnormal psychology two things help. They are individual differences and study of altered mental states. We may be tempted to assess individuals who differ markedly from ourself as 'abnormal'. Again in altered states of consciousness, including sleep and dreaming, there are occasions when we come closer to an understanding of psychosis, neurosis, and other forms of abnormality. In considering variations between individuals, pioneers like Sir Francis Galton found enormous diversity; parochial disbelief and intolerance between people who differed; and a continuum ranging from lack of capacity for visual thinking up to and including visual hallucination. Availability of altered states of consciousness to normal people has interested many psychologists. Among them may be mentioned Freud on dreams; Silberer on the drowsy pre-sleep hypnagogic state; Klüver and many others on the effects of mescaline and a variety of other hallucinogens; and many investigators of the hypnotic state from Mesmer to contemporary experimental researchers.

In a book that is entitled *Abnormal Psychology* we are thus much concerned both with variations of subjective mental life between normal people, and with altered mental states available to them. A provisional definition may be offered from this standpoint. 'Abnormal psychology is the scientific study of experiences and behaviour that seem to be, or are, abnormal.' The word 'abnormal' has several relevant meanings. First is its usage in a quasi-medical sense to refer to illness or disease. This has particular relevance to conditions like the organic psychoses, when the disturbances of experience and behaviour have direct relation to brain injury, infection, or toxic effects of chemical agencies such as drugs of misuse or alcohol. Second is a statistical usage in the sense of deviation from the norm. Some forms of 'abnormality' are unusual. Some vary from accepted social norms of a given geographical or temporal area of culture. What is culturally abnormal in one society can be both commonplace and socially acceptable in another. Even in the twentieth century there are many parts of the world where subjective experiences that we would interpret naturalistically are regarded otherwise. Violation of a taboo, antagonizing a witch, or spirit possession are accepted causal agents. Again, some forms of possession are socially valued. Third, by 'abnormal' we may imply some failure of adjustment. Conflict is closely associated with such maladjustment, and is of two main kinds: conflict with other people, and intra-psychic conflict within oneself.

It was intra-psychic conflict which mainly interested Freud, and he formulated his triad of ego, id, and superego better to understand it. The interactions of sub-systems within the person-ality will much concern us. Here we encounter concepts and constructs as devices that assist, and sometimes impede, the task of scientific understanding.

CLASSIFICATION, DIAGNOSIS, AND INDIVIDUALITY

Diagnostic categories and systems of classification have their uses and limitations. Such limitations apply to the longstanding traditional psychiatric categories of 'neurosis' and 'psychosis'. Neurosis refers to the 'lesser' syndromes or groups of signs and symptoms characterized by 'insight' on the part of the patient. Defined by enumeration these include anxiety states, hysteria, neurotic depressions, and a group of neuroses called 'anankastic'. Anankastic reactions comprise compulsions, obsessions, and phobias. By contrast, in psychosis or 'major' psychiatric illness, the sufferer 'lacks insight', for example because delusions impede thinking or hallucinations largely replace perception of external reality. Two sub-categories are in use. Along with 'organic psychoses' such as delirium tremens, or general paralysis (GPI) with a known pathology of brain lesions, are 'the functional psychoses' which lack a known cause. These are paranoia, the schizophrenias, and the manic-depressive psychoses. Many alternative diagnostic systems exist and define these or similar categories and sub-categories. Widely used is the diagnostic system of the American Psychiatric Association, the DSM III and its predecessors (DSM I and DSM II). In its third revision the 1980 DSM III system has incidentally dropped use of the category of 'neurosis' and the sub-category 'hysteria'. Many of the alternative systems retain both.

Immediately we encounter problems of diagnostic criteria that are cross-cultural or cross-temporal. To illustrate, the DSM III has greatly narrowed down the category of 'schizophrenia'. As Warner (1985: 17) points out, until the mid-1970s this was an extremely broad one. It meant that many patients labelled schizophrenic in the United States elsewhere 'would have been considered manic-depressive or non-psychotic'. Another accompaniment of this narrowing-down in the DSM III has been distinguishing multiple personality as a diagnostic sub-category within dissociative disorders. Until 1980 this was merely listed as a symptom (Coons 1984). Thus in the late 1980s American psychiatrists are now dealing with whole series of multiple personality patients hitherto believed to represent an extremely rare condition. Resulting incidence must obviously be seen in relation to changes in diagnostic criteria. Influential in establishing many of the categories of the classification systems in use was the work of the German psychiatrist Emile Kraepelin (1856–1926). There are very many such systems. In a study for the World Health Organization Erwin Stengel even in 1959 discussed no less than thirty-eight of them.

Within psychology, personality typologies share many of the limitations of psychiatric diagnostic systems. They are constructs. Like the geographer's lines of latitude and longitude on the map – possessing 'length but no breadth' – for some purposes they provide useful systems of reference. William James used the categories of 'tender-minded' and 'tough-minded' in relation to temperament and attitudes. Various studies by Eysenck (1961) used this James typology as the basis of a measurable attitude trait. Application of this is to be found in the fact that we can often predict a given individual's attitude to one issue from a knowledge of his attitudes to others. Thus a person who is tough-minded about the upbringing of children tends also to be tough-minded towards prison or mental hospital reform. A very large number of typologies have been thought up and often form the basis of tests of measurable traits. A good example is Spranger's approach to personality in the 1930s. Spranger saw personality in terms of six values or long-term motivations: they comprise a dominant concern with respectively truth, beauty, usefulness, human welfare, power, and religion. Best known of all is the typology introduced by Jung (1953) which involves not merely introverts and extra-verts, but also four function types. These relate to dominance or otherwise of the functions of thinking, feeling, sensation, and intuition as personality characteristics. In the research of Eysenck and his colleagues introversion–extraversion has received con-siderable attention as a measurable and basic dimension of personality.

Despite typologies and diagnostic labels, human beings exhibit some remarkable heights of inconsistency. Pressures from a given social situation may be influential, as when a person who is ordinarily a sociable extravert in the company of relative strangers behaves like a shy introvert. In these areas abnormal psychology has its experimental aspects. Hypnotically induced behaviour can closely resemble phenomena of the hysterical neuroses on the one hand, and also – it is claimed by some investigators – criminal actions on the other. Again in experiments with sensory deprivation or hallucinogenic substances it is possible to simulate, in otherwise normal volunteer subjects, not only hallucination but a variety of other psychotic phenomena. Both areas will be considered. 'Intelligence' is a word that refers not only to a trait difference between people, but also to the level of thinking of the same person on different occasions. Under the influence of emotion, for example fluster, an otherwise intelligent person may act in a remarkably stupid way. Likewise, emotional habits such as super-stitions, prejudices, and phobias ensure that levels of intellectual functioning are uneven. In one of his lesser-known works Freud makes this point, while also noting our tendency to ignore it. He refers to 'an astonishing fact, and one that is too generally overlooked ... people of the most powerful intelligence react as though they were feeble-minded' (Freud 1907, edition 1959: 71).

As constructs, nouns in typologies and diagnosis have a place. But along with them in considering behaviour it is realistic to take account also of adjectives and adverbs. Variability is all-important in actions, as in thinking. As regards the area of beliefs and opinions, we regularly encounter logic-tight compartments: however logically deplorable, this is psychologically commonplace. Inconsistencies of behaviour point to the fact that the degree of integration of a given personality is itself an important personality variable. Henry Murray (1938; 1943) uses the term 'conjunctivity–disjunctivity' as a name for this attribute. One of Murray's early collaborators, S. S. Rosenzweig, who became interested in the study of frustration, introduced a somewhat related concept. This is 'frustration tolerance', defined as the amount of stress a given individual can endure without developing psychiatric disturbance (Rosenzweig in ed. Murray 1938; Rosenzweig 1944). This is viewed by Rosenzweig in terms of the extent to which the personality 'holds together' with component parts organized into a well-integrated system. Under the stress of inhuman conditions of imprisonment it has been well established that powerfully developed master sentiments, like strong religious faith, have maintained morale and with it normality. In various hospitals I have interviewed patients who I believe would never have developed psychiatric breakdown but for severe ill-treatment during imprisonment under wartime conditions.

In attempting to understand neurosis or psychosis we encounter both predisposing and precipitating factors: personality and the pressures on it. Relevant is stress and the different kinds of stress that the individual concerned has endured, or is still enduring. On the side of personality, since it is mostly impossible to distinguish genetic from early learning factors, I will use the term 'constitutional' to refer to both. From 'constitutional predisposition' may be distinguished 'precipitating factors' operating from outside. 'Stress' is a very general term for one kind of environmental pressure: its different types include physical pain, humiliation, bereavement, loss of occupation, and being left destitute by riot, natural catastrophe, or war. There are also positive environmental forces acting on the personality: parents or good Samaritans who support, acquaintances who give encouragement, and friends or groups turned to at times of low morale. In elucidating the interactions of the individual with environmental forces, both positive and negative, I will here and later draw on one particular theory. It involves two basic concepts.

NEED AND PRESS

The theory, using these and other concepts, derives from the work of the Harvard psychologist, Henry Murray. He is well known also for his authorship of a widely used projective test, the TAT (Thematic Apperception Test). The two basic concepts comprise 'need', or motivational forces that operate from the side of personality, and 'press' or forces that stem from the environment (Murray 1938; 1943). Apart from needs that are common to the species are those which characterize the personality of a given individual. Thus 'need autonomy' (*n*. autonomy) may distinguish people strongly motivated to instigate their own actions, go their own way, and resist coercion by others. Again, '*n*. achievement' may be a dominant motive in some, but not other, people, while '*n*. nurturance' – to support, sustain and give comfort to others – is an often admired personality attribute.

The second concept is 'press' (plural press). Similar words to those employed to specify needs can often be used with press. Thus an individual may have to make adjustment to '*p*. achievement': a social environment of ambitious other people with whom he or she has to compete. Again, people may be subjected to '*p*. nurturance', strong support from mother, father, or friends, or alternatively '*p*. aggression', as negative environment forces in the home or at work. In taking a case history the sources of press can be specified. Thus a person may have had to adjust to '*p*. aggression' from being bullied at school, while also experiencing '*p*. counteraction' (don't give up, stand your ground) from the home. Positive press may stem from one parent, perhaps the father, and negative press from perhaps the mother, as happened for example in the multiple personality case of Sybil (Schreiber 1975). Recent studies of groups of patients diagnosed as multiple personality give evidence of association of this syndrome with a history of cruelty experienced as a child (Wilbur 1984). As regards this type of negative press it is well known to paediatricians that parents responsible for inflicting suffering on their children have often themselves experienced similar treatment in childhood. Here press seems to have generated a need towards its repetition. As in this case, suffering does not necessarily ennoble: on the contrary it may brutalize its victim.

There may be important differences between perception of environmental pressures and the realities. What has happened, or what is happening to a given person may be misperceived. False expectancy, rumour, stereotypes, and, in extreme cases, delusion and hallucination can all contribute to the discrepancy. Murray's press theory takes account of this in a distinction between 'alpha press' (perceived) and 'beta press' (actual realities). Interviews with a patient will reveal his or her perceived press, but where possible a check on the underlying realities of what actually happened is highly desirable. Behaviour takes place within the perceived environment: this involves a very basic concept of psychology, discussed later in this chapter, which I have called the 'Koffka Principle'. Murray's emphasis on these two types of force in mental life, needs from within the personality and press from the environment, has considerable relevance to stress in abnormal psychology. An illustration emerges from the study of juvenile excursions into criminality. In his classic investigation of this area, Sir Cyril Burt (1937) stresses individuality in punishment history: the under-punished child, the over-punished child, and the inconsistently punished child. As Burt argues, in dealing with offenders it is important which of these may be involved. Although his terminology is different, Burt's point is similar to Murray's. Other of Murray's kinds of press may also be relevant to treatment. Thus allies may be sought in the '*p*. nurturance' – of a kindly schoolteacher – or perhaps '*p*. counteraction' enlisted from within the home environment. We may also need to ascertain from which sources the probably highly relevant history of punishment stems. On the concept of press I suggest an intro-spective exercise. The reader might like to review the main types of press personally experienced during the past week, and perhaps also the needs which have erupted or been evoked by these environmental pressures, both positive and negative.

Others may not have been as fortunate as ourselves, and an example may be taken.

A FIELD STUDY

The field in question was the psychiatric hospital environment. Involved were imagination, deception, plus a considerable amount of courage. Rosenhan (1973) organized an experiment in which eight people with no obvious psychiatric problems gained access as patients to a number of psychiatric hospitals. Rosenhan himself was the first of these pseudo-patients, the deception being known only to the hospital administrator and the principal psychiatrist. The volunteers presented themselves at the admissions office, complaining of hearing voices, with a number of other non-existent signs and symptoms. Twelve hospitals were involved. Seven of the volunteers were diagnosed as schizophrenic, and one as manic-depressive psychosis. After being admitted to the hospitals, the pseudo-patients acted normally, and if questioned, related significant events of their life histories, dealings with parents, siblings, and other such matters as they had actually occurred. After periods in the hospitals ranging from seven to fifty-two days, all were discharged. Rosenhan asserts that the deceptions apparently were not detected during the time within the hospitals.

Among many thought-provoking features of the study is evidence it provides of how easy it is to confuse normal and abnormal behaviour. As Rosenhan put it, 'a psychiatric label has a life and an influence of its own' (1973: 253). Once an impression has been formed of 'schizophrenia' then expectancy influences subsequent interpretations. How were the pseudo-patients treated in the twelve hospitals? On the whole the press experienced was demoralizingly negative. Normal behaviour was constantly mis-interpreted. Both 'talking down' and a kind of 'acting down' were very common. Thus if one of the pseudo-patients approached the staff and asked a question, there was either no response at all, or a brief reply with head averted. Sometimes such encounters took what Rosenhan describes as a bizarre form. The pseudo-patient would ask about when he would be eligible for grounds privilege, to be greeted with: 'Good morning, Dave. How are you today?' The staff member would walk on without waiting for a reply. One aspect of the study involved the pseudo-patient asking questions in the form: 'Pardon me, Mr (or Dr or Mrs) X, could you tell me ... ?' In the case of physicians, 71 per cent moved on with head averted; with nurses and attendants it was 88 per cent. The pseudo-patients were regularly treated as unworthy of notice, as invisible non-persons. Like real patients they felt powerless, their freedom of movement limited, personal privacy minimal, frustrated in attempts to initiate communication. They were ignored. On one occasion a nurse unbuttoned her blouse to adjust her brassière in front of a whole ward of men. She wasn't being provocative. Rosenhan comments, 'She didn't notice us'. A group of staff might point to a patient and discuss him with animation as though he wasn't there. Of interest is how the participants regularly wrote notes: at first they did this unobtrusively. But as it became clear that nobody cared, they continued to write things down openly in public places like the day ward. Some of the actual patients noticed this and voiced their suspicions in such terms as 'You're not crazy,' 'not a patient', or 'you're a journalist'. The investigator comments that the fact that patients often recognized normality when staff did not, raises important questions. One physician did notice but missed the point: 'You needn't write it. If you have trouble remembering, just ask me again.' The records on three of the patients mentioned their note-taking. 'Patient engages in writing behaviour' was one such entry: no questions were asked as to just what he was writing.

Rosenhan is cautious about concluding that the negative press he and other pseudo-patients experienced coincides with that of true patients. He may be over-cautious. In psychiatric hospitals within several different countries I have often talked with patients recovering from their illnesses, waiting hopefully for their discharge. Their recurrent comment is how difficult it is to be seen to be acting 'normally'. As Rosenhan himself puts it, 'there is an enormous overlap in the behaviours of the sane and the insane'. He adds 'the sane are not "sane" all the time' (op. cit.: 254). And he emphasizes that the patient is 'shorn of credibility by virtue of his psychiatric label'. In the investigation he reports on how abusive behaviour towards patients quickly terminated when other staff members were likely to appear. 'Staff are credible witnesses. Patients are not' (op. cit.: 526). In the limitations of their credibility and thus relative defencelessness psychiatric patients are not unique. Those who have been patients in other types of hospital will need little convincing that in many respects, patients are socially at the bottom of the hospital hierarchy. But the Rosenhan experiment spells out how very much worse is the situation in hospitals that specialize in mental illness. This applies to even the more humane of them. There are others. It is understandable that many psychiatrists give vigorous support to the alternative of psychiatric wards in general hospitals, in progress from the old type of 'asylum' to the hospital atmosphere. Often this helps at least a little.

Experience and behaviour may be examined in their relation to the material and social environment. Here we encounter a paradox. This involves a principle that pervades psychology, with many applications. Many psychologists have recognized and used it, but I have named it after Kurt Koffka (1886–1941). In one of the great classics of the psychology of perception, *Principles of Gestalt Psychology* (1935), Koffka makes extensive use of the principle. Using largely a subject matter of visual illusions, the Gestalt pioneer questioned the seemingly obvious notion that behaviour takes place 'within the environment'.

THE KOFFKA PRINCIPLE

An alternative view may be stated in these terms: 'Behaviour takes place within the perceived environment.' We may be grossly in error in the way we perceive or otherwise apprehend environmental objects and events. Thus Koffka distinguishes the environment that interests the geographer from the one that interests the psychologist. Discrepancy between the 'geographical' and 'behavioural' environment is obvious in the case of visual illusions when we check them against realities. Thus in the Müller–Lyer or horizontal–vertical illusions, lines which are geographically equal look unequal. In Figure 1.1 I have combined them. If we visit Scotland we encounter, near Ayr, the 'Electric Brae', where a section of the road which geographically goes downhill is perceived as going uphill. Outside visual illusions we find many applications. Consider emotions. Anger is provoked not by insult, but by perceived insult which may – geographically speaking – not be present at all. Outside paranoid psychosis in everyday life we encounter 'unduly sensitive' people who are constantly provoked to anger or tears by fancied slights. Again in the phobias we have to deal with fear responses to a variety of objects and situations which are innocent of actual danger. Something very similar happens with the superstitions many people have, and the avoidance rituals that surround them.

In the world as we perceive it the sun rises in the morning and sets in the evening. Since the earth goes round the sun, and not

Figure 1.1   The Koffka Principle: The horizontal line is, in fact, of equal length to the vertical one. Perceived qualities of environmental things may differ from the actual realities.

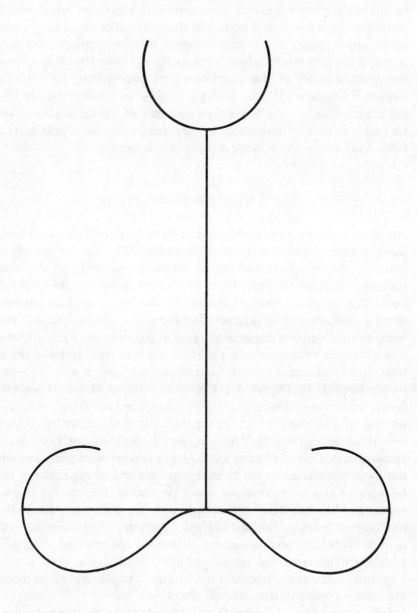

vice versa, this also is illusory. Or is it? It depends on one's frame of reference, provided in part by our firm belief in the Copernican solar system. If we travel by plane some problems arise from the inadequacy of our usual frames of reference for time. A simple question, 'What is the time?', is no longer simple, and has more than one answer on a long-distance flight in a modern airliner. Very many accidents can be seen in such terms as when, in Antarctica, a New Zealand passenger plane crashed into Mt Erebus. The sound recordings in the recovered 'black box' revealed that, almost up till the moment of impact, aircrew believed themselves to be safely over McMurdoe Sound, not flying into a 12,450-foot mountain. Tragic losses of life in aviation continue to take place when actual dangers of the real environment are either not perceived or under-estimated. They have included flying in fog or polar whiteouts; being in error over sensitive hostile territory; misperceiving engine fire as a burst tyre; and accepting disguised terrorists as innocent passengers. In driving situations expectancies based on established habits may intrude as when, with an unfamiliar vehicle, we find ourselves operating the windscreen wipers when we mean to give a traffic signal. A variation of this recently affected a driver unused to the vehicle he was operating, a double-decker bus. Behaviourally he acted in accord with the assumption that he was, as usual, driving a single-decker bus under a low railway bridge: geographically he was driving a double-decker bus into it. This incident, which occurred in 1987 in the north of England, was fortunately without tragic consequences – all the passengers were seated downstairs – or injury, not counting a scalped bus.

Maladaptive responses to the realities of the environment can be experimentally simulated in ways relevant to abnormal psychology. Thus during a walk through Victorian London, Sir Francis Galton sought empathy with the mental life of a persecuted paranoiac. He did this by imagining that everyone he met was a spy. The experiment, he recorded, succeeded only too well. Galton reported no difficulty in entering into a world of suspicion provided by his own imagination. Moving from Galton's Victorian England, consider a modern equivalent: how people indulge in imagination about the drivers of other motor vehicles when headlamps follow, with great persistence, at night. One woman driver told me recently, during a long journey at night in a remote part of the country, of the fear she had of cars following her. Very probably I suspect she, like Galton, had projected her fantasy on to the other drivers unseen by her, each going about his or her business in an innocent way. At any rate she gained some reassurance when I pointed out the next car we saw, its occupants being a woman and two children. Paranoid-like suspiciousness can occur in everyday life in a neutral, non-threatening environment. But consider a more subjective orientation. Viewed from the standpoint of the person concerned – and what is going on inside in terms of illusions of perception and belief – quasi-persecutory interpretations become more meaningful. The Koffka Principle is involved: behaviour occurs within the perceived environment.

In the case of a psychosis the hallucinations and delusions may transform the actual geographical environment of an enlightened hospital into something resembling one of Hitler's or Stalin's concentration camps. The perceived surroundings are those of threat, cruelty, and always-present danger. As regards the imagining of superstitious fear, in the *Rime of the Ancient Mariner* Coleridge writes of how, at night 'on a lonesome road', a person may 'walk in fear and dread' of some imaged personification of that fear. And cross-cultural differences can give rise to many misunderstandings when culture-bound assumptions that are now inappropriate are still adhered to. I take as illustration a person working in another country, within a very common work situation, an office. In an article on culture shock, Corinne Julius discusses emotional reactions and problems of adjustment. 'An office looks much the same anywhere in the world.' Yet in many countries of the Far East, for example, despite apparent similarity they are very different from those of Europe. The European may become angry and frustrated by the way eastern subordinates accept a decision without discussion but afterwards ignore it. 'The local subordinate views the situation quite differently.' If the decision appears to have been a bad one, 'rather than cause a superior loss of face ... it is far more polite to act as if no decision was taken, and therefore no action is required' (*The Times*, London, 23 January 1986: 40). Even an office, to say nothing of a psychiatric hospital or a prison, may create problems of this kind, stemming from the different assumptions of the people who work in it.

Among other applications of the Koffka Principle are those that stem from differences of age rather than of personality or culture. Time itself may be involved. In many work situations an older person perceives himself or herself to have inaugurated prompt action. But this may seem to a younger subordinate an unreasonable, even provocative, delay. As is well known, time passes more rapidly as age, and with it seniority, increases. Nor should we neglect the generation conflict at still younger age levels, and the fantasies that may provoke conflict in school, nursery, and home. Again the Koffka Principle is relevant. How toys are perceived can create such conflicts. To take a specific example: for a 10-year-old a laser beam torch is subject matter for a fantasy game of space travel. To a nearby 4-year-old it is merely a hammer that is perceived and used as such! Empathy with the perceptions and resulting needs and purposes of different age levels is involved; it may be taxed in coping with misunderstandings and conflicts. Parallel problems may occur in the regressions that may accompany psychosis. Yellowlees (1932) cites conflicts in a psychiatric ward over a chair which one grandiose deluded patient viewed as not merely a chair, but her personal throne.

There are many barriers to empathy between normal people. Some psychologists are themselves at fault in their readiness to neglect the often empathic ideas of thoughtful non-professionals. In this context we will consider contributions to the understanding of empathy from the resulting, often neglected, insights of literature.

THE PSYCHOLOGY OF EMPATHY

Empathy may be defined as an imaginative identification with another person for the purpose of understanding his or her experience and behaviour. Shakespeare's tragedy of *King Lear* is not only a study of deterioration of judgement and thinking in old age, or of the apparent insanity of Lear or Kent. It is also a penetrating treatment of repeated failures of empathy. Neither Goneril nor Regan had sympathy or empathy with their father's querulous demands and narcissistic needs. After all Lear had ruled as a king, and felt himself entitled to have about him some knights and courtiers despite his abdication. Cordelia – though ethically more admirable – was not much better at empathy than her sisters. She was wholly unwilling to reassure her father with what he craved, words of respect and affection. The psychiatrist Muslin (1981) discusses Shakespeare's play in these terms. Failures of empathy are considered in relation to Lear himself, his family, and others. Clearly Lear has indulged Cordelia in ways that alienated his other two daughters. Moreover, in dividing up his kingdom he makes his favouritism public, and in front of Regan and Goneril he is ready to offer her 'A third more opulent than your sisters' (I.i.). Hardly tactful? In fact Lear seems to have been conscientious in omitting nothing that would provoke sibling rivalry and deep resentment towards himself. As regards the sub-plot, the sufferings of Gloucester may evoke our sympathy and hostility towards Edmund, who is certainly one of Shakespeare's most unpleasant characters. Yet consider the 'press' he has been subjected to in his upbringing: repeated humiliation by his father. Edmund is illegitimate, which is obviously not his fault but something for which Gloucester himself has been responsible. But the father has often taunted his own illegitimate son, as Muslin points out, with his bastard birth. Sadism has seldom been better defined, and perhaps Edmund learned his from his father. On that father for these humiliations he takes revenge. Gloucester's preference for his other, legitimate, son and resulting sibling rivalry shape the form revenge takes. As regards the Lear family, one actress – Anna Massey – who has played Goneril makes a parallel point. She assesses Goneril as 'a victim, a terrible victim of being a child of Lear' (Interview reported in *The Times*, 11 December 1986). Thus as Muslin points out, central to the story is deep insight into 'the tragic consequences of empathic failures'.

This brings in a concept I have called 'the psychologist in literature' (McKellar 1979b). Sometimes authors invent a character whom they use as a device to express their own insights. In *King Lear* the best example is the Fool, who has profound understanding of Lear's strong self-destructive needs. Again we find it in the supposedly insane Kent, disguised as a psychotic beggar. Shakespeare uses the fool and the madman as vehicles of his own psychological understanding of human motivation. Elsewhere we find the psychologist in literature. Ibsen, for example, used this device a great deal. Again and again in his plays we encounter an invented character, revealing the dramatist's insights into the motivation of the other characters. One is there to unmask sentimentality in *The Wild Duck*. Another psychologist character is there to uncover the aggression accompanying puritanical fanaticism of the 'nought or all' kind in *Brand*. In ways parallel to Freud and Nietzsche, Ibsen thus reveals the seemingly admirable morality of Pastor Brand to be, as Nietzsche put it, something 'dangerous to life'. To consider the psychology of empathy itself we may turn to Edgar Allan Poe for another such character who is sensitive to the complexities of the psychology of thinking. Both its reasoning and imagination aspects are revealed in the insightful thinking of Poe himself, expressed through his psychologist character, Auguste Dupin.

The Mystery of the Purloined Letter and two other short stories involve Auguste Dupin. He has often been regarded as the forerunner of the modern detective in subsequent fiction. A stolen letter has been hidden somewhere, and the Paris police know by whom. They have searched the house, inch by inch, without success. Poe's fictional amateur now takes part. Dupin works out where the letter must be hidden, and does so from knowledge that the man who has so far thwarted the police's efforts is both a poet and a mathematician. A hypothesis about where such a person would hide something is formulated, and verified by Dupin's successful finding of the letter. In two other stories Dupin again appears, and again demonstrates his powers of empathy. In one he breaks in on the unspoken thoughts of his companion, and adds an appropriately relevant remark. This is achieved not by telepathy but by observation of the movements of the other person, and by step-by-step empathy with his processes of association. (Later Conan Doyle makes Sherlock Holmes repeat this exercise in the psychology of association of ideas – he makes rather grudging acknowledgement to Dupin – for the benefit of a much-impressed Dr Watson.) The Dupin stories have other things to say about empathy, for example in references made to a boy who, playing the game of 'odds and evens', succeeded in 'winning all the marbles in the school'. The contests involved one player who chooses either an odd or even number of marbles, and holds them behind his back while the other boy guesses. As Dupin explains, success depended on the winning boy's ability to assess the level of sophistication of his adversary. A simpleton would merely alternate odds and evens, and he would guess accordingly. But more experienced players could also be defeated by accurate empathy with their level of strategies like 'odds last time, he'll try odds again', or 'he'll now try a run of odds', or 'two odds, then two evens'. As Poe reveals through the mouth of his characters, guessing correctly again and again involved 'an identification of the reasoner's intellect with that of his opponent'. Similar processes of empathy play their part in other games of skill, as opposed to games of chance, though seldom have they been better described than by Poe – through Dupin – in these short stories. As such contests or acts of detection reveal, empathy does not necessarily involve sympathy. In empathy there is a 'feeling into' rather than a 'feeling along with' the other person. Sympathy may, or may not, also be present. Both concern us in the next chapter, which will consider variations of subjective mental life in their relation to insight into oneself and empathy with others.

SUMMARY

1   Psychology has a history, extending back over 2,000 years, of thought, observation, and introspection about experience and behaviour. Early beginnings and four aspects of that history relating to abnormal mental life are considered.

2   We shall be concerned with experience and behaviour that are, or seem to be, abnormal, their description and classification, and with principles that may help understanding the phenomena.

3   Approach to the motivation of the individual personality and pressures on it are considered in the context of Murray's 'need–press' formulation, and illustrated in terms of a field study.

4   A first basic idea, the Koffka Principle, is introduced: the notion that experience and behaviour relate to the environment as it is perceived and believed to be. The realities may be different.

5   The twin problems of insight and empathy will much concern us. It is argued that psychology can learn – and has sometimes learned – from other disciplines including anthropology, as cross-cultural differences create barriers to empathy. From literature, which can also make its contributions, empathy itself is discussed in terms of its failure and success.

Chapter Two

VARIATIONS OF SUBJECTIVE EXPERIENCE

We start by living, each one of us, in the solitariness of our own mind.

William Somerset Maugham

Two important psychological tasks confront every human being. One is achieving empathy with other people; the other is gaining insight into our own mental life. Psychology is the science concerned with the systematic accomplishment of these two tasks. A human lifetime resembles a long voyage on a ship: finding something to occupy time that is personally satisfying, and getting to know the other passengers. The personality itself provides resources. Regularly we use our own as providing a frame of reference for understanding similarities and differences between ourself and others. In his autobiography Somerset Maugham examines this process, the subject of this book. Some similarities and differences are obvious. The other passengers have beliefs and numerous emotional investments in attitudes, or pro and con sentiments including group loyalties which we may share or reject. 'Misguided' and 'ignorant' are the milder labels in use to accompany such rejections. Others include 'fanatical', 'perverted', 'mad', or 'insane'. These testify to unwillingness or inability to achieve empathy. Among similarities and differences of mental life are those that are less obvious: some are common, others relatively rare. Their lack of a name, or a name known to us, may lead to their being overlooked, or if noticed, to upsurges of anxiety.

The strong illusory experience – 'I feel as though I have lived through this before', while knowing one hasn't – has a name, *déjà vu*. But the illusion of 'already seen' points to a whole family of related subjective experiences. Its numerous variants, including 'already heard' or 'already touched', have been relatively recently spelt out by the psychiatrist Neppe (1983). These variants of *déjà vu* are common and innocent phenomena of normal mental life, and illustrate the problem of names and labels. Yet I have encountered anxiety, and even on occasion a sense of isolation and fear of 'going insane', because of a *déjà vu* experience. In his systematic study of the phenomenon Dr Neppe has provided names that alert us to notice sub-types. He has also systematically investigated it in relation to 'normal' people, diagnosed psychotic patients, and those whose belief systems lead them to give it supernatural interpretation. *Déjà vu* is but one example. There are others. Synaesthesia is another phenomenon, involving an upsurge of subjective imagery in one sense mode during perception in another. Its commonest form is having mental pictures of shapes or colours while listening to music. But synaesthesia resembles *déjà vu* in having a whole family of variants, some of them strange and uncommon: for some people pains have colour, while others respond to sights and sounds with strong imagery of texture and even taste. A number of years ago Lorna Simpson and I discovered that some of the oddities of experience that occurred in experiments with hallucinogenic substances – we used mescaline – were in fact these rarer forms of synaesthetic experience. We suggested a two-word convention for labelling these types of synaesthesia (Simpson and McKellar 1955; McKellar 1957). Consider finally a third kind of subjective experience, namely the illusion of 'falling' while we are dropping off to sleep. This is very common indeed. But what I shall call the 'falling experience' doesn't even have a commonly accepted name.

From work like that of Dr Neppe on *déjà vu*, and our own on the synaesthesias, three points emerge. First, there are many variations of mental life that some people report, but others lack, that are readily overlooked. Second, even in the elementary matter of naming them there remains much to be done. And third, perhaps we may – while seeking to escape from the solitariness of our own mental life – learn something from them that will assist understanding of the actually, or seemingly, 'abnormal'. Mental imagery has been mentioned and will be considered first.

Figure 2.1 Diagram form for dates: The subject regularly visualizes months of the year in such an image. 'Slowly revolving. I am always facing into centre of circle towards opposite six months.' (From McKellar (1957), *Imagination and Thinking*, p. 60.)

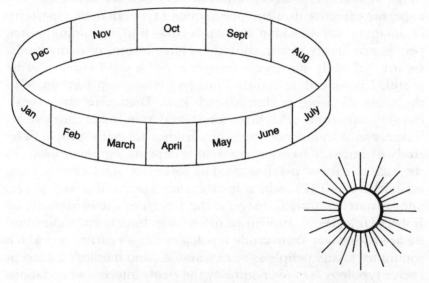

DIFFERENCES OF MENTAL IMAGERY

There is a temptation to assume that, in their equipment for thinking and remembering, others are similar. This may or may not be true. Access to 'mind's-eye' experiences is not universal. Nevertheless many researches, including some of my own, reveal that most people – in these activities – have and use visual imagery. Most also appear to have access to auditory imagery. Their mental life is equipped with subjective equivalents of 'looking' and 'listening'. Thus scenes and people previously perceived can afterwards be visualized, usually with recalled auditory accompaniments. Exceptions are also of some interest. I met such a person as a fellow passenger on a ship: he and his wife were travelling from Australia to visit England, Scotland, and Europe. Later I met him again in London. Only then did I learn that in his mental life he lacked any capacity for visual remembering. His tour of Europe had been a disaster, because he had somehow lost all the photographs he had taken. As he told me, without this substitute for his non-existent visual imagery he might as well have stayed at home. His wife – he could not visualize her with his eyes closed – was fortunately different. She possessed the more usual repertoire of imagery. Elsewhere I have suggested that such a repertoire involves three aspects (McKellar 1965a). They are range of available imagery; kinds present that are strong enough to permit effective use; and predominant type. In their repertoire of imagery for thinking, remembering, and imagining, some people are highly restricted. Others have images of many kinds. In strength only some such images may be vivid enough to be useful. Visual and/or auditory imagery tends to predominate in the sense of being preferred and used. Dreamlife also reveals imagery variations of all three kinds, and as in wakefulness visual imagery is obviously of great importance to many people. The study of imagery has now come to occupy its legitimate place in the mainstream of psychology. The *Journal of Mental Imagery* was established in 1977, and a little earlier appeared a key paper, appropriately entitled 'Imagery: the return of the ostracized', by Robert Holt (1964). Individual differences have been studied and we are a long way from crude typologies like an earlier one which sought to classify people as 'visiles, audiles, and motiles'. To accept such a typology is to over-simplify the richly interesting variations of imagery we find in exploring human subjective experience. Although such a typology has sometimes been wrongly attributed to him, the pioneer investigator in this area, Sir Francis Galton (1822–1911), resisted this temptation.

In considering the work of Galton himself, 'exploration' seems an appropriate word. He likened study of the differences between people in their mental life to exploring: visiting a new country whose inhabitants and customs may seem strange to us. Galton, Darwin's cousin, was a pioneer of anthropology as well as of psychology, and himself an explorer of considerable experience. His *The Art of Travel* (1855) is still a useful guide on such matters as crossing rivers, kindling a fire, safe drinking water, and making a bivouac. From his travels in Africa and elsewhere he was alerted to the tasks of making observations in other cultures. His attitude was similar in study of subjective experiences within his own. Galton's unashamed defence of introspection within psychology echoes both interests.

26

I do not see why the report of a person on his own mind should not be as intelligible and trustworthy as that of a traveller upon a new country whose landscapes and inhabitants are of a different type to any we ourselves have seen.

Less usual forms of imagery such as colour associations and number forms, together with the hallucinations of the sane, all interested Galton. Some of his subjects appeared to lack visual imagery altogether, while others could visualize with a vividness comparable to that of real perception. Some could 'read' from mental manuscripts, and some could project their imagery; it was visual imagery which mostly interested him. As anthropologist and traveller Galton took account of the ways cultural factors can affect visionary experiences. Under the influence of one kind of social norm 'the seers of visions keep quiet; they do not like to be thought fanciful or mad'. But with other norms that encourage, such imagery is openly admitted, and may indeed become more vivid by being 'habitually dwelt upon' (Galton 1883: 128). Of considerable importance is this process of alerting a person to notice what is going on within his own mental life. This may give rise to a kind of co-conscious evaluation of one sub-system of the personality by another.

Figure 2.2 Fear-arousing imagery: Claw with ring. Hypnagogic image reported by one subject who regularly experiences such imagery, often much more pleasant, and sometimes in cartoon-like forms.

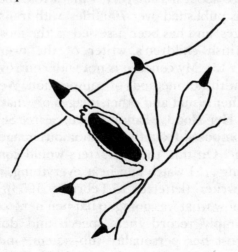

IMAGERY AND AUTHORSHIP

In elucidating hidden differences within the mental life of different people I turn to authors of books, as one kind of thought product. At the low-powered end of Galton's continuum I take first an author whom I will call C.D. He has written several widely read books with well-constructed plots that often deal with natural disasters and human responses to them. They are exciting, but it is the plot rather than the characters that provides the strength of a series of quite well-known books. In an interview I had with this author it emerged that C.D. was almost entirely without the capacity for visual imagery. His method of working compensated for this. He used his camera. Thus he would visit a suitable locality on his travels in some part of the world – he had been to many – and take very many photographic slides. These he would project, and as he worked with them plot and characters would emerge. This author resembled my ship-board acquaintance. Another such low-powered imager told me how he had long been puzzled when others told him about how they enjoyed re-living their holiday experiences. He simply did not know what they meant until, one day, he discovered imagery differences and his own lack of visual memory.

Enid Blyton (1897–1968), unlike C.D., can be named as she gave me her permission to do so when, following considerable correspondence about her imagery, I first wrote about it (McKellar 1957). She has published over 700 titles, with translation into 126 other languages, and has been assessed as 'the most commercially successful British children's writer of the twentieth century' (Mullan 1987: 13). My concern is not with controversy about her writings, but with her methods of composition. We corresponded on details of her visual and other images of what she called her 'undermind'. Her Noddy, Famous Five, Secret Seven, and other books were composed from the autonomous imagery of 'a private cinema screen'. On this 'the characters would come on and off, talk, laugh, sing ... I watch and hear everything, writing it down with my typewriter' (letter of 15 February 1953). She explained she did not know what was going to happen next to her characters but would simply record their speech and doings. She had learned to trust her personality sub-system, and if something appeared to be going wrong she regularly discovered 'it rights itself, falls into place – now I dare not alter a thing'. A feature of Miss Blyton's 'cinematographic eidetic imagery' – to give it a name – was its resort to humour. She comments on this in relation to the autonomy of the experience.

> Sometimes a character makes a joke, a really funny one,
> that makes me laugh as I type it on my paper – and I think
> 'Well, I couldn't have thought of that myself in a hundred
> years!' And then I think 'Well, who *did* think of it then?'

This mysterious source of subjective experiences dissociated from her mainstream of consciousness first began in childhood in what she called her 'night stories'. These, incidentally, she distinguished from hypnagogic imagery with which she was also acquainted. It did not, however, represent, as Mullan claims, 'the only way she could write' (1987: 147). On the contrary, as she explained in another letter, when writing 'something serious, abstract, or considered ... I think hard – deliberate – write a sentence or two – erase one – rewrite – think again, and so on.' Of interest were the difficulties she encountered when she first wrote a play. The imagery failed her. 'And then my mind cleared, and I saw a big stage, in all its details. I saw Toyland there ... I saw exits and entrances through which the characters could come. And of course they came.' Writing this play was accompanied by auditory imagery of about twenty-five lyrics. Of one she records, 'It was not a song I would have thought of myself, if I had tried to write it,' but one which 'seemed to burst out spontaneously from the characters then on the stage ... I saw them dancing to it, and heard them singing it.'

In giving her very lucid account of these products of her autonomous imagery, Miss Blyton adhered to a strictly naturalistic explanation. This was in terms of past perceptual experience. In several instances she was able to locate this in forgotten memories, thus siding with a standpoint many psychologists and philosophers have accepted. This will much concern us, and from one of its early exponents I shall refer to it as the Hobbes Principle. 'There is no conception in a man's mind, which hath not at first, totally or by parts, been begotten upon the organs of sense.' Thus Thomas Hobbes (1651) argued, and we may find it useful throughout the study of imagery, and waking or sleeping imagination. Although this notion of a sensory origin of all knowledge may have some important limitations, as a guiding principle it has considerable application to human thinking, however seemingly creative.

As the two instances taken show, authors, like other people, may differ markedly in their subjective mental life. It is unwise to overlook such differences which some authors have themselves admitted to in their account of their own creative processes. Some, like Robert Louis Stevenson, have recorded their use of autonomous dream imagery; and on one occasion Stevenson, like Mary Shelley in writing *Frankenstein*, is explicit about drawing upon a nightmare for subject matter. Not only in *Kubla Khan*, but also in *The Ancient Mariner*, Coleridge used dream material. Some, like Edgar Allan Poe and in more recent times Ray Bradbury, have drawn on hypnagogic imagery. Among scientific writers it is known that Charles Darwin was a good visual imager – doubtless something that helped in his studies of the detail of natural selection – and he was in fact one of the subjects of Galton's pioneer investigation of differences of visual imagery. In studying through products, whether art or science, we cannot safely lay down how their authors must have worked. We can, however, study individuals in terms of how they did work, and the diversity of their source material of both observation and imagery.

In seeking to understand these things, Freud in 1900 turned to literature, Schiller's advice to a young man who complained of being unable to produce original ideas. Schiller declared, 'The reason for your complaint seems to me to lie in the constraint imposed by your reason upon your imagination.' He went on to draw attention to the importance of upsurges of creativity and the fear of these leading people, as he put it, to 'reject too soon and discriminate too severely' (Quoted in Freud 1900: 103). Schiller was advising greater receptivity by the young man towards the subjective processes of his own mental life. Sleep and dreamlife may provide creative insights. In considering these and other altered states of consciousness, together with individual differences, a distinction may be introduced.

A-THINKING AND R-THINKING

Schiller, as cited by Freud, refers to both reason and imagination. The word 'thinking' is ambiguous and two of its manifestations may be noted. Elsewhere (1957) I have argued that processes of reasoning based on logical inference and relevance to evidence comprise only one kind of thinking. We may call it realistic, or more briefly, 'R-thinking'. Also important are processes prominent in dreaming and waking fantasy of the kind which Eugene Bleuler called 'autistic'. For brevity we may call this 'A-thinking'. Neither should be equated with either normality or abnormality. In fact, as I have argued elsewhere in discussing originality, socially useful thought products seem to depend on interactions of A-thinking and R-thinking. The A-thinking component may be likened to the activity of an author, and the R-thinking to the critical and evaluative activity of an editor (McKellar 1963b). For some A-thinking is easy, as we have seen in the case of the author of children's books, Enid Blyton, with her cinematographic imagery. Other authors have found it difficult, like for example Emile Zola, who resorted to writing himself letters about his characters for the purpose of stimulating his imagination. Reference has been made to Edgar Allan Poe in discussing 'the psychologist in literature'. Poe himself was remarkably skilled in both R-thinking, and A-thinking. Both aspects are prominent in his character Auguste Dupin as components of his empathy: he could follow through a chain of logical inferences, and he could certainly imagine.

For Eugene Bleuler, who introduced the concept of schizophrenia, autism was one of its defining characteristics. Fantasy-dominated consciousness, and A-thinking processes of the hallucination kind largely replace realistic perception. In dreams and nightmares A-thinking predominates and, with the interesting exception of lucid dreams, it is largely uncorrected by R-thinking. To a large extent the excesses of A-thinking are something that, in normal mental life, we are able to confine to sleep. Again there are exceptions. One is the phenomenon of hypnagogic imagery: this may be seen as an anticipatory invasion of dreamlike A-thinking into the drowsy state before sleep. Another exception is visual or other hallucination, and the circumstances under which it occurs are very numerous: they are by no means confined to psychosis. In several kinds of experiments hallucination and dominance of A-thinking can be artificially produced. They include sensory deprivation experiments, and others in which either a hallucinogenic drug or hypnotism is used to induce such experiences.

Altered states of consciousness, including dreamlife and hypnagogia, will concern us in later chapters. Consideration may now be given to some of the more usual, less usual, and 'seemingly abnormal' variations of subjective mental life as between individuals. Instead of assuming similarity with other people, an individual may become the victim of silent misery because of believing he or she is 'different'. Such a difference may be imaginary rather than real. I have mentioned anxiety of this kind over even the common phenomenon of *déjà vu*, which it is interesting to notice has sometimes been interpreted supernaturally. In the case of *déjà vu* we at least have a name which may help to reduce anxiety or fear of the unknown. But there are many such variants of subjective experience which either lack a widely known name, or have not been named at all.

THE VOCABULARY OF SUBJECTIVE EXPERIENCE

Much work remains to be done in the spirit of the psychologist naturalist in describing, classifying and naming innocent variants of mental life. Existing vocabulary is limited, and some of the words we have, like 'image', 'vision', and 'hallucination', are often over-worked. The generic term 'diagram forms' has been suggested for a family of atypical phenomena, involving a regular tendency to think of numbers, dates, months, or something else in a spatial way. We have number forms, date forms, and others, including in the case of one subject a diagram form for the Ten Commandments. Such diagram forms, which greatly interested Galton, are sometimes imaged in colour and may be three-dimensional. As Galton found, people with diagram forms do not agree, and two such people brought together may hotly dispute the lines, whorls, and angles they respectively image. One of the most interesting instances of number forms he found concerned the archaeologist Flinders Petrie. This took the form of an imagined slide-rule that could be mentally manipulated and with which Petrie could make calculations. Also very common are colour associations for days, months, and numbers. They also occur for names, e.g. 'Dorothy is a brown name, Ethel a red one, and Helen blue'. Needless to say, again there is no tendency for agreement between colours, this providing problems of communication (McKellar 1957).

Like Petrie's slide-rule number form, colour associations may on occasion prove useful in thinking. An example is one person I interviewed, a skilled linguist. He possesses and uses different colours for the vowels of the many languages he is able to speak and think in. But possessing number forms or colour associations may have disadvantages. One is fear of being different, and another is not noticing one is. Thus things may be made worse rather than better if a person makes an attempt to communicate some innocent variant of subjective experience. I quote one subject representative of many: 'Once or twice in my youth I attempted to describe some of these phenomena but met with scoffing ridicule. I did think that perhaps I was not quite sane.' Fear of being thought of as abnormal, or of being in fact 'abnormal', are both commonly reported. Frustration at attempts to communicate is another thing that may happen. This may occur with the phenomenon of colour association, though a frequent variant of subjective experience. One correspondent, writing to the *Listener* (11 April 1963), reported on her own colour associations for numbers. The number ten was, for her, a deep brown, 'the colour of strong tea'. In her letter she told how, when aged about 6 she had explained to somebody that her brother liked 'ten tea', and was told that she was talking nonsense. Another person has a somewhat more unusual form of colour association, a tendency to think of pains in colour terms. A burn and a sprain are for her differently coloured. In her attempts at communication as a child this variant of subjective experience created difficulties. If she reported pain her mother would ask, 'What sort of pain is it?' Replies she received, such as 'a yellow one', did not please her. To the child's way of thinking the colour–pain association was very real; to the mother it was meaningless. Hidden differences of these kinds may divide a child from a parent who simply does not understand. We may meet parochial intolerance of such variations even in students of psychology who ought, surely, to know better. Failure of empathy was well defined by one such student who expressed her scorn in the words, 'Anyone who arranges numbers in space and patterns, or who associates things with colours must be *peculiar*' (italics hers).

The term 'body image' refers to the impression a person has of his or her own body as a physical object with spatially related parts. In daily life we use our body image in dressing or undressing, and in deciding we can walk along a passage without bumping our head. Under a variety of circumstances some people experience illusions of change in the shape or size of their body image. Various hallucinogenic substances, including psilocybin from one specific mushroom, may produce this Alice in Wonderland experience. Interestingly enough, Alice herself had it after consuming a mushroom, but migraine, high temperature, and other circumstances also induce it: of possible relevance is the fact that Lewis Carroll was a sufferer from migraine. Very common is its occurrence in the drowsy pre-sleep hypnagogic state. Despite the resemblance to delusions of bodily change, the phenomenon is an innocent variant compatible with normal mental life. This is not always the interpretation put on it by, for example, a frightened child. One woman wrote to me about it; in recording the misery of many of her early years she reported, 'it is terrifying enough for a small child to face alone in the dark'. She added, 'I always thought it was the onset of madness'.

Illustration may be taken from a much less common form of subjective experience, namely crystal-gazing. Some people can project their visual imagery into a crystal globe. Throughout history this, and related activities with mirrors, pools of water or other liquids, and polished metals, has sometimes been given clairvoyant interpretations. Cohen (1964) lists no less than sixty-two such media for achieving these self-induced visions. The visions reported may be of complex scenes, faces, clouds, or a variety of objects. A comprehensive account is given by one anonymous author who, in her own case, reports, 'Just as a fanciful child will tell itself a story, I sometimes ... create a group of figures and put them in the crystal to see what they will do ... I watch the scene with curiosity and surprise' (Anon 1889: 5). On a number of occasions I have been able to study crystal-gazing visions with individuals who spontaneously have the experience, and others who reported it under the influence of a hallucinogenic substance. We used both lysergic acid and mescaline (McKellar 1957). None of these people incidentally placed any kind of supernatural interpretation on the occurrence: they simply regarded it as a more unusual form of mental imaging. All stressed the characteristic 'out-thereness' of the visions contained in the crystal we used. One young woman, a regular and spon-taneous crystal-gazer, described how the images 'appeared to come out of a pinpoint of light, and sort of grow, magnify and become clearer'. In 1957 I had reported in detail on her variant of subjective experience. Some years later, following her marriage and acquisition of a family she wrote to me, referring to her somewhat unusual mental life. 'It's funny this "but surely everybody thinks like me" feeling. It does cause quite a shock sometimes to find out that *nobody* in one's immediate environment does' (Quoted in McKellar 1965a: 176). The young woman concerned is perhaps a little unusual also in her insight.

Another variant of subjective experience is imaginary companions, who may be treated by a child as very real people. Such happenings are not reasons for parental anxiety, but rather a device through which some normal children explore inter-personal relations. Sometimes the imaginary companion appears to be 'seen' in the visual image sense. Adult members of a family may have to adjust to the imagined playmate, and indeed some adults admit that an imaginary companion may – in their own case – persist into later life. Childhood imaginary companions are more common than is generally realized. Pines (1978) placed their incidence from his study as high as 65 per cent. Some other studies would place it much lower, but give clear evidence of a sex difference, favouring girls over boys (e.g. Hurlock and Burnstein 1932). The point is that some children have the experience, others do not, and some adults report it retrospectively. Elsewhere I have discussed one such case in detail, involving a child I have called 'David' (McKellar 1965a). The time period the imaginary companions were present was from 2½–3 years. There were two. One was a 'Mrs Cornflake', a kind of imaginary, very wise aunt who knew all the answers. She exemplifies a usual characteristic of such companions as benign, helpful figures. The other companion was a tiger that David called 'Hallspeaker', of which – like his toys – he was very fond. This reminds us that imaginary companions are not necessarily humans, but may be animals. Companions persisting into later life was reported in her own case by a woman university lecturer (McKellar, op.cit.: 180). Hers was a blue fairy called 'Tinkerbell', traced to illustrations in a book seen as a very young child. This played a prominent part in her life until, aged about 5 years, the child realized Tinkerbell didn't really exist but 'I decided to have her anyway'. Here we encounter the phenomenon of half-belief which combines many of the features of belief and disbelief. In dealing with the category of the supernatural, it may combine intellectual rejection together with a weakening of disbelief. As elsewhere we find a continuum in that in some manifestations of religion spiritual beings perform functions of supporting and comforting, like those of childhood imaginary companions. Perhaps closing the eyes in meditation or in prayer assists being able visually to image them? Outside religion we find the deliberate use of something very similar, the 'inner advisors' deliberately used in some forms of therapy. These imagined figures of a wise and caring kind are evoked in imagery therapy. In discussing such techniques one such therapist, Martin Rossman (1984: 244), quotes therapy that stems from Jung's method of active imagination. They involve 'an internal talk of one person with another who is invisible, as in invocation of the Deity ... or with one's good angel'. Similarity does not necessarily mean identity, but resemblances of these phenomena that assist adjustment to childhood imaginary companions are of interest. In his consideration of a less usual phenomenon, multiple personality, Bliss (1984) discusses imaginary companions and invisible play-mates. By questioning his multiple personality patients he found many had had imaginary playmates with whom they had conversations that were 'audible and distinct'. To illustrate, one such patient created her first personality at about 4 or 5 years of age. She had wanted a brother and through such fantasy obtained one, a protector and friend. Then came two more such personalities, both female and equally helpful and protective. In one series of fourteen multiple personality patients all such imaginary companions had appeared before the age of 7 years. Although obviously the much commoner phenomenon of imaginary companions does not usually result in multiple personality, it is of interest to note that in the rarer phenomenon such companions are often to be found. We may encounter amiable sub-systems strongly reminiscent of imaginary companions. Dissociation as such will be discussed in a later chapter.

As we have stated, the words we possess to label and describe subjective experiences are often carelessly over-used. Such words as exist are not widely known, as in the case of imagery that belongs not to sleep but to states adjacent to it. Hypnagogic imagery sometimes takes the form of 'faces in the dark'. Consider this experience of the drowsy pre-sleep state and its fear-arousing character. The person who reported it to me added, 'this happened quite often when I was younger'. He reported 'Terrifying faces, one replacing the other ... They seemed too vivid and too extraordinarily evil not to belong to something real somewhere.' Often such imagery is of landscapes, or even amusing cartoon-like happenings, and by no means frightening. Alfred Maury, the investigator who provided the name 'hypnagogic imagery', experienced such faces. These hypnagogic acquaintances were always strange to him, people he did not know. They were often in his case distinguished by bizarre hair styles. Auditory imagery may also be frightening, resembling as it does hallucinatory voices which may call out the sleeper's name, or murmur in a threatening way. Relevant to such imagery is Galton's observation of the likelihood of supernatural interpretations. The fear, including fear of the unknown, associated with changes of the body image also in the hypnagogic state may be noted. There are also false awakenings, in which sleep continues with its dream accompaniments, though the sleeper believes himself or herself to be awake. Out-of-the-body-experiences, in which during sleep or in the hypnagogic state there is the illusion of departing from one's body, are yet another variant. All may contribute to the sense of isolation of a frightened child, to terror of the supernatural, or to fear of becoming insane. The result may be a child, or for that matter an adult, who is unaware of the normality of such experiences, enduring months or years of silent misery.

The phenomenon of lucid dreaming was named by Frederick van Eeden (1913). In this the sleeper retains awareness that he is asleep and having a dream. Earlier Hervey de Saint Denys (1867, reprinted 1982) described many of these atypical dreams, sometimes associated in his own case with out-of-the-body-experiences. In later work Celia Green (1968b edition 1982) distinguishes pre-lucid dreaming in which the sleeper is uncertain whether he is asleep or awake. Readers may be familiar with this experience, and of pinching themselves to see if they are awake or not, deciding they are, and then continuing to dream. Confusions about whether one is asleep or not are not confined to sleep: sometimes on return to full wakefulness there is uncertainty. The content of the experience may often decide the matter because of violations of natural law that some dreams involve. A conversation with a historical character or flying like a bird – recalled the afternoon of the next day – is testimony of sleeping or waking fantasy. But sometimes the situation is more ambiguous. An example of my own will illustrate this point. It concerned the news I received, in reality, through a letter from a former colleague of a tragic accident to a friend in another country. On the afternoon of the day following I recalled reading a newspaper report of the accident. This proved to be a false memory. The 'reading' of the report was part of a dream I had the night after receiving the letter, which dealt only in very general terms with the location of the tragedy. But the 'newspaper report', contributed by my dream, gave specific geographical information. The letter itself, which I carefully scrutinized, was bereft of such information. Because the accident occurred in another country – indeed another hemisphere – it was several days later that I was able to, in fact, read any newspaper report. The incident illustrates that confusions between waking and sleep do not necessarily involve improbable events. They may result in addition of plausible, but imaginary, details, despite efforts to recall events with accuracy.

In the case of accidents that may involve court proceedings, or in reports of allegedly supernatural events, such details may be highly relevant. There is a passage in Dostoevsky's *Crime and Punishment* in which Raskolnikov attempts to recall the sequence and 'exact date and duration of certain events' through 'piecing together the information he got from other people'. He discovers that he has mistaken one event for another while some have 'existed only in his imagination' (Penguin edition, part 6: 450). The events in question related to his crime and were of considerable relevance to the subsequent trial. Dostoevsky is alert to the contribution which dreamlife may make – as happened in my own case – to such details. Here also confusions occur because, earlier in a dream, Raskolnikov has anticipated the crime he later commits in fact. Dostoevsky's insights, expressed within literature, illustrate how sleep as well as waking imagination may add probable but false detail. Confusions between imagination, imagery, and fact are not confined to the hallucinations of psychosis, or the testimony of children. If we observe, and introspect, we can find parallel instances in everyday life.

In the less usual forms of waking fantasy, like the products of Enid Blyton's 'undermind', such imagery is typically autonomous. Though author, she had no knowledge of what the characters of her imagery would do or say. Another striking example of autonomous imagery, though in sleep rather than wakefulness, concerned John Livingstone Lowes. Lowes had been lecturing on the substance of his book about Coleridge's two poems, *The Ancient Mariner* and *Kubla Khan*. One night in New York he was rewarded for his scholarly efforts. In his dream he saw the palace of Kubla Khan hanging 'like a mirage on the remote horizon ... a shimmering golden dome ... a cataract of foam which sent up a luminous golden mist'. As the spectator in the dream he saw the dome, the deep romantic chasm, and the sacred river (Lowes 1927, edition 1930: 404). Later – with his own dream, as he had with the two poems of Coleridge – he was able to trace content to previous perceptual experiences and their re-arrangement by the processes of imagination. He points out that the imagery of the dream was highly original, and wholly unlike any of his visualizations about the poem during his studies of it. As is well known, the original Coleridge poem itself resulted from a dream, though the detailed study by Lowes makes it clear that many other things contributed.

SYNAESTHESIA

One of the most interesting variants of subjective experience certainly possesses a name. Yet 'synaesthesia' refers to not one, but a whole family. In its commonest form it involves visual imagery evoked by an auditory stimulus: parts of Walt Disney's *Fantasia* still represent its best-known expression in film. With the emergence of video-tapes in connection with music, new possibilities are constantly being explored. Among classic composers Bach often provides, for a synaesthetic person, imagery of complex shapes and patterns. Other musicians, for example Debussy – who was himself subject to synaesthesia, may evoke with their music colour as well. From the side of visual art note the names some have given to their creative thought products. Thus Paul Klee painted a 'Fugue in Red', while in Monet we have 'Symphony in Grey and White', and 'Nocturne in Blue and Gold'.

A colleague and I (Simpson and McKellar 1955) suggested a way of specifying some of the more uncommon types of synaesthesia. On our proposed two-word system, 'visual–auditory'

39

Figure 2.3 Types of synaesthesia: In the two-word language the image word comes first, as in the 'sight of a sound': this is visual–auditory synaesthesia. The 'sight of a taste' is visual–gustatory; the 'smell of a sound' would be olfactory–auditory; and the 'sound of a smell' would be auditory–olfactory. The grid allows for fifty-six theoretically possible types, and those found or reported in research literature are indicated.

	Visual	Auditory	Tactile	Gustatory (taste)	Olfactory (smell)	Kinaesthetic	Thermal	Pain
Visual	—	✓	✓	✓	✓	✓	✓	✓
Auditory		—			✓			
Tactile		✓	—					✓
Gustatory (taste)	✓			—				
Olfactory (smell)					—			
Kinaesthetic					✓	—		
Thermal	✓						—	
Pain		✓					✓	—

synaesthesis, or the sight of a sound, would specify the over-whelmingly most common kind. There are many others. One person already mentioned experienced, as we have seen, a 'visual–pain' synaesthesia: different types of pain for her evoked strong colour imagery. A study with a group of medical students revealed that this was one of the next most common types of synaesthesia. Some people, on hearing music, respond with imagery of touch and texture: the visual–tactile type. And some respond to voices in this way. In his study of one individual with remarkable powers of memory, the Russian psychologist Luria (1968) found that the mnemonist concerned often resorted to synaesthesia as an aid. The visual–auditory type was present and, as the subject explained, this could be a disadvantage. On one occasion he had gone to buy ice-cream, but when the woman selling it spoke, the horrible imagery of black coals that issued from her mouth put him off eating it. Present also was taste–visual synaesthesia, and this was helpful. The subject had no difficulty finding his way back to the laboratory because of a landmark, 'a briny-tasting fence'. The imaged 'sight' or 'sound' of a smell may seem a strange form of experience but we find it in a story by Sax Rohmer about a perfume blender. In this, two people are overcome by the fumes of a perfume which they both see and also hear 'speak' to them. These are rarities but I have found them in some highly synaesthetic subjects, as also independently did Luria in the mnemonist he investigated. Of some interest is the fact that even people who have some of the rarer types of synaesthesia sometimes assume that 'everybody is like me'. As I have mentioned above, Luria found an instance of synaesthesia involving the taste of a sight. For a long time I was looking for a case of the taste of a sound, and once in a radio talk I mentioned its apparent rarity. The response was a letter from a Scottish school teacher who expressed her surprise 'that you found it difficult to find people who tasted, or rather had the sensation of taste on hearing a sound'. She added, 'I have always had this sensation'. She went on to describe the different taste images evoked by the sound of a hammer against wood, against metal, and against earth (McKellar 1968).

Synaesthesia is of special interest in connection with empathy. Those who have the experience do not seem particularly liable to experience anxiety, or fears of insanity or the supernatural because of it. Yet the imagery-perceptual connections of their mental life, and actions that stem from them, may be baffling to others. Consider Luria's mnemonist subject. A man who goes to the trouble of buying something and then abandons it is puzzling. Puzzlement departs when we achieve empathic understanding of the synaesthesia of his mental life. To purely external observation, the ice-cream situation of Luria's subject, S, is puzzling. But from introspection we discover the explanation of visual imagery evoked by a voice. His powers of remembering of material like numbers, sometimes recalled correctly after two or more decades, were remarkable: unusually good imagery aided by synaesthesia was again involved. To consider other cases, one highly synaesthetic young woman I tested gained a great deal in her vocation from her many types of synaesthesia. She was a talented painter. Her synaesthesias involved imagery-percept connections with vision, hearing, touch, taste, smell, and pain. In the case of pain it may not be easy for others to understand her reactions. She actually enjoyed visits to the dentist and having her teeth drilled. Through synaesthesia the pain sensations gave rise to visual imagery of landscapes, sunshine, and other happy experiences. In discussing her case a colleague and I (Marks and McKellar 1982) drew attention to records of a seemingly related case of synaesthesia as an escape from pain and discomfort. It concerned Dr Edward Wilson, who recorded his subjective experiences in his diary of the Scott *Discovery* Antarctic expedition. Suffering the acute pain of snow-blindness, with bandaged eyes, pulling a sledge through icy temperatures, Wilson records his 'strangest thoughts or day dreams' of warm sunlit woods and 'all sorts of places connected with a hot sun'. There appears to have been a strong synaesthesia component. Wilson records how the 'swish-swish of the ski' would evoke the imagery of the woods 'brushing through dead leaves ... heather or juicy bluebells. One could almost see them and smell them.' He was in pain, he was cold, and was engaged in what to many people would be morale-reducing physical exertion pulling a heavy sledge. But Wilson adds, 'It was delightful' (diary of Saturday 27 December 1902). Again, once we become aware of the subjective accompaniment and the synaesthetic linkages, what he has to say becomes understandable. The utterances of synaesthetic people may be puzzling to others, as when Luria's subject referred to the psychologist Vigotsky as having 'a crumbly yellow voice', or when Edith Sitwell wrote of 'Emily coloured primroses'. At times they resemble the seemingly meaningless speech of people while waking up from sleep, which have been likened to the attempted communications of the schizophrenic. In these other cases the phrases used become understandable once the associative connections are understood. In the case of synaesthesia such connections are inter-sensory and this, to other people, provides an additional challenge to empathy.

Some of the more hidden differences between people have been considered with emphasis on thinking, remembering, and imagining. Awareness of their diversity may assist empathy with the mental life of others, and escape from the personal parochialism of our own. Often such variations are overlooked, or there is failure to recognize that what is characteristic of one individual does not necessarily apply to another. An example may be taken in the assertion by J. B. Watson (1928), pioneer of behaviourism, that 'thinking is sub-vocal speech'. Such a statement seems blind to the distinction between 'some' and 'all'. To consider it further I will draw on a concept from logic which will be used to elucidate variations of subjective experience.

THE SQUARE OF OPPOSITION

This concept is an elaboration of the 'some–all' distinction. The statement made by Watson clearly applies to some forms of thinking. On occasion a person may mentally compose a letter, or sub-vocally think through a problem in words. There are people for whom this way of thinking is characteristic. But there are alternatives involving those who can and do, visually or otherwise, use imagery when they think. Psychologists like Alan Richardson (1977) have been interested in studying this visualizer–verbalizer difference in both acts of thinking, and between individuals. Similar points may be made about what appears to have been Aristotle's own view that 'all thinking involves imagery'. The occurrence of imageless thought, and the variety of forms imagery can take, argue against this over-generalization. Yet from Aristotle and his successors in logic comes classification. The Square of Opposition relates to four types of statement that can be made.

Figure 2.4 The Square of Opposition

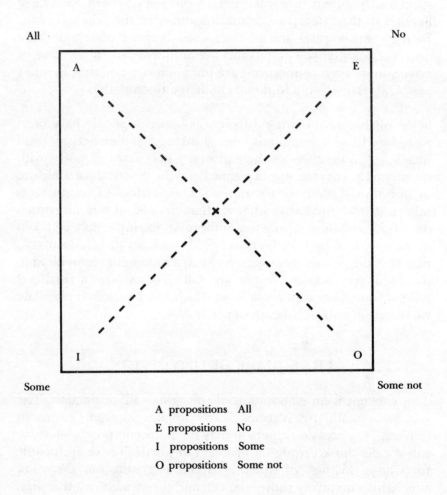

All

No

A

E

I

O

Some

Some not

A propositions   All
E propositions   No
I propositions   Some
O propositions   Some not

A propositions involving All (Universal affirmative)
E propositions involving No (Universal negative)
I propositions involving Some (Particular affirmative)
O propositions involving Some not (Particular negative)

Thus Watson was making an A-type assertion. If I wish to challenge it, as I have done, I respond with an O-type proposition:

some thinking is not sub-vocal talking. To take another example, if somebody wishes to argue with an E-type proposition that no people are able to project their imagery into a crystal, I may likewise deny this. The response is an I-type proposition, involving information that there are such people, and I have – like many others – investigated such imagery.

Although it is primarily a device for dealing with the form arguments may take, the Square of Opposition may also be applied to evidence about content. Immediately we come up against the difficulty of establishing universal statements, whether positive or negative. Since we cannot test all cases we can only state such propositions as probabilities, not certainties. The exception is statements that are true by definition, e.g. 'All psychiatrists are medically qualified,' or 'No true paranoiacs – as opposed to paranoid schizophrenics – are hallucinated' (in terms of the diagnostic criteria of true paranoia). As regards one important category of subjective experience we are now able to make the assertion 'All people dream.' This can be asserted, though only as probability, if we use as a criterion of dreaming the presence of recordable accompaniments like rapid eye movements (REMs). By the same criterion we may also assert with more confidence 'Some animal dream.' Marks (1986a) lists species in which REM sleep has been demonstrated, including for example the chimpanzee, elephant, sheep, kangaroo, pig, and mouse.

The Square of Opposition may be applied to subjective experiences of the kinds discussed, though sometimes only as probability statements. In discussing the body image my concern is with what I assume to be a universal form of subjective experience. Along with this A-type assertion it seems reasonable to advance an I-type statement that some people report body image distortions (e.g. while falling asleep). Do people dream in colour? From their introspective testimony we encounter O-type and I-type information: some say they don't, some say they do. The I-type proposition is particularly relevant to many phenomena I have discussed. This includes diagram forms, colour associations, lucid dreams, and visual synaesthesia for sounds. In the case of lucid dreaming, to be considered more fully later, we may be dealing with a phenomenon much more common than once believed. Once named, and people are alerted to notice it, evidence often accumulates about the relative frequency of a given phenomenon.

This applied even to the recognition of visual and other kinds of imagery. Galton's pioneer studies seriously under-estimated their frequency of occurrence. Most contemporary investigators report visual, auditory, tactile, and other kinds of imagery as very common indeed. One of my own investigations revealed that with a sample of 500 people, 97 per cent reported visual imagery, and 93 per cent reported the auditory kind. More than half the subjects had available to them in their mental life, in addition to these, imagery for movement, touch, taste, smell, and pain, and slightly less than half (48 per cent) could image temperature as well. In another part of the study it emerged that visual imagery (86 per cent) or auditory imagery (69 per cent) was the predominant kind: what they relied on most in thinking, remembering, and imagining (McKellar 1965a). In terms of contemporary evidence, denial of mental imagery is uncommon. Yet, in terms of their testimony we can make an O-type assertion: according to the people concerned themselves some people don't have it. Moreover the testimony of at least some such individuals as psychologists, should in fact be introspectively reliable. Among them was the claim of W. H. R. Rivers to know about imagery only through dreams and hypnagogic experiences. He declared, 'I am one of those persons whose normal waking life is almost totally free from sensory imagery, either visual, auditory, tactile or of any other kind' (Rivers 1920: 11). This did not prevent his contributing, as regards the imagery of sleep, a major book on the psychology of the dream (Rivers 1923).

Many of these phenomena permit O-type assertions, of the form 'some people – indeed most – don't have them'. Diagram forms, crystal-gazing visions and imaginary companions are seeming examples. As regards lucid dreams we should perhaps be cautious. Alerting to notice may again be relevant. In this respect hypnagogic imagery presents an interesting case. Early investigators claimed it to be a rarity, but later work indicated they were in error. Once alerted, a very large number of people report visual hypnagogia, and auditory equivalents are also common. As with dreaming, perhaps we are dealing with something universal. Much that happens in mental life is overlooked. Here we encounter what I will call the 'ladybird phenomenon', from an occasion when I found two ladybird beetles in the room while I was working. Is there another ladybird in this room? There may be, but I have not found one. It may be argued, but you have not looked properly! And I admit I have not. The ladybird phenomenon, failure to be alerted to notice, or to look for something in mental life, has been a common occurrence in psychology. Note also the degree of hostile disbelief many of these experiences provoke in people who deny having them. Some people are tolerant to such variants, others are not. I recall one occasion when a group of hypnagogic imagers were comparing their experiences with one another. An 'outsider' who denied having them remarked with great scorn, 'It sounds like a bunch of alcoholics discussing their DTs.' When asked to respond in a questionnaire, one subject indignantly wrote that because she was a Christian she 'didn't have' hypnagogic imagery. Similar intolerances even about diagram forms and colour associations have been noted earlier. As we have seen, if hostile disbelief is often encountered in relation to these variants of subjective experience, anxiety and fear may often be associated with aware-ness of one's own. From such emotional accompaniments of styles of thinking, remembering and imagining I turn to emotion itself, and its variants.

EMOTIONAL DIFFERENCES BETWEEN PEOPLE

Many variations between individuals are by no means hidden. Important among these are the opinions people develop about one another and social groups to which they and other people belong. 'Love', 'hate', 'dislike', and 'respect' are words of common use to refer to emotional habit systems. In the chapter to follow they will be examined in detail. Often such emotional investments are protected by what Bernard Hart (1936) has called logic-tight compartments. Hart uses Jung's term 'complex' for such systems. Such complexes – as systems of emotionally toned ideas – help to define an individual. They give rise to internal conflicts and inconsistencies of behaviour; they may be resistant to argument and evidence; and they provide major barriers to empathy. Hart's very wide category of complexes includes what Shand (1920) called 'sentiments'. These comprise emotional involvements like love and hate, liking and disliking, and loyalties to individuals, social groups, and causes. The justification for retaining the two terms 'complex' and 'sentiment' will be examined. They also exhibit similarities. As distinct from emotions, both point to individuality and differences between one personality and another. The mere arousal through provocation of fear or anger may tell us little about the individual concerned. To understand him or her as a person we need to know how learning has shaped the development of emotional habit systems. Such structures may be likened to coral reefs that have been built up through time: the emotions themselves resemble the organisms, the polyps that have been responsible for such structures. As C. E. Cory has put it, in emotion as such 'there is nothing that is worthy of the name individual.' He adds 'experience to be individual must be organised and stable', such structure 'ensures continuity' and a significance that 'extends beyond its existence . . . as an immediate experience' (Quoted in McDougall 1926: 531). These comments are in close accord with a distinction between specific emotions on the one hand, and sentiments on the other. We know a good deal about an individual in terms of his loves and hates, likings, and loyalties. These help to distinguish him or her as a personality. Sentiments and other emotional investments differ from emotions as such. Both will be considered in the chapter to follow.

SUMMARY

1   Variations of subjective experience are numerous, and even within the range of the normal the forms of mental life that differ markedly from our own may strain our credibility. Yet empathy with hidden differences between people provides a useful beginning to the study of apparent abnormalities.

2   Language to label such variants is limited, but some of those that have been named are discussed: *déjà vu*, synaesthesia, hypnagogic imagery, diagram forms, crystal-gazing, and lucid dreaming.

3   In the realm of mental imagery – subjective equivalents of looking and listening – we find wide differences that are important to thinking, remembering, and imagining. An illustration is taken of extremes of visual imagery from the cases of two authors.

4 'Thinking' is an ambiguous word, including both reasoning and imagination. A basic distinction is made between A-thinking and R-thinking whose interaction is important to normal thought products. Extremes of autistic or A-thinking are of importance in abnormal psychology, as well as to normal mental life.

5 The logician's concept of the Square of Opposition is introduced as a basis of classification of types of thinking, and of the commoner and less common variants of subjective mental life.

Chapter Three

EMOTIONAL SYSTEMS

No other emotion has had such general tributes paid to it; for love, its only competitor, is a sentiment.

Alexander Shand

Subjective experiences in which people differ from one another evoke a wide range of emotional reactions. Fear of the unknown and anxiety about becoming 'insane' may result in innocent variants being regarded as abnormal, even of supernatural origin. Emotions and emotional habits are of central interest in considering the neuroses and psychoses, and here we encounter depression, anxiety, and apathy in extreme forms. Many phenomena of abnormality can be seen as defences against anxiety: this emotional state may overwhelm the personality when such defences fail. Among such defences are the phobias, compulsions, and obsessions of the anankastic group of neuroses. Within the psychoses, the delusions and hallucinations may be highly charged with emotion. In everyday living with its struggle to achieve adjustment, conflicts may be acute between different emotional systems: loves, hates, and loyalties. We constantly encounter evidence that the human personality is, like the body, a set of sub-systems. The extreme case is the schizophrenic psychoses with a multiplicity of such systems operating in a shattered personality. In the case of depression it has been well said 'one part of us is standing by, and wouldn't miss the show for worlds.' Conscience is one such sub-system. And there are others within a personality: emotional habits like love and hate, which may, on occasion, overcome it. When this happens otherwise seemingly normal people may sometimes react with violence that resembles behaviour of the aggressive psychopath. Alcohol and indignation are two of the agencies in which the sub-system of conscience may well be said to be highly soluble. Indignation is dangerous. But there are other emotions.

The one to which Shand refers – and distinguishes from sentiments – is hope. Sometimes this, the optimistic emotion, is too closely involved in the excesses of wish-fulfilling A-thinking. As a bridge to reality it is not always reliable. Yet as Shakespeare puts it, 'The miserable have no other medicine' (*Measure for Measure*, III, i). The emotion of hope plays, at times, an important part as a 'balancing factor' of the personality: a resource to be called upon at times of stress and disappointment. La Rochefoucauld commented on the emotion: 'Deceitful as it is, it nevertheless carries us agreeably through life.' Again and again we encounter invocations to the optimistic emotion in expressions like 'I hope so' or 'I hope not', from people who at least half-believe that this verbal magic helps a little. With it a negotiator, for example, returns to his task.

Hope is one of the specific emotions. Fear, sorrow, amusement, and anger are others. Many words refer to emotionality. Yet despite this large vocabulary both everyday language and psychology itself often ignore an important distinction. Consider anger. Because of a widely accepted social rule strangers and acquaintances largely escape our anger and other negative expressions of specific emotions. By contrast anger is expressed against people we like, and even more against those we love. This does not mean that love turns to hate. The words a child, a lover, or a spouse speaks – 'I hate you' – often mean 'I'm angry with you'. Again, the expression 'making love' is used very loosely, and is better translated to mean that one or both are acting under experienced erotic emotion. Love may or may not be present, and tender emotion may play little part in it. An aid to tidying up such everyday misuses of words is the distinction emphasized by Shand in the words that head this chapter. Emotions like hope, fear, and anger are one thing. Emotional habit systems, like love and hate, are another.

AN ANATOMY OF EMOTIONAL LIFE

First is the category of specific emotions. They are many: along with fear, hope, sexual excitement, and anger, are others like surprise, relief, amusement, and sorrow. Some words refer to degrees of intensity, including terror as opposed to mere fear, or rage and fury as opposed to anger. Indignation is moralized anger. In all such instances the emotion, often accompanied by clear awareness of accompanying bodily changes, is prominent to consciousness and such changes can often be physiologically recorded. Some investigators have placed emphasis upon the disruptive effects of emotion, while others including Darwin have taken an alternative view. The fight or flight reaction of the anger and fear emotions may be biologically appropriate and conducive to survival. A human being experiencing emotion is very much aware of the fact, and of the object or situation to which that emotion relates.

Second, from specific emotions may be distinguished a variety of emotional habits. What Shand called 'sentiments' and Jung called 'complexes' are examples of these, as are the emotional habits which everyday language calls 'prejudices'. Following Shand, psychologists like Thouless (1935) have classified sentiments into the three categories of concrete particular, concrete general, and abstract. Loving, liking, or hating a specific person are instances of concrete particular sentiments; anti-semitism or colour prejudice are concrete general; and love of justice or hatred of cruelty would be abstract sentiments. Among abstract sentiments are those built round the notions of right and wrong, good and evil, justice and injustice: these are called 'moral sentiments'. Sentiments are emotional habits, complexes are systems of emotionally toned ideas of a habitual kind, and phobias are irrational habitual fears. A friendship or a phobia continues to exist, though neither the object nor the situation has been thought about for some time. When perceived or imaged the object evokes emotion, as though from some inner reservoir. As a mere fact, people do not go around all the time motivated by specific emotions. Indeed, as some investigators have proved for themselves by, for example, keeping a diary of instances of experienced emotion, civilization shields us from too frequent emotional arousal.

Table 3.1 An anatomy of emotion

Specific emotions	Being angry or indignant, surprised, frightened, or amused; experiencing hope or disappointment, sorrow, or regret.
	These result from either (1) immediate provocation; or (2) arousal of stored emotion from emotional habit systems like sentiments or complexes.
Emotional habit systems	(A) 'Tidy'. Sentiments. Liking or disliking somebody; being in love; parental affection; hostility or loyalty to a group; moral sentiments about the right, the good, and justice; sentiments about religion, social class, and one's national group. (These may be ambivalent.)
	(B) 'Untidy'. Complexes, prejudices, phobias, etc. They may comprise deterioration of sentiments into fanaticism; they include delusions, superstitions, and residues of emotionally traumatic experiences.
	Both A and B result from the interaction of emotions with learning experiences. Both help to define the individuality of the personality.
Other	(C) Emotional states, or moods. Examples are elation, depression, demoralization, and calm serenity.
	(D) Feeling tone. Degree of pleasure–unpleasure that accompanies mental states.
	(E) Guilt feelings, anxiety, and feelings of inferiority; exaggerated feelings of conviction, including free-floating certainty.

The Canadian psychologist D. O. Hebb has developed the theory that man is not merely the most intelligent of the animals, but also the most emotional. Yet this is not obvious. The reason is to be found in the norms and customs of human society, the rules and taboos which insulate us from fear and from anger. A diary of experiences of fear by Garwood (1961), together with one kept by myself on anger, provide evidence in support of this assessment. To amplify: having earlier kept an anger diary, I gave up keeping a fear diary because the experiences were so few; this is not because I am specially brave, but rather because – under normal circumstances – society organizes it that way. Dr Garwood persisted with the fear diary for the Ph.D. research he was doing. The fear experiences we both found related largely to being a pedestrian or motorist on the roads. Living in a modern city under normal conditions, neither of us was often frightened in other ways.

Failures of empathy that occur to observation – and sometimes to introspection – have been discussed earlier. But as regards empathy with the actions, and even safety, of others, sometimes it is 'interesting' to note how unemotional and law-abiding individuals act when driving a car. Researches by Parry (1968) of motorist behaviour reveal some frightening heights of aggression closely resembling psychopathic behaviour in unpleasant forms. One such subject reported to Parry, 'I drove my car right into the back of his. ... I would have smashed his face in too ... I'm sorry about my car being smashed, but it was worth it' (Parry op. cit., quoted in McKellar 1977b: 18–19). For much of the time social norms as rules of society restrain such upsurges of anger. Exceptions are frightening, and as Schopenhauer reminds us, human savagery can erupt when these rules break down. We see this happening in riot, panic, and disaster, and even in the road behaviour of apparently normal people.

THE TWO SOURCES OF EMOTION

Alexander Shand was the first secretary of the then newly formed British Psychological Society. Like Sir Francis Galton, a man of independent means, he valued good food and wine. At dinners of the society he 'would discuss the specific emotions as though they had vintage and bouquet', as Professor Pear once told me. Shand's major contribution, *The Foundations of Character* (1920), was an unusual book, a kind of historical symposium he chaired. Contributors were poets, dramatists, novelists, and philosophers selected for their sensitivity to often subtle complexities of experience and behaviour. Drawing on this material Shand develops his thesis: although we are sometimes motivated by specific emotions, much of the time the process is a more indirect one. It is through the sentiments as internal reservoirs of emotional energy. These sentiments give rise to a whole range of responses under different circumstances to the object of the sentiment. Many leading British psychologists took over Shand's concept of the sentiment. They included McDougall, C. S. Myers, Burt, Pear, Flugel, and Thouless.

Sir Cyril Burt (1937) contributed the idea that sentiments are often ambivalent. They contain strong components of both positive and negative emotion: thus in relation to their object they may impel towards both sympathetic and antipathetic feelings and actions. For his part Pear added the notion that the negative component is often hidden by repression. A rival concept interested some others, like Bernard Hart in his *Psychology of Insanity* (1936). This was Jung's notion of the complex as 'a system of emotionally toned ideas'.

Whatever terminology we use it becomes apparent that the sources of emotional arousal are two-fold. On the one hand external factors provoke emotion. These, in accord with the Koffka Principle, result from perception, accurate or otherwise, of actions by people and environmental events. But the second internal source of emotional arousal should not be forgotten. Internal habit systems like sentiments and complexes store emotional energy. They define a given individual's personality, and permit predictions to be made in everyday life situations. Thus an empathic host or hostess may introduce two strangers, knowing that they will get on as they have interests and sentiments in common. Clashes can occur if mistakes are made. Common interests may involve strongly opposing sentiments. Positive sentiments define a wide range of sympathetic responses to friends, love objects, and groups we identify with. By contrast there is also a range of antipathetic emotions towards social groups we reject and even individuals who – in the case of political opponents – we may not even have met. Characters from history or fiction – whom we cannot meet – may also become objects of strong sentiments, both positive and negative. Self-love – Freud's narcissism – and self-hatred – Flugel calls it 'nemesism' – are specific instances of sentiments.

We learn much about violence and aggression from study of both negative and positive sentiments. More than mere immediate provocation is involved. There are additional reserves of emotion that may well up spontaneously because of established hostility to some out-group or loyalty to one's own cause. It is because of these inner reservoirs of emotion from strongly held sentiments – both pro and con – that otherwise mild-mannered and law-abiding individuals may, on occasion, behave with aggressiveness, brutality, and cruelty suggestive of the pathological. The inconsistencies which characterize human beings may be seen in terms not only of immediate provocation of emotion, but also in terms of such personality sub-systems.

SENTIMENT AND DELUSION

One of the best known cases from forensic psychology may be taken to show how strongly held sentiments may shade into delusions. Consider the instance of Daniel McNaghten, around which the McNaghten Rules were later to be formulated. Perceiving a man he mistakenly believed to be Sir Robert Peel, McNaghten was provoked to the act of murder. The event took place in Whitehall, London, on Friday 20 January 1843. McNaghten's victim was actually a man called Drummond who seems to have physically resembled Peel. At the trial a system of persecutory delusions was uncovered. The accused had developed strong sentiments against Peel, who was at the time pursuing a policy sympathetic to Ireland and Irish nationalism. McNaghten had come to believe he was being persecuted by Catholics, Jesuits, and thus, ultimately, Peel and the Tory party. So he set out to kill the Tory leader by an act which he believed to be justified as one of self-defence. Here we encounter negative sentiments carrying their own morality, and moralized aggression stemming from it. History has judged McNaghten insane. The term 'monomania' was used at his trial: his subjective world revolved around grievance and fancied danger. In such a case we are not merely dealing with immediately provoked emotion. It was not an impulsive act, but one stemming from an emotionally charged habit system. Many assassins of leading political figures have been of this kind, and sometimes idiosyncratic political reasons have motivated their action.

Somewhat similar to that of Daniel McNaghten was a New Zealand case, again involving homicide. The man concerned, Lionel Terry, became almost certainly the most famous patient in New Zealand psychiatric history. Tall, highly intelligent, bearded, and highly educated, Terry had about him a dignity often associated with paranoid psychosis. He made several successful escapes from various psychiatric hospitals. After Terry's return from one of these, the superintendent, Sir Truby King – known for his own work in pediatrics – decided to make a deal with Terry. The patient, with his usual dignity, gave his parole and in return Dr King gave him wide privileges within the hospital grounds. Terry wrote poetry and did paintings that revealed considerable artistic skill; he had his own garden in which he made his own wine; he 'permitted' university students to visit him, and greeted them with an impressive presence not unlike that of a now white-bearded biblical prophet. This dignified, talented man, who of course adhered scrupulously to the parole he had given, was a murderer. His victim was an elderly and inoffensive Chinese whom Terry 'executed', as he put it, in a street in Wellington. The following day he handed himself over to the police authorities, who had been baffled at this seemingly motiveless crime. This was, in his own opinion, fully justified. For Terry it was not the Jesuits and Tories that were persecuting but the 'Yellow Peril', Chinese immigrants. He wished to make a public gesture, and did so by his – as he saw it – justifiable act of 'execution'. As his means he chose a Chinese man who was both elderly and in a poor state of health. Strong sentiments about 'race' and 'racial purity' were central to Lionel Terry's personality. 'He was a disciple of Hitler then?' I asked one medical student who had recently interviewed him. 'Only at first,' he replied. 'Later Terry saw Hitler as one of *his* disciples.' This historically interesting case brings out the fact that sharp distinctions between the pathology of legal-political offences and paranoid delusional systems are not easy to make. Terry had characteristics of an intelligent, highly talented, sensitive man, an artist, and – among other things – enlightened reformer of psychiatric hospitals. He was also, like Daniel McNaghten – because of the structure of his emotional life – a very dangerous man. In such cases 'sentiment' may not seem the most appropriate word for such emotional structuring.

SENTIMENTS, COMPLEXES, AND PREJUDICES

Half a century ago the first psychology professor in Britain – Professor T. H. Pear – invited Shand and others to his department at Manchester University. The occasion was a symposium to discuss the issue: 'Does psychology need both sentiments and complexes?' Many were by this time using the two terms inter-

changeably, though some defined complexes as 'repressed sentiments'. Jung had defined a complex as 'a system of emotionally
toned ideas'. Elsewhere in science we find the term 'complex', as
in biology for a group of cells or in geology for a mountain
system. Pear's own contribution was, I believe, the most psychologically interesting.

The host psychologist argued for preserving the distinction,
and for keeping both terms. We need to do this, he argued, to
take account of both 'the tidy and the untidy' aspects of emotional
life (Pear 1922). Sentiments are 'tidy' in that they figure strongly
in the normal personality: feelings and actions that stem from
them are largely predictable, and we are prepared intellectually to
defend them. Complexes are different. As another of the psychologists present, C. S. Myers, put it, they are characterized by
'surprise, irrationality, and unpredictability'. Pear himself stressed
their explosive all-or-nothing character. At best we excuse them
rather than rationally justify them. We may use words like 'I'm
sorry but I can't help it' or 'I've got a thing about so and so' or 'I
know I'm being silly and irrational, but. ...' In defending this
analysis Pear used many analogies to elucidate the difference
between these two kinds of emotional system. He likened sentiments to well-maintained, tidy gardens, and to properly serviced
electrical switchboards. But gardens may disintegrate into unkempt
jungles; electrical systems may become a mass of dangerous live
wires. Thus sentiments may similarly degenerate into complexes,
as when a normal patriotic sentiment turns into anti-social jingoism,
or a religious sentiment becomes intolerant fanaticism. A more
modern analogy may be added. A traveller just returned from a
recent visit to Tibet has made the point that although the Potala in
Lhasa withstood the wanton destructiveness of the Red Guards of
the 'Cultural Revolution', it is amazing that it has survived its
incredibly dangerous electrical wiring. The comment reminds us
of how nationalistic and political sentiments can degenerate
into motivation for irrational and destructive fanaticism. In the
destruction of much of the culture of Tibet in this period we again
encounter the influence of reservoirs of energy stored up within
explosive learned systems.

Pear further likens sentiments to music as opposed to loud
noise: a happy analogy in that what is music to teenagers is often
mere noise to their parents. Generation differences represent

only one of many areas in which sentiments of individuals or between groups may clash. Sentiments relating to animals comprise another such area. Thus conflicts have arisen in the United Kingdom over methods of killing animals for food supported by religious sentiments, notably those of Islam. Other conflicts, including some which have led to overt acts of aggression, have arisen over 'Animal Liberation'. Strongly held sentiments about animal experiments and vivisection have motivated acts of violence directed against human beings.

Everyday language makes use of the term 'prejudice'. This seems to refer to emotional systems with resemblances to both sentiments and complexes. Prejudices may be pro or con, or ambivalent in character. As regards animals, even outside the phobias we encounter many widespread negative prejudices, e.g. snakes and spiders. When human beings behave in particularly revolting ways others often describe them as 'animals' or 'wild beasts'. Yet rarely do such speakers have in mind the objects of pro-prejudices, such as koalas, pandas, and bush babies. As a whole, prejudices, whether about animals or humans, resemble delusions in their attributes of rigidity, strong emotionality, and resistance to evidence and argument. Yet like sentiments – as opposed to complexes – prejudices are sometimes intellectually defended, even with a degree of pride. As regards negative prejudices relating to human groups a distinction may be made between two types. Sometimes they are 'secondary', in the sense that they derive largely from taking over prejudices of other people, involving minimal contact with members of the group concerned. Some years ago, with a group of university students in New Zealand, I found the students as a whole were strongly prejudiced against Turks. Inquiry revealed that none of them had, in fact, ever met a Turk! It was purely secondary prejudice. With such a prejudice the appropriate advice is 'go and meet some'. Attitude change or appropriate therapy is different with 'primary' prejudices, which are based on over-generalization from individuals the prejudiced person has actually encountered. This is a different thing, to which the suggestion 'go and meet some more' is appropriate.

In considering national groups one has to be careful. To play safe I will make reference to Bouvet Island – a remote place in the South Atlantic, about 1,000 miles from the nearest land – which is uninhabited. In exploring the grammar of prejudice we can thus speak freely about the deplorable attributes of 'Bouvet Islanders'. We can accuse them of the usual failings regularly attributed to minority groups. And they have other uses, for example, in variations of subjective mental life of the kind earlier discussed: 'none of them experiences hypnagogic imagery', or alternatively, 'all of them experience synaesthesia', or are lucid dreamers. Such references to imaginary populations are by no means inappropriate. Enterprising social psychologists have found that it is merely necessary to invent some national group to find people prepared to be prejudiced against it. Along with my islanders such peoples belong to that interesting category of logic, the logician's 'null class'. Members of such a class may become the objects of strong sentiments, both positive and negative. A child may develop considerable fondness for its imaginary companion though it has no existence in reality. The last child I interviewed expressed her strongly positive sentiment towards fairies, and also ambivalence including a regrettable degree of positive emotion towards vampires. Social groups that undoubtedly exist also have some reference to the null class in that the ethically dubious attributes allegedly present in many minority groups are likewise non-existent. Similarly many of the characters of history, being merely stereotypes, never in fact lived.

ETHICS AND PSYCHOLOGY

The notion that it is a moral responsibility to assault, injure, or kill other human beings has its place in any thoughtful consideration of abnormal psychology. Here we turn to ethics or moral philosophy as a discipline. This has much to teach about the psychology of moralized emotional systems and their influence upon behaviour and experience. One important classic by the moral philosopher Sir David Ross has as its title *The Right and the Good* (1930). It distinguishes these two things. 'The good' relates to values which are psychologically important to long-term motivation, as when we pursue beauty, truth, or the welfare of other people. By contrast, 'the right' relates to notions like duty and morally reputable motivation. In terms of what people actually do, quite often some good — like financial support of an area of human welfare – may result from ethically neutral or even dubious motivation. By contrast, a sense of duty can result in suffering and human misery, the reverse of good in any value sense. Ross himself is vigorous in defence of his dual theory. In developing it he considers a number of '*prima facie* duties' on the side of the right, and also a number of different manifestations of the good. Thus in his psychology he adheres to the healthy doctrine: what people actually do involves multiple motivation.

At an earlier date a group of philosophers, the Moral Sense School, also argued the case for 'multiple motivation'. Important among these was Bishop Joseph Butler, who saw the body as 'a composition of various parts' and mental life also as a series of sub-systems: 'The principles of our mind may be contradictory, or checks and allies only, or incentives and assistants to each other' (Butler 1729). Among these principles are two which correspond closely to what Shand would label moral sentiments, or Ross would see in terms of *prima facie* duties. One is the principle of benevolence or altruism: concern for the welfare of other people. The second is prudence or cool self-love: concern about one's own long-term welfare, as opposed to the short-term advantages of impulsive emotional actions. Butler's prudence concept resembles Freud's reality principle which guides consciousness, and restrains the pleasure principle that dominates the unconscious. For Butler benevolence and prudence may often coincide, rather than oppose each other. Both are organized in a hierarchical way under a third principle, conscience, which approves or censors conduct in terms of its rightness or otherwise. A second thinker of this Moral Sense School was Adam Smith – also one of the pioneers of modern economics – who anticipated Shand's concept of the sentiment. Adam Smith's notion of conscience or moral sense was of 'an impartial spectator'. This internal sub-system of the personality overlooks impulses and actions, stands apart from them, and evaluates them as would some fair-minded, impartial bystander. A similar concept is to be found in the idea of the judgement of 'a reasonable man', a notion sometimes invoked in modern courts of law.

Some kind of moral sense – it has many names, of which 'conscience' and 'superego' are two – is one important sub-system of the personality. There are others, including influential master sentiments, and sentiments in general. Here we encounter an important principle relating to the functioning of sentiments and other emotional habits. Shand writes of the 'Relative Ethics of a Sentiment', its special emotions, its virtues, ideals, and duties acquired by the sentiment as it develops. It works for or against its object and functions in accord with the ends of that sentiment (Shand 1920: 116). This applies to both positive and negative sentiments, as when we make moral exceptions for our friends and the causes we favour, and against those of which we dis-approve. Sympathetic and antipathetic emotion operate in moralized forms and each sentiment tends to bring with it a relative ethics of its own. Objects of our negative sentiments, being morally despicable or evil, 'deserve what they get': we feel released from ordinary restraints in dealing with them. Hate may be in this way subject to this principle of relative ethics, and as Shand puts it 'tends to destroy all virtues, ideals and duties that restrain it from its ends' (Shand 1920: 119). We have seen emotions have not merely one source, but two. We may of course be provoked to moralized anger, or indignation. But there is also an internal reservoir of emotion locked up in emotional habits like sentiments. Thus indignation may erupt against some person, group, or institution towards which hatred has developed. When the relative ethics of such a sentiment operate the result can be extremes of behaviour, vindictiveness, brutal aggression, and cruelty at its worst. It is not only that the external rules of society have broken down: also relative ethics operate internally to weaken such restraints from within. Sometimes there is, instead, an interaction of the general morality – the moral sentiments of the personality – with this relative ethics of the sentiment. It is an understatement, as regards human behaviour in some of its most horrible forms, merely to say that such restraints do not always operate. Violence, aggression, and evidence about it, at for example the Nuremberg Trial, will be discussed in later sections. Shand's principle of Relative Ethics of Sentiments is of consider-able relevance to their understanding.

PERSONALITY INTEGRATION AND SUB-SYSTEMS

Recognition of sub-systems within the personality has characterized the work of many psychologists. In developing his theory of personality – he called it 'character' – William McDougall (1871–1938) drew on the work of Shand. Like Shand he distinguished sentiments, as enduring emotional habits, from specific emotions. Personality is a hierarchical system organized under some dominant sentiment or value system, exhibiting greater or lesser degrees of integration of the components. Important for McDougall as an integrating principle was the 'sentiment of self regard': this resembles Butler's 'conscience' or Freud's 'ego'. For McDougall acts of volition involve the personality as a whole, integrated under some such master sentiment. Internal conflicts can arise between other personality systems and are often resolved by this integrating principle acting like 'the dominant member of a society' in appeals to 'the sentiment of self respect' (McDougall 1926: 548). Lack of integration of the personality, conceived of as dissociation, is for McDougall a clue to much abnormal behaviour. Likewise, 'when I relax my control, in states of sleep, hypnosis, relaxation, and abstraction the subordinate systems ... replace the normal and harmonious co-operation of all members in one system' (op. cit.: 548). The automatisms of fugues, somnambulisms and the trance personalities of the seance room are conceived of in similar dissociation terms. McDougall conceives of 'a sentiment or complex as a structural and functional unity'. He adds that such a system 'may become relatively isolated from the rest of the structure of the mind; it becomes a "complex" in the pathological sense' (op. cit.: 159). He cites the famous case of Miss Beauchamp – to be discussed in our next chapter – as representing the extreme instance in which such a subordinate system acquires increasing influence over other members of the internal society.

The sub-systems of ego, id, and superego comprise the alternative language of psychoanalysis to deal with inter-psychic conflict and its byproducts of guilt feeling and anxiety. As Freudian theory developed, it came to recognize repression as but one of a large repertoire of mechanisms for coping with such internal conflicts. It is not repression itself, but threatened 'return of the repressed', that comes closest to the alternative concept of dissociation. Many other such mechanisms have been described and labelled by psychoanalysts. For example in 'projection' we avoid awareness of our own guiltiness by attributing blame to someone else. In 'identification with the aggressor' we reduce anxious fear by ourselves assuming a dominant and aggressive role. Anna Freud (1936), Flugel (1945), and others placed emphasis on a range of ego defensive mechanisms which may both reduce anxiety and contribute to self-deception. Among them, and allied to dissociation, is 'isolation': mental compart-mentalization. Ideas and emotions are isolated from one another. Isolation also performs important adjustive functions, as when we seek to exclude emotions and sentiments, and think in an un-emotional and fair-minded way. Magistrates, in administering the law, use it when they put aside sympathy they may feel for an accused. A scientist isolates when he excludes emotion and seeks to evaluate in accord with the evidence. In doing so he may have to isolate his judgement from irrelevant feelings of satisfaction at disproving some disliked rival, or confirming the work of another scientist he admires. In dealing with the main Nuremberg Trial we shall later consider how G. M. Gilbert (1948a), as psychologist observer, recorded instances of failure of these isolation defences. Sometimes members of the leading Nazi accused – when confronted with evidence of what they had been responsible for – would emotionally break down in open court. At other times tears of shame were observed in interviews with Gilbert later. Isolation may play its part in the training of a medical student when he is learning to dissect the human body, though the defences may prove inadequate later when first asked to perform a postmortem. Even professional pathologists have told me how difficult it can be at times to maintain objectivity because of upsurges of emotion.

LOSS OF THE 'AS IF'

Subjective experiences which erupt into consciousness may some-times seem wholly foreign to our own mental life. They may surprise us in that we don't feel them part of ourself. It is from 'somewhere else' they seem to come. As illustration I take an occasion when I was a subject in a series of experiments by Dr Hannah Steinberg (1956) on the effects of nitrous oxide. Having once before experienced 'laughing gas', I was interested in this opportunity to learn more about its effects in producing an altered state of consciousness. The previous occasion had been a dental extraction. In awakening from this I had undergone what I would now call a hypnopompic image of my dentist in fishing waders in the middle of a river! I knew he was a keen angler. It was a blend of R-thinking complicated by an upsurge of A-thinking. The dentist who was bending over me was real, but the river and fishing equipment were hallucinatory. Happenings in the Steinberg experiment were different, but equally strange and alarming. As she found also with her other subjects, abnormal psychology can be an experimental science. For me there was an upsurge of thoughts and images that seemed alien to my personality. It felt 'as if' somebody else was putting them into my mind. But soon this 'as if' disappeared, and in my clouded state of consciousness I heard myself speaking out loud the words 'enemies are putting thoughts into my mind'. Earlier I discussed this phenomenon as the 'loss of the as if' experience, arguing that retention of the 'as if' is one of the things that distinguishes sanity from psychosis (McKellar 1957).

Having recovered from the effects of nitrous oxide, I found myself likening this upsurge of alien ideas to tuning in to a different radio station. The wish to deny authorship may be emphasized, and the sense of some clearly external source was very real. In later experiments with hallucinogens my colleagues and I encountered similar phenomena. Thus, on looking into a crystal globe after taking mescaline, a subject would have visions of projected images. They would seem to emerge from, and be part of, the crystal, to belong there certainly not to come from the subject herself. As one of our subjects commented, 'I feel as if I could step back and they would still be there.' His retention of the 'as if' may be noticed, insight into recognizing he was taking part as subject in an experiment. In my own experience with nitrous oxide I lost such awareness, and so produced a fine simulation of paranoid schizophrenic experience and behaviour.

We may next turn to a more detailed examination of related phenomena in which dissociated sub-systems of the personality express themselves. In the more extreme forms of dissociation they may assume an identity of their own: here we encounter multiple personality.

SUMMARY

1 Emotions are distinguished from emotional habits, important among which are the sentiments. Sentiments comprise loves and

hates, likings and dislikings, and our pro and con emotional investments in individuals and social groups we identify with. Sentiments are 'tidy' and complexes are 'untidy' emotional systems.

2   There are thus two sources of emotion: immediate provocation, and emotional arousal that erupts from the stored reservoir of emotion in an emotional system. Prejudices are considered and their relation to delusions discussed in terms of two case histories: Daniel McNaghten and Lionel Terry.

3   Among the principles that Shand introduced with his treatment of the psychology of emotional systems was the notion of Relative Ethics of the Sentiment. Moralized emotional responses may occur – for example, in indignation as opposed to mere anger – and we tend to make moral exceptions for or against others in accord with our pro and con sentiments. Ethics itself has sometimes made contributions to psychology, notably to the understanding of how duties, and values influence motivation.

4   In some respects the personality may be viewed as a set of sub-systems, of component parts which may function with some degree of autonomy. Here we encounter the concept – which is re-emerging into contemporary psychology – of dissociation of the personality. Within normal mental life, sub-systems like prejudices may become influential: in more extreme cases we encounter dual and multiple personality.

Chapter Four

DISSOCIATION OF THE PERSONALITY

Two or more personalities, each of which is so well developed and integrated as to have a relatively co-ordinated, rich, and stable life of its own.

Taylor and Martin

Many analogies have been used to express the notion of unconscious mental life. Karl Menninger (1946) likens consciousness to the stage of a theatre, with groups of unruly actors all keen to make their often inappropriate appearances on it. Upsurges of A-thinking that feel alien to the personality may be seen in such terms, as eruptions from the unconscious. To get away from pervasive imagery of depth and darkness we might liken the personality to a large and complex social organization. Within it are numerous competing groups and ambitious individuals pursuing their various interests. There is also a remoteness – characteristic of many such institutions – between leadership and followers. Lack of empathy between component parts within the whole results from lines of communication which are primitive or non-existent. The individuals and groups concerned are largely unconscious of one another. Such may be a personality. Few organizations are more complex than the personality itself with its numerous sub-systems. During therapy there are indications that what is 'unconscious' is linkages between the sub-systems, each often highly charged with emotion. Gaining insight is less a matter of excavating what has been repressed, in the sense of wholly forgotten, but rather of establishing such linkages. Here we

67

encounter the concept of dissociation. Menninger (op. cit.: 233) defines dissociation in these terms. 'Groups of ideas, together with their emotional concomitants, may become split off from the main personality ... and continue a separate existence.'

In multiple personality, the extreme case of dissociation, we often – though not always – encounter prominent elements of hostility and conflict between competitive sub-systems. Such hostility figures prominently in three of the major literary anticipations of what might be called the 'Jekyll–Hyde syndrome'. They were in 1839 Poe's *William Wilson*; in 1846 Dostoevsky's *The Double*; and finally in 1886 Stevenson's own famous story. Dissociation in the form of a somnambulism induced by laudanum had also appeared in literature. This was in the Wilkie Collins novel, *The Moonstone*, of 1849, and it provided illustration of ways of gaining access to a dissociated store of information by returning the person concerned to a somnambulistic mental state. Alternative ways of tapping such content from a system that continues to function along with normal consciousness interested the Boston investigators Sidis and Goodhart (1905). Along with hypnotism they mention such techniques as automatic writing and crystal-gazing. In their own work they had encountered a remarkably interesting case to which they give a dissociation interpretation.

AMNESIA AND REV. HANNA

A young clergyman, Rev. Thomas Hanna, fell from a carriage. After a period of loss of consciousness he remembered nothing. He had no ability to recognize familiar objects, no capacity for speech, and is described by the investigators as acting 'like a newly born infant'. The original personality, which they call A, seemed to have disappeared and with it the knowledge previously possessed by a well-educated young man. Another system, a B-personality, seemed to have assumed control. This lacked knowledge and skills previously possessed but its capacity to learn was excellent for information fed in a process of re-education. Within a period of six weeks following the fall, B was able to engage in normal conversation, though this B-personality remained amnesic for A's past life. As one test, B was shown a long passage of Hebrew, familiar to the A-personality, and he was able to complete it by automatic speech. It had no meaning to him. Next he was taken to the city of New York in the hope that previous memories would be revived. The following morning he woke up in his original A-personality with amnesia for the B period and all events since the accident. Then, the next morning he awoke again as the B-personality with amnesia for A. Periods of alternation between the A and B systems followed. After a week of this the subject found himself confronted with the memories of both A and B and, as he reported, 'I decided to take both lives as mine.' A successful integration of the personality was achieved.

During their treatment the investigators used light hypnosis of the Rev. Hanna in his B-personality state in efforts to tap the forgotten memories of the original A-personality. Deeper states of hypnosis did not prove to be possible. Of interest was the spontaneous occurrence of vivid dreams about persons and places which friends were able to identify as familiar to the original A-personality. They were not recognized as such by the B-personality, nor were images that also occurred during the states of light hypnosis. The passage of Hebrew which the B-personality was able to complete through automatic speech frightened him. It felt, he reported, 'as if another being was speaking through me'.

These events in the life of the Rev. Hanna are less well known than those of other cases that emerged about this time in the Boston area. William James had been interested in another clergyman, Rev. Ansel Bourne. This famous case involved states of fugue, a 'flight' from one personality system, and way of life, to another that was entirely different. The alternating personalities concerned were treated hypnotically. We shall return to considering it in more detail later. The next happening was the First International Congress of Psychology in Paris, at which Morton Prince presented his paper on 'The Misses Beauchamp'. His report on perhaps the most famous case in the literature of multiple personality later appeared in 1905 as *The Dissociation of a Personality*. Fortunately the text of this classic study has become available again in a re-edited edition (Prince 1905, edition 1978). Miss Beauchamp will specially concern us. In all of these cases treatment of the altered mental states by hypnotism played an important part. The investigators frequently faced the criticism that the phenomena they reported were artefacts of hypnotism and its misuse. Morton Prince in particular was widely accused of gullibility. Hostility to hypnotism in therapy that grew up as the psychoanalytic movement became more influential, did not help. It may be noted that Pierre Janet, with his interests in fugues, somnambulisms, and multiple personality, had, late last century, visited Boston and Harvard and had lectured there. Janet's ideas had obvious appeal to the influential William James who makes reference to 'splitting of the mind into different consciousness'. James adds that Janet 'designates by numbers the different personalities which the subject may display' (James 1890, vol. 1: 210). We may choose alternative constructs in conceptualizing complex mental happenings. Thus one might explain the case of Rev. Hanna as an instance of amnesia brought about by his fall, and presumably registered in some way in his central nervous system. Then followed a process of recovery of functions – variable in appearance at different times – and finally a return to his normal self. I find Christine Beauchamp – discussed more fully below – more difficult to conceptualize without invoking the concept of dissociation. In parts of the world today very different concepts would be chosen.

POSSESSION AND MULTIPLE PERSONALITY

Neglect of phenomena that psychologists view in terms of dissociation and multiple personality has been only partial. Exceptions have included some major investigators of the paranormal. They include McDougall (1926) on trance personalities of the seance; Métraux (1972) on possession in the West Indies; Bourguignon (1973) on African spirit oracles; and Ian Wilson (1981) on instances of alleged reincarnation. Voodoo possession was re-examined by Karen Brown in 1976. In her thesis she argues that 'within a single person there are many selves' and adds 'in Haiti these manifest themselves through the various personalities of the gods' (Brown 1976: 289). Zusne and Jones (1982) discuss a whole range of allegedly supernatural phenomena in terms of dissociation. Subsequently Leonard Zusne has argued that there are many happenings 'from automatic writing to voodoo possession' that can best be seen in terms of 'dissociated states of personality' (Zusne 1983: 20). In analysing possession Ellenberger (1970) distinguishes two types: lucid and somnambulistic. In lucid possession the person is aware of the possessing entity; in somnambulistic possession the entity takes over, and there is loss of such insight. Elsewhere I have examined the parallel between these and two manifestations given the alternative interpretation of multiple personality (McKellar 1986). These will be reconsidered in similarly naturalistic, as opposed to supernatural, terms.

MULTIPLE PERSONALITY: RETURN OF THE OSTRACIZED

Does multiple personality exist as a reality, outside the imaginative literature of Robert Louis Stevenson and his various predecessors? Taylor and Martin (1944), whose definition heads this chapter, approached multiple personality in a mood of scepticism. In the research literature they found seventy-six such cases. By the time of Nemiah's (1975) study there was evidence for 200. Interpreted supernaturally as spirit possession, or sometimes reincarnation, multiple personality has a long history. The earliest case given a naturalistic interpretation is usually taken to be that of Mary Reynolds, recorded in 1817. In this there was an alternation between Mary's 'first state' and 'second state' that went on, with mutual amnesia, over a period of years until her death in 1854. Bliss (1980), however, refers to a report by Paracelsus of 1646 which involved a woman who stole her own money, but had complete amnesia for the occasions on which she did this. As regards both history and incidence, from the side of anthropology Erika Bourguignon (1973) provided an antidote to cultural ethnocentrism. She examined 400 non-western cultures. There was evidence of social and institutional support for some form of dissociation in 356 – that is, 89 per cent – of them. Rarity or otherwise depends on the social norms which encourage a phenomenon and alert us to notice or ignore it. Among such norms we encounter well-established psychiatric habits and criteria of diagnosis.

As Warner (1985) has reminded us, the tightening up of diagnostic criteria by the American Psychiatric Association has had several effects. With their 1980 revised manual now in use we are encountering numerous cases of multiple personality among dissociative neuroses. The revised DSM III (1980) manual accepts a category of multiple personality for which it lays down new diagnostic criteria. Individual cases like Miss Beauchamp, Spanish Maria, Rev. Hannah, and Eve with her three faces, recorded in at least four books, now have a context. In this study of a series of thirty-three such cases Kluft (1984) argues that the development of the treatment side has 'hardly begun'. Cruelty towards the patient in childhood, so revoltingly present in for example the case of Sybil (Schreiber 1975), now emerges as a frequent causal factor. Also from the side of press and apparent in the Sybil case, there is some evidence of pressures on the patients from a narrow, primitive and intellectually limited religious background. Many of the famous cases have been women rather than men. The incidence studies now possible support this: R. B. Allison, for example, gives a sex difference of 85 per cent female and 15 per cent male. Many investigators are now able to report on study of whole populations of cases rather than just individuals. Bliss (1984) strongly questions the claim that multiple personality is rare, as was once supposed. On the overall assessment of evidence available to him, from a polling of psychiatrists, Braun (1984) estimates no less than approximately one thousand such people now in the United States. As regards his own experience, Kluft (1984) reports having interviewed within his own practice 171 such patients during a period of ten years, these involving referrals from over fifty sources.

The general picture now emerging provides a frame of reference for the famous individual cases like Miss Beauchamp, Eve, and Sybil. High hypnotizability seems to characterize such individuals, and contemporary investigators follow Morton Prince himself in using hypnotism in therapy. Spiegel (1984: 101) describes the syndrome as one which involves individuals who are 'both highly hypnotizable and have a history of severe developmental abuse and neglect'. Characteristically such patients report periods of 'lost time', as happened with Christine Beauchamp, Eve, and Sybil. One such patient told me of repeatedly being accused of 'lying' about actions she didn't remember. They learn about their doings in other ways. In the Miss Beauchamp case, for example, the personality B.I observed herself through crystal-gazing in the Sally personality. Sally was smoking. The violently anti-smoking B.I reacted with horror. 'Other ways' in the case of Eve involved the use of films and tape recordings through which it was possible to make the personalities of Eve White, Eve Black, and Jane aware of one another. A history of headaches and hallucinatory voices regularly recurs in the numerous cases now being reported. As happened with the sixteen personalities of Sybil, the sub-systems may differ in their body images. Two of Sybil's subliminal selves were male, Mary was plump with dark brown hair, Vanessa was a tall redhead, 'with a willowy figure', while Ruthie was a baby (Schreiber 1975). In the contemporary research literature we find many instances of body image differences as between the personalities and sometimes also differences of handedness. Sybil Dorsett and Eve White emerge as colourless, 'depleted' people, and the same picture of the primary personality is now regularly reported. Thus Clary *et al.* (1984) refer to 'lack of vitality in the host personality', and 'depletion or impoverishment of the central ego'. This they explain in terms of the identifications that comprise the subsidiary personalities, who draw off emotional energy. These investigators side with Freud in one of his rare references to such cases and the notion that 'different identifications take hold of consciousness in turn' (op. cit.: 89).

In the writings of psychiatrists interested in the therapy of such cases are discussions of how to cope with the often mutually hostile personalities concerned, and of the temptation to take sides. Watkins and Watkins (1984) stress the need for extreme diplomacy in coping with the numerous disputes likely to occur. Hostility to the therapist is, they point out, a hazard and may involve actual physical danger. In his study of the case he called 'John Smith and the One Fifth Man', Bernard Hart (1939) had to cope with a secondary personality strongly antagonistic to himself, a kind of 'crystallised resistance' to the treatment. Contemporary investigators deal with dangers of physical violence to themselves, also violent and self-destructive behaviour of the personalities towards one another. Coping with the problems of both positive and negative transference was also of concern at a much earlier date in the work of Morton Prince with Miss Beauchamp. To this extremely interesting case we may next turn.

A DISSOCIATED PERSONALITY

Miss Christine Beauchamp has been identified as a young Radcliffe student studied in Boston by Morton Prince (1901–1905). (Later, in 1912, she became 'Mrs Waterman', having married Dr G. W. Waterman, one of Prince's younger colleagues.) In this case of multiple personality there were three main systems, B.I, B.IV, and Sally. Morton Prince described them with the code-words of 'The Saint, the Woman, and the Devil'. Sally was the 'devil' in the sense of being a personality that enjoyed teasing, sometimes tormenting the other personalities. She had contempt for B.I, the prim 'saint', and was often in conflict with the 'woman', B.IV, who made vigorous efforts to control her. Sally retaliated in ways that resemble a kind of poltergeist phenomenon, sometimes with physical violence. The treatment was conducted mainly by hypnotism, but Morton Prince also used techniques of automatic writing and crystal-gazing. In terms of diagnosis the case would today fit the DSM III criteria of multiple personality: 'Existence within an individual of two or more distinct personalities, each of which is dominant at a particular time.' The survey conducted by Taylor and Martin in 1944 distinguished two main sub-categories of multiple personality. On one hand is 'alternating personality', as in the early case of Mary Reynolds cited above. On the other hand is 'co-consciousness'. Both occurred in the case of Christine Beauchamp. The B.I and B.IV personalities alternated, and later Sally emerged to take control for periods of time. Sally was also co-conscious, and able to overlook both B.I and B.IV when they occupied the stage. On one occasion she even intervened to prevent suicide by a depressed Miss Beauchamp. Sally seems to have been a younger version of Miss Beauchamp, possessing many of the characteristics of a delinquent child; in this she strongly resembled Eve Black in the Eve case. Among her delinquencies was automatic writing in the form of scribbling on the letters of the other personalities, and otherwise interfering with their mail. They also included posting spiders to them, over-spending money, preventing their sleep and imposing her imagery upon them in the form of hallucination. Morton Prince reproduces some of the letters of the various personalities. The originals I have seen in Boston, together with an unpublished biography of Morton Prince written by his daughter. This records that Miss Beauchamp, in one or other of her personalities, was 'always turning up' at their house. Of interest is Prince's own testimony that he had no difficulty in recognizing which of the Misses Beauchamp turned up in temporary control of the body.

The study and treatment of Miss Beauchamp was conducted within a robustly naturalistic framework, even though, at times, Morton Prince seemed somewhat obsessed with his pursuit of 'the real Miss Beauchamp'. There was no question of 'possession', nor of 're-incarnation' which, as Ian Wilson (1981) has suggested, may sometimes be explained in dissociation terms. Sally and B.IV 'kept up a mutual correspondence', and the automatic writing when Sally was co-conscious was interpreted naturalistically, though Sally herself referred to it jokingly in such terms as 'the spooky messages' (op. cit.: 241). Of her own periods of time loss, B.I complained of 'missing' the letters from Sally that kept her informed of events. Such messages were helpful when the other personalities found themselves in strange places without any idea of how they had come there. The personalities of B.I and B.IV were markedly different in choice of food, clothes, and preferences for people. Thus meals, dressing, washing, and taking of baths created endless problems. On one occasion Sally changed back to B.I, leaving the unhappy woman naked on top of a pile of furniture. After a struggle with B.IV Sally was induced to agree to an ultimatum which B.IV composed. Its contents are revealing. They included 'no more' hallucinations, spiders, or interference with the post and the keeping by Sally of her weekly allowance of money.

In the introduction to his edition of the Morton Prince book, Charles Rycroft (1978) discusses the issue of transference and counter-transference. Clearly Morton Prince became fond of Sally, as with an exasperatingly difficult but attractively amusing young delinquent. The temptation to take sides, which contemporary investigators have found a problem, also concerned Morton Prince. In the end he achieved, to his satisfaction, the integration of Miss Beauchamp by the suppression of Sally, who was not 'the real Miss Beauchamp'. For his part Rycroft is not so happy about this decision, and he points to therapy in other cases ending in a taking over of the personality by one of the later emerging sub-systems. At the time when he published this edition of Morton Prince, Rycroft argued for 'the rarity' of multiple personality: he cites four cases since the end of the Second World War. Now, as we have seen, many are being reported. In another area of psychology, Robert Holt in 1964 published his paper 'Imagery: the return of the ostracized'. Perhaps now we have been alerted to notice, dissociative phenomena including multiple personality are emerging from similar ostracism.

DISSOCIATIVE PHENOMENA

Some of the distinctions defended by Pierre Janet need to be re-emphasized. He did not, for example, identify somnambulism with sleep-walking. Somnambulistic behaviour may begin in a state of wakefulness, as in one of Janet's famous cases, Irène, who would suddenly begin to re-enact events relating to her mother's death, in a spontaneously occurring altered mental state. Elsewhere (1979b) I have described a similar diurnal somnambulism involving a middle-aged woman who suddenly began to re-enact a traumatic experience in her early life when, as a 12-year-old child, she first learned of her father's death. Again she became, for a period of about ten to fifteen minutes, a 12-year-old, pleading with her father not to die. Collapse and sleep ensued, with subsequent amnesia for the somnambulistic episode. Diurnal somnambulisms may occur during therapy in the form of abreactions, or emotional re-living of distressing events. To illustrate, Spiegel (1984) reports on such an episode during hypnotic treatment of an army NCO who had served in Vietnam. It related to the discovery of the body of a Vietnamese child whom he had cared for over a period of years and who now had been killed in a rocket attack. He would start to speak in the voice of the dead child, re-live the burial scene, and then start to re-enact events at a party he had given for the boy following his recovery from an earlier injury. Highly traumatic past experiences, like the death of a parent and other forms of press of a distressing kind, seem to be closely associated with diurnal or nocturnal somnambulisms. As in Irène's case, and in somnambulistic behaviour that can sometimes be induced hypnotically, amnesia for the period of lost time tends to occur.

Pierre Janet was also careful to preserve the distinction between somnambulisms and fugues. Somnambulisms, according to Janet, are of short duration and the accompanying behaviour is bizarre or otherwise attention-attracting. Fugues differ in being much more complex. During the dissociated period the individual concerned acts normally and without attracting attention. One of

Janet's fugue cases involved a young Frenchman who was reading a newspaper in North Africa. The paper reported the disappearance of a young man from France, and the complete mystery of his whereabouts. Suddenly he realized that the missing person was, in fact, himself. He had amnesia for the intervening events. As Janet reports of such cases, 'they take railway tickets, they dine and sleep in hotels, they speak to a great number of people.' He adds 'they are not recognised as mad' (Janet 1901: 60; McKellar 1979b: 18 ff. and Glossary of Terms). A fugue is a flight in the sense of an escape to a different state of consciousness, and also in that it often seems to involve actual travel. The famous case of Rev. Ansel Bourne, studied by William James, seems to lie on a continuum between a fugue and dual or multiple personality. The Rev. Bourne drew out a sum of money on 17 January 1887 from a bank in Providence, Rhode Island. Two months later on 14 March a man woke up in a flat above a shop in Norristown, Pennsylvania. It was a confectioner's shop in which the man, known to his neighbours as Mr A. J. Brown, had quietly carried on his business. In the interim he had done nothing eccentric or unusual. But now he declared he was Rev. Ansel Bourne, knew nothing of shopkeeping, and had – it seemed only yesterday – drawn out 55 dollars in the town of Providence. The case, which interested William James, was treated by hypnotism, during which the Mr Brown personality was re-activated, reacted to Mrs Bourne as a stranger, and declared he had heard of, but not met her husband! As is apparent in this case the fugue or secondary personality is not necessarily of a Mr Hyde anti-social kind. Instead it may perform the function of escape from a way of life to a different one, perhaps fed by the fantasies of the primary personality system. Nor, as we have seen, are such dissociative phenomena confined to female patients.

Cornelia Wilbur (1984), who was the psychiatrist in the well-known case of Sybil, reports on the functional survival characteristics of such a personality in a male patient. At the age of 7 he was attacked by three boys, larger than himself. He was afraid of being killed. A secondary personality emerged and when interviewed in the adult man revealed its character as violent, aggressive and omnipotent. At times during service in the army this personality would take over on going into combat. It would volunteer for dangerous missions. Finally it took up a position on a hill with a machine gun, and not only pinned down the enemy, but also its own allies. The primary personality had amnesia for ever being in combat, though the secondary personality could give full details of the experiences. Wilbur finds that this and other male cases parallel those of female patients who have responded with defensive rage to childhood cruelty. The individual has had to repress its angry affect, but builds up a reservoir of emotion 'that creates the potential for explosions of feeling when repression breaks down', expressed through this secondary personality system (op. cit.: 6). In Cornelia Wilbur's Sybil case many of the personalities were better able to look after themselves than the original 'depleted' and frightened Sybil. The survival aspect of the functioning of the secondary personality is emphasized by many investigators. Somewhat different is one of the classic cases involving dual personality, 'Spanish Maria', discussed by McDougall (1962) and studied originally by Cory. In this instance the A-personality differed little from Maria's own. But there emerged a B-personality which claimed to be the reincarnation of a Spanish gypsy dancer. This sub-system was self-assertive and colourful, and differed markedly from the usual timid Maria. She spoke English always with a foreign accent, and gave evidence of sometimes being awake when the A-personality slept. She could force her imagery on the sleeper in the form of dreams. There was a marked difference between the two in body image and in place of Maria's slight figure, B saw herself as 'large and voluptuous, a fascinating beauty' (McDougall 1926: 496). This secondary personality seemed better able to cope with living, and expressed the self-assertive, exhibitionistic and sexual aspects of Maria. These had been strongly discouraged in the convent where Maria was educated. The B-system may be seen less in terms of repression than as potential or actual 'return of the repressed'.

MECHANISMS OF DISSOCIATION

While examining the mechanisms of the major, and more minor, forms of dissociation we may notice their portrayal in literature. In this I am indebted to the psychologist Dr Henry Murray, who was not only Morton Prince's successor at the Harvard Psychological Clinic, but also an expert on Herman Melville. Dr Murray drew my attention to one of Melville's books previous to *Moby Dick*, namely *Mardi and a Voyage Thither* (1849). One of the characters in this is the talkative philosopher, appropriately named Babbalanje, who from time to time is interrupted by a 'mysterious indweller' called Azzageddi, 'locked up' inside his personality. On occasion other characters in the novel are aware that they are interacting with this named personality sub-system, and not with Babbalanje. The philosopher himself – like Socrates – had a co-conscious awareness of an internal sub-self. He reports on his awareness of 'something going on in me that is independent of me'; he likens himself to 'a blind man pushed from behind'; and he records 'many a time have I willed to do one thing and another has been done.' The sub-system also reveals its presence in other ways: 'it is he who talks in my sleep, revealing my secrets' (Quoted in McKellar 1979b: 38–9). Babbalanje, like Sybil, is on amiable terms with this dissociative aspect of himself: evidence of Melville's early awareness that named dissociative sub-systems are not necessarily of the malevolent Mr Hyde kind. Melville explored these issues thirty-seven years before the publication of Stevenson's own imaginative novel. Also early in the field was Wilkie Collins, who wrote *The Moonstone* (1868). Like his friend Charles Dickens, Collins was much interested in the psychology of altered mental states. The plot of his novel depends on a somnambulism induced by administration of laudanum. Collins himself expresses through his characters his awareness that somnambulistic episodes may be diurnal, as well as nocturnal. He is quite explicit on this point, as on the possibilities that a 'sensory impression which has once been recognised by the perceptive consciousness ... may be reproduced at some subsequent time' despite absence of conscious awareness 'during the whole intermediate period' (Collins 1868: 371). In *The Moonstone* there is also a clear reference to the work of Dr Elliotson – who had instructed Dickens in hypnotic inductions – and specifically to Elliotson's *Human Physiology*. Here we encounter anticipation of the notion of 'state dependency' which has recently much interested experimental psychologists. The passage concerns 'an Irish porter ... who forgot, when sober, what he had done when drunk; but, being drunk, again recollected the transactions of his former state of intoxication' (op. cit.: 372). Thus on one occasion when drunk he had lost a parcel of some value, but was later able to find it when he was next in a state of intoxication. In *The Moonstone*, the Wilkie Collins 'psychologist in literature' – Ezra Jennings – is able to solve the mystery of the disappearance of the moonstone. In the novel a similar instance of what we would today call 'state dependency' was involved. It depended on laudanum not alcohol. When the opiate was re-administered the lost stone was retrieved by restitution of the somnambulistic state of consciousness. In the normal state amnesia was present, but when the opiate-induced system took over, memory returned.

DOSTOEVSKY ON DISSOCIATION

The insights of the great Russian novelist impressed many of those who contributed to what Ellenberger (1970) has called the great 'unmasking tradition', including both Nietzsche and Freud. Dostoevsky (1821–81) did not merely observe people and intro-spect. As one of his major biographers has emphasized, he also took a considerable interest in informing himself, through books on medical and psychological matters (Grossmann 1974). And he was specially interested in abnormal psychology. From these sources of information and his own abnormal traits, illuminated by genius, he had much to contribute in his novels. Too rigid a dichotomy between 'science' and 'literature' should not mislead us. Some great writers were well informed about scientific matters – Coleridge is a good example – and Dostoevsky, the son of a medical father, clearly prepared himself by reading for his major novels. Some day I hope a psychologist will examine Dostoevsky's note books (now available in translation), and contribute a study of this potentially rich store of psychological information about experience and behaviour, a study comparable to the one done by Lowes (1927) on Coleridge. To tempt, I can only briefly indicate a few of Dostoevsky's penetrating insights to which I have referred in other publications (McKellar 1957; 1968; 1977a; 1979b). In *The Brothers Karamazov* we encounter a striking example of the psychologist character in literature through whom Dostoevsky expresses his understanding of dissociation in its relation to fugues, somnambulisms, multiple personality and hallucination. Earlier, in *The Double*, a short story that was an apparent failure at the time, the novelist dealt with duality of personality. Dostoevsky's own comment was 'Why should I forfeit an excellent idea, a character type of supreme social importance, which I was the first to discover and which I heralded?' (Quoted in Grossmann 1974). Deep intra-psychic conflicts continued to fascinate Dostoevsky and sometimes in ways that involved co-consciousness and dissociation. As the translator of his note books for *The Brothers Karamazov*, Wasiolek points out he 'showed great candour and courage in what he dramatised' through the personalities of Raskalnikov of *Crime and Punishment*, and Stavrogan and Peter Verkhovensky of *The Possessed*. 'What his nihilistic heroes attack is what Dostoevsky himself believed in' (Wasiolek in Introduction to *The Notebooks for The Brothers Karamazov*, 1971: 2). Moreover, as regards character types, there were many rehearsals in earlier writings. An interesting re-example of this is the saintly Alyosha who, in the note books for the later novel, is first labelled 'the idiot', an echo of the earlier Prince Myshkin in the novel of that name (Wasiolek, op. cit.: 14). Thus the 'character type' explored in *The Double* recurs in the dissociations of his outstanding psychologist-in-literature creation, Ivan Karamazov.

Following the murder of his hated father, Ivan experiences dissociation, his dissociated sub-system taking the form of visual and auditory hallucination. He sees and talks with the devil, but at times retains co-conscious awareness that the hallucinatory figure is nevertheless part of his own mental life. The depth of conflict along this line of cleavage is profound, resembling the alleged influence in the life of Luther to which reference is made. In his struggle to resist, and dissociate himself from this threatened 'return of the repressed', during a period of co-conscious insight Ivan says to his brother, 'And he is myself, Alyosha. All that's base in me, all that's mean and contemptible.' But this insight is fragile. He adds, in an earnest and confidential tone, 'I should be awfully glad to think that it was *he* and not I' (Garnett translation 1945: 692). On another occasion he tells Alyosha who is, like himself, preoccupied with the problems of good and evil, 'I think if the devil doesn't exist, but man has created him, he has created him in his own image and likeness' (op. cit.: 244). In both the note books and the novel the hallucinatory figure echoes the same chilling thought, and in Latin: '*Satan sum et nihil humanum a me alienum puto.*' From his own sufferings, and observations in Siberia recorded in *The House of the Dead*, Ivan's creator was profoundly preoccupied with this grim assessment of human cruelty: 'I am Satan, and nothing human is foreign to me.'

Through Ivan's moments of insight Dostoevsky provides his own analysis of the place of conflict in dissociation; establishment from the resulting cleavage of a functioning sub-system; rejection of aspects of self, but threatened return of the repressed. He also provides understanding of how repression as a mechanism provides content to the dissociated sub-system. Thus at one stage the hallucinatory figure relates an anecdote. Ivan is triumphant. He recognizes this as a short story, a product of his own imaginative thinking, but up till now forgotten. Now he has proof that the apparition is not a reality: 'You are a dream, not a living creature.' But Ivan's devil continues to taunt him – as her own alter ego tormented Miss Beauchamp – with words 'From the vehemence with which you deny my existence ... I am convinced that you believe in me' (op. cit.: 345). Then follow words of scorn at 'hesitation, suspense, conflict between belief and disbelief' that can be 'such torture to a conscientious man' (op. cit.: 346). Guilt feelings play their part also in Ivan's dissociation, guilt about the murder of which he is factually innocent, but which he has nevertheless committed in fantasy and also through his influence on the actual murderer.

Sub-systems like Ivan's alter ego sometimes play their part in hallucination, as in multiple personality. They may often be interpreted as possession. But 'possession' may also be benign rather than demonic, and sub-systems may, as we have seen, be of a more amiable type. Sally Beauchamp was by no means a malevolent Miss Hyde, though there are instances of physical injury to the other personalities, as when B.IV showed Morton Prince her badly scratched arms. But mostly, though delinquent, she seems likeable. Some multiple personality cases fit the picture of Ivan Karamazov dissociation. In others we find, instead, the child within, as imaginary companion, or a Jungian animus or anima figure representing the other sex. The mechanism of an internal imaginary companion, better able to cope than the primary personality with problems of living, seems to operate in many of the cases. As recent studies of series of such cases tend to show, the secondary personalities tend to emerge – like imaginary companions – at an early age. Investigators like Bliss (1986) find that in multiple personality cases they have studied, there is very often a history of imaginary companions. Such companions in childhood seem to be relatively common. Multiple personality is a rarity, though perhaps, as we have seen from the work of recent investigations, not as rare as once supposed. There appear to be many related phenomena to which the concepts of degrees of dissociation and personality sub-systems seem highly relevant.

Multiple personality cases provide a psychological reference point. The exaggerations they provide may help to alert us to notice ways in which the sub-systems of normal people may develop a measure of autonomy. As investigators of belief systems, from Hart (1936; 1939) to Rokeach (1960; 1968), have shown, these may function with impenetrable barriers to contrary evidence. That images are products of the personality itself may sometimes not be recognized, and in extreme cases we label them 'hallucination'. Master sentiments and prejudices may become powerful and unruly components of mental life, and as Pear (1922) suggests, may deteriorate into Jungian 'complexes'. Still more extreme failures of personality integration are encountered in the schizophrenias and in these – as in multiple personality cases – 'time loss' and episodes of amnesia may be accompaniments. However rare or common, multiple personality provides a rich source of information of great value to both normal and abnormal psychology.

DISSOCIATION AND PAIN

The grim history of major operations including amputations before the development of anaesthesia defies, one hopes, our powers of imagery of human suffering. But later, hypnotism was used by surgeons like Elliotson in England, and others throughout Europe, as a method of coping with pain. I cite as illustration the Frenchman Courmelles (1°91), who discusses its uses in his own country. He makes explicit reference to successful production of hypnotic insensitivity to pain in operations that included amputation of the arm, the leg and the thigh. Many investigators in this period interpreted such hypnotic effects in dissociation terms. The relations of spontaneous forms of dissociation like multiple personality to experienced pain are also of some interest.

During an interview one young woman, diagnosed as a multiple personality, told me of her own experiences. On one occasion, while in the personality system I will call 'C.1', she experienced severe toothache. This took her to the dentist, but she arrived in the personality of 'C.2', which felt nothing. While this sub-system was in control she found herself unable to locate for the dentist the source of pain. Very ruefully she told me that by evening she was now back again as 'C.1', again experiencing the pain of toothache. In this case we encounter not co-consciousness, but rather the alternating personality form of a major dissociation. Some years ago, after conducting a related hypnotic experiment of our own, we became interested in these issues, and by no means disposed to reject a dissociation view of the hypnotic state (McKellar and Tonn 1967). Then followed the further questions which we asked ourselves: 'Are there not degrees of dissociation? Must we continue to regard it as an all-or-nothing phenomenon?' Our own experiment concerned hypnotic induction of negative hallucination, but hypnotic induction of anaesthesia to pain seems to present some parallels.

Later (1979b) I discussed an experiment that was carried out in 1960 by Kaplin, involving hypnotism, pain, and automatic writing. The hypnotized subject was given the suggestion that his left hand would be insensitive to pain, and his right hand would engage in automatic writing. The subject was blindfolded and the left hand was pricked by a needle. At this the right hand wrote, 'Ouch, damn it, you're hurting me.' It was some time later that the subject asked the experimenter, 'When are you going to begin?' The important 'hidden observer' experiments of E. R. Hilgard (1977) have involved systematic study of such paradoxical happenings.

THE HIDDEN OBSERVER

In the Hilgard experiments pain was induced by immersion of one hand of the volunteer subject in icy water. Following this the hypnotized subject would report no pain, suggestions of anaesthesia having been given. But by automatic writing there was evidence that pain was in some way felt. Such writing also provided quantitative assessment on a scale of degree of pain. In interpreting these experiments Hilgard was led to develop his 'neodissociation theory', and in this he makes reference to two systems of cognitive awareness. 'Cognition A' would experience and assess the pain, while 'cognition B', in accord with hypnotic anaesthesia, would feel no discomfort. Thus in cognition A we have 'a hidden observer'. Hilgard makes a plea for serious reconsideration of dissociation as a concept in psychology. It is noticeable that the reports obtained from various of his subjects give additional substance to the notion of a hidden observer. Thus one such subject reported, 'There's Me 1, Me 2, and Me 3.' He added to this: 'Me 1 is hypnotised, Me 2 is hypnotised and observing, and Me 3 is when I'm awake' (Hilgard 1977: 210). Although he argues for re-habilitation of the concept of dissociation, Hilgard is justifiably cautious about it being important 'not to claim too much'. He points out that 'it was possible hypnotically to establish a "hidden observer" in less than half his subjects, and only in those who were highly hypnotisable' (Hilgard 1982). Like many other psychologists, I believe these experiments are important and far-reaching in their implications, and none the less so because of the revival of interest in multiple personality by psychiatrists, and the numerous cases now being studied. Through some kind of co-conscious awareness these 'hidden observers' provide evidence of dissociated systems capable of cognitions not available to the other sub-systems of the personality.

AWARENESS OF DUALITY

Mental life sometimes presents us with a sense of duality, as between its component parts. Thus we may say, 'I was tempted but I resisted.' On the one hand is the 'I' and on the other the impulses that 'I' experience. Or again, 'conscience was giving me a bad time.' There seems to be within the personality a more restricted part to which pronouns like 'I' and 'me' appear to be particularly appropriate. With imagery also this ego system may seem co-consciously to 'observe' the images, and perhaps make use of them in thought and imagination. Such co-consciousness was noticeably present in the creative writing activities of Enid Blyton discussed earlier. She could 'watch' her characters appear as though on an internal screen and 'hear' what they said. The recorded end-product provided one of her stories. Imagery can also provide occasions when this awareness of duality is absent. Thus it is commonly reported how, when falling asleep or waking up, it is confused with real sounds. It is wrongly attributed to outside sources in these common hypnagogic and hypnopompic mistakes. Recognition that it nevertheless does come from one's own personality may come later as when, on return to our bed, we ruefully accept the imagery sources of the purely hypnagogic door-bell we have got up on a cold night to answer. As in the hallucinations of the psychoses, auditory images play a prominent part in the mistakes of hypnagogia. Retaining co-conscious awareness of duality is not necessarily a bad thing.

In the case of 'depersonalization' one aspect of the personality seems to be watching the actions of another self. Mild instances of depersonalization are often reported in everyday life, as when, for example, an exhausted walker or mountaineer finds himself observing his wretched self struggling homewards or upwards. Somewhat different was the case of one marathon runner studied by Morgan (1978). The woman athlete concerned used her awareness of duality. She would think up images of the faces of people she heartily disliked and mentally step on their faces, one by one, for the next 26 miles! Less satisfying was the experience of another person who reported a period of depersonalization of 'watching himself' for a whole day. Although it happened many years earlier he remembered it vividly from his childhood: it had occupied one whole Christmas Day! During a period of depression there is sometimes – perhaps usually – this sense of a shadowy other part of the personality which is not merely 'observing', but also actually enjoying the experience. There are similarities, and differences, to the clinically abnormal as when the Sally system of Miss Beauchamp found satisfaction in discomfort of her other selves: she teased B.I, and subjected B.IV to near-persecution. There are differences in that co-consciousness was one-way. Sally was co-conscious, but Miss Beauchamp herself lacked any direct sense of duality. In one place Morton Prince records a demoralized Miss Beauchamp coming to him with a strong 'as if' feeling that she might somehow be 'possessed'. From his own robustly naturalistic standpoint he was able to reassure her. In some cultures and sub-cultures such reassurance is not forthcoming.

Studies of alleged invasion of the personality by spirit forces have led to a distinction between 'lucid' and 'somnambulistic' types of 'possession'. In the lucid case there is retention of a sense of duality, an ego system that has awareness of some invading entity. With somnambulistic possession there is no such awareness, and it is as if that entity has wholly taken over mental life. There is an interesting passage in which Alfred Binet (1896) discusses similar happenings in the hypnotized individual. Sometimes he argues the people concerned are 'by no means the dupes of the suggestions given', and these are carried out 'because they are unable to resist' (op. cit.: 258). Despite readiness to act in the ways required by the hypnotist, such people 'never forget who they are, their identity', so in accord with suggestions given they will perform in such roles as a priest, a general, or some other specified person. 'But they know they are playing a part.' In other circumstances, and with susceptible hypnotic subjects, they become 'complete victims of the suggested behaviour'. Of these artificially produced somnambulisms Binet adds, 'the memory of their former ego is for the moment entirely obliterated' (op. cit.: 260). For their part professional actors and actresses may vary in the extent to which they retain a co-consciousness of their identity while performing. Autobiographical accounts by introspectively literate people like Shirley MacLaine (1986) suggest awareness of duality despite a huge variety of different roles. As regards altered mental states, a variety of neuroses, psychoses and conditions like drunkenness are regularly portrayed on stage or screen by psychiatrically normal and sober professionals (see also Chapter 16). In the case of multiple personality itself we have noted the distinction which Taylor and Martin (1944) made between co-consciousness and alternating personalities. Thus as we have seen co-consciousness was absent in the fugue states of Rev. Ansel Bourne. By contrast with this, in the case of 'Spanish Maria' the secondary personality, when co-conscious and awake, could inflict her imagery as 'dreams' on the sleeping primary personality. Lucid dreaming represents an interesting variant of dreamlife in which, despite sleep, co-consciousness seems to be retained.

It is sometimes difficult to draw a sharp distinction between actual dreaming in its more usual form, and another type of subjective experience, hypnagogic imaging. There are intermediate phenomena. The notion of co-consciousness may help.

Figure 4.1 States of mental life

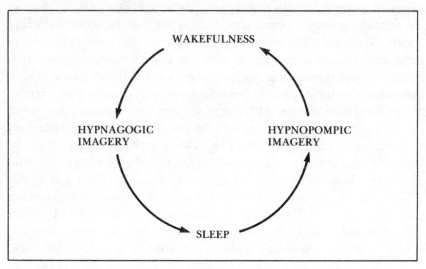

Visual hypnagogic imagery is often likened to a display of lantern-slides with an impression of being apart and 'watching' them. By contrast dreams are experiences in which the dreamer seems to participate, rather than observe from outside. Carrying this analysis further we are led to a distinction between what might be called 'hypnagogic sequences' or displays, and 'hypnagogic episodes' in which there are momentary losses of waking consciousness. These latter mini-plays seem to herald the approach of sleep and actual dreaming. On occasion, however, they are sufficiently dramatic to evoke a return to full wakefulness, rather than a drifting towards sleep. Hypnagogic imagery – whether visual, auditory, or of other kinds – is considerably more common than once supposed, or even than some people admit in their own cases. The mystery of its incidence will shortly be considered. Such processes may be going on all the time, though frequently unnoticed. The occurrence of the half-awake state that precedes sleep itself may provide us with more information about the functioning of dissociated systems. Once we have been alerted to notice such imagery it reveals itself with one advantage over mere dreaming: we can study it introspectively. By contrast, dreams – with the atypical exception of lucid dreams – permit only retro-spective study. Characteristic of hypnagogic imagery is co-consciousness, and awareness of duality during its occurrence. In hypnagogic sequences at least, there is an ego system operating observing the imagery with interest, surprise, amusement, or fear. The imagery itself is characteristically autonomous: it seems to erupt from some system of the personality that is different from, and perhaps dissociated from, this ego system. We shall now turn to a fuller examination of hypnagogic experience as an intrinsically interesting variant of normal mental life.

SUMMARY

1   Sub-systems of the personality may function autonomously with only primitive or non-existent linkages between them. Literature provided us with the 'Jekyll–Hyde Syndrome', and in fact Stevenson's novel had its predecessors. Do we in reality encounter equivalents?

2   Cases of multiple personality are considered. Such cases are now in the United States being very frequently reported, and within psychology the concept of dissociation is again being given serious attention. It seems timely to re-consider this area, defined at the time by Morton Prince's important case of Christine Beauchamp, and often neglected perhaps partly as a result of the development and influence of psychoanalysis.

3   An alternative to the 'di-psychic' division of mental life into conscious and unconscious, is the 'polypsychic' view of a number of dissociated systems. The exaggerated manifestations of such systems in multiple personality may provide reference points for a fresh re-consideration of normal and abnormal psychology in non-Freudian terms. The tradition of Pierre Janet, as well as that of Freud, merits consideration.

4   Within literature the understanding of dissociation and other issues by Dostoevsky is of great interest. The concept of 'the psychologist character in literature', whom a writer uses as a vehicle for his own psychological insights, is introduced. Foremost among such characters is Dostoevsky's Ivan Karamazov, who seems well to understand the psychology of dissociation.

5 A variety of lesser dissociative phenomena are considered along with experiments involving hypnosis and pain in Hilgard's 'hidden observer' studies. In these something resembling the co-consciousness of some multiple personality cases appears to occur. These point us to a more detailed study of hypnagogia.

Chapter Five

BETWEEN WAKEFULNESS AND SLEEP: HYPNAGOGIA

A twilight condition of consciousness in which pseudo-hallucinations which are neither waking visions nor dreams can occur.

Mrs F. E. Leaning

I feel as if I were a mere spectator ... and in no way concerned with the getting up of the performance.

Rev. Henslow (Galton's subject)

Resemblances between the fantasies of sleep and psychosis have often been noted. Yet poverty of language has not always permitted distinctions to be made between dreams and other types of imagery. Two thousand years ago Aristotle commented on hypnagogic experiences, and noted their tendency to evoke anxiety and fear in young people. In the seventeenth century Thomas Hobbes distinguished them from dreams and discussed them as rich sources of subject matter for superstitious beliefs. It was not until the year 1861 that Alfred Maury provided psychology with the name, 'hypnagogic imagery'. Warren's *Dictionary of Psychology* (1934) defines it: 'Imagery of any sense modality, frequently of almost hallucinatory character, which is experienced in the drowsy state preceding deep sleep.'

The imagery, when visual, has often been likened to a display of lantern-slides. This is the commonest kind. Voices, music and other sounds are also frequently reported. Like the visual type, they enjoy a life of their own, erupting without warning from some seemingly dissociated part of the personality. There are also, less often, images of touch, movement, temperature, smell, and pain, and even on occasion hypnagogic electric shocks. Such phenomena may be likened to an invasion of drowsy consciousness by anticipatory dreamlike imagery. These pre-sleep eruptions may be distinguished from rather similar experiences that follow sleep, perhaps a continuation of dreaming: these have been labelled 'hypnopompic imagery'. Andreas Mavromatis (1987) uses the generic term 'hypnagogia' to cover both. The imagery and other phenomena of the realm of hypnagogia will be considered in this chapter. My own interests have been especially in hypnagogic imagery.

Content varies enormously. Often it takes the form of landscapes or scenes, though because of peculiarities of lighting the term 'moonscapes' is sometimes used. One subject likened the visions to glimpses 'as through a gap in a curtain of misty cloud' (Leaning 1925: 325). The images are spontaneous and their content is often surprising to the imager concerned: 'like scenes from the kind of travel books I don't read,' declared one of my subjects. Of 400 people, 48 per cent of men and 61 per cent of women reported this visual kind of imagery (McKellar 1979b).

MODE OF APPEARANCE

Whether they are landscapes, scenes, or something else, typical visual hypnagogic images are something that their author watches rather than participates in. Henslow described himself as 'a mere spectator'. Their content is extremely diverse. In her important pioneer study, Leaning (1925) was led to distinguish five categories: (1) Formless, e.g. light-charged clouds 'seem to float between eye and eyelid'; (2) Faces, sometimes kindly but sometimes grotesque and frightening; (3) Designs and objects, e.g. 'complex patterns like those of a carpet'; (4) Landscapes; (5) Scenes, e.g. 'a throng of happy people clad in gay clothes' (op. cit.: 309–27). Some hypnagogic visualizations have a quality which Freud (1900) also attributes to dreams, as 'something alien as though from another world'. This applies to some, but not all, of the visual experiences.

We were led to distinguish two types: what we have called 'perseverative' on the one hand, and 'impersonal' on the other

Figure 5.1 Glass and eyeball hypnagogic image

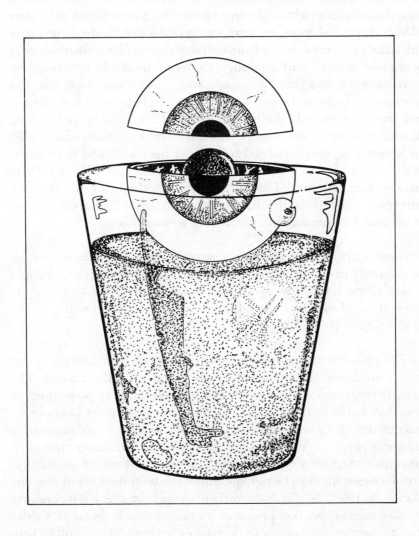

(McKellar and Simpson 1954). The perseverative kind is imagery of previous events that can readily be related to past perception. Thus on a night following a period of gardening a person may be entertained by a perseverative imagery of weeds and other plants. Flournoy, a pioneer investigator of dissociation, had visions of the board and pieces after playing chess; the physiologist Johannes Müller reported perseverative imagery of the field of view in a microscope, after work in the laboratory. One of my own subjects, a regular imager and a science student, could often predict his perseverative imagery. On Tuesdays, after three hours in the laboratory, he would again see what he had been working with: 'It will be a night of shells' (McKellar 1979b). The second or 'impersonal' kind of imagery was different, exhibiting the quality of 'something alien'. Indeed some have been tempted to describe it in terms like 'glimpses of another world', or 'visions from a previous incarnation'. One of my subjects, though rejecting such interpretations, found what loomed up from some dissociated system of her personality surprising in its content.

> I was seeing green cockatoos swaying on soft bamboo ... I distinctly saw and heard a jungle sort of noise – bright sunlight and those birds waving up and down: green and brown, and vivid, vivid yellow ... bamboo trees and undergrowth.
> (McKellar 1957: 37)

The example quoted is a reminder that other imagery – in this case sound and temperature – may accompany the visions. The literature provides many instances of such imagery possessing an impersonal, at times a sort of 'archetypal', quality. In Leaning we encounter 'a desert scene ... yellow, brown sand beneath a burning sun ... underneath each of the arches a horse ... beautiful creatures with flowing manes and tails'. And then in front 'rises a small pyramid, gleaming white in the rays of the sun' (Leaning 1925: 341). Characteristic of such imagery is its creative quality, seemingly composite in its perceptual origins, and difficult to locate from memory of past experience. From numerous investigations into hypnagogic visualizations my impressions are that about half may be classified as perseverative, while about half are of this impersonal or 'archetypal' kind. The perseverative vs. archetypal classification applies to visual hypnagogia, though not readily to imagery of other modes. In my study of 500 subjects cited above, 31 per cent of men and 38 per cent of women reported auditory hypnagogic experiences; as regards 'other' sense departments, they were reported by 21 per cent of men and 35 per cent of women (McKellar 1979b). But how often does such imagery, whether visual or other kinds, occur but pass unnoticed?

THE INCIDENCE MYSTERY

Does hypnagogic imagery represent a hidden difference between people: an affair of those who have and those who lack the experience? Considerable mystery surrounds the question of incidence. In this context, since psychology is about people, including psychologists, I will mention two. My original collaborator Lorna Simpson, when we first became interested in it, failed to find such imagery in her own mental life. Later, during our researches, she realized she quite often had it (McKellar and Simpson 1954). Something similar also happened with David Marks, a psychologist deeply interested in imagery, who much later on discovered his own hypnagogic experiences. Hypnagogic imagery is certainly very common but, like many subjective phenomena, often overlooked. It has a name which helps alert us to notice it but that name is not widely known, and errors of exclusion also seem to be extremely common. As regards the alerting-to-notice process, of interest is a third person, Sylvia Sutherland (now Mrs Scullard), who also experiences crystal-gazing imagery. On one occasion she – who is not a psychologist – happened to visit while I was deep in a pile of questionnaires. These related to hypnagogic and hypnopompic imagery. I asked my visitor to help sort them out, and she did while expressing interest in this experience other people had. It was unknown to her. A few days later she called again with the information that she also had hypnagogic imagery: she experienced it regularly, and quite often nightly! Hers was often of an amusing kind with cartoon-like characters enacting a mini-play. It had some resemblances to the cinematographic imagery of Enid Blyton. This, it will be recalled, occurred in full wakefulness, and Miss Blyton distinguished it from hypnagogic imagery which she also experienced. Here are three discoveries of the imagery through a process of being sensitized to notice it. Yes indeed, as Somerset Maugham observed, we do live first 'in the solitariness of our own mind'. And we may also overlook a resemblance between our own mental life and that of other people: many people seem to forget their hypnagogic imagery just as they forget their dreams.

Researches in this area accord with the three illustrations taken. Early studies found the imagery to be a rarity: Müller (1848) found it in only 2 per cent of a group of Berlin University students. Leaning (1925) estimated it to occur in about one-third of the population. A research of mine on all types yielded the figure of 76 per cent, very close to that of an independent study by Owens (1963) of 77 per cent. Still more recent was an investigation by Richardson *et al.* (1981) in which the late Mrs Owens took part. These investigators found that of the people questioned only 25 per cent denied its occurrence. Subjects were a panel of 600 normal people aged between 20 and 80, drawn from the general population. There is a substantial difference between the initial 2 per cent and an incidence of around 75 per cent. One suspects that among the remaining 25 per cent of people who denied the experience are at least some – perhaps many – who failed to notice it. The Richardson *et al.* investigation incidentally confirmed findings of my own and other investigators that hypno-pompic imagery is less often reported than that of the hypnagogic kind.

My own experience of the process of being alerted to notice may be of general interest. It happened during a series of experiments at Aberdeen Medical School with mescaline (McKellar 1957). Several times I was myself the subject. In the first experiment I experienced a flood of visual imagery of the kind produced by mescaline, like LSD, psilocybin and other hallucinogens. In seeking to communicate this, I looked for a reference I could make to some type of experience the two experimenters might have themselves known. I likened them to what happens while falling asleep: at the time the term 'hypnagogic imagery' was unknown to me. Later we found that very many investigators, for example Klüver (1928; 1942), had independently noticed this same resemblance. Three things followed. First, studies by Lorna Simpson and myself on hypnagogic imagery as such; second, a paper my psychologist colleague, the late Dr Amor Ardis, and I gave to the (then) Royal-Medico-Psychological Association, comparing mescaline and hypnagogic imagery; and third, more experiments with mescaline itself with its hypnagogic-like imagery display. It may be noted that many substances of the hallucinogen kind have both a similar chemical structure in possessing an indole nucleus, and also remarkably similar psychological effects. Mayer-Gross *et al.* (1954) are representative of many investigators in their conclusion that mescaline and lysergic acid diethylamide are 'virtually identical' in the phenomena they produce. My own personal discovery – duplicated independently by many other people – of the resemblances of hypnagogic visual imagery to these hallucinogen effects may be summarized. First we have an individual alerted by mescaline to an imagery phenomenon and seeking a way of communicating about it. Next he relates it to a spontaneous occurrence of normal mental life which, he later discovers, has a name. The question arises, how common is this seemingly normal subjective experience? In what ways is his own mental life similar to, or different from, other people's? By questionnaire and interview he finds out that the experience is common, commoner than many people who have it suppose. And some of those who deny having it later realize that it is, in fact, part of their mental life hitherto ignored. In building up a frame of reference to the hypnagogic experience the investigator, myself, comes to suspect that the phenomenon may in fact be a universal one. One of the most useful lessons that can be learned from experimental abnormal psychology may be how it can alert us to notice what is going on all the time in normal mental life.

Despite the diversity of content we encounter in hypnagogic imagery, certain regularities can be found. In his own studies of mescaline-induced imagery Klüver (1928) called these 'form constants'. They apply particularly to patterns and designs with their kaleidoscopic arrangements of colour and shape. Klüver (1942) was to find a recurrence of such form constants in a wide variety of visualizations, both in imagery and hallucination. In the case of hypnagogic phenomena Leaning refers to lattices and spirals, as does Klüver himself. Of interest also is Leaning's references to cases of 'micropsia' or 'lilliputian' imagery, also mentioned by Klüver in the case of the hallucinogen. Examples of hypnagogic micropsia included 'hosts of little people', 'miniature wagons and horses', 'tiny people in ordinary incidents of daily life', and 'always as minute as pins, or even pin heads' (Leaning

Figure 5.2 Visual and verbal introspection: Page from hypnagogic notes provided by Rob Guyton, giving his drawings and sketches from a sequence of images he experienced.

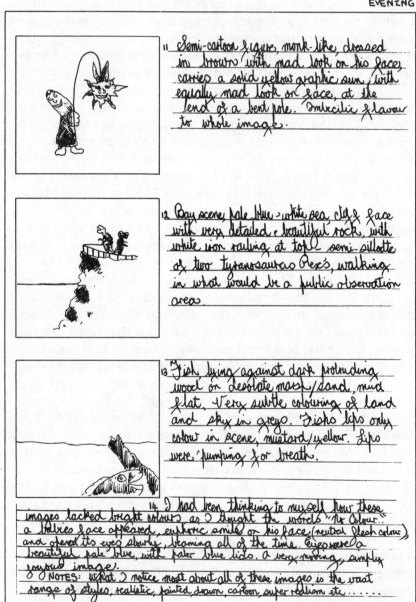

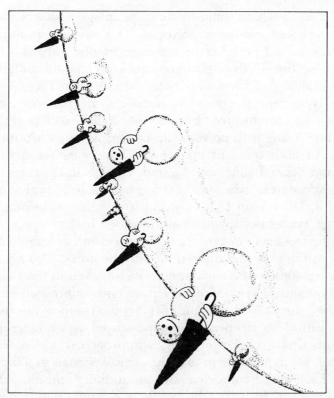

Figure 5.3 Polyopia in hypnagogic imagery (Rob Guyton)

1925: 333). Instances of such microscopic imagery occurred in our own experiments with mescaline and in this we encountered also the microscopic clarity of detail that can be a feature of hypnagogic imagery. Such impossible clarity led many of our own hypnagogic subjects to liken their imagery to surrealist paintings. It may be noted that both Max Ernst and Salvador Dali are known to have used hypnagogic imagery in their paintings. Other surrealist characteristics are strange juxtapositions of objects, and peculiarities of lighting and colour.

Another feature which some hypnagogic imagery shares with hallucinogen-evoked visions is polyopia. This involves multiple reproductions of a figure, as in the case of one subject who reported seeing 'hundreds of pink cockatoos, on an outdoor table by a hedge, talking'. I have also noted instances of these 'hall of mirrors'-type reproductions in instances of psychotic art. Perhaps these also are inspired by images or hallucinations of the polyopia kind? Along with polyopia and micropsia, we encounter synaesthesia in both types of imagery. It is very common with mescaline and other hallucinogens, and, though much rarer in the hypnagogic state, Ardis and I (1956) were able to find some instances of it. Much later Rob Guyton provided a good instance of hypnagogic synaesthesia, and sound-recorded his introspections while listening to Ravel's *Bolero*. He saw a succession of bubblelike figures that ran in slow motion in time with the music, also a pale skeleton figure, and later a stick insect which rocked in time with the bass. Hypnagogic synaesthesias I have encountered all tend to be of the common visual–auditory type. Another instance involved a would-be sleeper who experienced a sequence of purple clouds that grew larger as they approached and passed over his head. He likened them to Indian smoke signals or a flight of aircraft. Each cloud coincided with an auditory stimulus, the individual snores of his wife who lay there sleeping beside him! Hypnagogic and hallucinogen imagery may summate, as seems to have happened with one investigator, Weir Mitchell (1896), who, after consuming peyote buttons, lay down and relaxed seemingly into a hypnagogic state.

Before discussing hypnagogic imagery further, I shall consider the characteristics of the hypnopompic phenomena of hypnagogia.

HYPNOPOMPIC IMAGERY

Subjective experiences of vivid imagery may follow sleep: a perseveration of a dream. These were named hypnopompic by F. W. H. Myers (1904), who distinguished them from the hypnagogic kind. They may result in interesting confusions with reality and many subjects report believing themselves to be awake and acting accordingly, while still lying in bed and waking up. False wakings with imagery accompaniments are a feature of these blends of A-thinking and R-thinking. One subject, typical of many, reported, 'Often when I am waking up I imagine I am really up and going about the morning's work, washing, shaving, etc.' These happenings testify to the fact – of some interest in studying the allegedly supernatural – that insight into whether one is awake or asleep is fragile and variable. Closely related problems occur, not in the confident state of lucid dreaming when one knows one is asleep, but in 'pre-lucid dreaming' when one doesn't know whether one is or isn't. This distinction between lucid and pre-lucid dreaming is maintained by Celia Green (1968b). Both types will be discussed in the next chapter. In the pre-lucid case one may be puzzled, and have to ponder over this issue. A psychologist colleague of mine during one night became much interested in this problem when he woke up, or thought he did, to find a fox terrier beside his bed. His wife lay sleeping beside him. He knew he had a wife, but not a dog. He must still be asleep? During this interesting interplay of A-thinking and R-thinking he in fact woke up, to verify the reality of the wife and the hypnopompic nature of the dog. These hypnopompic perseverative intrusions of imagery into the waking-up period may be very frightening. Thus O. H. Myers – another Myers – reports the case of a woman who, for a short period after waking, had to 'pick her way through a mass of crabs on the carpet'. Eventually she would reach the light to switch it on 'to reassure herself that they were not really there' (Myers 1957: 70). Sometimes during this recurrent hypnopompic experience she would continue to see the hallucinatory images in full light.

That words are available to label such experiences can be reassuring. Yet terms like 'hypnagogic', 'hypnopompic' and 'false wakings' are not widely known today. They did not even exist in the seventeenth century when Thomas Hobbes noticed hypnagogia and distinguished it from dreams and nightmares. Despite the superstitious age in which he lived, he recognized a huge subject matter for supernatural interpretation, in seeming 'events' in dreams and hypnagogia. In these all things are possible. Moreover even in our own sophisticated society we find uncertainties about whether one is awake or asleep. In Africa, Asia and parts of Europe and America there are many cultural norms that encourage rather than discourage supernatural interpretations. Consider, for example, levitation and flying. I confess to being myself pretty efficient at both, though only in sleep and adjacent mental states. Leaning (1925) reports on a Professor Newboldt who recurrently experienced 'flying face downwards, about twenty feet above the ground ... it is always night and I am following a road, trees, fences, fields dimly seen by the roadside.' He assessed his experiences, as I do mine, as phenomena of sleep and hypnagogia. At other times, and in many other places today, different interpretations might be made.

Events of the seventeenth century concerned Thomas Hobbes who, of course, lived in it. In this context we meet what might be called the 'History–Geography Principle'. In a sense it is possible historically to move backwards in time by travelling geographically around the twentieth-century world. Witchcraft and possession still flourish. Even in Europe and America people compete to tell their stories of the supernatural: stories are modified and dramatized in the process. Many oddities of experience occur in hypnagogia including, for example, appearances of people dressed in the garments of a former age, sometimes viewed open-eyed approaching one's bed. Apparitions are traditionally associated with darkness, fear and accompanying drowsiness. The will to believe is often strong, and short of full belief we encounter the phenomena of half-belief. We do not necessarily have to travel far in search of instances of the History–Geography Principle. Many, perhaps most, people entertain at least half-belief superstitions well catered for by the media: the astrology columns of many newspapers, to say nothing of the recurrently appearing astrologer on British television. Two important empathy bridges may be noted. On the one hand is the bridge which links personal superstitions with delusion; on the other is the bridge between normal hypnagogia and phenomena diagnosed as 'hallucination'.

HYPNAGOGIC IMAGERY REVISITED

In considering the fascinating realm of hypnagogic imagery I will draw on three sources, together with the published research literature. These comprise first, my own introspections; second, numerous studies with questionnaires, interviews and sometimes tape recordings; and third, a detailed investigation by two regular hypnagogic imagers who use drawings as well as words to communicate about them. This third source involved systematic work by Rob Guyton and Phil Scadden. In a reminder of the error of identifying introspection with 'verbal report' they made considerable use of drawings and paintings as part of these communications. These various sources of information support the distinction made earlier between two types of hypnagogic imagery: perseverative, and impersonal or archetypal. The second kind of imagery, the archetypal kind, might be likened to suddenly tuning in to a very strange, and irrelevant, television programme. It seems unrelated to thoughts or other perceptual experiences going on at the time. In one experiment with a regular hypnagogic imager we were even able to get the subject to respond by thinking up another, non-hypnagogic image. This co-existed but did not blend with the flow of hypnagogic visualizations going on at the time.

Hypnagogic imagery has the characteristics of an interruption, an invasion of consciousness by processes of the kind we ordinarily are able to confine to sleep. If one's usual time for sleeping is delayed the imagery may become noticeable not merely because of tiredness, but also because then sleep and dreaming 'should be' happening. As one investigator, cited by Mavromatis (1987), put it, 'I was able to watch myself dreaming.' Yet it differs from dreams in this characteristic of irrelevance. To use an analogy, dreaming resembles a lecture illustrated by slides which form part of it; hypnagogic imagery is more like a display of slides meant to illustrate some other lecture. Moreover the slides have been mixed up, and follow one another in random order. But often criterion problems arise in distinguishing the imagery from onset of actual sleep and dreaming. Here another distinction may be made between two rather different kinds of hypnagogic imaging. Sometimes it is sequences of objects, faces, or landscapes. But it may also take the form – as one progresses closer to actual

103

Figure 5.4   Hypnagogic visual joke
Sometimes they are 'like visual jokes worked out for my amusement', not
thought up – they happen to their author who watches as a passive spectator.
This one – original coloured – was mobile. The bridge proceeded to 'walk' across
the river (Rob Guyton).

dreaming – of an episode or mini-play. One sequence was of a
snowscape, a wharf, head of a bird, old Victorian building, marine
shells, a tall tree, then more shells. The alternative kind, the mini-
plays, were often entertaining and amusing. One example con-
sisted of a 'cartoon sabre-tooth tiger', moving forward on its hind
legs 'paws held up near face' and then suddenly 'a striped tiger's
arm comes around from behind and covers the sabre-toothed
tiger's eyes' (McKellar 1979b).

A number of different subjects experienced these cartoon-like
sequences of imagery or isolated figures. One reported 'a very
stern Humpty-Dumpty with hat and cane', another 'a dachshund
dog dressed in a tartan coat and breeches with a puppy dressed
the same', yet another a block of clear resin 'with a picture of
Paddington Bear upside down in it'. For the most part the
imagery, unlike dreams, was experienced as something one
watched rather than took part in. An exception was reported to
me by Phil Scadden on one occasion. Although he ordinarily
enjoyed his hypnagogic imagery this sequence was alarming and

fear-inducing. He found himself as one of a group of sheep standing outside a slaughter-house. 'I was one of them. We moved up the gangway. I could feel what all the sheep felt.' In the mini-play image he saw the slaughterman's face. He found the image very frightening.

Introspections by Mr Scadden and Mr Guyton support my own that would indicate more seems to be 'there' in the imagery than can be attended to and taken in. There are resemblances to a tapestry or large painting with only glimpses of detail at the margins. I quote Scadden's comment:

> There appear to be layers and layers of the imagery. Beneath those in the foreground are additional ones to be examined. There is the strong impression that the imagery is, in some sense, there to be noticed or overlooked. (McKellar 1979b:194)

In addition are the attributes of movement and change which also complicate efforts to study the imagery. Apart from the rapidity of change in the sequences, happenings during the hypnagogic episodes may be disturbing. On one occasion I experienced such an episode in my imagery concerning a Siamese fighting-fish which – in reality – lived in a tropical fish-tank at my university office. In the image the fish jumped out of the tank, on to the floor. I was very concerned. Although aware I was at home, in bed, and not in my office at work, I felt it my responsibility to sink back into the imagery, 'look for' the fish on the floor and 'put it back safely' into the tank. One has some peculiar hypnagogic responsibilities!

In his very important contribution to the study of hypnagogia, Mavromatis (1987) is critical of the distinction originally made by Lorna Simpson and myself (McKellar and Simpson 1954). He suggests that our 'impersonal' category should include not only plausible content, for example of faces or places 'outside the subject's conscious memory', but also implausible and fanciful items like monsters, angels and devils. My inclination is still, using the Hobbes Principle as a guide, to assume and wherever possible seek such perceptual origins. I take as illustration a rather strange image reported by the Scadden–Guyton team of a woman feeding a blackcurrant pie to a fish. Free associations helped. That evening a little girl had shown the imager her new dress with a fish design on it. The meal that night had included blackcurrant pie. Hypnagogic juxtaposition had done the rest. The word 'hypnagogia' provided by Mavromatis is a useful generic term. If within this concept we retain a distinction between hypnagogic and hypnopompic there is one trap to be avoided. The words do not necessarily relate to night and morning. It is, for example, wholly possible to drift off again towards sleep in the morning and have hypnagogic imagery. Similarly in the evening or during the night there may be wakefulness after sleep, accompanied by hypnopompic imagery. Preserving the distinction, Richardson, Mavromatis, Mindel, and Owens (1981) report a considerably higher incidence of hypnagogic than hypnopompic imagery. Relations to actual dreaming are interesting. I have a tape made by Mr Scadden embracing experiences of hypnagogia with gaps that occurred when he actually fell asleep. Introspections on the tape include the words: 'carrying over things I had been dreaming about ... oscillating between half consciousness and unconsciousness'. Resemblances of hypnagogia to states of meditation are discussed by Dr Mavromatis, and he cites a Tantric Buddhist text. This refers to the desirability of being able to hold oneself 'at the junction of all the states, i.e. in the half asleep state', something Scadden on this occasion achieved only spasmodically. Some investigators provide information on duration of the imagery. One reported an image of 'an alligator for 2½ minutes'. Scadden developed a technique of time measurement using his own breathing. On one tape he reported, 'I've just watched one which lasted 10 breaths.' Duration of imagery varied greatly. Some came and went with a speed that defied timing. Others we have seen could last minutes. We shall also later encounter hypnagogic mini-plays as longer or shorter episodes of hypnagogia. There are many ways of classifying the experiences and duration provides the basis of some of them. It is difficult to over-emphasize the beauty, often involving vivid and unusual colour, of some of the images of the visual kind.

Sometimes visual hypnagogic images occur open-eyed in a darkened bedroom. After-images of previous sensory stimulation may contribute to the visualizations, particularly when the dark-adapted eye is involved. An 'inadequate stimulus' to vision, in the form of eyeball pressure, may also influence it. One subject described this producing 'a yellow blob' in the field of the hypnagogic imagery going on at the time. Many investigators have supported the theory that the sensory activity of the eye itself may contribute to the structure and content of the imagery (Schacter 1976). Mavromatis is critical of this emphasis on peripheral sense organ explanations and instead places his own emphasis on central brain processes, 'activities of areas of the brain', the thalamus and electromagnetic processes in various different 'brainfields' (op. cit.: 265–6). The underlying physiology of hypnagogic imaging is a study in itself on which various investigators differ. Certainly there is, as I have suggested elsewhere, much 'visual noise' going on in the eye itself (McKellar 1979b). Granit, for instance, refers to this 'spontaneous activity of the sense organs' which makes them 'one of the brain's most important energisers' (Granit 1955).

EMOTIONAL RESPONSES

A range of emotional responses is encountered in hypnagogic and hypnopompic imagery. They include interest, amusement, fear, anxiety, surprise, and even anger. Guilt feeling has been noted in my own image of rescuing the Siamese fish. From my introspections I can also testify to anger. The image in question involved a group of people standing there, when suddenly an intruder appeared, drew out a hand-gun and shot several of them. I was most indignant about the activity of the 'Mr Hyde' within myself, which had some resemblance to the hostility that the other Misses Beauchamp must have felt towards Sally. Yet it was a product of some sub-system of my own mental life, outside consciousness. As regards amusement, several imagers told me that they laughed out loud at what their dissociated sub-systems produced: 'like visual jokes worked out for my entertainment', reported one. In the psychoses we sometimes encounter hallucinations of lilliputian-like figures which the patient complains persecute him. The instances of micropsia encountered hypnagogically seem mostly to have been accompanied by interest and sometimes amusement, rather than by negative emotion. Fear is often a response to the grotesque faces that can occur in sequences of imagery. On occasion ghostlike figures of a traditional kind, or apparitions dressed in the garments of a former age, are reported.

Hypnagogic imagery means different things to different people. At times it assumes a nightmare character, involving fear of the supernatural or anxiety about becoming insane. On occasion one encounters such reactions to the imagery in children who are also too frightened to tell their parents. Many people seem to accept the imagery as an interesting variant of normal mental life. I have sometimes had the salutary experience of discussing the imagery with deluded and hallucinated patients who also interpret it in this way. It was merely accepted as 'one of those things that happens before sleep', and as something that did not happen to fit into the patient's delusional system. On the other hand, sometimes it does fit in, and this phenomenon – shared with normal mental life – may provide subject matter in the development of psychosis. Auditory hypnagogic imagery in particular merits emphasis in relation to such happenings. Some with appropriate beliefs may interpret the visual or auditory imagery as glimpses of, or sounds from, some other world. Nowadays not only religion but also science fiction may encourage such interpretations. Many artists and writers have not merely exhibited interest in the imagery, but have also made deliberate use of it in painting and writing. It may be noted, in the cases of Mary Shelley and *Frankenstein*, and Stevenson's Jekyll–Hyde story, that such use did not exclude being frightened by it. In the field of science well known is the occasion when the chemist Kekulé used two instances of hypnagogic visualization as the basis of his benzene ring concept. Both Kekulé himself and this structural formula have – like Breuer's famous patient, 'Anna O' – been commemorated by West Germany on its postage stamps.

HYPNOPOMPIC SPEECH

Hypnagogic and hypnopompic imagery are not the only things we encounter in the realm of hypnagogia. We have already noted that illusions of change in the shape or size of one's body, or its parts, are a common phenomenon. Along with these body image changes may be mentioned another happening that lacks a well-established name. Among those who have noticed it have been Mintz (1948) and Kenneth Craik (1966), and I have suggested the name 'hypnopompic speech' (McKellar 1968). Before or after sleep in these drowsy states people often murmur very strange things. Mintz suggests they involve loosening of the thought processes of a kind reminiscent of schizophrenic utterances. Like instances of thinking of the 'knight's move of the schizophrenic' kind there is sometimes a kind of logic that can be decoded. Once when half-awakened from sleep I was asked the question: 'What is the time?' My reply was: 'I'll rub together two clocks and tell you.' Since it involved myself I can provide associations that help with this dark saying. When drowsy and still trying to attain full wakefulness, a look at a badly designed clock face – particularly one with roman numerals – is unreliable. The obvious thing is to check with both clock and watch, though only in the hypnopompic state would one describe looking at both as 'rubbing them together'. A subsidiary association involved recall of the joke about lighting a fire by 'rubbing together two boy scouts' (scouts are only allowed two matches). One of the examples given by Mintz involved a young wife murmuring in a sleepy voice to her husband, 'light the towel'. This, it emerged, meant 'raise the window shade': 'lighting' means 'provide more light'. A towel and a curtain are the same shape: thus, to the kind of thinking which Arieti calls 'paleologic' – to be discussed later, they are identified (see Chapter 11). The resemblance of such utterances to those of schizophrenic thinking impresses Mintz, who adds that schizophrenic thinking lies 'within the behaviour repertoire of the normal individual' (McKellar 1968: 107). In his discussions of both dreamlife and hypnagogia, Hervey de Saint Denys considers similar identifications under the heading of what he calls 'abstractions'. He argues that objects possess a number of attributes such as, for example, shape and colour. These 'abstractions are the most common form of link between ideas' in both wakefulness and sleep. But in the sleeping and related drowsy states 'there is frequently a fusion or confusion between two ideas which have been brought together by the process of abstraction' (Saint Denys 1867, edition 1982: 128–9). Comparison of the ideas of Saint Denys on sleep and of Arieti on schizophrenic thinking suggests some interesting future areas of inquiry into their similarities and differences. In a paper published posthumously in 1966, Kenneth Craik gives further illustrations of hypnopompic speech and decoding its meaning. He notes relevance of each associated idea to the previous idea but not to the total context. In this he likens hypnopompic speech to the activity of an inefficient secretary who cannot file things correctly, being unable to grasp the principle of classification involved. There is, as Silberer found in his studies of hypnagogic thinking, a switch to an easier mode of mental functioning.

AUTONOMY AND VOLUNTARY CONTROL

Resemblances between upsurges of A-thinking in imagery of hypnagogia to hallucinatory experience are considerable. Many investigators have stressed the autonomous character of hypnagogic experiences. Mrs Arnold Foster declared, 'No exertion of will can summon them at our pleasure ... they are wholly independent of our control' (Quoted in Leaning 1925: 364). Although such autonomy appears to be usual, there are exceptions. One of my own subjects reported being able to 'step into the play as an actor might walk onto the stage' and found himself sometimes 'able to act the part of a magician, affect the action, even change the characters, after which the play proceeds normally' (McKellar 1975: 20–4). In considering the variants of such imagery, Marks and McKellar (1982) found it necessary to distinguish 'primary autonomy', relating to onset of the imagery, from 'secondary autonomy', in the sense of being able to change the imagery once it had begun. Individual experiences vary. Thus one of the subjects cited by Leaning experienced imagery of a tree trunk with small white objects at its base. What were they? She thought, 'Mushrooms perhaps?' Immediately they became mushrooms. Her next thought was: 'Playing cards?' and as a result, 'they became playing cards.' She began to think, 'Now can I get these plants to bloom?' and no sooner had she formulated the thought than flowering buds 'grew by degrees and unfolded'. Persisting in her efforts she thought, 'if it comes again I'll try to get something alive.' Then followed imagery of a number of creatures, including a small rat-like animal with its mouth open and a pink tongue (Leaning 1925: 367–8).

Indirect influence on the imagery seems, on occasion, to be possible. As Rob Guyton, a careful introspectionist, reported with reference to this and secondary autonomy, 'I can't say "I'll have a square cloud," but I can say "I'd like a different one, thanks." And a different one will come. You can't specify' (McKellar 1979b: 193). In his emotional responses to such imagery we may note his genuine gratitude in the word 'thanks'. In this instance, as in the case cited by Leaning, we might invoke Freud's notion of the 'omnipotence of thought', which has relevance to his analysis of seemingly supernatural happenings. But a subtle difference between the two instances may be noted. In the Leaning case the subject made a demand over the imagery, requiring 'it' to do something in accord with her will: the analogy is with magic. Mr Guyton made a request, permitting a range of things to occur: the analogy is more closely with religion, even reverence and prayer. These and other exceptions to the more usual primary and secondary autonomy of hypnagogic visionary experience provide much food for thought. Sometimes the dissociated system responsible for the imagery, like the Jungian unconscious, has 'its message' for us. Like those from the bicameral mind which Jaynes discusses in relation to the Old Testament prophets, we should not be impatient in what we demand but wait to see what comes. Julian Jaynes (1976, 1982 edition) thus seeks a psychological explanation of both the oracles of Ancient Greece and the utterances of the Hebrew prophets in these terms. It seems likely that hypnagogic imagery played a part in both types of visionary experience, the message being available not through consciousness but perhaps from some dissociated system outside it.

Transitions from hypnagogia to dreamlife are of interest. So also are similarities and differences between hypnagogia and other altered mental states, like typical dreaming and atypical lucid dreaming. This leads to a distinction that may be made between two differing types of hypnagogic experience that I have called type A and type B (McKellar 1979a). Type A are 'hypnagogic sequences': like a display of lantern-slides, randomly presented, which the imager finds himself 'watching' as though on an internal screen. Type B are different: they are 'hypnagogic episodes', resembling mini-plays that characteristically go on longer. Thus one of my subjects reported an upsurge of his imagery of 'a family of skulls in a car, driving along'. He added, 'I could tell it was a friendly family. No, it wasn't at all frightening. On the whole it was rather jolly' (op. cit.: 190–1). For those who have difficulty experiencing – or noticing – hypnagogic imagery, whether type A or type B, I suggest a technique which sometimes

111

seems to help. In the drowsy pre-sleep state, form a visual image of a television screen and 'watch' what appears on it. If autonomous imagery does emerge this 'watching' process is difficult to maintain. There is likely to occur a transition from hypnagogic sequences to hypnagogic episodes, and these in turn shade into dreamlife and full sleep. Initially, like Rev. Henslow cited at the beginning of the chapter, we are a 'mere spectator' and a degree of co-conscious awareness of ourself as distinct from the imagery is retained. But the hypnagogic episodes that follow seem to herald actual dreams, with imagery we participate in rather than merely co-consciously 'watch'. As Havelock Ellis once put it, in his book appropriately titled *The World of Dreams*, 'dreams are true while they last.' The exception is lucid dreaming, in which it is possible to retain a degree of co-conscious awareness of a self which is in some way different from the dream's imagery of events.

In moving from hypnagogia to dreamlife we encounter the work of Freud and his predecessors. Outstandingly important among these was the French investigator, the Marquis Hervey de Saint Denys (1822–92). Although an Orientalist rather than a psychologist, Saint Denys made a lifelong study of his own dreams. Mostly in the case of dreamlife as opposed to hypnagogia we have to rely on subsequent retrospection rather than introspection. Here we encounter an exception. Although he did not name the phenomenon, Saint Denys observed in his own case lucid dreams: he was aware of being asleep and dreaming, and thus while asleep could introspect. His book, published in 1867 (edition 1982), deals in detail with dream imagery in its relations to perception, memory and association, and with the substantial control over dreams he achieved. On the basis of studies of himself and others, Hervey de Saint Denys concluded 'there is no sleep without dreams.' Evidence for this included his investigation of one individual who persistently denied dreaming, and it reveals Saint Denys' imaginative, often experimental approach. One night, after the man had been asleep for about half an hour, Saint Denys woke him up just after having spoken the words 'Present arms! Shoulder arms!' and other military commands. On waking the man denied dreaming. Saint Denys asked 'Are you sure you didn't see a soldier?' Now the dream memory came back. 'Yes, now I remember. I dreamed I was watching a parade. How did you guess?' (Saint Denys, op. cit.: 42). The observations were verified on another occasion. Again there was denial at first, but when he was prompted the man recalled a dream 'suggested by the spoken words'.

In such ways Saint Denys sought to verify that his own dreamlife applied also to others. In his own case he reports that having been awakened 160 times during sleep, 'each time I noted that some thought accompanied by an image occupied my mind' (op. cit.: 42). Many of these experiences were lucid dreams. Because of Maury's previous work, Saint Denys was familiar with the name 'hypnagogic imagery'. His observations on the transition towards sleep from hypnagogia refer to an onset of drowsiness in which reality is forgotten and 'the mind sees more and more clearly the tangible images of the objects with which it is preoccupied' (op. cit.: 36). He explained the content of dreams and hypnagogic imagery by past perception. They are 'formed by materials already contained in the dreamer's memory', though recombinations of these may be creative. Saint Denys experimented on this by repeated close examinations of paintings in a Chinese album. Subsequently in several dreams he experienced scenes from the album 'in movement mixed with innumerable images and incidents of different origin'. And in other dreams he saw scenes and people that had been associatively evoked by the album's paintings, that – like the pictures in the album – transformed themselves into 'engravings and watercolours' (op. cit.: 155). For him dreams and hypnagogic experiences, however creative, were natural not supernatural phenomena.

SUMMARY

1   The often surrealist-like images which erupt into consciousness as pre-sleep anticipations of actual dreamlife have interested investigators from Aristotle onwards. Such imagery may also be auditory and of a hallucinatory kind, often confused with real sounds. There are also, more rarely, images of touch, smell and temperature, and they may be composite, covering several sense modes.

2   In content they vary enormously and they may evoke fear and other strong emotions; they are characteristically autonomous rather than 'thought up' by the imager; and sometimes they have been given supernatural interpretations, for example as 'glimpses of another world'.

3   There is some mystery about their incidence. Once they were thought to be rare, but are nowadays recognized as a common subjective experience, and like dreams themselves possibly universal. Once alerted to them, people are often surprised to notice that they have the experience. Hypnopompic experiences, which follow rather than precede sleep, appear to be more unusual.

4   There are other subjective experiences of states adjacent to sleep, such as illusions of changes in the body image, and 'hypnopompic speech' with its strange and schizophrenic-like utterances. In addition the dichotomy between perseverative hypnagogic imagery with obvious sensory origins, and the impersonal and 'archetypal' type, seemingly remote from past perceptions, is considered.

5   Such classification leads to a statement and defence of a basic concept, the Hobbes Principle which incorporates the notion of a sensory origin of mental content, however creatively imaginative. A further classification distinguishes hypnagogic sequences from hypnagogic episodes which seem to herald onset of sleep and actual dreamlife.

Chapter Six

DREAMLIFE

'What shall we do with you Socrates, after your death?'
'Whatever you like – if you can catch me.'

Plato: *The Phaedo*

Crito, the disciple who asked the question, was thinking of the body. Socrates, about to die, was thinking of the soul. Psychology is literally the study of the soul. Pre-existence before birth and survival after death were convictions held with passion by Socrates and Plato. Their successor Aristotle was less interested in survival than in some vital principle that distinguishes living organisms. He distinguished the organic from the inorganic and brought classification to both. Often assessed as the greatest psychologist of ancient times, he claimed the phenomena of thinking, perception, learning and habit formation as subject matter for naturalistic inquiry. Aristotle accepted the fact that mental life continues during sleep. For him dreams were not the result of temporary absence of the soul from the body, but natural happenings meriting investigation as such. For thousands of years mankind has been confronted with opposing theories of dreamlife.

TWO THEORIES OF THE DREAM

Two theories have emerged, both widely accepted today. One is of considerable interest to anthropology; the other comprises the

Figure 6.1 Sleep and adjacent states: In the mid-seventeenth century Thomas Hobbes, like many later thinkers, regarded dreamlife and hypnagogia as providing the source of supernatural imagining about spirits, benign or malevolent. Did the gods and goddesses of polytheism arise from dreams? Anubis was regarded by the Ancient Egyptians as the 'Bringer of Dreams'.

standpoint of psychology. The 'supernatural theory' views sleep as departure of the soul, or some aspect of the self, from the body. This departure is temporary, and dreams are memories of people encountered and places visited until the soul returns with wakefulness. Death results if the soul fails to return. In our own society many superstitious beliefs and half-beliefs reflect this fear of loss of soul. A sleeper should not be suddenly awakened; sick room windows should be closed; mirrors should be covered and, as something which an optical image can be projected into, should never be broken. As anthropology teaches us, fear of loss of soul in sleep, or even wakefulness, is widespread in the twentieth-century world. Insensitive tourists with their cameras have sometimes discovered this. The myth of Narcissus and the pool of water is a reminder that other things than mirrors and camera lenses have been, and remain, subjects of widespread taboo and ritualistic avoidance.

The alternative 'naturalistic theory' of dreamlife follows broadly the standpoint of Aristotle. Dreams are an expression of the personality of the dreamer; they reflect his emotions and emotional habits; and they draw their content from past perceptual experiences. Dreaming is the thinking of sleep. Individual theories differ in their emphasis on the extent to which dreams are regressive on the one hand, or disguised expressions of emotion and motive on the other. But overall for the psychologist, the mental life of sleep, like that of wakefulness, is a biological not a supernatural subject. As Hervey de Saint Denys puts it, 'When the eyes of the body are closed ... the eyes of the mind are opened to the world of fantasy and recollection' (1867, edition 1982: 46). The relation of the reactivated memories and associations that make up a dream's content to biological structure and functioning may be emphasized. The organism has been modified in some way by previous sensory experiences which have been registered and somehow stored in the brain or elsewhere. As William James wrote, 'No mental modification ever occurs which is not accompanied, or followed by a bodily change' (James 1890, vol. 1: 5). Since theorists sometimes overlook the fact that social influences, traumatic experiences, and memory, forgetting, and learning have this biological basis, the point he is making is important. Learning, no less than genetic endowment, is biological in character; this was recognized also by the early behaviourist E. B. Holt when he wrote of learning, 'the resistance of any synapse is lowered by use' (Holt 1931: 28). In the case of imagery, the relations of this to the biological processes possibly underlying learning and conditioning are considered in a symposium by seventeen contemporary psychologists (Bugelski *et al.* 1982: 1–92). A later contribution by Marks (1986b) surveys mapping of the topography of regions of the brain in terms of recent electroencephalogram (EEG) studies of specific areas of the cortex. Much has happened since William James, yet his early emphasis on the biology of mental life, 'that states of consciousness are the vehicles of that knowledge, and depend on brain states' (James 1890), provided an orientation which psychology as a whole has taken. Accepting this orientation as fundamental, I will give a name to this guiding principle, a reminder of biology, as the 'William James Principle'. It has considerable bearing on abnormal psychology even when we are particularly concerned with its subjective phenomena.

In an early paper G. T. Ladd (1892) discussed the retinal sensations that occur with closed eyes. Various names have been given to them: 'luminous dust' (Wundt), 'idio-retinal light' (William James), 'phosphenes' and '*Eigenlichten*'. In introspection Ladd noticed these changing visual patterns and shapes, and his suggestion is that they provide the basic structure of dream images. He wrote, 'there is no shape known to me' that has not 'been schematically represented by the changing retinal images' (op. cit.: 300). Hervey de Saint Denys earlier noticed these retinal sensations and was interested in their transition into actual dreaming and hypnagogic imagery. Some, he declared, 'resemble fireworks more than real objects' (1867, edition 1982: 136). And some are 'little suns that whirl rapidly round'. These he described as 'the forerunners of better framed images' (op. cit.: 135). This aspect of Ladd's own study was frequently noticed and commented on by other investigators. Perhaps in these sensations we have the beginnings of an explanation of the varied forms of hypnagogic, dreaming, and hallucinatory experiences. But if Ladd's paper was widely read, one aspect of it was largely overlooked. This was a clear reference to ocular-motor movement of the eyeball during dreaming, detectable even through the closed eyelids.

It was half a century later that Aserinsky and Kleitman (1953) again noticed this, and made good use of these rapid eye movements or REMs in their experimental work on dreams. Through this they established that a great deal of human dreaming is lost through forgetting. But earlier, and seemingly independently, another person had made the observation that in sleep dreaming seems to go on much of the time. This observer's mentor, Morton Prince, recorded her observations with some reservations as to whether this applied to the dreamlife of other people as well (Prince 1905).

SALLY AS INTROSPECTIONIST

The observer in question was the 'Sally' sub-system in the dissociations of Miss Christine Beauchamp. Sally remained awake while the B.I and B.IV personalities slept. Like a person experiencing a lucid dream, she was thus able to introspect during such sleep. Sally was puzzled. According to her the sleeper would imagine 'all sorts of things'. Morton Prince was inconsistent. 'If she remembers them you call them dreams, and the others you don't' (Prince, op. cit.: 327). Sally added, 'It never stops the whole night long' (op. cit.: 329). She regarded it as most illogical 'to call dreaming only what one remembers because the same thing is going on all the time' (op. cit.: 330). Finally she asks, 'If you call one thing dreams why shouldn't you call the other dreams?' Morton Prince records these observations by the Sally personality in direct quotation marks. He adds his comment that to her, who remembered the whole dream, the mere remembering of a part of it was 'an inconsequential fact' (ibid.). He was, we have seen, cautious about generalization regarding people as a whole.

Sally herself was much more emphatic. She was aware of the continuity between wakefulness and sleep, the contributions of perceptual experiences to dreamlife, and the fact that in sleep fantasy goes on, whether we remember it or not. In making such observations, as we now know from vigorous researches into REMs that have since taken place, Sally was substantially correct. Although those available REM occurrences are not a certain criterion that a dream is taking place, they are a valuable one. Wakened during an REM period a sleeper tends to report a dream; after such a period, fragments of a dream; and some

119

time later no dream memory at all, presumably as a result of forgetting.

Inadequacies of language become apparent in consideration of one sub-system within a multiple personality claiming to be 'awake', and introspecting, while the other personalities are 'asleep'. There is a similarity to the other known occasion on which sleep permits introspection – as opposed to mere retrospection – to occur. This is lucid dreaming. In a way independent of Hervey de Saint Denys, van Eeden, and others, did Sally Beauchamp discover lucid dreaming? Should we classify these aspects of Christine Beauchamp's mental life as lucid dreaming?

LUCID DREAMS

In a book which has alerted many investigators to this area, Celia Green (1968b, edition 1982) makes a distinction between pre-lucid and lucid dreams. In lucid dreams the sleeper knows he is asleep and dreaming; in pre-lucid dreams he thinks he may be asleep. She points out that both lucid and pre-lucid dreams 'appear to take a certain delight in humorously exploiting the situation': we frequently encounter situations in them about whether a dream is, or is not, taking place. An example concerns Celia Green's 'Subject B' who reported in a lucid dream talking with her mother. They were walking along a road and in the dream the dreamer said, 'We are in a dream *now* Mother.' The mother agreed. Next the dreamer had an idea. She asked, 'If I tell you something now, will you try to remember it when you wake up?' The mother was doubtful about being able to do this. 'But you would *try* wouldn't you, Mother?' (Green, op. cit.: 65–6, italics hers).

At Celia Green's Institute of Psychophysical Research at Oxford, and elsewhere, lucid dreams are receiving considerable research attention. The name 'lucid dream' was provided by Frederick van Eeden (1913). In an analysis of 500 of his dreams he found 352 to be of the lucid type. Another early investigator was Mary Arnold-Foster, who was also talented at flying during her lucid dreams. On one such occasion she found herself at Burlington House, London, in the Rooms of the Royal Society. The company included physicists and other scientists, including Lord Kelvin.

She was invited to explain her method of flying and proceeded to do so, giving a demonstration of gliding, floating, and circling around the rooms of the Royal Society. Then – still in the dream – Lord Kelvin came forward and remarked, 'The law of gravitation has probably been in this case temporarily suspended.' The other physicists agreed. As a final demonstration Mrs Arnold-Foster showed that flying 'is not really difficult', and by taking a by-stander's hand she succeeded in raising him from the ground – but only a few inches (Arnold-Foster 1921: 71–2). Some of the impressive things that happen in lucid dreams and out-of-the-body experiences may tempt those who experience them towards a supernatural interpretation. Perhaps in sleep the soul does, for a time, leave the body but later return? In considering this hypothesis it may be noted that some investigators who emphatically reject it, also have such experiences.

Hervey de Saint Denys maintained a consistently naturalistic approach. Dreams, however strange, were for him psychological not supernatural phenomena. Thus when he reported one such experience in the words, 'Last night I dreamed my soul had left my body,' it was a phenomenon of the 'as if' kind. What followed is the report Saint Denys gives of the landscapes and people he encountered in this lucid dream. He retained his identity and some control over the dream events. After a while he decided to return to earth. Now back in his own bedroom he had 'the strange sensation of looking at my sleeping body before taking possession of it again' (Saint Denys 1867, 1982 edition: 162). During his experiments on his own dreamlife Saint Denys achieved a considerable amount of control over his dreams and what happened in them. But such control was not absolute in that he decided that lucid dreams obey certain laws, comparable to laws we encounter in waking life. Thus he decided, during one lucid dream, that if he put his dream hand in front of his eyes he would be able to blot out surrounding events. He would be able to see, to image, other things. So on one occasion in his dream he did this, and was thus able to blot out a country landscape, this being replaced by visual images of 'dreadful monsters'. Charles McCreery (1973) translates this incident from the original French text, and discusses it in terms of dream control. An additional comment may be made, namely that the incident in question showed that in doing this Saint Denys was able to experience visual imagery separate from the imagery of his dream. McCreery goes on to consider the subsequent lucid dream experiences of Saint Denys which even the latter is prepared to describe as 'curious'. In one lucid dream he travelled in a hackney coach. From this dream he woke up, and noted the time. Then after about ten to fifteen minutes of wakefulness he fell asleep again. Now he dreamed he woke up in the carriage with the impression of having dropped off to sleep for about fifteen minutes! In other words, in his dream of having been asleep the period of sleep coincided with the intervening period of wakefulness. These experiences suggest that while asleep we can even dream that we sleep and dream. In Saint Denys' case wakefulness was, to lucid dreamlife, sleep.

On the complex inter-relations between lucid dreaming and wakefulness, Celia Green (1968b, edition 1982) adds some observations. She reports on the introspections of her 'Subject C', who described the effort of maintaining lucidity in a dream as 'like trying to keep awake when one is dreadfully tired' (op. cit.: 172). The same subject reported conflict during a lucid dream while looking for a book: 'pursuit of the book was leading back to non-lucidity.' As a result 'I realised the two aims were incompatible' and thus 'decided to sacrifice the book and focus on maintaining lucidity'. Most people are familiar with, during sleep, asking the question, 'Am I dreaming?' Investigators of lucid dreaming like Saint Denys and van Eeden conducted some tests on themselves in such situations. Thus Saint Denys on one occasion – during his dream – licked his finger and made with his dream-image saliva a wet cross on his hand. This was followed by a false awakening in which he verified that the mark was still there, and finally a real awakening when he discovered it wasn't. Frederick van Eeden made many similar attempts and seemed to enjoy doing dangerous or self-destructive things to himself, being confident he was asleep and dreaming. Of special interest are his attempts to cross the barrier between sleeplife and waking reality by shouting and singing in his lucid dreams. His wife testified that despite such efforts the breakthrough was never achieved: never did she hear his voice, and he continued to sleep peacefully.

The rarity of lucid dreams, and of lucid periods within dreams, seems to have been exaggerated. Once alerted to notice them, many people report these experiences, among them some who assume that everybody else has them. In sleep it is well said 'all things are possible' and the possible seems to include evidence of some complex hidden differences between individuals. The variety of subjective experiences reported in relation to sleep and adjacent states, like the variants of waking subjective experiences, is impressive. Dreams are reported by people who are lucid in the sense of knowing they are asleep and dreaming. Dreams are reported by others who think they are awake but are not (false wakings). There are occasions when a person while dreaming is uncertain about whether he is having a real or dreamlife experience (pre-lucid dreams). Dreamlike experiences intrude on the falling-asleep process and we call them hypnagogic, and dreamlife may continue to operate as hypnopompic experiences into waking up. In the technique I have suggested of imaging a television screen and hypnagogically 'watching' what happens on it we have imagery within imagery. Having a dream within a dream – the experience reported by Saint Denys – is probably a rarity, yet it is reported by an unusually careful introspectionist. Both he and van Eeden also report a range of imagery, including touch, taste, temperature, and smell, along with vision and hearing in actual dreams. Finally flying in dreams is reported by many.

Not surprisingly many investigators have turned to dreamlife and its mechanisms in attempts to understand subjective experiences in general, and the apparently abnormal in particular. A feature we recurrently encounter is concretization: rapid transition of thoughts into visual or other imagery form. Thus Saint Denys defines dreaming as 'the representation in our mind's eye of the objects that occupy our thoughts' (1867, 1982 edition: 26). Again and again he produces illustration of how 'the image connected with each idea appears as soon as the idea arises'. In view of the emphasis he places upon this transition to concrete imagery, for brevity I will refer to it as the 'Saint Denys Principle'. An example may be taken from one of Saint Denys' dreams. He was sitting down to dinner, and on being served a particular dish murmured in his dream 'It's as hard as shoe-leather.' Immediately there appeared on his plate a piece of shoe-leather (op. cit.: 141). We encounter the principle in action outside dreaming. In our experiments with hallucinogens we found many instances of the principle: when the subjects felt hostile to the experimenters they would often hallucinate us in uncomplimentary ways. One of my co-experimenters became old and witch-like. And on another occasion I was hallucinated as a crumpled piece of card ready to be thrown into a wastepaper basket (McKellar 1957). In the naturally occurring psychoses, as opposed to experimental attempts to simulate them, the highly concrete nature of responses has been much emphasized. Thus Julian Jaynes describes the schizophrenic as 'almost drowning in sensory data ... they see every tree and never the forest' (Jaynes 1976, edition 1982: 427). As regards concrete imagery he cites the case of a patient who 'saw the word *poison* in the air at the very moment when the attendant made him take his medicine' (op. cit.: 92–3).

The mechanism of what I have called the Saint Denys Principle greatly interested Herbert Silberer after he first encountered it in hypnagogic imagery. He was lying on a couch in a drowsy state comparing two sets of ideas and, on losing the thread of one of them, experienced a vivid image. It took the form of a morose and unhelpful secretary from whom he sought information, and who greeted him with 'an unfriendly and rejecting look' (Silberer 1909: 196). On another hypnagogic occasion his inability to remember a sequence of ideas took the form of an image of 'a piece of typesetting with the last few lines gone'. These 'auto-symbolic' phenomena, as he called them, led Silberer to systematic experiments. He would lie on his couch, drift off into drowsiness, and await the imagery: it would regularly assume these highly concrete, often cartoon-like forms. Under such conditions, as Silberer puts it, 'The tired consciousness ... switches to an easier form of mental functioning' (op. cit.: 198–9; McKellar 1957: 102ff.).

Before considering further the psychologists' naturalistic theory of dreaming I turn briefly to one very strange phenomenon. It lies literally not between wakefulness and sleep, but between life and death. The 'near-death experience' is suggestive of the comment of Socrates which heads this chapter. It is related to resuscitation of people who have nearly died, perhaps have even 'died', since death is not necessarily an all-or-nothing happening. I had the opportunity to interview one person – a young American woman journalist – who had undergone it. Moody (1975) has studied more than a thousand cases of it over twenty years. My informant told me of vivid imagery and of seeming to move away from her bodily self towards clear light, and of eventually – by medical and nursing power – returning with reluctance to living again. Dr Moody reports not encountering the phenomenon with EEG electrical brain silence, and he is interested in its relation to cardiac arrest. 'Resistance to return' to bodily existence and imagery associated with vivid light during this struggle are character- istic. He is quoted as emphasizing 'the consistent and repeated patterns' encountered in his years of study of these strange experiences, and their 'internal coherence and order'. There may be some similarities with hypnagogic and drug-induced experi- ences, but he himself is critical of this suggestion. Overall Moody accepts, with reluctance, 'the conclusion that a different level of reality is being experienced' (*Independent*, London, 26 October 1987).

DREAMS AND THE DREAMER

Dreams do not merely reveal mechanisms: they are also a source of information about the personality of their author the dreamer. Freud's approach to dreamlife involves his wish-fulfilment theory. The motive of the dream is a wish; its content the fulfilment of that wish. Content comes from re-activated past perceptual experience. Both the motivation and the content thus provide information about the sentiments and emotional preoccupations of the dreamer. Some dreams – notably those of children – are simple wish fulfilments. In others there is a discrepancy between the manifest content of the dream and its latent content. Dream mechanisms intrude to produce this discrepancy and, through free association, the dream has thus to be interpreted. Freud's *Interpretation of Dreams* is not merely an account of the psychology of dreams as such, but also a detailed introspective study by Freud. In a sense it is the record of Freud's self-analysis: Freud's own testimony confirms this, as does his correspondence with Wilhelm Fliess at the time. The English translation became available in 1900. That was a long time ago, and as we have seen, there has been important scientific progress since. Yet it remains one of the outstandingly important classics of psychology and in Freud's own view his most important work.

The Interpretation of Dreams has been widely criticized, sometimes apparently without what it actually says being noticed. In this book at least Freud is very explicit about what his recommended method of dream interpretation is *not*. What he argues for, and indeed insists upon, in this book is more sensible than frequently heard loose talk about 'Freudian symbols' implies. Freud's method is one of free association: to interpret a dream the first thing needed is presence of the dreamer. From his or her free associations it is ascertained what each item of the dream means in terms of the emotional life of the dreamer. Symbolism may occur, but a given symbol may mean different things on different occasions, and to different individuals. There is no short cut through some kind of standardized key to dreaming in some dreambook. Freud is emphatic on this point. In other words he advocated, instead, in dream analysis a linking of the dream's content with the personality. This linkage with thoughts, motives, and emotional problems must be achieved through free association. It is not an affair of 'Freudian symbols'. A dream of my own – permitting such free association – will illustrate this method. My 'writer's problem' dream involved learning, during the dream, that a cardinal with a complicated foreign name had written a book I wanted to cite. Again in the dream I possessed his book, but discovered that – as sometimes happens in reality – there was no author's name in it. By a dream telephone call I discovered the name. But it was a long foreign name and I knew I had the spelling wrong. Next, in my dream, I saw the cardinal but found myself too shy to go up and speak to him. The dream ended with a decision to omit the reference.

When I woke up my free associations led me to associative linkage of this imaginary foreign cardinal with a Frenchman, whose full name was the 'Marquis Hervey de Saint Denys'. As will be apparent, I have not omitted reference to his many important insights into dreamlife. But he creates a problem. There are so many different ways of referring to him by name, as many writers have found. In my own author's problem dream this was represented by the complexity of the cardinal's name, and my inability to spell it. As regards omission of the reference to the book, this led to association with Freud, who refers to his inability to obtain a copy of the Saint Denys book (fortunately now readily available). My own efforts to obtain it – represented in the dream by the phone call – were considerable and in the end involved rather complex co-operation of at least three different people.

Again as regards omission there is a strong association in my mind, through a French postage stamp, between Cardinal Richelieu and Descartes. Descartes is a thinker whose ideas – unlike those of Saint Denys – have little appeal to me. I remember how often I have wished to be able to omit reference to him in courses I have taught on the history of psychology. The dream as a whole represents the intellectual and emotional preoccupations of a person engaged in writing. Moreover as a thought product it differs very little from what might well occur in the waking thoughts of such a person concerned with such an activity.

In his emphasis on free association, and the process of linking a dream through it with the personality and activities of the dreamer, Freud is lucid in his rejection of dreambooks and standardized 'Freudian symbols'. Among many who misunderstood Freud on this point was the surrealist André Breton. When Breton invited Freud to contribute to an anthology on dreams, Freud refused. His refusal is consistent with what he wrote in *The Interpretation of Dreams*. In replying to Breton he declared, 'A mere collection of dreams without the dreamer's associations, without knowledge of the circumstances in which they occurred tells me nothing.' For emphasis he added, 'I can hardly imagine what they would tell anyone' (Quoted in Gombrich 1954: 2). As elsewhere we can also notice the concern of Freudian psychoanalysis with individuality, and the use of the fantasies of sleep as a method of investigating a personality.

If Freud was interested in dream mechanisms as a clue to neurosis and the normal personality, Jung had a special interest in their relation to psychosis. It was individual people rather than diagnostic categories that concerned him. This is also apparent in his experiments on word association as a technique for revealing complexes, systems of emotionally toned ideas that define the interests of individuals. Analytical psychology views consciousness as consisting of an indefinite number of such complexes; for its part the unconscious embraces a more finite number of archetypes. Both may reveal themselves in dreams. Along with free association Jung used other techniques, and on return to wakefulness the dreamer would be encouraged to draw, paint, and actively imagine around his dreams. Jung's preference was to analyse where possible not one but a series of dreams. In these modifications we have a bridge via Jung to a different technique of personality research. It is Henry Murray's TAT, or Thematic Apperception Test. This technique is used in psychology to investigate individuals by analysing their imaginative thought products, and relatng these to emotional preoccupations (Murray 1943). Murray's concepts of need and press have been considered earlier and they form an important part of the scoring of a TAT.

Henry Murray, who had his own dreams analysed by Jung, dedicates his major book to both Freud and Jung. *Explorations in Personality* (1938) is an intensive study of a group of normal subjects investigated by Murray and his Harvard colleagues. Murray's TAT deals with waking fantasy rather than dreams as thought products. It reflects Jung's preference in dealing with not one but a series of instances of imaginative creation. A TAT testing involves twenty standard pictures. (Sub-sets are available for men, women, boys, and girls.) The subject responds to each in an interview-type situation, by making up a story: what is happening, what led up to it, and what is the outcome. The twenty thought products are then analysed for the light they throw upon personality: its ways of thinking, emotional preoccupations including sentiments, and memories. That co-operation is involved between subject and tester in this process may be emphasized. If, for example, one of the stories merely reflects a film recently seen or a book recently read there is no reason why the subject should not volunteer such information. Together with his TAT thought product he is there to be interviewed. Many psychologists find this method of using a series of waking imaginings elicited by the TAT a useful way of eliciting information not readily available to ordinary recall. Interpretation of the manifest content of the thought products resembles Freud's recommended method of dreams interpretation, and association is heavily involved. The TAT is one derivative of dream interpretation. As with dreams, sources in previous perception and motivational aspects – in this case Murray's 'needs' – can be ascertained. Methods of a similar kind have been used in the study of other thought products more permanent than recorded dreams or TAT responses. The outstanding example in literature is the work of Livingstone Lowes (1927) on two of Coleridge's major poems. There is the study by Taylor (1952) of Lewis Carroll; the recent comprehensive investigations of Rothenberg (1979); and the work by the imagery psychologist, Akhter Ahsen (1984), on the myths of Cronus,

Uranus, and Rhea. There seems no reason, as I have tried to show, why hypnagogic imagery should not, like dreams and waking imagining, be studied in this way (McKellar 1957). Although, like dreams, works of literature and mythology have been widely studied, the content of another type of thought product, hallucination, still awaits intensive investigation.

Granted the occurrence of a dream or other act of imagination, there arises the question of why it is so and not otherwise. Study of related associations reveals that condensation is much involved. As Freud puts it, referring to dreams, they are 'brief, meagre and laconic in comparison with the range and wealth of dream thoughts' (1900: 279). The people and the incidents that form part of a dream may be examined in terms of such condensation. Sometimes in analysing a dream we are aware of how much we over-simplify when we attach a name to a person in that dream. He is, we come to realize, mostly the individual thus labelled but also possesses characteristics of other people. Something similar often happens in a TAT story or other waking imaginative production. Authors frequently reveal in print, or in interview, their awareness of condensation and the composite nature of their characters and incidents. Friends and acquaintances may ask a writer the question, 'Am I in your novel?' Doubtless the response such questioners receive is sometimes, 'Bits and pieces of you are, but as usual my characters are composite.' This diverse use of prior perception seems to be characteristic of human imagination.

On this issue I can contribute some testimony of my own. Having written – as perhaps all psychologists should – an as yet unpublished novel, I have some introspective evidence on this point. My associations about my central character, a young woman from the Scottish Highlands possessed of occult powers, reveal her composite origins characteristic of imagination. Of the twelve people she is based on, ten I have known and two come from history; one of the subsidiary characters derives from six people. Doubtless other 'models' contributed, but this is as far as I have been able to trace the perceptual origins. There is evidence that professional authors imagine in a similar way. Sherlock Holmes is largely based on the Edinburgh surgeon Bell and his powers of 'deduction', but certainly – as we have seen – his predecessor, Poe's Auguste Dupin, and his actions, added something. Dr Watson was doubtless Conan Doyle himself but, one suspects, other people as well. Consider again the distinction I have drawn between two types of hypnagogic imagery: repro- ductive and perseverative, as opposed to archetypal and im- personal. These differ in the amount of creative imagining involved, which may be seen in terms of number of sources in past perceptual experience. Those of Coleridge, tracked down by Lowes in his classic study of *The Ancient Mariner*, proved to have been remarkably numerous. The more imaginative, the more the sources.

ORIGINALITY IN DREAMLIFE

Many investigators make comment on the highly creative character- istics that dreams sometimes assume. Like impersonal hypnagogic images they seem to come from somewhere else and are not products of one's own mental life at all. A partial explanation may be found in this diversity of perceptual origins. In wakefulness perception is going on all the time; much perceiving, like much thought, is lost through forgetfulness. Yet in some way or other it is stored up, and can in dreams make its presence felt. Hervey de Saint Denys, in his wholehearted acceptance of the perceptual origin of dreams, has much to say about the processes involved. Memory of past events carries with it a background of informa- tion about the location in which the original sensory input occurred. This background 'remains in shadow'. It begins to appear 'in daydreaming and emerges clearly when we are com- pletely asleep' (Saint Denys 1867, edition 1982: 36). Saint Denys illustrates from one of his dreams in which he found himself present at a bullfight, the matador having been fatally wounded. In the dream, through association of ideas, he is transported to Normandy where he once saw an angry bull. The result in the dream is seeing a wounded matador now lying in the middle of a peaceful French country landscape. To develop his point Saint Denys uses an analogy: projection of lantern-slides. I take the example he uses. If we put in a second slide without removing the first, one of two things can happen. There is either 'an incongruous ensemble in which Bluebeard, let us say, faces Tom Thumb; or they are superimposed ... Bluebeard appears with

Figure 6.2   Selective perception and attention: Events are happening all the time. What we perceive as 'figure' stands out; though the 'ground' also present is ignored it may be somehow registered by us. It may re-emerge in dreams that are based on past perception. This diagram may be seen as four planks of wood. But when a figure–ground reversal occurs the four ends become diamond-shaped and three-dimensionality is lost. There are numerous other alternative perceptions possible: the octagon figure, for example, is camouflaged.

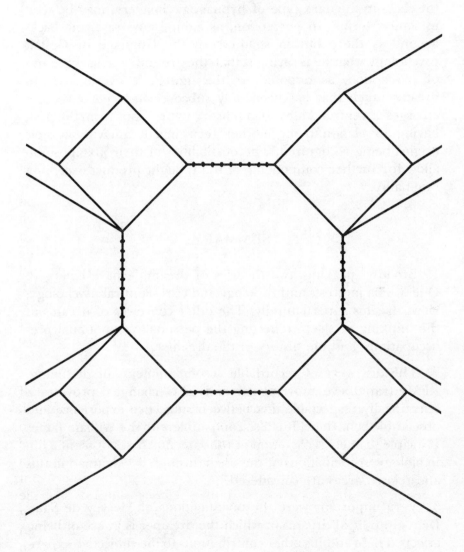

two different heads, four legs, and an arm emerging threateningly from his ear' (op. cit.: 37). It is thus that we may in dreams experience such oddities as a wounded matador lying unnoticed amid a family who are chatting peacefully having tea. Such juxtapositions occur often in dreams as well as – we may add – in surrealist paintings and hypnagogic imagery. The people unknown to us, and the strangers characteristic of the faces-in-the-dark type of hypnagogic imagery, may be seen in similar terms. In perception, as Saint Denys says, the background is there but in shadow. In the language of Gestalt psychology what he is saying is that 'the ground', the background of perception, as opposed to 'the figure', is overlooked. In dreams much that has been only subconsciously perceived re-emerges as central. Many such sensory impressions from the past, having no relation to one another, recur in a dream without their origins being recognized. The possibilities of their juxtaposition allow for further components of the thought product's seeming originality.

SUMMARY

1   Broadly speaking, two theories of dreamlife have emerged. One, which interests anthropology and cross-cultural psychology, views dreams supernaturally. The other conceives of dreams as the thinking of sleep, reflecting the personality, emotional pre-occupations, and life history of the dreamer.

2   The discovery of recordable accompaniments of dreaming, REMs (rapid eye movements) and EEG changes, provides a scientifically respectable link between subjective experience and observable behaviour. It is also compatible with the William James Principle, namely recognition of fundamental bases of mental life in biology. Anticipations of the breakthrough by Kleitman in this and related areas are considered.

3   Very important were the investigations of Hervey de Saint Denys into lucid dreams in which the dreamer is aware of being asleep. These and his other contributions to the subjective experiences of dreaming are examined.

4   Relations of the dream to the personality of the dreamer are considered with particular reference to Freud's work. The Freudian approach to dreamlife, with its emphasis on free association rather than on 'symbols', has been widely misunderstood. Uses of waking fantasies as an approach to the personality by Murray with the TAT present a parallel to the psychoanalytic use of dreams in personality studies.

5   If the Hobbes Principle of origins in sense experience is to be maintained, the apparent originality of dreams presents problems. These are considered in relation to creative thought products more generally, dream studies of Hervey de Saint Denys, and concepts from Gestalt psychology.

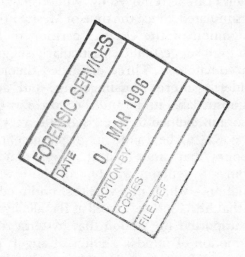

Chapter Seven

HYPNOTISM AND HYSTERIA

This disease is not more remarkable for its frequency, than for the numerous forms under which it appears, resembling most of the distempers wherewith mankind are afflicted.

Thomas Sydenham (1624–89)

Hysteria as a diagnostic category has had a long history, going back to Hippocrates and indeed earlier. In the later period the sensory, motor, and memory accompaniments of hysterical neurosis have been closely associated with hypnotism. Many phenomena are common to both. Typical signs and symptoms of hysteria can be removed by hypnotism, and can also be hypnotically simulated. Since the time of Mesmer there has been a growing recognition of the close association of the hysterical neuroses with high suggestibility, particularly suggestibility towards bodily symptomatology. Three discarded theories are of interest: 'the wandering uterus', 'malingering', and 'animal magnetism'. The diagnostic label itself, and the word's association with the female sex organ, helped to give rise to the very ancient theory that the cause was to be found in displacement of the uterus, and/or 'vapours' that came from it. The seventeenth-century physician Thomas Sydenham was one of those who demolished this explanation – which nevertheless continued to recur – by pointing out that he had male, as well as female, hysterical patients. Instead he supported the notion that hysteria results from 'some great commotion of mind ... either of anger, grief, terror or the like passions' (Hunter and MacAlpine 1963: 223). Today this concep-

134

tion of the neuroses – physical symptomatology resulting from emotional and psychological factors – remains broadly accepted.

If Sydenham and others had difficulties with the wandering uterus theory, later physicians found the malingering hypothesis hard to dislodge. The patients themselves didn't help, as they often gave extremely convincing evidence of apparent malingering. During the First World War psychiatrists who had to deal with so-called 'shell shock' in victims of trench warfare bore an additional burden in the charge that their patients were malingering. Fear emotion often expressed itself through such signs as paralysis, blindness, and deafness, seemingly a deliberate attempt to escape from the firing line.

William McDougall (1871–1938), as a psychologist who was also medically qualified, was one of those who dealt with such patients, using hypnotic therapy. As regards physical injury he points out that in a few cases postmortem examinations 'revealed numerous small haemorrhages in the brain tissue', but in the majority of cases of so-called 'shell shock' there was, in fact, 'no history of concussion' (McDougall 1926: 3). Mostly, he concluded, it was a matter of stress and fear. His hypnotic therapy included retrieval of memories, removal of paralysis or other signs and symptoms when hypnotized, and post-hypnotic suggestion. As illustration of war neurosis of the hysteria type consider one of his patients. McDougall's 'Case 6' was a soldier sent home from the Gallipoli front with paralysis, an anaesthesia in the legs. When hypnotized he could, however, move these limbs. During treatment McDougall mapped out the limits of the areas of anaesthesia. In a series of sessions he was able progressively to reduce the affected area and in this way he 'drew off the anaesthesia like a pair of stockings' (McDougall op. cit.: 245). As with other skills, individuals who have learned the technique vary in their skill as hypnotists. The important leader of the Nancy School – which entered into controversy with Charcot in Paris – Hippolyte Bernheim was scornful of those who found they were only able to hypnotize certain individuals. At Nancy they were able to hypnotize virtually anyone. McDougall's clear and interesting writing on this subject is suggestive of his own skills. Certainly his striking personality would have been an asset in the authoritarian kind of hypnotic induction he seems to have used. The late Professor Pear once told me about McDougall in action at a British Psychological

Society meeting, 'standing like a Roman senator' and – as Pear put it in synaesthetic language – speaking 'in a rich mahogony voice'. Perhaps, as in Bernheim's and McDougall's case, skill in hypnotism had something to do with readiness to make use of it in therapy, particularly with the hysterical neuroses. Also relevant is the hypnotizability of the individual concerned, and various scales for the measurement of this are now available. Related to this is suggestibility which, as the work of Eysenck and Furneaux (1945) has revealed, is of more than one kind. Other researches, like those of Barber and Wilson (1978), provide evidence that imagery and creative imagination also have some important relations to hypnotizability. Receptivity towards one's own mental life, and a somewhat adventurous attitude towards altered states of consciousness, seem to be favourable to hypnotizability. Nevertheless we find that individuals diagnosed as exhibiting hysterical neurosis also tend to be highly hypnotizable.

THE HYSTERIA NEUROSES

Phenomena that can be experimentally induced by hypnotism characterize the hysterias. These sensory, motor, and memory happenings of hysteria are spontaneous and thus different, however close their resemblance to hypnotic phenomena. A distinction may be made between two sub-categories of 'hysteria' which may represent opposing ends of a continuum. In an earlier chapter we have considered dissociation of the personality, fugues, somnambulisms, automatic writing, crystal-gazing, and multiple personality. These are sometimes classified as 'dissociative hysterical reactions'. To illustrate from recent work, Eugene Bliss (1980; 1986) finds in automatisms, multiple personality, and hypnosis a triad whose elements have much in common. Multiple personality cases, he argues, 'qualify for the diagnosis of hysteria'. Such individuals develop early in their lives 'the capacity to go into a deep trance'. This is a defensive reaction to stress and often, as a child, to cruelty at the hands of adults. Thus they 'resort to this hypnotic tactic as children when confronted with danger'. For Bliss such automatisms are a defensive self-hypnotic reaction, resembling hypnosis in its more usual forms but occurring spontaneously. The multiple personality type of automatism Bliss views as 'a primitive tactic and when carried into adulthood seems to be simple-minded and infantile' (Bliss 1980: 1395). Its cultural context seems often to be associated with religion of the hell-fire type and other primitive forms.

While there are similarities there are also important differences between these dissociative neuroses and another sub-type, namely 'conversion hysteria'. Dissociation of the personality may also be involved, though psychoanalysis would look to other mechanisms: conversion of anxiety into some physical sign or symptom. It is in this area that we often encounter scepticism if not downright hostility to the 'hysterical' patient. The signs and symptoms he – or she – produces tax sympathy and credibility. In some very transparent way this type of hysteric seems to gain from the symptomatology and in ways that seem to be designed to deceive other people. To illustrate, on two occasions I observed a student who developed paralysis of her writing-hand during finals exam-inations: she recovered in between but during the next exam her hand again became paralysed. The behaviour that takes place is likely to attract, even to demand, attention. Conversion hysteria is histrionic, and with some justification has been called 'the great imitator'. In their performances such individuals often simulate physical illnesses with a known organic basis. Hypnotism can be used to unmask such imitations. In hypnosis hysterical blindness and deafness disappear, and paralysis and anaesthesias depart. It is diagnostically relevant that in hysterical as opposed to epileptic fits and convulsions the individual, if he or she falls, does so in such a way as to avoid being hurt. The phenomena encountered give other indications of being 'not real': for example, areas of anaesthesia or paralysis follow popular ideas about anatomy and physiology and not underlying biological realities. They are also variable. Pierre Janet uses an analogy: the affected areas of the body are like those variably exposed to the cold by a person trying to sleep with too short or too narrow a blanket. To illustrate, once in dealing with a patient thus diagnosed I tried to induce him to do a pencil and paper test: his immediate response was paralysis of the wrist. I abandoned the first task for one involving walking along a chalked line. Then followed paralysis of the legs. Not for nothing are bystanders often much more sympathetic to other types of neurosis – depression, anxiety states, and phobias – than to hysteria.

To the tough-minded it is 'obvious' that such people are 'not really ill'. In military life, under conditions of war, they are likely to have a very hard time indeed. The scholarly study by Ilse Veith, *Hysteria: the History of a Disease* (1965), deals mainly with conversion hysteria. She finds a close association of this with being the underdog – often by being a woman – throughout history. Variants of attention-attracting by fainting or 'fits of hysterics' are also considered by her. One aspect of hysterical reactions that should not be overlooked is the way in which there may be a hysterical overlay to a clear-cut physical condition. Thus in the area of actual head-injuries Brosin (1959) points out that a patient of this kind may have 'little or no hesitancy in utilising the injury as a reason for obtaining secondary gains'. This may incude not merely sympathy and attention but also monetary gain from compensation payments. Despite such possibilities Brosin stresses that a neurosis of the hysteria kind that is triggered off by an accident is nevertheless 'a real clinical condition'. It also needs treatment. Here we encounter a manifestation of the Economy Principle: making use of sense data and the realities and building on this framework. Consider, for example, deafness with a clear-cut basis of injury to the inner ear. Others may react with impatience towards an organically deaf person, claiming that he is 'using' his deafness by selectively not hearing. This may well be the case. There is a definite physical pathology, but along with it are psychological factors that have affinities with both hysteria and malingering.

Since hysteria of the conversion type taxes sympathy and credibility I will attempt a bridge towards greater empathy. The illustration taken is a more prosaic one than the First World War soldier who becomes paralysed before 'going over the top' in battle. In a lesser way mechanisms of hysteria are nevertheless involved. It concerned a schoolboy, now an adult without any noticeable psychiatric abnormality. He told me of his time at school when aged about 10 or 11. This concerned his experiences in being taught mental arithmetic. Teaching involved a blackboard, a teacher with the attributes of impatience and a bad temper, and a long rod of wood. The boys would be made to stand in front of the blackboard on which numbers were written in a circle. With his rod the teacher would point rapidly from one number to the next, demanding they be added by mental arithmetic. If responses were too slow the rod would be used on the hands of the pupils, often with force. As a result of this barbarism the mornings of certain school days became occasions for anticipatory terror. The emotion was bottled up: the boy did not tell his parents. As with other kinds of bullying, anxiety about retribution for reporting on a bully was an additional source of fear. Sometimes the boy in question, now a man, told me he would bang his head on the pillow on 'mental arithmetic days' to induce a headache. This physical symptom would enable him to avoid having to go to school. Sometimes a headache would occur without the head-banging. And sometimes the boy would lie to his parents, pleading illness. No kind of general 'school phobia' was involved: it was not a general avoidance of the school, but was specific in its aim to avoid mental arithmetic teaching sessions. Here we have a typically physical symptom – headache in this case – and avoidance of an emotionally distressing situation. As we have seen, the emotion would sometimes convert itself, without assistance, into a physical symptom. We also encounter the uncertainties about whether malingering is or is not involved. Sometimes deceit and lying played a part. Variability of symptoms also occurred, as when the 'I feel too ill for school today' involved a variety of other imagined, alleged, or actually experienced illnesses. It may be added that the mental arithmetic teacher also taught music. In this case his methods were less brutal, but also demoralizing. The would-be learners were divided into the categories of those who 'could sing' and the 'growlers' who couldn't, who would sit for the duration of the class doing nothing. There was no quasi-hysterical attempt by my informant to avoid such classes which, though boring, involved no fear or physical pain. But the man concerned informed me, 'I'm not much good at music either.'

THE BODY–MIND: ADLER, GRODDECK, AND DUBOIS

It was out of the study of hysteria that psychoanalysis developed. Primacy is important in the early case histories encountered by major theorists. The study by Freud's associate, Joseph Breuer, of 'Anna O' heralded the movement, and Breuer and Freud's *Studies on Hysteria* (1893–5) remains an influential, important classic.

Breuer used hypnotism in his treatment of Anna. Freud had studied hypnotism both with Charcot in Paris, and with Bernheim at Nancy. Like Breuer he initially used it to excavate repressed memories. Repression of whole incidents characterized the hysterical patients discussed in the Breuer–Freud book. Freud rejected hypnotism as a way of uncovering repressed memories, in favour of the free association method. As a psychoanalyst once put it to me, there developed a preference for dealing with patients in their normal rather than altered mental state. For Freud and his colleagues in the case of hysteria, the prevailing mental mechanisms were repression, and along with it denial: failure to perceive and accept painful information.

Initially psychoanalysis viewed the unconscious as the storehouse of repressed, emotionally charged memories. Later developed the notion that there were aspects of the unconscious that had never been conscious: the concept of the id was added. In this Freud was influenced by another man, and he acknowledged his debt to George Groddeck. This highly original pioneer of psychosomatic medicine has often been neglected. Groddeck argued that Freud began his work in an area midway between physical and mental illness: the study of hysteria. He could have moved either way, towards the physical or the psychological. Groddeck himself explored the neglected alternative direction in, for example, works like *The Book of the It* (1923). Groddeck's central concept, 'the It', differs in certain respects from the Freudian 'Id' which it helped to inspire. Groddeck's It is a vital principle which comes into existence at the moment of conception, and from then on living is determined by this 'unknown self'. It may express itself in physical or psychological ways, or in both. The concept is Groddeck's way of reminding his medical colleagues that people are neither disembodied minds nor mindless automata. Thus, as a physician, he saw no reason to avoid treating both aspects at the same time. Groddeck's use of this central idea is highly original, and at times even alarmingly so. He argues, for example, that the It may utilize the bacteria normally present in the body to create a fever, and in this way discharge accumulated emotional tension. In the treatment of infant feeding problems he claimed that it was always necessary to find out what was wrong with the mother, who would be giving involuntary signals to the baby of hostility or some other aversive emotion. These would express themselves by the It of the suckling parent. Respiratory conditions and skin complaints were dealt with by Groddeck in a similar way. Somebody once said of Alfred Adler that if he were called in to a case of ptomaine poisoning he would probably suspect the patient of embezzlement, or marital infidelity. This seems to be something of a caricature of Adler: the remark applies much more appropriately to Groddeck.

Adler, like Groddeck, explored areas between physical and mental illnesses and thus was also a pioneer of psychosomatic medicine. There is a difference. Often what Adler wrote is passed over as mere common sense: today we take it for granted. Thus Adler saw no argument against using psychotherapy and physical treatment in combination. Likewise, in dealing with disturbed children and parents he would interview them together. The pragmatic sweet reasonableness of Alfred Adler often leads us to under-estimate his contribution. If such things still need to be said, the need was even greater at Adler's time and among patients with whom he worked. Although the concept of 'the unconscious' mattered little to Adler, it is appropriate that Ellenberger's (1970) monumental history in this area of psychology has underlined the importance of his – at the time – very original contributions. Human beings are often preoccupied with their body image; in the case of the hypochondriac, unreasonably so. About it they may develop feelings of inferiority which certain types of advertising often shamelessly exploit: adolescents have spots on their faces, a man is of short stature, a girl's bust is felt by her to be too large or too small. Even the possession of freckles may needlessly worry their owner. Others may be surprised at what individuals may use as a focus for illusions of 'organ inferiority'. Bodily signs and symptoms play, we have seen, an important part in the hysterical neuroses. Adler was sensitive to their place in mental life more generally. Groddeck, a younger man for whose original ideas Freud himself had obvious respect, was different. There is little of Adlerian common sense about him. Overstatement and imaginative speculation characterized his work. His ideas were in advance of psychoanalysis which, by comparison, appears almost pedestrian in its orthodoxy. Like Adler he had his contribution in this area of the continuum that extends from clear-cut organic illness, through hysteria, into conditions with no known physical pathology.

In the year before there appeared the English translation of Breuer and Freud's *Studies on Hysteria* came another contribution, this time from Berne, Switzerland. Paul Dubois was Professor of Neurology in the Swiss capital, and he provided, as Goshen (1967: 870) puts it, 'a sorely needed contribution to the subject of psychoneurosis'. An often forgotten pioneer of psychotherapy, Dubois was also interested in classification, and he tackled in a spirit of robust common sense the body–mind unity of the personality. On the one hand he stressed that the 'scientific ground' should not be abandoned, and that it was essential 'to study man with all the precision of modern biology'. And in doing so he pointed out how certain conditions – he instanced tetanus – should be struck from any list of 'neuroses', being due to 'a pathogenic micro-organism acting directly upon the nerves' (Dubois 1904, quoted in Goshen 1967: 872). But on the other hand he opposed rituals as unsatisfactory alibis for appropriate treatment, regularly engaged in by physicians who remained blind to the influence of emotional factors on illness. In vigorous language he attacked 'stupid materialism' in medical treatments and argued that 'there ought to be more place given in medical studies to psychology and philosophy.' It was now, he argued, 'absolutely necessary' to extend the breadth of courses of instruction in psychiatry 'to allow students to enter the insane asylums'. While physical methods of treatment – but not therapeutic rituals – had their place there were other things often more appropriate. Thus, in general medicine, sometimes 'a heart to heart talk with these patients would be worth considerably more than the baths, the douches, or the choral' (Dubois 1904: 881). While recognizing relevant pathologies and surgery when appropriate, he spoke out strongly in support of recognizing psychological factors and for 'treatment by psychotherapy' (op. cit.: 882). Today, of course, schools of medicine in universities accept this standpoint, and we may also note similar recognition of the place of psychology by schools of dentistry (McKellar 1971). Though we accept the fruits of their work today, it was more than necessary for reformers to say such things. Their writings were timely, as were their efforts to implement them in the actions of individuals and institutions.

At a very early date we encounter thoughtful recognition of the psychosomatic standpoint that is now accepted widely in modern methods of treatment. This preceded even the biologically orientated Aristotle. David Kalupahana (1987) was led to write his own book because of what he assesses as frequent misconceptions about the traditions of Buddhist psychology. He finds close affinities between the psychology of William James and that of Gautama himself in, for example, the concept of 'the psychophysical personality'. Thus for the Buddha 'mind' is 'contact with concepts' (in Pali *adhivacana-samphassa*), matter being 'contact with resistance'. With this neutral notion of 'contact' there was an early avoidance of the rigid body–mind dichotomy that has much troubled later thought. It also makes sense in terms of a notion that has influenced modern psychology, in Kelly's view of the influence of 'constructs' we choose in coping with the basic issues of experience and behaviour (Kelly 1955; 1958).

With renewal of interest in imagery has come concern with its place in therapy (e.g. Horowitz 1934, revised 1983; Ahsen 1965; 1968). Its applications vary. This includes its use in the treatment of physical as opposed to psychiatric illnesses (e.g. Sheikh, ed. 1984). Techniques of 'relaxation' that sometimes shade into full hypnotic induction have important applications to many physical conditions. Such a recognition does not commit us to abandoning hard-earned achievements from the side of biology and replacement of bacteria, viruses, or genes for vague and undefined 'psychological factors'. It does mean that something can often be contributed by suggestion, relaxation, hypnotism, or even at least more humane and careful choice of words. Thus in the 1940s there was a movement in obstetrics which placed emphasis on how words can be used to induce relaxation rather than anxiety during childbirth. One of its leaders, Read (1948), was sensitive to the use of words to convey information about 'contractions' rather than 'pains' and about what was likely to happen next. Within the realm of general medicine and surgery it is difficult to exaggerate the intensity of anxiety, apprehension, and fear patients experience either during examination or when awaiting the results of a laboratory test.

Things said or not said by the professional concerned, and often unwitting non-verbal signals, can increase or reduce avoidable emotional distress. The point I am making is obvious, but I will make it. With medical students it is often best communicated with reference to dentists for whom they too are 'patients'. Dentists sometimes use hypnotic induction, but even when they don't they can easily increase or reduce fear and anxiety. Dentists in the presence of their patients try to avoid words like 'digging into', 'grinding', or 'gouging out' and likewise avoid saying to their nurse things like 'hand me the excavator'. Other words are available to suggest, in a matter-of-fact way, cleaning, polishing, and tidying up the mouth and its teeth (McKellar 1971). Words similarly have a part in hypnotic induction. Very noticeable is the fact that those chosen are usually expressed in the language of sleep and relaxation.

HYPNOTISM: HISTORICAL ORIENTATION

Hypnotism's long pre-history preceded Mesmer and his 'animal magnetism'. Franz Anton Mesmer (1734–1815) was one of those who sought to apply concepts of physical science – in his case wrongly – to psychology. His methods of treatment of organic and mental conditions received infiuential support when he moved from Vienna to Paris, from among others Louis XVI and Marie Antoinette. Many of his patients were to perish in the French Revolution. His influential disciple, the Marquis de Puységur, who became interested in hypnotically induced somnambulisms, was for a time imprisoned but survived the Reign of Terror. Then followed the conflicts between the rivals of two different traditions, the 'magnetizers' on the one hand, and 'exorcists' on the other. The place of suggestibility rather than either magnetism or possessing spirits was next recognized. James Braid's words 'hypnotism' and 'hypnotic' came into use. Braid defined 'neurohypnology' in terms of his concept of 'nervous sleep': 'A peculiar condition of the nervous system, induced by a fixed and abstracted attention of the mental and visual eye, on one object not of an exciting nature' (Braid 1843, in Goshen 1967: 831). In France there developed the opposing schools of Bernheim at Nancy and Charcot in Paris. Sigmund Freud studied at both, and Pierre Janet was to succeed Charcot. Earlier we noted the longstanding use and association of hypnotism with the relief of pain in operations. John Elliotson (1791–1868), who held a professorship in London, made much use of it and was sufficiently influential to take a stand against hostility. Opposition took the usual form that we continue to encounter today with major medical advances: it was argued that to control pain in such a way was 'unnatural'. There was also the use of hypnotic anaesthesia by James Esdaile, who worked in Calcutta. In his case it was claimed that his Indian patients actually enjoyed the pain of amputations and other major operations, deceived Esdaile, and simulated anaesthesia to please him (Bliss 1986). In considering this period Eugene Bliss points out that nevertheless 'a parallel between "artificial hysteria" (hypnosis), and hysteria was recognised.' But he mentions another case in which a surgeon called Ward had amputated a leg under hypnosis. In this instance critics claimed 'that the patient had been trained not to experience pain, and contended he was an imposter' (Bliss, op. cit.: 28). There are different kinds of 'ignorance', including simply not knowing, but in resistance to advances that have helped to alleviate pain and suffering we repeatedly encounter what might well be termed 'vicious ignorance'. Hypnotic techniques became less relevant with the development of general anaesthetics. This was at times also opposed by some, again on the grounds that 'it was unnatural'.

Bernard Hart (1939) suggests a summary of the history of advance in psychological medicine. First, was the realization – associated with Hippocrates in Ancient Greece – that psychiatric syndromes should be approached and treated by the methods of orthodox medicine. The second – associated with Anton Mesmer and his predecessors – was realization of the limitations of such an approach. Dr Hart may have over-simplified scientific history, but in doing so he gives appropriate recognition – often not accorded – to Mesmer's contribution, which was closely orientated to parallels between hysterical neurosis and hypnotism.

PHENOMENA AND MECHANISMS OF HYPNOSIS

Some readers will themselves have introspected while being hypnotized. Others may have proved resistant to hypnotic induction. Some may be firmly determined that nothing of the sort will ever be allowed to happen to them. Three things may be said at the outset. First, anybody – or at least most people – can be hypnotized, and/or learn to hypnotize. Individuals differ in hypnotizability, and hypnotists differ in how skilled they are in the techniques. Second, though light hypnosis – closely akin to relaxation – can readily be induced, some of the more spectacular hypnotic phenomena require optimal conditions. Some involve subjects who have been trained hypnotically, i.e. have been hypnotized on a number of earlier occasions. There are safeguards against becoming, through such experience, too readily hypnotizable. One is by giving a post-hypnotic suggestion that the subject will not allow himself/herself to be hypnotized again without signing a paper giving such consent. This is a safeguard responsible hypnotists can use. Third, many of the alleged dangers of hypnotism are myths. Obviously it is sensible for volunteers in any hypnotic experiment or demonstration to work only with a responsible hypnotist. On occasion there are abuses, as when some stage hypnotist – such happenings are rare – allows subjects to make fools of themselves in front of an audience. The notion – a derivative of the plot of the novel *Trilby* – of 'loss of mind' or soul to some sinister Svengali figure, is also largely misguided. The *Trilby* story is discussed in Chapter 16. There is now good evidence that its author, George du Maurier, was much better informed about hypnotism than often supposed. There is also the fear, having been put into a hypnotic state, of 'not being able to come out of it'. In connection with some recent experiments, my colleagues and I sought, for ethical reasons, information on this point from several experts. We were reassured by what we learned from others, and this reassurance confirmed our own personal acquaintance with the hypnotic state.

Traditionally hypnotism has tended to be considered in books about 'abnormal' psychology, though nowadays there are many exceptions. Some of the best discussions in earlier writings on hypnotic phenomena and experiments are those of William James (1890) and William McDougall (1926). Among books may be noted those reporting important research on ways of overcoming pain, for example the Hilgard experiments (Hilgard and Hilgard 1975; Hilgard 1977). Relations of hypnotic states to relaxation, and continuity between hypnotic behaviour and phenomena of normal mental life, have received much attention from T.X. Barber and his colleagues (Barber 1970; 1984; Barber and Wilson 1978). In his own carefully controlled experiments Martin Orne has been led to develop the concept of 'trance logic' to take account of the paradoxical thinking that hypnotized people often reveal (Orne 1959). In negative hallucinations – being hypnotically induced not to perceive some object actually present – there is a paradox in that one aspect of the subject appears able to see in order to permit another aspect to discriminate what not to see. Hilgard's 'hidden observer' experiments (1977) and modified dissociation theory suggest a way in which such paradoxes can be explained by two different perceiving systems.

Consider the process of being hypnotized and the subjective experience of the hypnotized person. Suggestions are given that he is becoming drowsy, and having difficulty in keeping his eyes open. He is permitted to close them, and told he is sinking into a state of comfortable deep sleep. As drowsiness overtakes him he listens to the hypnotist, who by counting sinks him more deeply into a sleeplike state. When he is asked to place his hand on a surface he finds himself responding to the suggestion that he is unable to raise it. He feels he could, but it is not worth the effort. Similar experiences accompany inability to unclasp the hands, or lower his outstretched arm. Arm levitation may occur: under suggestion he finds his outstretched arm rising as though attached to a helium balloon. At some stage he is told he may open his eyes, but will remain hypnotized. If sufficiently 'deep' in hypnosis he may be required to stand up and move about the room. The suggestion is often given that somebody actually present has left the room. He is encouraged to move into this 'empty' space, and finds himself experiencing the paradox of somehow both seeing and not seeing this 'absent' person. Subjectively he responds to this, but manages as far as possible to avoid this area of the room. A dream under the influence of hypnotic suggestion may follow, and appropriate imagery wells up inside him. In deeper hypnosis he may experience positive hallucination. A torch shown to him seems to glow, or objects which he somehow realizes remain stationary, seem to 'move'. Plasticity of the limbs may occur, and he leaves his arm without effort in the strange positions in which it is placed by the hypnotist. Throughout he finds himself with a kind of mental tunnel-vision focused on the words and commands of the hypnotist. Through this rapport he finds himself disregarding things such as the doings of other people. He may be given a post-hypnotic suggestion that, after 'waking up', he will – on some agreed signal from the hypnotist – respond to this. He hears the instruction not to remember this suggestion but that he will be able to remember everything else that has occurred. Finally

147

he listens to the hypnotist, who tells him that following a count to ten he will be fully awake. When he hears this number he finds himself blinkingly aware of being his usual self, having emerged from the altered hypnotic state.

Some or all of these happenings are likely to occur. To illustrate post-hypnotic suggestion; in one experiment with a colleague in my office at the university I gave him the suggestion that, on waking, he would open the cupboard and look in it for a packet of cigarettes. Having found it he would light up one of these. The actions were performed faithfully following the signal I gave. This is not at all the sort of thing people usually do in someone else's office, with furniture and property that do not belong to them. In another experiment I witnessed – the colleague I have previously hypnotized was on this occasion hypnotist – a subject was given the post-hypnotic suggestion to use a typewriter. He was also told that the 'a' key would be absent from the keyboard. The results were interesting. The subject typed away quite rapidly. He did his best. Mostly he responded to the 'absent' key by sub-stituting the letter 'S'. Post-hypnotic suggestions resemble the phenomena labelled 'determining tendencies' that were much studied in the early experiments of the Würzburg psychologists. Flugel (1945) suggests a small experiment that may assist in uncovering the continuity between the two: the experiment may be of some practical use. If having difficulty getting up out of bed in the morning, set yourself the task of counting after pre-deciding that when the number twelve is reached you will be in the act of getting up. On a suitably cold morning begin to count, as slowly as you like. But when the magic twelve is reached, as Flugel puts it, 'we have risen automatically and without further exercise of will.' The task is accomplished 'without strain or effort – almost it might seem, without our own complicity' (Flugel op. cit.: 28) The pre-arranged signal to respond is given by oneself and not a hypnotist, but the subjective accompaniment of 'it's easier to do it than not' of the determining tendency is like post-hypnotic suggestion. In hypnotic experiments it is important that the subject be allowed to perform any post-hypnotic sugges-tion and not prevented. The alternative is intense anxiety very like that of the compulsive neurotic when he is restrained from his rituals. This is illustrated in one of McDougall's experiments when the post-hypnotic suggestion was that the subject be the last person to leave the room. When play-acting attempts were made to push him ahead through the door he struggled until the experimenters allowed him to carry out the post-hypnotic suggestion (McDougall 1926). If challenged, subjects tend to rationalize their reasons for such actions.

THE LIMITS OF HYPNOTIC INFLUENCE

Because of some of the remarkable happenings reported, questions arise about the limits of hypnotism. Is it, for example, possible to induce a law-abiding person to perform a criminal act? A great deal of evidence is available on this and related issues. This is difficult to evaluate and it is always possible for a critic to challenge the controls of another hypnotist's experiments. Careful researches by investigators like Martin Orne are tidying up some of the issues: Orne makes considerable use of comparing the behaviour of actually hypnotized subjects with that of other subjects who are instructed to act as though hypnotized. In this difficult and intellectually exciting field it is my own opinion that the alleged limitations of hypnotic influence have been overstated. To this area the Square of Opposition, discussed in Chapter 2, is again relevant. To combat an E-proposition that such and such an effect cannot be achieved, what is needed is merely one good experiment defining an I-proposition that in one such instance it can. If others fail to replicate, supporters of the I-proposition can always question the other investigator's hypnotic skills. A failure is only a failure and does not refute a well-established success. There may or may not be a ladybird beetle in this room in which I am working: my denial 'there isn't,' may merely mean I haven't looked properly.

As mentioned earlier, certain of the more striking hypnotic effects involve optimal conditions, a trained subject, and a skilled hypnotist. It is in the area of attempts to produce hypnotic crime that many of the experimental studies have been conducted. Among such experiments have been some which have involved a hypnotic suggestion to steal a sum of money from the experimenter and spend it. Some investigators have claimed success – advanced an I-proposition – in producing this. Their critics have responded by saying that as subjects they would have had no moral objection to 'stealing' from the experimenter a small sum of money, especially if he had somehow signalled to them this was what he wanted them to do! There are, however, limits to what even the most dedicated scientist is prepared to have happen to him. I find convincing an experiment by Rowland (1939) which took the form of inducing the hypnotized subject to throw acid in the experimenter's face. (I hasten to add that there was, in fact, glass between the two but this fact was not known to the subject. Critics can always claim, 'But yes, it was.') As regards self-destructive behaviour, in another experiment Rowland induced the subject to make persistent efforts to reach out for a very lively rattlesnake. Again I stress the presence of glass. In this area of what can and cannot be achieved hypnotically, much has been made of an alleged incident. On one occasion it is reported that the hypnotist departed from the room leaving the hypnotized subject, a young woman, with a class of students. They asked her to remove her clothes. The report claims that she refused, and woke from hypnosis in a state of indignation. Yet, as Eysenck (1983) has pointed out with justification – if this incident ever in fact took place, there are many circumstances in which undressing would be appropriate to a virtuous young woman. Eysenck mentions 'suggestion to the effect that she was in her room all by herself, that it was late, that she was ready to go to bed' (op. cit.: 30).

Similar additional suggestions could apply in acts of violence. The subject might be told it was his duty to protect some innocent person from a homicidal intruder, or fight with an enemy on the battle-field. We have seen in many situations that people respond to their surroundings as they perceive and believe them to be. It is certainly possible to inject imagery into a situation that is misleading as to the realities. Here the powers of hypnotism, as of suggestion, are strong. As we have seen there are, outside the laboratory, many situations like those involving the processes of suggestion in an angry crowd that produce violent, brutal, and sadistic actions in seemingly normal individuals. Under the influence of suggestion – as of hate or moralized anger – anti-social acts of violence may be carried out by most unlikely people.

Can a person be hypnotized against his or her will? My own experience leads me to another I-proposition. I have seen it happen in ways that convinced at least me. Can a person be hypnotized when he doesn't know he is being hypnotized? Again the answer is 'yes'; indeed it has been done quite often. And what about a person being hypnotized when the hypnotist himself doesn't realize this is happening? I leave aside reports I have had on two occasions of somebody walking in from the next room to a hypnotic session, having been hypnotized through the thin wall. By accident I once achieved this effect myself on a colleague who was standing behind me when I was engaged in hypnotizing someone else. Among demonstrations I have seen I would mention another instance involving hypnotic influences on the systems of the body, heartbeat, and respiration. A psychologist colleague was the hypnotist. He gave the suggestion to the subject that he would see a rabbit and would chase it a long way across a field. The room was a small one. Afterwards the pulse and breathing of the subject suggested not the two or three strides, confined by the room's size, but evidence of having run a much greater distance. On another occasion the same colleague suggested to his hypnotized subject that the drink he was being given was strong alcohol: his intoxicated performance was very convincing. These events I found interesting as I had myself filled the glass with water from a nearby tap. Such incidents, and others which readers may have observed themselves if they have witnessed hypnotic demonstrations, give evidence of the power of hypnotism to bring considerable illusion into the environment of the hypnotized person. In most demonstrations anaesthesia of the skin is introduced. One hand is made anaesthetic, while the other remains sensitive. Out of sight of the subject the anaesthetic hand is pricked with a pin without the usual withdrawal response and the subject reports feeling nothing. This demonstration replicates the 'glove anaesthesia' phenomenon found in some cases of conversion hysteria. A variant is to give the suggestion that some, but not other, parts of the hand will be insensitive to pain. The subject is asked to say 'yes' when he or she feels it and 'no' when he doesn't. Then the hand of the blindfolded subject is pricked in various places. Of interest is the fact that sometimes when insensitive areas are pricked the response is 'no'.

THEORETICAL INTERPRETATIONS OF HYPNOSIS

Different theorists give emphasis to one or other of the main components of the state of hypnosis. These are: increased suggestibility, rapport with the hypnotist, role-playing, and being in an
altered mental state. There is very little controversy about the first
two of these components. Clearly we are dealing with an area in
which qualities of the suggestibility kind play a leading part, and
in this the relationship to the hypnotist and the suggestions he
communicates are of major importance. Earlier theorists often
interpreted hypnosis in terms of dissociation of the personality,
particularly of its perceptual aspects, into different functioning systems. Among major contemporary psychologists Ernest
Hilgard (1973a; 1973b; 1977) has given substantial support to a
'neodissociation' standpoint. In this he gives emphasis to being
in an altered mental state. Opposed to this in many respects is
T.X. Barber, who sought to show that many alleged hypnotic
phenomena can also be produced without hypnotism. Some
theorists have stressed the importance of role-playing, while
admitting that this behaviour does take place in a state different
from normal consciousness.

One explanation is that the hypnotized subject is concerned to
act as a hypnotized person, and does so in accord with the
guidance of the hypnotist as to how a hypnotized person is
required to behave. The psychologist T.R. Sarbin stresses that the
way the hypnotic subject interprets the cues from the hypnotist is
of major importance. To this I would myself add that the
hypnotist may unwittingly insert signals to the subject, as to what
he expects of him. In this way he can do much to influence the
kinds of response that do, or do not, occur. When this happens it
resembles the 'therapeutic compliance' of a patient during treatment. In therapy as in hypnotism good rapport is involved, thus
for example it is not surprising if a patient during a Jungian
analysis produces evidence of archetypes in his dreams. This is
the way his analyst conceptualizes the problems and there are
powerful, unspoken incentives to behave accordingly. In the case
of hypnosis many suggestions are given in the language of sleep,
or progress towards it. It is sleep plus 'attend to my voice and the
suggestions I give.' Thus so far as the role-playing component is
involved, the subject acts like a sleepy or sleeping person, but one

alert to the hypnotic rapport. Such identification with sleep is only partial: physiologically we know the hypnotized person is awake, not asleep.

Of interest are the comments of the leader of the Nancy School, Bernheim, in comparing spontaneous and hypnotic sleep: 'the spontaneous sleeper is in relationship with himself alone' (Bernheim 1900: 862). By contrast, in induced, hypnotic sleep 'the subject's mind retains the memory of the person who has put him to sleep, whence the hypnotist's power of playing on his imagination' (op. cit.: 863).

Many were to interpret the hypnotic state in dissociation terms, and in doing so placed emphasis on the altered state of consciousness component. In this case, with a hypnotist who takes this view, there are likely to be signals to the subject to act as an automatism of the somnambulistic or multiple personality kind. These unwitting cues are received and interpreted by the subject who does his best to act in such ways. One of those who adopted this view of hypnotism was Morton Prince, who wrote 'sleep, trance, epileptoid states, hypnosis, etc., are forms of dissociation' (Prince 1905, edition 1978: 193). He adopts the view that 'a normal personal consciousness may be disintegrated in all sorts of ways,' thus 'any group of memories, and even functions and faculties' may be lost, and all sorts of combinations of them may be formed (op. cit.: 475).

If we give due weight to suggestions made under strong rapport, and for the subject to respond to cues given, some of the mysteries of hypnosis disappear. Different hypnotists, like different therapists, vary in their interpretation of the phenomena they are dealing with. Subjects are highly receptive to not merely the words of the suggestions given but also to what is meant by them in terms of the hypnotist's expectancies. It is inevitable that some of the signals given will be involuntary and unintentional. If the expectation thus signalled proves too 'difficult' to handle, the subject can escape in one of two ways, either of which can happen: he can 'wake' from hypnosis, or fall asleep. As regards hypnotic experience and behaviour we have noted that Barber argues that they are very similar to those of normal, unhypnotized mental life. His theory is not exempt from the interpretation I have suggested. Clearly holding such a standpoint, he is unlikely to give signals – wittingly or unwittingly – to the subject to behave like a dissociated automatism. On the contrary, the suggestions given, and the accompanying messages they convey, are to act in ways resembling normal states of consciousness. Any subject has a lifetime of experience to draw on in doing this. The cues are received, and acted on accordingly. And so further evidence of the 'normality' of hypnosis continues to accumulate. Other ways of conceptualizing what happens during a hypnotic induction may seem less convincing: return to infancy or pre-natal times. Despite this they can be accommodated. Consider such 'hypnotic regressions'. These may be to earlier stages of development or, as some investigators believe, previous states of incarnation. The role-playing of subjects expected to behave in such ways is not beyond the powers of suggestible human beings whose hypnotic behaviour is 'shaped' by expectations during hypnotic rapport.

HYPNOTISM AND EXPERIMENTAL PSYCHOPATHOLOGY

From the standpoint of research, leaving aside therapy uses, hypnotism is a powerful experimental technique. In conversion hysteria and dissociative reactions it permits many of the phenomena to be simulated. From such simulations we may learn more about mechanisms and principles. There are the various kinds of amnesia. The somnambulisms of dissociative conditions, and Hilgard's 'hidden observer' experiments, relate to occurrences that have strong resemblances to co-consciousness. In typical hypnotic inductions the apparent inability of the subject to resist the suggestions given provide an experimental analogue of aboulia – incapacity to perform willed actions – that we find in the hysterias and in many neurotic conditions. The category of conversion neurosis overlaps with some, but not all, of the 'war neuroses'. With hypnotism it is possible to produce anaesthesias, paralysis, deafness, and a variety of visual effects such as tunnel vision, colour blindness, and blindness itself. Negative hallucinations are perhaps a special case of these. Many phenomena of hypochondriasis can readily be induced through hypnotic suggestions, and other body image phenomena encountered in the psychoses, like delusions of bodily change, can be temporarily established. The phenomena of trance logic may help understanding of oddities of psychotic thinking to be considered in a later chapter. Experimentally it is difficult to produce auditory as opposed to visual hallucinations by other means, but not difficult hypnotically. The waxy plasticity that is to be found in the catalepsy encountered in catatonic schizophrenia can also be simulated with a good hypnotic subject.

A distinction has often been made between two major categories of neuroses, 'hysteria' being one of them. Eysenck (1947) early distinguished hysteria or extraverted neuroses, from dysthymia or neurotic introversion. Among the dysthymic neuroses we find neurotic depression, anxiety states, and the sub-group of the various anankastic reactions. In his work Morton Prince did not confine himself to neuroses of the dissociative, hysteria type. His famous 'bell-tower case' is a good illustration of the dysthymic and self-frustration type of syndrome, in this case a phobia (Prince 1929). The patient exhibited strong phobic reactions, accompanied by acute grief and despair at the sight of any bell-tower. If she saw such a tower it would arouse intense emotion to the extent of terror. Even hearing the words for such a building would awaken inner stored emotion. Consciously she was unable to explain the source of the phobia. Morton Prince used hypnotism, and also automatic writing. From the repressed memories uncovered it emerged that as a girl of 15 the patient had waited in a room near a bell-tower. The bells had marked the quarter hours of her long wait while her mother was undergoing an operation. Fear and anguish after her mother had died during the operation had persisted – even after the interval of twenty-five years – and were evoked by the sight or sounds associated with such a tower. In addition to having repressed the traumatic memory, the patient had, throughout this period, tried to avoid looking at churches, schoolhouses, and any kind of tower. She had sought to avoid hearing the ringing of their bells, or even any talk about them, thus keeping all thoughts about them out of her consciousness.

The 'anankastic reactions' – phobias, obsessions, and compulsions – seem to involve defences that differ from those of the hysterias. There is, however, an interesting similarity to one of the phenomena of hypnosis. Given a post-hypnotic suggestion the subject exhibits a strong inner compulsion to carry out the required act. A similar internal system seems to motivate the actions and avoidances of the anankastic neuroses, and in this also thwarting results in a powerful upsurge of anxiety. This upsurge also resembles closely what is likely to happen during therapy when ego defences are themselves analysed. There are also resemblances to the acute emotional tension that overwhelms the personality in the anxiety states. A re-orientation in the area of diagnosis was provided by Suttie (1935; reprinted 1945), who classifies these anxiety states, together with depressions, as 'self-frustration syndromes'. They provide clear and abundant evidence of distress and absence of escape from it in any kind of internal equilibrium. In the anankastic reactions a defensive equilibrium is achieved through compulsions, phobias, and obsessions.

SUMMARY

1   Historically there have been links between the study of phenomena artificially produced by hypnotism, and those which occur spontaneously in the hysterias. Broadly speaking, the symptomatology of hysteria involves things which can be removed hypnotically, as in the treatment of First World War cases mis-named 'shell shock'.

2   Hysterical neuroses are discussed with reference to the two categories of dissociative and conversion reactions. Patients diagnosed as 'hysterical' are often viewed harshly by those who have to deal with them: their signs and symptoms seem to be 'not real' and they be misdiagnosed as 'malingering'. A case history is offered in support of a more sympathetic reaction to such people.

3   It was with this seemingly unrewarding group of patients that psychoanalysis began. Along with Freud's own work we encounter that of Adler and Groddeck, which in many respects pioneered a more psychosomatic approach to patients. Advances in medical knowledge in, for instance, virology add to uncertainties of diagnosis.

4   The phenomena of hypnotic states are considered, and it is argued that under ideal conditions some very remarkable effects can be produced. It is suggested that we should be cautious in accepting the alleged 'limitations' of hypnotism, and that a single success invalidates the claim that such and such an effect 'cannot be produced'.

5 Theoretical interpretations of hypnosis and hypnotism are considered, and with them the present and future uses of hypnotism, not only in treatment but also in experimental psychopathology.

Chapter Eight

ANANKASTIC REACTIONS

'I know it's irrational but I just can't help it: there's something inside that makes me ...'

We recognize anankastic reactions from words like those that head this chapter. Compulsions, obsessions, and phobias are often closely inter-related. The psychiatrist Kretschmer provided the generic term 'anankastic' for these 'internally forced' reactions. Compulsions are anankastic actions; obsessions are anankastic thoughts; and phobias are anankastic fears. Failures to conform to them result in severe emotional distress, anxiety, and some-times guilt feeling. Eysenck classifies these conditions as 'dysthymic', that is, within his category of neurotic introversion. His *Encyclopaedia of Psychology* describes their motivation towards minutely ordered, pedantic control over oneself and others, plus awareness of some inner process forcing them. Anankastic reactions are a common accompaniment of normal development, through childhood and adolescence, and often extend into adult life. Superstitions which feature in the experience and behaviour of any otherwise normal people seem psychologically to be closely related. Distinctions between irrational phobias and legitimate fears are sometimes not easy to maintain. And socially accepted rituals play an important part in many different systems of religion.

Inter-relations between obsessive-compulsive reactions and phobias may be close. This can be seen in the commonly occurring fear of contamination with its accompanying avoidance rituals. The picture is one of endless acts of hand-washing and obsessive thoughts about dirt and disease. Any connection between the resulting behaviour and realistic standards of hygiene may be exceedingly remote. In one such case, tissues or plastic gloves had to be used when touching doorknobs; in another, any object that fell on the floor had to be boiled, with disastrous effect on a travelling clock which was not excepted! It never worked again. An anankastic neurotic in whom such ritual-building has become well developed may dominate, indeed terrorize, a whole household. The amount of hostile feeling and aggressiveness in action that anankastic reactions can embrace has, on the whole, been under-estimated. We may note that 'phobia' is a word that comes from Greek mythology and the god Phobos who had the ability to terrorize. Again adolescents and children can punish or terrorize parents with their repertoire of phobias and compulsions. The behaviourist B. F. Skinner coined the term 'mand' to refer to one whole category of language: demands and commands are typical examples. An anankastic neurotic may become a veritable walking and talking mand, issuing to others commands and counter-mands, demands and prohibitions all the time. In the case of a housewife this form of almost perpetual 'press', in Murray's alternative terminology, may become extremely tiresome to others. This may involve insistence that everybody else avoid going into certain shops because somebody associated with them is ill, or has died; avoidance of chemists and doctors because of their contacts with sick people; and, of course, in shopping, rejecting anything that is near to, or falls on, the floor. One patient discussed by Kisker (1972) deviated from this. While out shopping she did not avoid chemists, but would have to go into a chemist shop to ask for a glass of water she would use to wash her hands. Some people will go to very great lengths in their rituals, fed by phobic contamination fears, to avoid shaking hands or otherwise touching almost everybody else. They may also undergo agonies of anxiety with money, even their own change, if it drops to the floor of a shop, for fear somebody present may pick it up and hand it to them. Much sooner would they not see and abandon it. One woman with tendencies of this kind made to me the interesting suggestion about 'not seeing' that washing the hands is a kind of 'washing out the eyes'.

In both compulsive and superstitious behaviour we encounter, among ego defences, the mechanism of isolation. Mental life is compartmentalized: emotion is isolated from thoughts and impulses to action in ways that permit the recurrent remark 'I know it's silly, but I can't help it.' Many psychologists find the concept of a repertoire of mental mechanisms provided by Freudian thought more acceptable than other aspects of psycho-analytic theory. It is frequently claimed, for instance, that obsessive-compulsive phenomena relate to the history of toilet training, and sometimes to 'regression to the anal stage' of development. And in contamination obsessions and phobias there may be hidden sexual connections between, for example, 'germs' and 'sperms'. But experimental evidence on such issues is far from conclusive, indeed very mixed. While suspending judgement on this issue I add two observations. First, many people seem to find it necessary to put down toilet paper on a lavatory seat. In extreme cases this happens even when it is their own, or a close relative's, from whom 'catching something' would seem improbable. Such improbability may be admitted in appeal to the patient's rationality. Second, in a somewhat related matter of hygiene there are cultural differences. Rituals relating to hand-washing differ as between peoples of Soviet Russia and some other East European countries, and those who live further west. This difference may help to unmask a minor irritation to travellers who are advised to pack a plug in their luggage: plugs are proverbially absent from Soviet wash-basins. But norms are different in these countries. Hand-washing should take place in running water under the tap, since 'only dirty people' would think of washing in a plugged basin of still water. In an atmosphere of misunderstanding this 'hot and cold war', as we might call it, continues.

As a general term like 'anankastic' implies, there may be functional connections between compulsions, phobias, and obsessions. Obsessive thoughts are likely to accompany ritualistic compulsions. Karl Menninger was not alone in finding many examples of both among students as well as patients of the famous Menninger Clinic. Among more exaggerated reactions were those displayed by one of his patients, who was obsessed with the idea that there might be broken glass in her food (Menninger 1946). Accompanying this obsessive anxiety were rituals she 'had' to perform. Together with her contamination phobic avoidances – she also had to cover up door handles with paper in her house – was the necessity to sift foods before meals. Without such filtering she was unable to drink a cup of coffee for fear there might be a pin in it. Water entered the obsessive mental life of another Menninger patient, though not in the context of hand-washing. The man concerned constantly faced the obsessive fear that if he washed his face he might get water into his ears, and this would give him an infection. Driving a car provided this man with other obsessional trials. He reported on one occasion having to drive back 10 miles for fear that a vehicle he had passed might have been accidentally grazed by him. Each night he made elaborate precautions in case of his unexpected death. This severely obsessed man had a persona: to the outside world he appeared tough and hard-boiled. But, he confessed, behind this exterior was 'a cringing and tortured worm'. During development from childhood into adolescence, and sometimes extending into adult life, I suspect behind many personas we will find similar obsessions and compulsions. Most of us will be familiar with having to get up again – though we know it is silly – to check having locked the front door and turning off the electricity or gas. Having to trace words or diagrams with one's tongue on the roof of the mouth was one of the more original oddities Menninger found among his students. Having to touch bars or fences or lamp-posts as one passes is common, as are other manifestations of the 'walk on the squares of the street' mechanism. The 'bears' at the corners symbolize the penalties of anxiety or guilt-feeling for non-conformity. As regards childhood, Anna Freud (1936) observed a greater tendency to indulge in compulsive rituals at night before bed and the unknown anxieties of sleep. Adults likewise may engage in more careful and elaborate folding or other arrangement of clothes before bed, on the night which precedes some important anxiety-evoking enterprise. The rituals of actors and actresses before stage performances are well known, but these are 'superstitions' not obsessive-compulsive happenings. But are they so very different? There are many places where the phenomena of anankastic neurotic experience and behaviour are continuous with others we regularly encounter in everyday life. The 'isolation mechanism' may play its part in compulsions and obsessions. It also operates when a scientist attempts to be impartial, or when members of a jury exclude emotion and reach a judgement in terms of the evidence presented. As regards phobic fears, if when climbing a ladder or crossing a narrow bridge you 'don't look down', is this an irrational phobic fear of heights or simply sensible? The falling 'pot of paint' theory of not walking under ladders has been much ridiculed. Yet students who have worked on building sites in vacations tell me that under-ladder avoidance makes real sense in terms of very probable falling objects. 'Ritual' is a word we encounter outside the obsessional neuroses and it plays a part in many human religions, as well as public ceremonies and other events. Social norms, sometimes in the form of strong taboos, govern many normal areas of human behaviour.

Norms about eating may be part of a religious tradition, as in the Jewish and Islamic avoidance of eating pork. These are well known, but in hidden differences between people are others we may not know about. They can result from religious traditions affecting people who are no longer religious. Early learning may be influential. An example I encountered concerned the publisher Victor Gollancz who told how, having been reared in an orthodox Jewish environment, he learned in the home the taboo about meat and milk in close proximity. Years later, having long abandoned his religion, he found it an ordeal to have lunch with a person who ordered steak and a glass of milk. This remained a trial for him, and mostly unknown to his dining companions (McKellar 1968). Meals sometimes provide a fascinating area permitting exploration of cross-cultural differences and empathic attempts to take account of norms that may – to the outsider – appear ritualistic. 'When in Rome live in the Roman style' was the advice of St Ambrose to Augustine. For this kind of reason guests in the Arabic world at meals are both empathic and wise to eat with one hand and not both; to thank the host, not his wife; and certainly not to give her a gift of flowers. One event involved my psychologist colleagues and I attending a meal with a visiting Buddhist missionary from Asia. The restaurant, doubtless impressed by Mr Mahinda and his companion's saffron robes, rose to the occasion and provided a strict vegan meal. The restraints on what this permitted us to eat were strange to my carnivore colleagues but the occasion was a memorable one. At a different meal my Japanese hostess instructed me in another hitherto unknown area: although I could use chopsticks I was till then wholly ignorant of the hidden differences of the norms – some subtle – that define their use in polite table manners. In driving my visitors in my car to the meal in question it emerged I had myself been guilty of having, through ignorance, violated polite-ness. The visitors – they were psychologists – were sufficiently confident of their own social norm to explain this to me, as they did with some amusement. I had placed the husband in a low-status seat (beside the driver), and given higher status to the wife by placing her behind the driver. The amount of emotion locked up in culturally different norms should not be under-estimated nor upset from non-conformity to such ritualistic acts and avoid-ances. Thus in therapy, treatment which seeks to remove anankastic defences in individuals is a matter involving great skill and care. Do not even the meat-eaters largely confine themselves and avoid the flesh of carnivorous animals? Such food is served cooked rather than raw. For some the prospect of eating snails or semi-raw steak evokes repulsion and anxiety, followed by flat refusal. There are many things normal human beings much prefer not to eat. Bridges to empathy with the anankastic reactions of neurosis are many.

Many investigators have sought an explanation of fears and phobias in terms of emotional conditioning. In this way a previously neutral object or situation may become fear-arousing through association, but there is the possibility that humans, and other animals, may in some way be biologically programmed to certain things as fear stimuli. Representative of researches in this area is the work of Bennett-Levy and Marteau (1980), who studied specific fear of twenty-nine species of animals. Their subjects proved 'disproportionately more fearful' of the rat. Overall their emphasis was on perceptual qualities, and certain configurations representing discrepancy from the human form were associated with fear. These included ugliness, being thought slimy, and being liable to make sudden movements. Their study supported clinical observations they had made of patients' vivid descriptions of what it is they fear that also emphasized perceptual qualities. Relatively 'harmless' animals as fear-objects were studied: the ladybird beetle and the rabbit were at the bottom of their scale. Sex differences – more fears by women – emerged. Whether associative learning or biological programming is involved, there are many fears which are hardly irrational. There seems to be a larger number of things many people prefer not to do. Examples include handling snakes, even harmless ones; travelling in submarines; and standing on the extreme edge of high cliffs.

'Acrophobia' or fear of heights, though not universal, whether rational or not, is widespread. Here we encounter the 'walking the plank phenomenon'. There are no problems about walking along a solid 4-foot-wide plank placed 3 feet above the ground. There are few problems at 4 or even 5 feet. But when raised still higher and higher the causeway starts to provoke fear emotion, sometimes accompanied by imagery of oneself falling. Everyone is said to have his price, but the fee for being willing to cross a chasm on a long 6-foot wide bridge without railings rises sharply. Eventually the 'I wouldn't do it for any price' reaction emerges. There are of course exceptions, including professionals. But for many people using swing bridges to cross over the chasms or rivers of the Himalayan countries, climbing the north face of the Eiger, and the ascent of the Matterhorn by any route remain firmly outside their ambitions. Fear of falling is amplified by vividness of imagination. Here we encounter one of the most interesting of the phobias.

FEAR OF HEIGHTS

An often biologically inappropriate, exaggerated fear of heights is widespread. In the statistical sense 'abnormality' may lie with those who don't, rather than those who do, have such fears. It is reassuring to know in a high wire circus performance that there is a safety net. Acrophobia has been much exploited visually in the film, from Harold Lloyd clinging to the face of a clock and the horrors of Hitchcock's *Vertigo*, to the skyscraper antics on a narrow ledge of the love-struck young man in *Thoroughly Modern Milly*. Audiences are made to hold their breath as they identify with dangers that rationally they would accept as imaginary, involving characters they know to be purely fictional. These vicarious fears are experienced and paid for, in the name of entertainment. Aircraft and boats provide some interesting variations. If we exclude fear of flying as such, it seems that an aircraft's remoteness from the distant earth's surface is in some way different. Again cliff-top or swing-bridge-over-chasm reactions seem to be absent with hot air balloon experiences, as with aircraft. In testifying on this point, one experienced expert told me that the instructor from whom he himself learned, suffered severe vertigo and inability to climb ladders but nothing of the kind in a balloon. The relation of fear to being 'connected' and 'disconnected' to or from the ground remains an interesting but unsolved mystery. Sometimes clouds by their proximity seem to provide fancied security, and in the case of small boats the close-up waters may provide similar comfort and perhaps even momentary half-belief that they could be 'walked upon'. They couldn't. It is only in dreamlife that clouds can be used as stepping stones, or something to float or fly through. Earlier, in considering dreamlife and lucid dreams, we noted that its flying achievements are bereft of fear. Mary Arnold-Foster (1921) used flight – without aircraft – to escape in her nightmares. She was able by training to increase the number of her flying dreams by observing and meditating on the flight of birds during wakefulness. The emotion of fear accords with the Koffka Principle: it results from perceived or believed dangers which may be illusory. By association, fears of actual dangers may be transferred to neutral objects and situations. In this context we meet one of the famous phobia case histories with a number of features of interest.

CLAUSTROPHOBIA

In an important book about unconscious mental life Rivers (1920) dealt in detail with a case of claustrophobia. He treated this with hypnotism. The patient had no conscious memory for what had led to his terror of enclosed spaces. In hypnosis he recalled his experiences as a soldier in trench warfare, living in dugouts during the First World War. Fear emotion was locked away with these memories and therapeutically released by hypnotism, but the claustrophobia nevertheless continued. In further sessions hypnotism uncovered more deeply repressed memories of earlier events. The patient recalled childhood experiences of having to sleep at nights in a confined bed with his brother, and his terror on the occasions when he had had to sleep on the wall side. Despite further release of the fear emotion the claustrophobia continued. There is evidence in these two recalls of repressed material that, although they were charged with emotion, both were what Freud was to call 'concealing memories'. They were defensive alibis against becoming conscious of still more terrifying recall. Rivers continued his hypnotic treatments. With this he was

165

able to recover an incident from childhood that was deeply repressed and wholly unconscious. On one occasion as a young boy the subject had gone to sell some things to an old rag-and-bone merchant. As he moved up the dark and narrow passage to the house, the gate had closed behind him. He was in the closed space with a fierce dog. The patient re-lived the experience in a state of extreme terror. After this abreaction of the final and most deeply repressed memory, the claustrophobia was cured. In terms of depth psychology it would seem that this complex, or system of fear-saturated ideas, had somehow fed into the two less deeply repressed ones that hypnotism had initially re-activated. In Pavlov's terminology the emotion had exhibited 'generalisation'. To use the language of conditioning, after his experience of an enclosed space together with a stimulus to fear, the man had responded claustrophobically to all such places. He continued to react as if the fear provocation was present.

Whichever way we conceptualize there is evidence in this case of different depths of repression. Traumatic experiences first uncovered may not be sufficient to remove the symptoms. In this respect the causation of a neurosis may be more complex than it first seems to superficial investigation. Causal factors may be more than sufficient, this surplus producing what Freud called 'over-determination'. The investigator Rivers was an unusually gifted man. He made important contributions to anthropology and to the establishment at Cambridge of its first psychology laboratory. His attitude to ideas was not to demolish them, but rather to make some constructive use of them. Rivers was on a field-trip when the English translation of Freud's *Interpretation of Dreams* appeared. The late Professor Pear had many discussions with him about it on return. When Rivers first encountered the Freud volume, Pear told me of how he was infuriated by it. He threw the book across the room. But then, he explained to Pear, 'I had to pick it up and go on reading it.' The result was his own book on dreamlife. His constructive re-evaluation of Freud's work led him to place emphasis on the type of dreams which exhibits anxiety rather than wish-fulfilment. Never, with *Conflict and Dream* (Rivers 1923) in my hand, have I been tempted to throw it across the room. On the contrary each time I have consulted it I've had to re-read it. It is that kind of book. Here also, as in his careful study of the repression mechanism in the case considered, Rivers took unconscious mental life very seriously. And he had something original of his own to add to its study.

In the Rivers claustrophobia case there is no reference to subsequent fear of dogs, only of enclosed spaces. But it raises again the issue of the narrow line between rational fears and irrational phobias. People who have been chased by a bull – as some of us have – may end up more cautious about such animals. This is testimony to the fact that human beings learn. Habits of caution, like phobias, are learned. In psychology criterion problems often arise. But on analogy with Pear's argument (Chapter 3) about sentiments, learned fears may like sentiments degenerate into untidy emotional systems like complexes. If a person has been attacked by an Alsatian dog – it once happened to me – he may from this traumatic experience learn to have a dislike of the breed of dog concerned which also embraces fear of that breed even though prepared to admit over-generalization. Criterion problems arise also with other fears. The plague years of the England of Charles II resulted in widespread fear, with accompanying avoidance rituals and inhumanities towards the victims. Fears of disease are still with us, new ones. The Acquired Immune Deficiency Syndrome, or AIDS, has been assessed by one specialist as 'probably the most important public health problem of the century', involving an estimated 1,750,000–2,000,000 people infected in the United States (Davie, M., *Observer*, 15 June 1986: 56). Thus again in the mid-1980s we encounter avoidance rituals and considerable inhumanity to victims. Some such rituals are phobic and irrational, and some are not. To provide introspective evidence I recall walking around the back streets of a town in one very poor country where leprosy and plague are still to be encountered. On return to base I took some of every medicine I possessed, washing it down with bottled beer and not the local drinking water. The upshot: this made me heartily sick. In retrospect I detect components both rational and irrational. Again, during a polio epidemic I observed one mother hang small bags of camphor round the necks of her three children. Where rationality ends and fetishism begins is not easy to determine in such cases. During a time of plague the famous prophet, Nostradamus (1503–66), showed no fear in entering houses and dealing with patients. This was attributed at the time to his magical powers, but Laver (1942: 25) refers to evidence about 'a mysterious powder which he used to purify the air', and concludes that the medically-skilled Nostradamus probably possessed some kind of disinfectant.

SUPERSTITION

In superstitions, as in neurotic anankastic reactions, we may also encounter the familiar words 'I know it's silly, but I can't help it.' Again anxiety accompanies failure to observe the avoidance rituals. One interesting thing emerged in a study by my former colleague, Dr John Clark (1976), who introduced some startling originality into the study of magical thinking and belief. Clark found that he only had to invent a new superstition to find people immediately prepared to believe in it! He assessed superstitions as involving erroneous views of cause–effect relationships, and commented on the similarities and differences between super- stitions and psychiatric phenomena. Along with the 'John Clark Effect' may be mentioned several studies of my own on the existing ladder superstition as a social norm to which the majority of people conform (McKellar 1979b: 164). With well-known superstitions we may construct a series of J-shaped curves with various slopes indicating degree of conformity and non-conformity in actual observance. Interviews reveal that among the conformists are many who do not believe, or only half-believe, the super- stition. Accepting their irrationality they nevertheless conform. As illustration I take one man who would regard himself as 'normal', and I see no reason to disagree. It brings out some of the similarities that hold between anankastic reactions we might assess as neurotic, and superstitious experience and behaviour.

Asked about his superstitions, the man C. D. mentioned ladders and the rituals concerning spilling salt. He admitted usually to throwing spilt salt over his shoulder. Asked about others he mentioned opals as allegedly unlucky stones. Once he explained he had just bought an opal in the United States. Immediately afterwards his car had broken down on a desert road. After this he declared he had been careful never again to own an opal. But of course he didn't believe he was being rational. His 'master- superstition', if we might call it that, concerned Friday the Thirteenth. He declared, 'I've got a thing about it. More than most people, I think.' On this date he would avoid making any major decisions, and would avoid writing cheques or letters. He explained he would be very anxious if he did. To this he added 'Yes, it's an obsession. I brood on it, if that date is going to turn up.' He knew of no basis, no painful experience he had ever undergone on a Friday the Thirteenth, just that of somehow having learned the superstition. His next comment was 'I know it's irrational, but I just can't help it. The alternative is a lot of worry and anxiety.' When questioned he declared he knew the theory which explained it in terms of the thirteen people at the Last Supper on a Friday. But, he added, there was nothing religious about his own irrational behaviour. Finally he referred to his attitude to horoscopes. He avoided reading his own, though he had no belief in astrology. This avoidance he defended as 'not irrational'. It removed any temptation to act in accord with the content of the horoscope or to brood in a perseverative, obsessional way on it. There are occasions when institutions exhibit rather similar behaviour, taking account of superstitious beliefs. Examples are hotels whose bedrooms and restaurant tables omit the number thirteen, and ships which avoid sailing on Friday the Thirteenth. Anxieties are avoided and the super-stitions of guests, passengers, and crew are in this way catered for.

Three areas in which superstitions flourish are science, religion, and medicine. First consider science. The incident in New Jersey, when a radio play, *War of the Worlds*, purporting to be an invasion from Mars, was believed by many to be a real Martian invasion, was not unique. On a later occasion, when *War of the Worlds* was thus presented in Ecuador, the angry public reacted violently on learning that it was 'only a play'. In the riot that followed they burned down the broadcasting building. A study by Cantril (1940) followed the New Jersey occasion. Among its findings was that a superstitious attitude towards science, readiness to be suggestible towards it, and the belief that to science anything is possible, were among factors responsible. Gullibility about religion also contri-buted in those susceptible to the notion of 'the end of the world'. In the chapter following I will deal critically with aspects of the alleged supernatural. Religion as such is not necessarily involved: there are many kinds of religion. In this area some may side with the view of the Ancient Greek monotheist, Xenophanes, in his criticism of Homer, who had attributed all sorts of unworthy doings to the gods. In history there have been many reformers – sometimes highly religious people – who have agreed with Xenophanes, critical of superstitions advanced in the name of religion. As regards medicine we encounter the often misleading notion that a given illness is 'contagious'. In the realm of the phobias the notion of 'catching' something by mere touch has much to answer for. Apart from people as agents of infection there are also often far from irrational beliefs about fomites – things or substances – through which illnesses can be 'caught'. There are of course fomites but this attribute is often irrationally extended to neutral objects. Health is a major area in which superstitions flourish.

EXORCIZING THE NEUROCRACY

The two words may be defined. A 'neurocracy' is a group of people who are neurotically anxious, and exhibit ritualistic or phobic behaviour about their own health. 'Exorcism' means removing something that shouldn't be there: in this case not evil spirits but hypochondriacal worries. I refer to an unpublished paper my colleague Peter Bradshaw and I gave at one New Zealand Psychological Society Conference (1978). Our full title added the words '. . . with garlic and the control group'. Garlic is a useful substance to have around for an exorcism, but in the case of a 'neurocracy' the control group is often more appropriate in dealing with the bad science and misuses of statistics it depends on. As we have seen, hypochondriasis involves excessive pre-occupation with one's body image in health matters. Exaggeration through journalistic over-simplification and human gullibility is only part of the story. Often also involved are 'scientific' findings of dubious value. Statistics have their place but may also be a temptation towards premature publication of anxiety-arousing, unconfirmed researches on health matters. One notorious example involved epidemiology – medical statistics – about the potato: it was claimed that potato blight was the 'cause' of the tragic condition of spina bifida. The two epidemiologists concerned produced a map of the world showing a relationship between incidence of the condition and consumption of potatoes as food.

A causal relation was claimed. That high potato consumption is related to areas of poverty, and people who are under-privileged in matters of health and hygiene, does not seem to have been considered. Perhaps we should look to these facts rather than potatoes which incidentally, in former times, were once asserted to be the 'cause' of leprosy. The result of publicity following the epidemiology study was widespread anxiety. A neurocracy emerged. Some people would not only avoid having potatoes in their house, but would avoid entering the homes of potato-eaters! We encounter many similar half-baked reports of alleged 'scientific' findings, seemingly endless sources of irrational hypochondriacal anxiety. If they start to look for them readers will be able to find many more such instances of anxiety-provoking alarmism needing exorcism. My colleague and I found a report in one responsible English newspaper relating to an interesting condition called 'Kwok's disease'. This is apparently 'caused' by eating fried rice in Chinese restaurants, and among other things produces the distressing phenomenon of 'wobbly chin'. Later I was able to find out more about this condition which derives from a letter written in 1968. A man called Robert Kwok reported, after his dinner in a Chinese restaurant, that he suffered from muscular weakness, numbness in the hands, and palpitations. Following his letter many began to report similar phenomena after Chinese restaurant meals, or meals containing monosodium glutamate. Subsequent searches revealed people are ten times as likely to report such signs and symptoms if they have heard of the syndrome than if they haven't. In its 'Medical Briefing' column, *The Times* (10 October 1986: 15) included a neurocracy exorcism conducted by Dr R. A. Kenny using proper control group studies. This helped to deflate the myth, and found that 'monosodium glutamate is, despite its reputation, an innocuous substance.'

Among the cases Bradshaw and I found in our own inquiry were upsurges of anxiety about the report that one can catch avian tuberculosis from feeding the pigeons in London's Trafalgar Square. St Mark's Square, Venice, was not mentioned in this hypochondriasis-provoking press report. We should also, we learned elsewhere, be careful about drinking water. This didn't relate to its bacteriological content but rather its 'hardness' or 'softness'. Both are dangerous, we learned, in relation to hypertension, heart conditions, and probably much else. As one critic of

171

this thesis pointed out cynically, the only safe thing to drink is distilled water, never of course tea and certainly not coffee. Prominent among such body image concerns is being overweight: a happy hunting ground for advertisers with products to sell, pseudo-researchers, and journalists who over-simplify. In this area of illusion we again meet what Alfred Adler called generically 'organ inferiority'. This includes anxiety and suffering by people who are underweight by statistical standards and who starve themselves. Anorexia nervosa, which can lead to death, represents one end of this continuum. Good health is one thing, but much unchallenged nonsense gets published in its name, based on unconfirmed researches that belong more to the category of superstitions about science and medicine than to science itself. This is not merely a source of avoidable anxiety but also a nuisance to general practitioners of medicine, and sometimes also to psychiatrists. Much has been said in this book about the silent misery of people who feel in some way different and isolated from others: this source of it must also be mentioned.

Corresponding to any disease, actual or imaginary, is a category of people who wrongly believe they have it or – if they don't perform the appropriate rituals – may 'catch' it. There are many physical illnesses which are believed to be infectious but aren't and others which, though infectious, aren't transmitted in the ways believed. The notion of a contagious disease that can be 'caught' from mere touch is one which links anankastic avoidance rituals to superstitions about medicine. We will encounter it again in relation to the supernatural, and Frazer's analysis of 'contagious magic' in *The Golden Bough* (1911). Perhaps, as one expert on the cinema has suggested, the film versions of *Ben Hur* should have ended – though the book did not – with the chariot race. As a result of seeing in childhood the later sequences of the outcasts, 'the unclean', one person told me of his years of phobic fears of leprosy as a 'contagious' disease. I suspect there have been others like him. Terror of the leper and his illness, once widespread in the world, pervades history. It is probable that up till the time when the bacillus responsible, the *Mycobacterium leprae*, was discovered there was confusion with many other conditions. Leprosy itself, now known as 'Hanson's disease', can be treated with sulphonamide drugs. Its transmission is by prolonged physical contact. Like other conditions that are not 'caught' from mere touch it nevertheless remains a potential basis of irrational fear and potential phobias. In these matters we encounter not merely often unjustified anxiety but also problems from 'serial reproduction': the transmission of information from one person to another and in over-simplified form. This may happen even with scientific experiments and the ways they are reported. One particular case history involving a phobia merits mention. Although it has been cited in numerous text-books of psychology I make no apology for again bringing in the story of 'Albert B.'. It has many features of interest.

ALBERT AND THE WHITE RAT

The experiment concerned the pioneer behaviourist J. B. Watson, his assistant Rosalie Rayner, and an 11-month-old Albert B. Watson and Rayner set out to establish in the infant a conditioned fear reaction to a white rat. Initially the animal evoked no fear. By pairing presentations of the rat with a loud noise created by striking a steel bar, they eventually succeeded. Finally when the rat was presented alone the child would whimper, cry and crawl away rapidly. Generalization also occurred. The fear reaction was also evoked by a number of other stimuli, including a rabbit, a fur coat, a dog, and cotton wool. The amount of fear shown was in proportion to the resemblance of these other things to the rat: the rabbit produced the strongest reaction, second only to the rat. Watson set out to explain childhood fears, for example of darkness, by a similar conditioning process. The experiment, reported in 1920 and in other of Watson's writing, created considerable interest. It is cited again and again by psychologists. Very remarkable is the degree of inaccuracy that has crept in. Harris (1979) has provided an entertaining account of some of these variations. For example, many later writers have Albert conditioned to a phobic reaction to a rabbit. Much imagining has also been indulged in about the various other things to which, allegedly, the fear generalized. Most interesting of all is the account in these various secondary sources of how Albert 'was cured of his phobia'. No therapy experiment ever in fact took place. It is a sheer invention.

An explanation can be found partly in a quite different experiment conducted by Mary Jones (1924). This was in fact supervised by Watson. It involved another child, Peter, who turned up with a fear of a white rabbit. By deconditioning techniques – resembling those now widely used in behaviour therapy – Peter was cured of his phobia. Since Watson very naturally also later wrote about Peter and the rabbit, as well as Albert and the rat, we have another aspect of the causal explanation. There are other aspects also. The notion of a still-phobic Albert, frightened by white rats, rabbits and other things, going about untreated may have troubled some. Watson was also a controversial person. When divorce proceedings against him began he was asked to resign from his post at Johns Hopkins University. In the end he withdrew from academic psychology, married Rosalie Rayner, and became a pioneer of the subject in the realm of business advertising. He continued, however, to write books and articles supporting the doctrines of early behaviourism. The emotional climate perhaps also had contributions to make to the confusions about Albert, the rat – not the rabbit – and his conditioned phobia.

The story of Albert B. has found its place in numerous books about psychology. Even granted its many misreportings, taken along with the Mary Jones experiment with Peter and the rabbit, it has been influential. And rightly so. Despite the limitations of early behaviourism, J. B. Watson, by his own experiment and through his supervision of the second experiment, provided a theory and a therapy. Behaviour therapy, much used for example in the treatment of phobias, owes much to this pioneer work. But the other message of the Albert B. story is also important. If errors occur, and continue to occur, in reports of a classical experiment within science, what of other past events? History itself becomes suspect. What we most closely associate with certain historical characters in popular history are often things they didn't do, and events which never occurred. Here of interest is the climate of Europe, and notably its winters. During such times past military exploits were often planned, but in the summer that followed never carried out. But history records these 'winter campaigns' sometimes as real happenings. Some 'events' of history are products of imagination, not of fact. Many of its characters have come down to us as stereotypes of 'good' and 'evil'. What did or did not occur, and even more the motives and causes that led to them, are difficult to ascertain at a much later period of time.

Particularly in the area of motives it is extremely difficult to approach this, taking account of the full complexities of multiple motivation.

As regards past events there is a related area presenting even greater difficulty than mere history. It is the realm of the supernatural. As portrayed by Homer, the deities of Mount Olympus constantly interfered in the Trojan War and its aftermath. During medieval times many strange and seemingly supernatural things are reported as happenings. As we move from the past towards the present, and from areas of illiteracy to better education, such happenings become rarer. Yet even today, within prosperous, well-developed, and highly educated societies, most of us have stories to tell which invite at least half-belief in the supernatural. The question arises of how far such 'happenings' can be explained in terms of known science. Stated differently, to what extent is it possible to explain apparently supernatural happenings in terms of the principles of normal and abnormal psychology?

POSSESSION AND EXORCISM

It was largely from West Africa that slavery brought its captives to the Caribbean islands and America. The parthenon of West African spirits or 'loa' reappears in the Caribbean not only in Haiti, but also the Dominican Republic, Trinidad, Jamaica, and elsewhere. A metaphor is widely used. The possessed person is said to be 'ridden' by the possessing entity, for example in Haiti the formidable female loa, Ezulie. There are a large number of different loa that may possess. And possession may be invited with, for example, the choice among the various vèvès, the figures drawn on the ground personifying each of the spirits thus summoned. A diversity of spiritual forces offers a parallel to the notion of differing functioning systems that make up the personality as a whole. As one investigator, the anthropologist Karen Brown, puts it, 'within a single person there are many selves ... these manifest themselves through the various personalities of the gods' (Brown 1976: 289). In considering multiple personality we have seen how a sub-system may emerge to function in defence of an oppressed and demoralized individual.

175

When possessed, the individual concerned becomes an object of awe and reverence to others. It is not difficult to understand this wish-fulfilment component in, for example, a socially and economically deprived woman. Possession brings liberation and attention and as a mechanism permits manipulation of other people. Ezulie, for example, personifies sexual love, eloquence, vanity, and demands for attention and expensive presents. In his classic study of possession in Haiti, Métraux (1972) describes an ordinarily shy and retiring girl becoming possessed by Ezulie. She begins to dance, gyrating slowly, confident, provocative, and sensuous. Other witnesses have testified to the remarkable changes that occur with voodoo possession. In the instance reported by Métraux the period of change suddenly comes to an end and is followed by a total amnesia for the whole episode. Sometimes, as in multiple personality cases, the possessing entity suggests the sub-system which Jung called the 'animus' or 'anima' and represents the other sex. In another of his descriptions Métraux gives an account of a wedding. During the ceremony itself the girl behaved in a restrained, timid way. But later her features changed.

Figure 8.1   Vèvè for Ezulie: My drawing of this device – laid out with cornmeal on an earthen floor so unlikely to be symmetrical – relates to possession by the voodoo love-goddess. There are alternative vèvès used to summon up other loa. In this case both the sexual symbolism for the female and the Catholic sacred heart may have contributed to the traditional design used.

She began to utter violent oaths, she stamped her feet with indications of fury and the possessing loa inside her began to demand rum. The girl is no longer a quiet young bride – a male animus figure has taken over; she is possessed by the spirit of the soldier-loa Ogu. During this period, Métraux reports her tongue, long and purplish, stabs out: her hands have become claws. The episode – which we might be disposed to label a somnambulism – came to an end, and the girl's face resumed its normal expression 'as though she had torn off a mask'. Amnesia followed. Other investigators, for example W. and F. Mischel, have described possession of a woman by Ogu, in this case in Trinidad. Again they emphasize the remarkable change of personality.

As regards Haiti it is difficult to ascertain – in the transition following the ejection of the Duvalier family and 'Baby Doc' – the present status of voodoo. Haiti seems destined to remain a country of extreme poverty and illiteracy of the kind in which supernaturalism is likely to continue. Of the earlier period in which he studied possession, Métraux underlined the wish-fulfilment character and the pleasure it gave 'to poor souls ground down by life'. Métraux himself refers to multiple personality being given, in such places, strong encouragement by the social norms of the culture concerned. In her Ph. D. study, Karen Brown (1976) refers to possession as permitting people to 'take a mental holiday'. She likewise endorses the dissociationist standpoint, adding that this permits them 'to explore the multiple possibilities of being'. As at least temporary escape from poverty, drudgery, and hardship – and in recent times a particularly oppressive political regime – motivation towards becoming possessed is readily understandable. Métraux placed emphasis both on the matter-of-fact way in which such a taking-over of the personality by the loa was accepted, and also the power and prestige it, for a time, provided. Within our own areas of culture we can find parallels. There are occasions involving alcohol when, at some social function, a person acts and speaks in a way that is 'not himself'. Bystanders may tolerate this, and even name the 'entity' responsible with words like 'too much gin' or 'he's drunk.' Or by implication the intoxicated individual may – like the bride possessed by Ogu – name it himself, demanding more alcohol and stating which kind he wants: gin, whisky, wine, or perhaps rum.

In studies of cultures or sub-cultures in which possession

occurs, two types have been distinguished. In 'lucid possession' there is an awareness of the invading spirit entity. By contrast, in 'somnambulistic possession' it takes over, wholly controls the organism, and amnesia follows. The Caribbean examples taken illustrate somnambulistic forms. An interesting case of lucid possession involved a German, Professor Ludwig Staudenmaier. This man, who taught chemistry in Freising, 'remained self-aware while his personality was controlled by a succession of entities' (Eban 1974: 228). It was after experiences of seances that he became interested in spiritualism. He started to engage in automatic writing. Visions and auditory experiences began to occur and while lying in bed at night he saw 'devilishly grimacing faces with total clarity and sharpness' (op. cit.: 230). Resemblance to the commonly reported 'faces in the dark' type of hypnagogic imagery seems obvious. Elsewhere I have discussed a public inquiry by a coroner's court in England. This related to a tragic case involving alleged possession, an attempted exorcism, and a subsequent murder (McKellar 1976). During an interval of the inquiry I had opportunity to discuss such hypnagogic visualizations of faces with the expert witness on exorcism called by the court, Dom Robert Petitpierre. Dom Robert acknowledged the existence of such imagery and distinguished it from evil spirits seeking entry and waiting to possess. Perhaps this distinction was not made by the German chemistry professor in his anxiety about these nightly, malevolent, apparently possessing forces. Moreover, in other respects than the beliefs of the allegedly 'possessed' man, his experiences resemble closely those of co-consciousness in multiple personality cases. There seems to be a parallel between somnambulistic and lucid possession on the one hand, and alternating personality and co-consciousness on the other. As regards differences of interpretation we may distinguish between the beliefs of the individual concerned, those of the area of culture in which he or she lives, and those of the investigator or therapist. As regards 'possession' there remains the alternative interpretation in terms of naturalistic concepts. Related phenomena are well known to anthropologists. When anankastic compulsions drive an individual to perform destructive actions including murder, principles familiar to abnormal psychology may also be highly relevant.

SUMMARY

1   Obsessions, compulsions, and phobias are often inter-related. They have the characteristic of a sense of being forced on a person by something within the personality. Anxiety is the usual accompaniment of failure to conform to these internal demands.

2   These anankastic reactions are common in everyday life, but a well-developed neurosis of this kind can inflict considerable strain on other people because of the demands and prohibitions it imposes. Resemblances can be found to other kinds of ritualistic behaviour, and also to common superstitions.

3   Phobias, anankastic irrational fears, are discussed with particular reference to fear of heights. Case histories are considered, along with the famous experiment concerning Albert B., and its relation to the development of behaviour therapy of patients. Two important lessons emerge from the experiment.

4   Obviously not all fears and avoidances are irrational. But phobic fears, hypochondriasis, and compulsive-obsessional pre-occupations can be fed by exaggerated reports of often prematurely published statistical studies. This applies particularly to medical and health matters: here 'exorcizing the neurocracy' is discussed.

5   Suggestion and gullibility may also occur in areas relating to religion, and the influences of spirit forces. In preparation for an examination of the psychology of the allegedly supernatural, included is a consideration of 'possession' to which sub-systems within the personality may have important relevance.

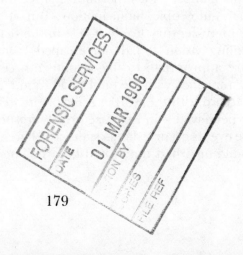

Chapter Nine

THE SUPERNATURAL

The mind as modern science has revealed it, was a sealed book in the Seventeenth Century ... the science of psychology ... must be banished if we are to enter the world of 1660.

W. G. Moore (1961)

I am climbing a stairway. The building is strange to me but I know I am in London. Near the top the stairs divide and from the landing I choose the right-hand stairway. Another figure appears. It is a man, he confronts me and bars my way. Trying to elude him by stepping to the side I am defeated in my efforts. He moves with me, still obstructing my path. Getting angry now I look more closely at this man. My anger turns to amazement, then to cold fear. The man confronting me looks back with recognition. He is myself.

It was not a dream, not a Doppelgänger experience from German literature. Hofmann in particular made much of the Doppelgänger: the supernatural appearance of oneself. Nor was it an autoscopic hallucination. But it did happen to me in twentieth-century London. Yet in the fear that accompanied this seeming vision I had not escaped from superstitious emotion more appropriate to the seventeenth century. Amazement and fear remained with me until I had found a naturalistic explanation. In accord with the Koffka Principle my reactions took place within the perceived – in this case grossly misperceived – environment. The events occurred on a stairway I had not previously climbed in a building I had not visited before. The stairway did not divide

180

but on the right-hand side of the dark landing near the top was a long mirror in which I saw my optical image. In magic as practised by stage magicians mirrors also play a prominent part, creating illusions in an environment different from the geographical realities. Expectancy and – as in this incident – haste can also contribute to a supernatural interpretation. Among stage magicians both Harry Houdini and, in recent years, James Randi report the difficulties they have had in convincing some people that everything they did depended on purely naturalistic principles. The will to believe that there is a residual 'something else' is a strong one.

In this context the Swiss psychologist Flournoy brought in what he called the Hamlet Principle. His reference is to Hamlet's words to Horatio: 'There are more things in heaven and in earth ...' In certain situations we encounter, if not belief, at least a weakening of disbelief in the supernatural. We are less ready than usual to dismiss apparitions, magic, and spirits as 'just superstition'. Half-belief is an interesting state of mind, carrying with it some features of belief and some of disbelief. Many of us have superstitious half-beliefs, and some situational factors like those in the incident related may arouse the Hamlet Principle. Even those of us – and I am one of them – for whom spirits usually fail to perform can recall incidents. To illustrate, once in New Zealand together with a companion I was standing in front of a tree near Rotorua regarded by the Maoris as sacred. My companion began to speak scornfully of the way in which branches of fresh green leaves had been placed by believers, as offerings to the tree and the spiritual forces it personified. Then suddenly, after uttering these words of disbelief, he was lying flat on the ground, prostrate in front of the sacred tree he had scorned. The scoffer was humbled. Of course he had tripped on a root. But had he? The two of us departed rapidly from the area. Some places have an 'atmosphere'. Once I lived in such a house and was not comfortable in it alone at night. It was in St Andrews, Scotland, a town which has many legends of the supernatural. It has a 'white lady', a haunted tower, a screaming skull which appears in the vicinity of the ruined cathedral, and also a monk who throws himself from the top of St Rule's Tower. Moreover, there is a phantom coach which drives at midnight along South Street: students and others in this old university town tended to avoid both this and the vicinity of the haunted tower in the late evening. With passage of time and the development of a strong department of psychology at the university things may have changed. But when, years ago, I taught at the university in this atmospheric old town, I could not find anybody prepared at night, to pass his arm through the hole in the wall of its famous haunted tower.

Fears of the supernatural are more closely associated with night and darkness than with daytime. Of interest in this connection are some of the autobiographical writings of Jung (1961) about his travels in Africa. He was impressed by the very great cheerfulness of the people in the villages, despite their poverty. But with the onset of night and darkness this cheerfulness would vanish. Then emerged anxiety and fears projected, as it were, into the invisible surroundings. With dawn a happier attitude towards the environment returned. As Jung in his travels moved northwards towards Egypt he began to understand better how the sun itself had become an object or symbol of worship. Fears of the night are commonplace outside Africa and projections of imagination imagery into the darkness have much to do with often related superstitious beliefs and avoidance rituals. Imagery has also its contributions to make in daylight under conditions of full wakefulness.

FACTS AND PAST EVENTS

Psychologists share with lawyers and historians a longstanding interest in the problem of establishing the facts about a past event. Selective perception and selective remembering create many difficulties: both interact with imagery and imagination. In telling an anecdote with supernatural overtones there can be a strong tendency to dramatize, with resulting distortion of detail. As the psychologist Wilhelm Stern put it, 'remembrance rapidly becomes personal mythology.' Many myths have accumulated about some of the better-known stories that involve mystery and suggestions of supernatural happenings. Consider for example the famous ghost ship, the *Marie Celeste*, found drifting in the Atlantic without captain or crew. There never was, in fact, a *Marie Celeste*. But there was a *Mary Celeste* found in this way on 5 December 1872 between the Azores and Lisbon. Having twice sailed over this area

I confess to momentarily scanning the horizon and nearby sea for supernatural or other non-existent things that were offered as explanations of the mystery. Much of the detail that those who prefer other explanations are asked to explain proves, on examination, to be as imaginary as the things that happened to Coleridge's Ancient Mariner. Fiction accumulated around the mystery, being first contributed by Conan Doyle, whose short story published in 1884 added details allegedly provided by a 'survivor', and introduced the name *Marie Celeste* for the ship. His explanation involved mutiny and murder of the captain by the crew. In 1904 another writer provided a sea-monster explanation, and the following year a 'message in a bottle' found beside a skeleton on an island was added. In 1913 and again in 1931 appeared other tales from alleged survivors, and in 1926 an astrology magazine claimed that the crew had been 'dematerialized'. There had in fact been three months of proceedings of a court of inquiry in Gibraltar, and at this the imagery and lively imagination of the Gibraltar Attorney General had made its contribution. Careful examination of the ship by an official admiralty surveyor had resulted in discovery of a sword that appeared to have been smeared with blood. Subsequent forensic tests of this, and of other scrapings of alleged blood, revealed that it was in fact rust. This evidence was suppressed. There is very much less to explain about the mystery than the legends that grew up would suggest. Imagery about fictional details had made many contributions. There was no half-eaten meal with still warm cups of tea in the cabin of Captain Briggs, nor an open bottle of cough mixture, nor half-smoked sailors' pipes, and certainly no chicken still cooking in a pot! Imaginative fiction was helped by the belief that the ship's boat was still on board. In fact it was not, suggesting a perfectly natural avenue of departure from the ship, possibly because of danger of explosion from the cargo of commercial alcohol. It seems improbable that the crew would have drunk this unpalatable liquid and then murdered the captain: also improbable – though this was suggested – is their all being hauled overboard by some giant octopus. Details were added, with demands for their explanation, despite the more mundane possibility of departure in the absent ship's boat.

What after all is an event? Events that require explanations are going on all the time. Some reach the newspapers, some the history books, and some – with added detail – become allegedly supernatural 'happenings'. Here we encounter what has been called in psychology 'the gatekeeper'. Reporters, editors, and others who decide what is 'the news' – to be noticed, reported, and recorded – are gatekeepers. Selective observers are gatekeepers who open or close the gate on information about things they notice. So also was the caliph who destroyed the books and library of Alexandria in Egypt. There is in fact a whole chain of gate-keepers between events, newspaper selection, reports, mention in books, and ultimate passage into history. Sources of distortion at every stage are numerous. They include misperception, prejudice, gross over-simplification, plain lying, misremembering, dramatization, and censorship. One event which has certainly passed into the history books – though we are still far from understanding what actually happened – was the assassination of President Kennedy: it achieved at the time world-wide attention, and also resulted in what has come to be known as the 'flashbulb effect'. Because of its emotional importance, even after a long period of time people can still recall what they were doing when they first heard the news. Let me contrast with this another undoubted event: something that really happened. It took place at Brisbane, Australia, in late November 1986. During a visit to that city the Pope escaped an apparent assassination attempt. A man called Richard McLaughlin, aged 24, recently discharged from a psychiatric hospital, was apprehended. He had with him a box containing five bottles filled with petrol with which he had planned to kill the Pope because 'he has too much money' (*Independent*, 27 November 1986). Had this attempt succeeded this would have resulted in world-wide interest and the man concerned would have become at least as well known or infamous as Lee Harvey Oswald. What is, and what is not, a major crime may be largely a matter of accident, or in this case of vigilance on the part of the Australian police. Because it didn't happen it seems eccentric even to record McLaughlin's name.

Let me be even more eccentric about 'events'. Some are un-important to others, yet may be noticed by individuals. Thus on Wednesday 17 September 1986 I was in the garden awaiting the arrival of the postman. I had a premonition about a desirable item arriving in the mail. A spider was about to pounce on a trapped fly: my momentary impulse to save it was too late. This mattered to the fly and the spider, though less to me. Then about 11.30, while still waiting, I found a four-leaf clover. The mail arrived, without the hoped-for item, though it contained a cheque which is always welcome. As regards coincidence of events, a hit or a miss? Had my premonition, or the lucky clover, or death – of the fly – in my vicinity anything to do with it? My belief is 'no'. I've been in aeroplanes with premonitions that they were going to crash, but they didn't. But the next day, at approximately 11.20 a.m., the hoped-for item arrived by the mail. Again, a hit or a miss? And as regards time or date, how chronologically precise are premonitions? When hits occur – or with imagining around them, seem to occur – such trivial events are remembered. The will to believe in the occult and supernatural is vigilant, and ready to pounce. In this area imagined 'events' are bad enough. Actual events are numerous and mostly forgotten. Imagining around the coincidence of two actual occurrences also creates numerous opportunities for subjective verification that a 'hit' has in fact occurred.

Next we encounter the 'acceptable evidence' problem. On what basis are we prepared to accept something as having actually happened? If the event is probable we accept it on relatively little evidence. The reader will probably accept my spider and fly incident on my mere assertion that it happened. They would be likely to reject my added assertion if I said that the spider remarked to me that 'it was a particularly tasty fly.' Apparent violations of nature of this kind invite scepticism, whatever the authority. David Hume, in his well-known discussion of miracles, expressed his own conviction about 'the knavery and folly' of human beings rather than in violations of nature. Yet Hume himself as an historian, despite his scepticism, was prepared to accept the traditional Tudor-biassed history of the many crimes of King Richard III. This we have all heard about from, among others, Sir Thomas More who, though a Tudor courtier, as a canonized saint must be trusted? It has emerged that the much-maligned king's reputation has suffered from the biassed history written about him by the Tudors, his political enemies. As one investigator has put it, the king thus emerged as an archetypal villain, 'a caricature of a human being which the genius of Shakespeare embalmed and mummified' (Potter 1983: 144). But perhaps Potter, as Chairman of the Richard III Society, is himself biassed though – for what it is worth – I add that my own looking into Thomas More's writings suggest that the hunchback was, as Potter puts it, 'a figment of Thomas More's fertile imagination'. In this and other aspects of the story Shakespeare drew heavily on More's work. Richard III will concern us in a later section, but of interest is some of the other information about him – retold by Shakespeare – that we learn from St Thomas. We may be disposed to accept the physical deformity, but what of the information, again recounted by Shakespeare from his earlier source, that he spent two years in the womb, and finally emerged from it with long hair and a full set of teeth? Together with the authority and integrity of those who relate such things, involved are also issues of probability and limits of credibility. The psychology of sentiments and bias on the one hand, and our elementary knowledge of biology and embryology on the other, seem to be relevant. Because they possess and use a robust frame of reference in relation to the allegedly supernatural it has often been stage magicians from whom we have had to learn. From Harry Houdini through to James Randi there have been many such people professionally sensitized to human gullibility and techniques of deception. It is, for example, easier to 'saw in half' a woman who later emerges whole and smiling if the act involves not one but two women. Magicians know all about how to make people believe objects can vanish, or appear out of thin air, or that spoons can be bent by will-power. Such things don't happen though, undoubtedly, forks and spoons can be bent in the ordinary way with physical force. Marks and Kammann (1977; 1980) have shown distraction of the attention of an audience or having a ring on one's finger helps in performances of spoon-bending. Both psychologists themselves became skilled in this aspect of stage magic. A professional magician once explained to me, 'people will say you did so and so.' He added, 'I didn't. It is physically impossible, but that's what they thought they saw me do.'

Controlled experiments in telepathy and clairvoyance are one thing. They are likely to continue to interest mathematicians and students of probability for a long time. Uncontrolled demonstrations are something quite different. If an audience of people is asked to draw a simple geometrical shape or some object and 'send it by telepathy' certain regularities of choice occur. These are called 'population stereotypes'. In the simplest case of geometrical figures, or two such figures, we encounter possibilities like a circle, triangle, or a square, and a limited number of other such drawings. The stage magician will 'receive correctly' some of these sendings from 'those who have these telepathic powers'. In other words he chooses from among the limited number of alternatives, and his choice agrees with some members of his audience. The others, it is sad, lack these psychic powers! In the case of figures inside sealed envelopes there are other techniques. Moreover, as regards what are 'hits' and what 'misses', subjective verification of 'hits' is often involved.

Consider the actual phenomena of what happens in the case of the visions in crystal-gazing. To my regret I have never personally experienced it, not even during experiments with hallucinogens. But on the evidence available I accept is occurrence in others as some kind of projection of visual imagery. On several occasions in experiments conducted by John Smythies at Cambridge I did experience, from flashings of a stroboscope on to a glass screen, hallucinatory phenomena resembling hypnagogic imagery, but never crystal visions. In what respects are the two kinds of projected imagery similar and different? And do people 'really see' visions in a crystal globe? On several occasions I have experimented on this with different people. One occasion involved a 'reliable' psychologist colleague, who described her visions as being like a photograph held up against the crystal and seen from the other side. Absence of the supernatural also disposes me to accept the testimony of a responsible elderly lady I know, who as a young woman was offered a lift in a car by two people. They said, 'But you'll have to share the back seat with Fenella.' She did, exhibiting some courage, as Fenella was a tiger! There was such a friendly tiger in the Yorkshire town she lived in, and children used to play with it; a book documents this seemingly improbable pet that lived in a field (Overend 1977). Documentation and testimony of others gives plausibility to the incident. Testimony of one or more 'reliable' people is something we rely on in absence of 'evidence of our own eyes'. Normality, and not being subject to hallucination, are also valued.

Yet a famous study, a 'census of hallucinations', investigated a total of 17,000 people. The question was asked: 'Have you ever, when believing yourself to be completely awake, had a vivid impression of seeing, or being touched by a living being, or hearing a voice, which impression, so far as you could discover, was not due to any external cause?' It will be noted that the question explicitly excluded hypnagogic, hypnopompic, or dream experiences, and also excluded other than visual, auditory, or tactile types of hallucination. (Sidgwick 1894). The investigations resulted in the answer 'yes' from 9.9 per cent of the respondents described as 'sane persons' of 21 years of age or older. The conditions under which hallucinations occur are very numerous. I suspect that with stroboscopes, sensory deprivation, hypnotism, or hallucinogenic substances they could be produced in virtually anybody. Among the circumstances in which they occur are spontaneously, sometimes, in full wakefulness, in apparently normal people. Galton's early investigation (1883) of 'visionaries' and their experiences resulted in numerous cases of daylight visions being reported by many responsible people. These included scientists and editors of influential newspapers. In addition to the experiences themselves as pseudo-perceptions are other relevant factors. They include report after passage of time, memory, and exaggerations of testimony. Much interest in recent years has turned to eidetic imagery: vivid and stable imagery which creates criterion problems in distinguishing it from 'hallucination' (e.g. Ahsen 1965; Marks and McKellar 1982, with peer comments by other psychologists). In occurrence of hallucination and related phenomena among 'normal' people we may well find subject matter for very critical evaluation of the 'with my own eyes' kind of testimony about the seemingly supernatural.

Apparitions are closely associated with night and darkness; conditions which favour misperception when drowsiness may also play a part. There are exceptions, to which Green and McCreery (1975) draw attention, involving daytime and full wakefulness. In considering apparitions in their possible relationship to eidetic and hallucinatory forms of imagery, these investigators introduce a concept which may have some explanatory power. This is 'metachoric experiences'. They point out that eidetic or hallucinatory images usually appear to be in some way superimposed on the normal environmental surroundings. Elsewhere I discussed one famous example, namely the figure of the 'Ancient of Days', which appeared to William Blake 'above the stairs' of his house (McKellar 1957). Eventually he decided to record it, a well-known work of art. Along with such visionary apparitions with this quality of superimposition, Celia Green and her colleagues argue that something different may occur. They use their term 'metachoric experiences for hallucinatory experiences in which the whole of the visual field is replaced by an hallucinatory one'. In this they add that this hallucinated background may 'provide a close imitation of the actual physical environment' (Green and Leslie 1987: 67). There seem to be parallels in other kinds of subjective experiences. It may be suggested that very frequently during sleep we have imagery of a prosaic kind of a familiar setting in which strange dreamlife events take place. In fact this is a very common experience. Yet the background itself, not less than the dream happenings, is just as much 'hallucinated'. The concept of metachoric experiences introduces this mechanism into wakefulness also. At the Oxford Institute of Psychophysical Research there has been a longstanding interest in apparitions. From the numerous cases available to Celia Green as its director, it is of interest that this new concept should have emerged. A classification is also offered of three different types of apparition: being seen 'in mid air', seen as 'projected on to some flat surface', and seen 'within some variety of frame' (Green and Leslie, op. cit.: 71). On the basis of the collection of cases examined at the institute it is argued that at least some of them are of this metachoric kind. 'The entire environment seen ... may be hallucinatory, not just the apparitional element' (op. cit.: 69). A naturalistic explanation is thus advanced.

SCIENCE AND THE SUPERNATURAL

It is a sobering fact that in the world of the twentieth century naturalistic interpretation of human illnesses is probably the exception. Other interpretations prevail. Here we encounter what might be called the 'History–Geography Principle'. It is that we can readily study beliefs and practices of past history by travelling in the modern world, within the geography of the present. Anthropology has much to contribute to this from Africa, India, the Caribbean, and elsewhere. Later I will return to this in connection with the generation differences between younger people and parents in the American Southwest. They told of how, in their own Spanish-speaking homes, they first had learned about mental illness in terms of possession, the evil eye, and witchcraft. By now most were themselves sceptical from their school and university education. Yet such beliefs remain widespread in remote villages of the American Southwest. In this they are not alone. In the United Kingdom, as elsewhere in Europe, we regularly encounter astrology and horoscopes in many daily newspapers. On a visit to India I found, in the lobby of a hotel in Calcutta, the resident astrologer at work. He was advising a young couple from his knowledge of the stars about the best date for their wedding. Soon afterwards I was in England. In the newspapers and in morning television programmes I encountered similar advice being given to the local people on how to conduct their lives and affairs. As regards Africa, in the mid-1980s I was reading a newspaper – one which omits an astrology column – and a report on how even civil servants in a country where witchcraft prevails often use charms as protections. Others, guerrillas fighting tribal wars, would protect themselves with tattoo on the skin; the blood and liver of a chicken that has been strangled is also considered particularly effective for very dangerous missions (Mary Fitzgerald, writing from Nairobi, *Independent*, 28 November 1986). The article also discussed voodoo and zombies in Africa. And I read all this just after watching London Television's zodiac-based advice.

Africa and India are not all that unique, but the widespread beliefs about witchcraft and fear of malevolent magic to be found in Africa have some less obvious side-effects. Writing of his work as a forensic scientist during the Second World War in the country that was then Rhodesia, John Thompson (1980) refers to one of these. Because of such fears villagers are careful about disposing of anything associated with themselves, including the waste products of their own bodies. These could be used in witchcraft. In this anxiety 'never to leave lying around anything which might be used to harm him' the villager will accordingly relieve himself in streams and rivers. Thus bilharzia and other widespread water-borne parasitic illnesses infect water which is used for washing and drinking (Thompson op. cit.: 24). Thompson assesses this as one of the less obvious evil effects of tribal beliefs and fears of magic.

Consider another part of the modern world. Of great interest is 'kuru', a condition found in remote parts of mountainous New

Guinea. This physical and mental illness I first heard about when, as secretary of a university open forum society, I invited our newly appointed Vice-Chancellor to speak to it. Our committee anticipated a competent but dull account on some subject like 'The future of universities'. Instead our speaker, (Dr) Sir Hugh Robson, spoke about 'Medicine and witchcraft'. During his time in New Guinea Dr Robson heard from local people that kuru, with its characteristic tremor and mental deterioration, is caused by malevolent magic. He responded by a challenge: prove the theory by giving me kuru. An image of him was made, placed in a rippling stream, and as it trembled in the ripples appropriate incantations were said over it. Despite this he survived. At the time he and his medical co-workers accepted an alternative explanation of kuru as a genetically determined condition: its confinement to certain specific areas seemed to support this. Both this naturalistic explanation and its supernatural alternative proved to be wrong. Transmission of the disease was neither by witchcraft nor genes, but occurred in other ways. Kuru is caused by a slow virus as happens also in a somewhat similar condition, scrapie, which affects sheep. Residual cannibalism in some of the remote parts of New Guinea helps in this transmission. Kuru represents an interesting stance of rival attempts to understand the unknown by supernatural and naturalistic explanations.

In such explanations what I have called the William James Principle – namely a reminder of the importance of the biological organism – applies. In the well-developed and richer parts of the world the advent of antibiotics has contributed also to mental health. Important have been treatments with them that have largely removed the bacteriological causes of one psychiatric scourge of the past, GPI or general paralysis of the insane. But bacteria, virus, and – as we have seen – parasitic infections remain major problems in many countries. All three have considerable bearing on illnesses that are often given supernatural explanations. Take one example. An article published in 1987 discusses one people, the Yanomami Indians, who survive in a remote part of Brazil. They, it is reported, engage in 'constant inter-group warfare' that results from raids to avenge sickness among tribal leaders. This is attributed by the Indians themselves to 'witchcraft by rival groups'. The investigator concludes that 'the true cause is almost always white epidemics' (Richard House, *Independent*,

191

19 February 1987). At an earlier period introduced diseases did much to destroy the idyllic culture of the South Seas. Consider a more contemporary problem, the virus infection that has become a problem of world-wide concern in the mid-1980s. Its origins are attributed to Africa. In 1986 a heterogeneous group of people got together in Africa to consider the Acquired Immune Deficiency Syndrome, or AIDS. Present were scientifically trained medical men and also traditional African healers, including witchdoctors. Various explanations were offered. 'It's probably the work of wizards,' was one opinion. Some attributed it to animals that had become infected and had spread the disease to humans through polluted water. Some – understandably in a continent where there are several such diseases – regarded it as caused by the bite of the mosquito. The meeting also included virologists, who seem to have successfully convinced some of those with alternative explanations, of causation by a known virus.

It has been well said that – because of payload problems and for other reasons – the only commodity worth trading in outer space is not gold but information. Advances in computing science and with them video and audio-tapes already offer much health information. Thus in a more developed and richer country like the United Kingdom, by the mid-1980s there is now 'Healthcall'. This provides recorded information on some 300 topics relating to health, includng neuroses, psychoses, and many other such topics. For example, the tape on schizophrenia refers to it as 'a group of conditions'. (Bleuler, who cointed the term, likewise wrote of 'the schizophrenias' in the plural.) Although the tape I heard does not deflate the widespread confusion with multiple personality it does contain much relevant information. With this is reassurance to the many young people who, in the course of their development, think they have 'got schizophrenia' when, in fact, they haven't. The *Healthcall Directory* that is available lists, on my assessment, fifty-four subjects relating directly to mental health problems, and dozens of others of more marginal relevance.

INDIANS OF THE AMERICAS

The American Southwest – Arizona and New Mexico – has interested me for many decades. In the vicinity of Santa Fe, capital of the state of New Mexico, are many Indian pueblos; and further west we encounter the nomadic Navajo in their reservation. It is paradoxical that we know more about the religion, ceremonies, and healing rites of the Navajo than of the pueblo or village-dwelling Indians. In pueblos like Taos or Zuni we may as visitors attend certain ceremonies. But there are others. What goes on in the kivas, the underground meeting houses of the villages, remains in many respects mysterious. On my second-last visit to Taos I found the pueblo closed for the day to non-Indians. Ceremonies were going on, in this case above ground. The village was open in its usual way on the day following.

Quite a lot is known about Navajo psychopathology. In his discussion of 'Indian America' Highwater (1976) lists five types of widely accepted supernatural causal agencies. They are: breaking taboos, being possessed by evil forces, loss of soul, witchcraft, and invasion of the body by some alien force. Diagnosis is by a 'hand trembler' who ascertains the cause of the malady and recommends the appropriate treatment. As Highwater explains, from the movements of his hand and arm he will 'locate illness much as a divining rod is said to indicate the location of water' (op. cit.: 225). Among the taboos whose violation may bring physical or mental illness are some that relate to bears, some to knives, and one particularly strong taboo to snakes in proximity to fires. Outdoor fires are of importance to these nomadic people, as of course are poisonous creatures like rattlesnakes and Gila monsters. The much-maligned large 'tarantula' spiders also found are harmless despite their reputation. Navajo psychiatric conditions include forms of psychosis that resemble the schizophrenias found elsewhere. Seizures resembling epileptic or hysterical fits appear to be common. Though having antagonized a witch or breaking a taboo may have been thought responsible, the actual agent is of a different kind. The conditions are known as 'moth sickness', and are thought of in this physical way. It is believed that a moth has entered the brain. As it moves about it induces movements of the body of its victim, thus producing the convulsions. Since the moth is naturally attracted to fire it can happen that the sufferer, during his seizure, will throw himself into it. Vigilance to prevent this is necessary. Methods of treatment among the Navajo include physical ways of handling possession by spirits. The techniques of trephination involve making an incision in the brain area to release something, perhaps evil spirits. Archaeological evidence indicates these have a long history. One Navajo patient told me of how a sharp arrow-head had been inserted into his skull – he showed me the mark – to secure such release. He had himself come to reject this kind of primitive psycho-surgery and more orthodox was the treatment he was receiving in the New Mexico hospital where we talked together.

Navajo therapy takes the form of a ceremony called a 'sing', with community involvement, drums, a professional specialist, and the making of sand-paintings. There are different types of sings, all involving expenditure that seems obviously thera-peutic in a morale-building way for the patient. Navajo sand-paintings – though visually very different – have some functional resemblance to the vèvès of the Caribbean discussed earlier. Both are magical devices used to summon the help of spiritual forces; both are accompanied by rhythmic drum-beating. Music plays its part, with chanting and dancing. Among the pueblos Cochiti is famous for the drums it makes. My only visit to Cochiti pueblo was rather disappointing. Although I was introduced to a witch, regarded as a respected member of the community, my hosts entertained me in their home. We watched baseball on television! Such aspects of visits to different cultures are often not men-tioned. Yet despite outward things much that is different from 'western' daily life goes on. The famous mid-winter ceremony, the Shalako of Zuni pueblo, is a reminder of the surrounding atmosphere of sincere belief in the supernatural. On one occasion I had the privilege of attending. At sunset the various Kachina gods arrived, portrayed by men in elaborate and colourful masks. Throughout the night the Shalako, equipped in tall masks of a bird-shaped kind, dance in buildings specially constructed for the occasion.

There were two dancers to each of the Shalako masks. Because of the height of these bird-like masks the dancers, 7 or 8 feet tall, towered over the watching audience. The dancers are taboo and must not be touched. Photography is of course forbidden, as also – I learned to my cost – is consulting a book. At one stage the copy of Ruth Benedict's *Patterns of Culture* I was surreptitiously glanc-ing at was noticed, and confiscated by the Zuni police! (I retrieved it in the morning.) The ceremony – which is attended by Indians from Navajo reservations and from other pueblos, dressed in

Figure 9.1   Shalako masked dancer
At the Shalako in Zuni pueblo, photography of the dancing and of the various
Kachina who take part is strictly forbidden.

colourful turquoise beads and bracelets – is impressive. So also is the hospitality of the Zuni, who feed their guests and the Kachina dancers through the night with bread, mutton, and much coffee. The carved Kachina dolls, that visitors associate particularly with Zuni pueblo of New Mexico and the Hopi Indians of Arizona, perform a specific function. These wood carvings, which portray the scores of different Kachina spirits, are used to teach the pueblo children the theology of their very complex system of religion.

Some Indian ceremonies perform therapeutic functions. Others like the Shalako have a different purpose. As regards therapy in relation to psychiatric conditions, or other medical problems, we encounter an important principle. There are, in any treatment, numerous uncontrolled variables, and a person may be recovering anyway. The principle is that the success of a therapy does not prove the theory – naturalistic or supernatural – on which that therapy is based. In the 'West' we know far too little about even such things as acupuncture, to say nothing of therapeutic ceremonies like the many 'sings' in all their variety. Writing of her related work in Trinidad and Tobago, Colleen Ward – as a cross-cultural psychologist – refers to the many things which play their part in therapeutic rituals. She refers to sensory bombardment, including chanting, slapping, and stroking; sensory deprivation; and also 'hypnopompic, hypnagogic and trance states' that evoke upsurges of mental imagery. She underlines the importance not only of these but of 'recognition and prestige, and the support and encouragement by the community [which] also affords psychological benefits for the participants' (Ward 1983: 19–20). In Navajo sings, and other such therapeutic rituals, she suggests 'a cross-cultural perspective may assist in understanding relationships between dissociative states and mental health' (op. cit.: 20).

Universities of the American Southwest, as elsewhere, have their departments of psychology. Those who have worked in them – as I have done twice – will have encountered many students of Spanish-American cultural background. In the home it is Spanish which is the spoken language. Important are generation differences and belief on matters relating to psychopathology. It has been well said that it is possible to study sixteenth-century Spain in the remote mountain villages of New Mexico. From Spanish-American students I learned about some of the distinctions traditionally made in the area of supernatural causes. Physical or mental illnesses called '*malefico*' are the result of witchcraft, malevolent magic used against the victim. By contrast is '*mal oje*', which involves the 'evil eye'. This may be inflicted unintentionally upon a child, resulting in sudden changes in its personality or well-being. Other causal factors my informants were brought up with in their homes included 'punishment by God'. Forces of nature, including for example eclipses, could also have effects on mental health. On the more physical side we encounter '*enceno*', which involves the festering of wounds caused unintentionally by specific individuals known as '*enconadores*'. In this area of the United States we meet architecture – a composite adobe type – which is a blend of influences, Spanish, Indian and 'Anglo'. Similarly composite are surviving traditional beliefs and attitudes relating to matters of health. As regards differences between generations, the problems of adjustment for younger people like my informants are well summarized by the comment of one such student. At the university he would speak and be taught in English. On return to his home it would be necessary for him to communicate with his parents, and also younger siblings, in Spanish. Not merely language, but different concepts and systems of belief provide their problems in this dual existence. Another type of problem of adjustment was somewhat of a surprise. One graduate student told me about his Navajo student room-mate. They shared their accommodation amicably. But, the young Navajo student explained to him, such a room-sharing, though possible with an 'Anglo', would not have been possible with another Navajo. Both of them would have been perpetually anxious about supernatural happenings, including fears of witchcraft.

The American continent, like Europe, Asia and Africa, has through its plant life contributed to belief and imagination about the supernatural. In this area of inquiry the standpoint of naturalistic science is defended by the discipline that has come to be called ethnobotany (Efran 1967). This uses evidence from anthropology about customs in more remote parts of the world as a guide in search for plants used therapeutically or to produce altered states of consciousness. The Amazon and Orinoco rivers have proved particularly fruitful areas of study by ethnobotanists. To illustrate, a number of hallucinogenic substances used as snuff by South American Indians have been found and now have a known pharmacology. Again from a particular vine found in Colombia a harmine alkaloid, caapi, has been studied by ethno-botanists in terms of its 'fantasy enhancing' properties (e.g. Naranjo 1987). The work of Schultes (1966) indicates that in addition to substances used since the time of the Aztecs, many more hallucinogenic substances of botanical origin remain to be found. It may be stressed that a given plant may contain more than one imagery-inducing substance. Also of interest is the fact that among the known hallucinogenic alkaloids are several – harmine is one of them – that share a similar chemical structural formula. Thus we have at least the beginnings of scientific understanding of at least one aspect of the biochemical basis of visual hallucination. Among the known hallucinogens one in particular will be examined in fuller detail.

PEYOTE AND MESCALINE

The Native American Church was established in Oklahoma in the later part of last century by the Cherokees. Central to its religious rituals was taking peyote to induce visions and mystical states of consciousness. It was about this time that researchers like Prentiss and Morgan (1895), Weir Mitchell (1896) and Havelock Ellis (1897) became interested in experiments with this hallucinogen. Mescaline is the main active principle of peyote or 'mescal buttons', dried pieces of a specific cactus, *Lophophora williamsii* (formerly known as *Anhalonium lewinii*). The hallucinogen was one of several known to the Aztecs of Mexico but may have come from still earlier civilizations, Mayan, Zapodec, or Toltec. A principal effect of mescaline, whether of botanical origin or in synthetic form, is a huge upsurge of vivid imagery. As Havelock Ellis puts it, mescaline produces an 'orgy of vision'. There are other effects also, to be considered in the following chapter. This small and rather nondescript plant, the 'dumpling cactus', has powerful influences on consciousness. Because of these it has been used for religious, scientific, or other purposes, and also widely misused, over a long period of time. The monograph by Klüver (1928) has probably been influential on others, as well as myself, in stimulat-ing researches that explore possible ways of producing a 'model psychosis' in normal people.

Various medicinal properties have been attributed to mescaline or peyote, but main uses among the American Indians in Oklahoma's tepees or Navajo hogans have been religious rather than therapeutic. From the reports available it is clear that the taking of mescal buttons in an American Indian ceremony is a solemn and dignified matter, and in no sense any kind of orgy. Obviously many things are different when peyote or other hallucinogenic substances are taken in an Indian religious ceremony, and when their usage is in a laboratory scientific experiment. Unfortunately, in recent years, perhaps dating from the publication by Aldous Huxley of a mescaline experiment on himself, controversies surrounding misuses of hallucinogens and other substances have created difficulties for both religious and scientific uses in this field. One specific phenomenon that occurs with mescaline, lysergic acid diethylamide, psilocybin, and probably other hallucinogens may be mentioned. It is the strong sense of what might be called 'free floating certainty' that some people encounter. Dogmatic certainty seeking a subject-matter may attach itself to one or other feature of the hallucinogen experience. Sometimes it assumes a quasi-mystical form as a sense of significance, of grasping or nearly grasping an understanding, at last, of 'truth', 'time', 'reality', or something else. The term *presque vu* refers to the impression of being on the edge of, but not quite achieving, such a realization. Under the influence of mescaline, there may be a strong conviction that the barriers that ordinarily divide specific things are mere illusion. All is one great spiritual unity. A world is seen, as Blake would have it, 'in a grain of sand'. It is possible to see the appeal of this kind of experience to American Indian religious traditions, like the notion of a great world spirit expressing itself through nature and natural forces. Hallucinogen experiences are not all of this kind and, on the whole, individual differences between people tend to have been under-emphasized. Some people simply don't think in these ways. Neither mescaline, nitrous oxide, alcohol, nor anything else will evoke any kind of mysticism in them.

But mystical or not, the phenomenon of certainty often seems to occur. It may be related to the belief some psychologists, including myself, have that hallucinogens can contribute to our understanding of psychosis. As we have seen, Mavromatis (1987) has expressed the view that in hypnagogia we have probably the only naturally occurring state of consciousness through which non-psychotic people can gain 'an insight into the nature of insanity' (op. cit.: 160). Earlier I have argued that artificially created states, like those produced by nitrous oxide or through hypnotism, may make parallel contributions to such understanding. Hallucinogens provide another line of inquiry, especially into the thought processes of schizophrenia. Such parallels will be considered in chapters to follow, though first it is necessary to give attention to perhaps the most central and complex of all conditions that concern abnormal psychology and psychiatry. It is here that we encounter schizophrenia, or perhaps 'the schizophrenias'.

SUMMARY

1 The question arises of the extent to which we can explain the supernatural in terms of the principles of normal and abnormal psychology. Here we encounter problems of memory and testimony as regards 'the facts' of a past evnt. And what, in any case, is 'an event'?

2 The acceptable evidence issue is considered with reference to imagery and hallucination, phenomena like crystal-gazing, and concepts like the notion of 'metachoric experiences'. Interpretation of physical and mental illness in terms of witchcraft is not a matter of the seventeenth century. In accord with the History–Geography Principle, it is very much part of the modern world.

3 Illustrations are taken from Africa and other places, but a more detailed consideration is given to the interpretations and beliefs of Indians and others in the American Southwest. Other cultures have their methods of treatment, and rituals like Navajo Indian sings may have their own therapeutic value.

4 Among Indians of the Americas we encounter the uses of substances of botanical origin with hallucinogenic properties. One of these substances, mescaline, has been used experimentally for other purposes. It will particularly concern us in our approach to the schizophrenias in terms of 'model psychoses'.

Chapter Ten

THE SCHIZOPHRENIAS

The schizoid does not get on in a crowd. The pane of glass is always there.

Kretschmer

Mescaline produces every single major symptom of acute schizophrenia, though not always to the same degree.

Osmond and Smythies

Unpredictability characterizes the schizophrenias. Traditionally psychosis is assessed as involving 'lack of insight'. Yet even here the schizophrenic is unpredictable. I have talked with many patients who have described lucidly the 'voices' they hear, and sometimes also their visual hallucinations. Some have even kept diaries of these upsurges of autonomous imagery. Such insight is difficult to maintain all the time. Delusions may also be accompanied by a degree of insight sometimes resembling half-belief rather than full beliefs. Unpredictability of emotion; oddities of thought, like 'the knight's move of the schizophrenic'; and unexpected impulsive actions become understandable if we can penetrate the 'pane of glass' to reach subjective experience. In terms of Mowrer's (1950) analogy, the personality, a walled city, has fallen to invasion: within consciousness there is loss of central control by the ego or self system. Anarchy has taken over. Systems of thought, feeling, and impulse go their own way, creating fantasies in which auditory and visual hallucinations largely replace perception of external realities. Consider as an example one of Jung's patients, an intelligent man, an archaeologist by profession. During progress towards recovery he was able to report retrospectively about what Jung describes as 'being in the chaos of an overmastering dream'. During his period of active psychosis the patient declared 'the world was out of joint, everywhere conflagrations, volcanic earthquakes ... enormous battles.' He found himself in the midst of it, defending himself: the external accompaniments of this were impulsive violence towards the hospital staff. Following two episodes the patient made a good recovery. As Jung puts it, 'gradually the gate of the underworld became closed' to him (Quoted in McDougall 1926: 379).

After discussing this patient, McDougall sides with Jung's view that such a psychosis resembles a waking nightmare. 'Schizophrenia is a dream state, a prolonged half-waking dream or fantasy.' He adds, 'as in sleep he has lost contact with the world about him' (McDougall, op. cit.: 380). In the light of the intensive studies by Mavromatis (1987) of hypnagogia, of interest are McDougall's further comments that such a patient's 'state is one between day-dreaming and night-dreaming' (op. cit.: 380). Mavromatis agrees that some schizophrenics 'find themselves locked in terrifying "nightmares" ', and goes on to suggest that 'hypnagogic and schizophrenic experiences may at times be indistinguishable phenomenologically' (op. cit.: 184). Mavromatis elaborates on the resemblance between the schizophrenias – he employs the plural – and hypnagogia. His argument is that 'practically all of the schizophrenic thought disturbances are encountered in hypnagogia' (op. cit.: 163). He cites numerous investigators in support of this view. In the more frightening kinds of hypnagogic and hypnopompic imagery, nightmares, and anxiety dreams, we can find empathy bridges between psychosis and normal mental life. As regards the subjective experiences of patients like the one considered, a distinction may be made between active episodes of psychosis and their aftermath. In interviews I have often found it desirable to use the past tense even with an only partially recovered patient. During therapy in the aftermath attempts may be made to reconstruct the personality by examining with the patient what has previously happened and trying to make sense of it. In periods of active psychosis a patient may himself seek to find an explanation and in doing so may develop delusions of influence from outside, or of persecution.

The same dominance of mental life by upsurges of A-thinking described by contemporary patients is to be found in earlier times. One great pioneer of modern psychiatry, Esquirol, writes of such patients: 'sensibility is exalted, or perverted ... no longer in relation with external or internal impressions. They seem to be the sport of the errors of their illusions' (Esquirol 1845: 318). He illustrates with one of his cases, an officer aged about 46 who had suffered disappointments in the army. One morning in Paris he persuaded himself that rebels had entered the city and threatened the government. He stationed himself on the Louis XVI bridge ready to defend it, and proceeded to arrest those who sought to pass over it. When guards appeared, he proceeded to defend himself – like Jung's patient – and the bridge. Eventually he yielded, but only to numbers. In accord with the Koffka Principle there was a marked discrepancy between the reality of this struggle on the bridge, and his delusory belief and perception of it. Hallucinatory voices or visions may add their component of unpredictability, and provide apparent 'evidence' in support of delusions. As one patient, diagnosed schizophrenic, explained to me in interview, he would not only 'hear' but also 'see' people speak 'when they never said a word'. Despite his awareness of being subject to such hallucinations, such insight was difficult to maintain. The result was a number of attacks by him on others in response to imagined 'insults'.

PROBLEMS OF DIAGNOSIS AND INCIDENCE

Discussion of 'schizophrenia' involves some formidable problems of communication. The variety of subjective accompaniments is not easy to talk about in ordinary language, and patients them-selves sometimes invent their own words. These 'neologisms' with their highly private meanings, may become meaningful to others in detailed study of individual cases. Another very basic difficulty is that 'schizophrenia' almost certainly refers to more than one condition. Bleuler, himself, who introduced the diagnosis, used the word in the plural. The full title of his book, *Dementia Praecox, or the Group of Schizophrenias* in the 1950 English translation, accurately reflects Bleuler's own usage. Before Bleuler, Kraepelin's concept of 'dementia praecox' implied a probable basis of these related psychoses in the physical pathology of the organism. As Jenner and Damas-Mora (1989) have recently reminded us, both before and after Bleuler many have taken the view that here are 'essentially physical diseases'. These two investigators use 'schizophrenia' as a diagnostic term in the plural and in doing so take account of the relatively known biochemical differences in subtypes like periodic catatonia (e.g. Gjessing and Jenner 1976). Although modern researches would not necessarily make distinctions in the same places, earlier diagnostic constructs are still widely used to refer to sub-types of schizophrenia. Among them are 'hebephrenia' and 'catatonia', along with 'paranoid schizophrenia', although, as Langfeldt (1976: 496) has pointed out, 'the paranoid syndromes can appear in almost all types of psychosis.' These three categories are at least of classificatory use as 'types of schizophrenia' in trying to make sense of syndromes within the huge range of symptomatology encountered. One such sub-type may spontaneously or under treatment change into another, particularly in institutionalized long-stay patients. In interviews I have had opportunity to conduct in four different countries, I have repeatedly found that there can be little resemblance between the patient actually seen and the case-notes relating to past history of that individual's psychosis. With the perspective of their scholarly study of the history of psychiatry, Hunter and MacAlpine (1963) point out that 'similar cases present different symptoms at different times'. Moreover, they add, 'identical symptoms by no means imply identical pathology' (op. cit.: 744). Thus it may be noticed that a patient who enters the hospital in an agitated, fantasy-dominated state of defensive aggressiveness – like Esquirol's patient mentioned above – may later on be co-operative and communicative. He may have much to tell the interviewer about his delusory beliefs, which may in fact be the product of his way of making sense, to his own satisfaction, of his hallucinations and fantasy.

In variability, and changes through time that can occur, we cannot over-estimate the effects of the institution itself. Thus Warner (1985) emphasizes the similarity of 'many of the negative features of chronic schizophrenia' to the demoralization effects of long-term unemployment. He refers also to 'the clinical poverty of institutionalism' (op. cit.: 134). Earlier, Goffman (1961) had much to say about the grim realities of existing in a possibly locked ward of an institution, whether we call it an 'asylum', or 'mental', or 'psychiatric' hospital. Such 'living' virtually defines the opposite of the living conditions which would be willingly chosen by a rational person, or a patient able to summon up residual rationality.

With the numerous unknowns – psychological, genetic, biochemical, and pathological – that surround the schizophrenias it is not surprising that we find unpredictability in outcome, as elsewhere. Studies of prognosis usually show that about a third of patients thus diagnosed show recovery; another third reveal temporary remission but recurrence; and the remaining third persist without apparent cure. Such variability becomes meaningful in terms of basic pathology resulting from postmortem studies. From these a distinction has been made between 'positive' and 'negative' phenomena shown in schizophrenic mental life. On the positive side of this dichotomy are put hallucinations, delusions, and thought disorders. By contrast, on the negative side are marked intellectual deterioration, apathetic withdrawal, and flatness of emotion. In this second group Crow (1980) suggests we should look to cell loss and changes in brain structure, rather than biochemical causal factors. Seidman (1983) finds evidence of physical pathology in some of the schizophrenias consistent with such brain deterioration. He also reports on extreme variability in occurrence of brain rhythm EEG abnormalities in patients thus diagnosed. 'The schizophrenias' rather than 'schizophrenia' seems the more appropriate term for a whole range of probably very different conditions.

While next considering the varied forms of experience and behaviour that are reported in the schizophrenias, of note is the comment by Osmond and Smythies that heads this chapter. Their contention is that these phenomena can be produced experimentally by one specific chemical substance, the hallucinogen mescaline.

PHENOMENOLOGY OF THE SCHIZOPHRENIAS

Pathological variants of perception, thinking, belief, emotional life, and of speech are all encountered. A patient may be mute, apathetic, and withdrawn, or by contrast voluble and communicative about delusions and hallucinations. In this respect – despite Kretschmer – 'the pane of glass' is not always there. When a deluded patient begins to explain – about changes in his body image, his persecutors, or interference with his mind by improbable people or forces – what he has to say is often intellectually and emotionally disturbing, and a shock to any interviewer. Enormous significance may be attributed to trivial events, or innocent actions by others. Freud used the analogy of the 'medieval monk' who saw 'the finger of God' in everything that happened. On the other hand, speech may be a 'word salad' of seemingly disconnected phrases or may exhibit 'echolalia', like one such patient who monotonously kept on saying, 'yes, that's right, yes, that's right ...' Neologisms, either invented words or familiar words given strangely new meanings, may figure prominently in speech. By contrast the patient may remain mute. Such silence may result from a wide variety of reasons: preoccupation with inner fantasy and fear of imagined persecution are only two of many. Hallucinatory imagery, particularly of sounds, is a prominent characteristic. Yellowlees (1932) contends that in all schizophrenias there is hallucination some of the time, and in some patients all the time. Such imagery may be of voices of a depressing, nagging kind: as one patient reported to me, hers 'never said anything pleasant'! They may take the form of commands from God or some other spiritual agent, as in one such case, a divine command to 'go out and shoot somebody,' fortunately prevented in good time. Non-verbal hallucinations like sighs and grunts, or animal noises may be experienced. A running hallucinatory commentary on the doings of the patient may occur. Hallucinations may distort the environment of an enlightened psychiatric hospital into something resembling a grim concentration camp. They may be highly specific, as reported by Esquirol (1845), who records that some patients are unable to read 'because the letters appear to be mingled in a confused mass', resulting in inability 'to arrange them in such a manner as to form syllables and words' (op. cit.: 318). On several occasions in model psychoses experiments our subjects likewise reported this 'jumbled print' phenomenon. And sometimes words and letters, like other small objects, moved and seemed to 'crawl' about, or – as one subject put it – 'marched'. In the natural psychoses, as opposed to these experimentally produced analogues, hallucinations of taste and smell are also reported. These may have reference to the frequent claim that the hospital authorities, or others, are attempting 'to poison' the patient.

Along with these disorientating and alarm-inducing phenomena subjectively experienced are others. Among them can be amnesic gaps and a sense of discontinuity in the passage of time, or time itself may seem to elapse more rapidly or more slowly. It may be difficult or impossible for a patient to assess whether seconds or minutes have elapsed since he or she last spoke, or since some other event. The overall influence of autistic fantasy – which greatly interested Bleuler – helps to provide some understanding of the neglect and apathy towards environmental happenings. In these psychoses there is, as Bleuler emphasized, considerable alteration of processes of association. The extremely interesting consequences in the thought disorders of psychotic thinking will concern the next chapter. Within this huge range of schizophrenic phenomena, marked changes may occur at different times in a given patient. Thus we often find that what is recorded in the case-notes differs markedly from the actual experience and behaviour of a given patient in interview. Moreover, representatives of the 'classic' sub-types of the psychoses concerned may later change and exhibit a quite different sub-type. These nevertheless retain some use for the purposes of classification and as reference points.

TYPES OF SCHIZOPHRENIA

From among the numerous constructs of the past, 'catatonic', 'hebephrenic' and 'paranoid' survive. Emile Kraepelin (1856–1926) brought these together within his single category of 'dementia praecox'. Since Bleuler they have continued to be used, together with the addition of 'simple schizophrenia', as sub-types of the psychoses involved. From psychology we may take the traditional constructs of 'cognition, affection, and conation' as of some help in relation to these manifestations of the schizophrenias.

Paranoid schizophrenia involves, thought, belief, and cognition. Such patients exhibit delusory beliefs, and their readiness to talk about them is sometimes a feature. As in a different form of psychosis, 'true paranoia', the delusions may be persecutory or grandiose, and delusions of bodily change are also common. Delusions of influence may involve supernatural agencies, but nowadays very often reflect superstitious notions about popular science: telepathy or visitations from outer space may play their part. Sometimes hallucinations built round radio or television may feed such delusions. One such patient frequently received personal 'messages' from these sources. When they ceased she attributed this to intervention by her psychiatrist with the BBC. The delusory ideas and accompanying hallucinations of paranoid schizophrenia tend to be variable and bizarre: in this they differ from the well-systematized delusions, with absence of hallucination, of true paranoia. Conversation with the paranoid schizophrenic patient tends to be a fascinating experience. Psychologist interviewers are very likely to forget to do such mundane things as administer tests or ask questions they meant to put. With tact, reasonably good rapport is possible, and there is the strong impression that such a patient is mobilizing his cognitive resources to make sense of the subjective phenomena he is experiencing.

In hebephrenic schizophrenia it is affect, or emotion, that is the most striking variant from the normal. Here belong the unpredictable and inappropriate emotional responses, the strange grimaces and 'silliness' (in the sense that is different from 'stupid'), and echolalia. Communication with hebephrenic patients is largely impossible. Several times two such patients when observed together appear to be engaged in a 'conversation', but this is illusory. Both are speaking, but neither is socially responding or listening to the other. By drugs or other physical therapies it may be possible to transform the hebephrenic into another kind of schizophrenic reaction. Then rapport and some kind of communication becomes possible.

Catatonic schizophrenia is characterized by impulse, action, or inaction. Psychologically it is associated with the category of conation: overt action and accompanying volition and motivation. Patients in states of catatonic stupor are much rarer today and physical treatments are used to get them from this into other states as far as possible. It is grim to think about catatonics in parts of the world where begging on the one hand, and minimal facilities for psychiatric care on the other prevail. Even in relatively recent years I have seen some pretty distressing exercise yards and wards in hospitals in what are accepted as prosperous, as opposed to under-developed, countries. The catatonic is likely to be lying around, mute, withdrawn, seemingly out of touch with what is happening around him or her. In some places he or she may be, as also happens with severely sub-normal people, left with a begging bowl during the day, it and him or her being collected when night comes. It is important to remember in connection with these and other helpless people that dramatic recovery can occur. Physical treatments can be very effective. Seemingly absent of conscious awareness at the time, many such patients report nevertheless memory of the events, including both acts of kindness and brutality. In catatonia we also encounter – sometimes unexpectedly from a state of stupor – catatonic excitement. After months of stupor, such a patient may suddenly perform an impulsive act, often returning to apathetic withdrawal. Periods of stupor and near-normality may alternate in this syndrome and with a regularity that may be studied, even predicted, from changes in their body metabolism (Jenner 1970).

The fourth and final type was later added by psychiatrists to the original three kinds. This is simple schizophrenia. Its phenomena tend to be less dramatic, and onset of the psychosis is slower and more insidious. Prognosis tends to be poor.

In addition to the four types mentioned are two others both relating to age. Childhood autism is a major, psychotic-like abnormality in children. Use of the word 'autism' in this context was a much later development than Bleuler's with his notion of autistic thinking. The childhood condition is sometimes interpreted as representing an early version of schizophrenic psychosis. The other type to be mentioned is late paraphrenia, a condition of early old-age, in which delusions of a schizophrenic kind are a prominent accompaniment.

ANALOGIES AND THE SCHIZOPHRENIAS

Many analogies have been used in attempts to communicate about this baffling group of psychoses. Patients who respond to their auditory hallucinations have been likened to a person at one end of a telephone conversation. In adjusting to what they hear, but others don't, they behave and speak in unpredictable ways. Their emotions are similarly unpredictable. For Kretschmer 'a pane of glass is always there,' difficult or impossible to penetrate in entering into the mental life of the patient. As regards adjusting to other people, the analogy of a 'fixed throttle' response has been used. The schizophrenic resembles a motorist driving along the road at the same speed but ignoring completely what other vehicles are doing, as McDougall puts it, 'out of rapport with persons about him' (McDougall 1926: 380). Schizophrenia has been described as 'suppressed mania', the words referring to the flood of associations and imagery which inwardly preoccupy the schizophrenic. This notion may help with another analogy, 'the knight's move of the schizophrenic' used by Freud. Reference is to the strange absence of connections between words uttered, resembling moves of the knight in a game of chess, jumping over the intervening square.

For Jung the behaviour is that of 'a sleeping person in a waking world'. Many have drawn analogies between dreamlife and the psychosis. McDougall described such patients as people who never find their way back from their dreams. As in sleep such a person 'has lost control with the world about him ... all sense impressions are apt to be interpreted in terms of the imaginative preoccupations of the moment' (McDougall 1926: 380). Often it is nightmares rather than dreams, but not always. Sound recordings of the therapy of one such patient interested me when I heard her complain bitterly of the therapist's attempts to 'take away' her 'dream world'. The wish-fulfilment content of such psychoses is likened by Bleuler to 'a fairy tale'. Bleuler adds there is a difference: it is not a tale that is told, 'it is a fairy tale that is lived.' There is, as I suggest elsewhere, a 'loss of the as if'. The autonomous nature of the internal fantasy processes seem to resemble closely those we encounter elsewhere in mental life, in, for example, the hypnagogic state. Interestingly enough Freud (1900) reports investigators who have identified the phenomena of the psychosis with the hypnagogic rather than the dream state. Although there are many differences there are also resemblances, in some diagnosed schizophrenics, to patients exhibiting multiple personality. Shakespeare, himself an experienced actor, referred to the world as a stage in which one man in his time plays many parts. One patient I interviewed used a related simile. He likened the chaos of his internal mental life to many actors playing their parts inside him.

Kraepelin used the words 'shattered into a multiplicity of warring factions' to describe the consciousness of such patients. In contrasting schizophrenic 'split' with hysterical dissociation Bleuler described that of the schizophrenic as 'more lawless, worse determined, more massive ... the schizophrenic psyche is infinitely more split than the hysteric' (McDougall 1926: 395). McDougall stresses 'the essential difference' between the two. Another difference is often overlooked. Some schizophrenic patients are colourful and as such likely to attract attention and interest. Many are not and, having become institutionalized, are cared for in 'back wards' of psychiatric hospitals. They are very different indeed from the multiple personality patients, in terms of the times they are interviewed. Books are not written about them as individual people and they continue to exist as sad, grey background to the major problems of psychiatric medicine. Outside hospitals they may become derelicts with low morale, perhaps 'sleeping rough'.

Freud likened spoken or written communications to letters which have passed through the hands of a political censor: the remaining message becomes meaningless. In psychoanalytic thought we find frequent resort to a kind of 'cypher hypothesis': the notion that the patient is trying to communicate something but is unable to do so in plain language. Thus decoding has to be resorted to, as in seeking to uncover the latent content of a dream from its manifest content. Of great interest has been the work of investigators like Arieti, who have attempted – as we shall see in the next chapter – to work out the principles, different from ordinary logic, on which such thinking depends. In treating such thinking as a survival of the 'bicameral mind', a residue of earlier and pre-literate forms of mental life, Julian Jaynes (1976) refers back to classical times. He points to four types of insanity: prophetic madness due to Apollo, ritual madness due to Dionysus, poetic madness deriving from the Muses, and erotic madness due to Aphrodite (op. cit.: 406). This is a reminder that the forms of thinking which we find in both the schizophrenias and mythology have sometimes been given high cultural valuation. The identification of schizophrenia and its thought products with unrecognized genius has appealed to some contemporary thinkers. Obviously creative talent and psychosis may co-exist in a given individual, but examination of the drawings and paintings of schizophrenic patients suggest that, as among normal people, mediocrity is more usual. Creativity and psychosis should not be identified.

The widespread confusion between the Jekyll–Hyde syndrome and the schizophrenias is doubly unfortunate. There are indeed some resemblances between the molar dissociations of multiple personality and the molecular dissociations of the shattered schizophrenic personality. An analogy from astronomy may help. In molar dissociations we are dealing with something like a planetary nucleus with one or more satellites. In the schizophrenias it is more like the asteroid belt, with no nucleus but with tiny bits of matter moving at random, or guided by principles we do not yet understand. The result: sub-systems of personality, numerous in number, giving rise to images, upsurges of emotion, and unpredictable impulses to action. Our own age, with space travel, computers, holograms, and atomic science, will doubtless continue to produce new and additional analogies. We are now a long way from the cog wheels of the Industrial Revolution. But with this earlier age in mind of interest is the thought of one great physicist.

'I can never satisfy myself until I can make a mechanical model of a thing,' declared Lord Kelvin. 'If I can make a mechanical model I can understand it' (Quoted in Bridgman 1927: 45). Models play an important part in contemporary scientific thinking. They may be verbal or mathematical rather than actually built. One of psychology's own most important theorists of the modern period is no exception to this emphasis on models. The late Professor D. O. Hebb was also emphatic in not identifying the model we use with scientific understanding. Earlier I argued that for psychology Hebb's point is fundamental (McKellar 1957: 177 ff.). Hebb argues there are two components of scientific understanding: they are possession of a model, and being aware of its limitations (Hebb 1953). With this standpoint in mind – leaving mere analogies aside – we may examine the task of finding a model that assists understanding of the schizophrenias. In this area we encounter the discipline of psycho-pharmacology, and within it a family of substances – originally of botanical origin – known today as the 'hallucinogens'.

The peyote cactus, *Lophophoria williamsii*, is the source of several chemicals with hallucinogenic properties. Most important

212

of these is mescaline. Early investigators like Prentiss and Morgan (1895) used slices of the cactus itself – which look rather like dried apricots – known as 'mescal buttons'. In this they were preceded by the Aztecs who used these and several other hallucinogens in religious ceremonies. In 1943 the chemist A. Hofmann discovered the hallucinogenic properties of another substance, lysergic acid diethylamide, or LSD-25. Psilocybin and other active principles were later extracted from one specific mushroom. Many more hallucinogens are known, and as the developing science of ethnobotany is revealing, numerous other plant hallucinogens remain to be discovered (Schultes 1966). I turn to experiments in this area.

MODEL PSYCHOSIS

Osmond and Smythies, cited at the head of this chapter, have been important investigators into experimentally produced model psychoses. The first of their two major papers was entitled 'Schizophrenia: a new approach' (Osmond and Smythies 1952; Hoffer, Osmond, and Smythies 1954). They used mescaline, and later other hallucinogens. Initially their reason was the known chemical resemblances of some hallucinogens to substances that naturally occur in the body and which could possibly be a guide to the chemistry of schizophrenias. Biochemistry may be highly relevant, but I shall leave it aside to focus on a second justification for this approach. It is use of mescaline and other such hallucinogens to throw light on phenomena and mechanisms that simulate those of psychosis. Being aware of the limitations of such a model is highly relevant. As yet any available models are only crude approximations. To illustrate: hallucinations in the schizophrenias are mainly auditory, while those experimentally produced by mescaline, LSD-25, and other well-known hallucinogens are mainly visual. In this respect the model is an imperfect fit, but may nevertheless prove revealing.

The peyote cactus was earlier known as *Anhalonium lewinii*, named after Louis Lewin's work with it in 1888. Prentiss and Morgan (1895), Weir Mitchell (1896), and Havelock Ellis (1897) were early experimenters. Some of the experiments were casual but informative. Thus Weir Mitchell reports taking mescal buttons, bicycling home, and lying down to observe what happened. His experiences have sometimes been assessed as hypnagogic, though Ardis and I (1956) suggest they comprised a summation of mescaline-induced and hypnagogic imagery. Probably many people were led by the monograph written by Heinrich Klüver (1928) to become interested in mescaline. Klüver (1942) further developed his concept of specific 'form constants', regularities in the imagery produced by mescaline and other agencies. At any rate – and even leaving possible clues to the biochemistry of psychosis aside – the 1952 Osmond and Smythies paper suggested that mescaline was well worthy of intensive investigation. We have noted their emphasis that the substance appeared able to replicate 'every single symptom of acute schizophrenia'. Our own psychologist-psychiatrist research team at Aberdeen University became much interested in this area, for which the term 'experimental psychosis' had been introduced by Mayer-Gross (1951). Our own experiments began at Aberdeen Medical School in 1951. On the first two occasions, as well as several later ones, I was myself the subject. Synthetic mescaline rather than peyote buttons was used in our research, though in some experiments we used LSD-25 instead. A fuller account appears in my earlier book (McKellar 1957). The experiments were basically exploratory rather than of the kind which involve tightly controlled variables. We also, as has often happened in psychology, used mainly ourselves as subjects. Despite limitations of this method it permitted observations to be made by an experimenter that were often enriched by empathy based on recall of his own experiences as subject. Thus at least a sketch map emerged. One form of 'control' was however essential, namely careful medical supervision, which was maintained throughout. In view of the problems that can arise about 'drugs', it seems appropriate to underline this point. Twice I have been concerned with human experiments in psycho-pharmacology. First were these at Aberdeen Medical School in the early 1950s. Later, in New Zealand, colleagues did controlled experiments with cannabis under government licence. These studies were at first approved, and later financed, by the N.Z. Medical Research Council. Overall I assess the hallucinogens like mescaline as considerably more interesting psychologically than cannabis. Two other areas of interest grew out of the mescaline experiments. One was the curiosity they evoked in

Lorna Simpson and myself about hypnagogic imagery (McKellar and Simpson 1954). The other was our interest in relations to synaesthesia (Simpson and McKellar 1955). We later were able to present a detailed analysis of similarities between hypnagogic and mescaline subjective experiences (Ardis and McKellar 1956).

Much serious exploratory research followed the Osmond and Smythies (1952) paper and its 1954 follow-up 'after a year's research' by this team. The uses of reserpine and other such substances in therapy were being investigated, and LSD-25 was itself being put to use in psychiatric treatment. A book edited by Cholden (1956) published a symposium of the American Psychiatric Association on the subject, and it reflected research progress in many places, not least Canada where Osmond and Smythies began their own experiments. To many serious investigators it seems unfortunate that there now appeared a book, and later a second one, by Mr Aldous Huxley about an experience with mescaline he had undergone. The spelling 'mescalin' and the word 'psychedelic' were accompaniments of the 1952 book, which Hearnshaw records 'described the mind-enlarging influence of the drug mescaline' and also 'popularised the taking of hallucinogens' (Hearnshaw 1987: 254). There was a great deal of 'psychedelic' enthusiasm and in particular LSD-25, and various synthetic versions of it, became widely used and misused. Jaffe (1965) was led to make a distinction between 'drug experimentation', 'drug abuse', and 'drug addiction'. Commenting on this, Buchman (1976) pointed out that though LSD and other such substances were not pharmacologically 'addictive', they had become closely associated with other things, notably generation-conflict types of rebellion. None of these happenings around the hallucinogenic drugs was of much help to scientific researches with them. Many were critical of the 'mystical' reactions Mr Huxley reported in himself, and regarded his two books as of little scientific – or religious – interest. Overall the wide individual differences that occur in response to hallucinogens has probably received insufficient emphasis. A related point emerged in one scientific study by Ward (1957) with lysergic acid. This established how very different can be the subjective experiences of the same individual, to the same substance, on different occasions. He is likely to have developed a frame of reference on the basis of earlier administrations. A similar point was made by Grinspoon (1971) in the case of cannabis.

With the frame of reference provided by this historical context itself, I return to our own researches. Since my own introspections are involved I add that I have never myself taken LSD-25, and my comments on this are confined to those of experimenters. In the case of mescaline I am, however, familiar with accompanying subjective phenomena. But the parallels between the two seem to be very close. Mayer-Gross (1951), among others, stresses this similarity. As regards subjective effects we ourselves found it helpful to distinguish four classes of happening. I use our original terminology of 'Category I, II, III, and IV effects'. This may help sort out apparent overlaps with psychotic-like phenomena.

Category I

This refers to what might be called 'alcohol-like effects'. Many agencies, along with hallucinogens – like nitrous oxide, oxygen lack, and alcohol itself – produce them. Physically and mentally the organism becomes less efficient. Studies carried out later in New Zealand, with alcohol, cannabis, and combinations of cannabis and alcohol, dealt with similarly impaired performances in tasks resembling the driving of a motor vehicle. Loss of muscular co-ordination and skills, motor ataxia, is accompanied also by what might be called 'mental ataxia'. The individual attempts to do or think something, and something else gets done or thought. With hallucinogens some colourful interpretations may be made, as when I as subject declared – with conviction– that I was now experiencing new and interesting gravitational forces.

Category II

These were the effects assessed by us as specific to the effects of the hallucinogen used, mostly mescaline in our own experiments. The pioneer investigators Prentiss and Morgan (1895) postulated a 'stimulation of the centre of vision in the brain' by the drug. One of these most striking effects, interesting in itself but not specifically relevant to the study of psychosis, was synaesthesia. Like many of the hallucinogens, mescaline produces synaesthesias

216

– sometimes unusual ones like 'the sight of a touch', or the 'sound of a smell' – in people who do not ordinarily have such experiences. Some of the bizarre phenomena that occurred may be seen as these atypical types of synaesthesia.

Category III

Central to our purpose, this will be discussed below: it comprised phenomena seemingly relevant to the psychology of psychosis.

Category IV

This is related to the personality of the subject. If we administer a chemical substance to a person, he or she will still express that personality. The two books by Mr Aldous Huxley about his own experience with mescaline seem to have been of limited general interest in that they failed to take account of these Category IV effects. For example, Mr Huxley responded mystically. Mystical thinking may be induced in a variety of ways – for example with alcohol or nitrous oxide – in people so disposed. Our own series failed to produce it in some, though succeeded in other subjects. Moreover, as the work of Ward (1957) with lysergic acid revealed, the same individual may respond differently on different occasions.

Our own subjects would often exhibit frame-of-reference effects, being often relieved when the expected occurred. Again what is, and what is not, a genuine 'mystical' experience is not a simple issue: and as regards art we may feel critical of Huxley's alleged 'seeing the chair' exactly as had Van Gogh. Also some personalities tend to be suspicious, and under the influence of any agency used, respond in a persecutory rather than mystical way. The crucial Category III effects may now be considered.

EXPERIMENTALLY-INDUCED PSYCHOTIC-LIKE PHENOMENA

The quotation from Osmond and Smythies that heads this chapter postulates considerable overlap between the experiences of subjects in mescaline experiments and patients diagnosed as schizo-phrenic. They also admit by implication that the model of psychosis produced in such experiments has its limitation. It is not perfect. At a symposium of the Royal Medico-Psychological Association in which Dr Smythies also took part, I explored the theme that such experiments also help us 'in the investigation of human thinking' more generally (McKellar 1963a: 15). John Smythies did not dissent. The process of insightful noticing of what we often overlook in everyday subjective mental life may be most central to what these hallucinogens have to teach. Thus earlier Stekel discussed what he called 'the polyphony of thought'. He wrote 'I picture thinking as a stream of which only the surface is visible; orchestral music of which only the melody is audible' (Rapaport 1951: 313–14; McKellar 1957: 99–100). Mescaline may help us to notice what is often ignored as the insignificant background to normal subjective mental life.

Following an interval of time, administration of mescaline results in a chaos of subjective experience. In this it resembles the mental life of the schizophrenic. But the subject possesses an ego, an awareness of himself, of having been normal 'yesterday' and of going to be normal 'tomorrow'. The result is, as with a paranoid form of schizophrenia, an attempt to make sense of these happen-ings. What is going on inside is much more absorbing and attention-arousing than the efforts of the experimenters to administer tests of time estimation, take pulses and blood pressure, or perform other mundane tasks. Social surroundings tend to be ignored because, as in catatonic schizophrenia, so much is going on internally. Bleuler viewed schizophrenia as characterized by a disturbance of associative thinking. He referred to the fact that such patients 'lose themselves in the most irrelevant side associa-tions' (Bleuler 1911). Our subjects made frequent reference to the same phenomenon: of losing the pathway of thought and trying, with limited success, to get back on to it. Of interest were occasions when, instead of answering a question asked, they would respond to another question that was, for them, associatively linked with it. Because of this we would sometimes encounter responses of the 'knight's move of the schizophrenic' kind. In this area we can study the phenomena of what Arieti was to call 'paleological' as opposed to 'logical' thinking, discussed in the next chapter. We encounter this also in dreams in which associative interferences play an important part.

218

Saint Denys (1867) discovered in his studies of dreams the range of meanings that stem from a given word or idea, this creating considerable confusion. An image may start a whole train of other associated images, leading a long way from the original starting point. Our mescaline subjects frequently experienced blockages from such images, or intruding hallucinations of a highly irrelevant kind. A question asked would evoke interesting subjective experiences, and the question itself would be ignored or forgotten. As in dreaming and in hypnagogic states, there would be regression from R-thinking to an easier kind of mental activity, A-thinking fantasy. Accompanying and often unpredictable changes of emotion would take place. The analogy I have used earlier, of seeming to be responding at one end of a telephone conversation to a 'voice' – in this case visualizations – not perceived by external observers has relevance. The flood of visual imagery which mescaline produces is often colourful and sometimes extremely beautiful, and outside happenings are by contrast uninteresting and unwelcome. When pressed to respond, our subjects would describe these, and sometimes other, visual phenomena like the 'crawling print' of a page in a book, 'moving crumbs' of bread during a meal or, on another such occasion, 'a snake' exercising itself under the table-cloth.

Highly concrete responses, often of an unreasonably literal-minded kind, have been associated with the schizophrenias. Sometimes the subject would respond to unwelcome intrusions of experimenters by having unflattering hallucinations of them. Either we would become grotesquely old and ugly, or we would be seen as otherwise disposable. When I questioned one subject too closely at a time she preferred to look at her imagery, this happened to myself. The subject proceeded to an uncomplimentary hallucination of a flat, cardlike figure – resembling the card-people in the later part of *Alice in Wonderland* – but all crumpled up. I had become a piece of scrap paper. On another occasion when a psychiatrist friend agreed to take mescaline, he stipulated no sound recordings, and only me as experimenter. His imagery cancelled any implied compliment. What he visualized was a beautiful swan, and nearby a tousled little duck 'writing furiously'. Psychiatrists sometimes feel hostile to their psychologist colleagues, and the concretization mechanism of mescaline can – like that of hypnagogia – neatly summarize this in pictorial

219

ways. Very characteristic was hallucinated movement of stationary objects, as when the walls of the laboratory would move backwards and forwards, or things would pulsate. The language of living things as opposed to inanimate matter would often be used, as when hallucinated dots would not merely move but 'march' in formation. The material surroundings of the subject would also exhibit hallucinatory movements. Often they would expand and contract around their usual shape.

One difficulty in interviewing, testing, or treating patients is when they fail to respond. They say or do nothing. A very interesting aspect of the experiments was the information they provided on the wide variety of reasons for these blockages of thought. With the aid of sound recordings played afterwards we would discover why they occurred. Sometimes the mind was blank, there was simply nothing there; alternatively there was so much going on that – because of it – response was impossible. Vocabulary would sometimes deteriorate: words usually available would be lost. And sometimes a suspicious paranoid-like response would occur. The subjects felt that whatever they said, even in response to a seemingly innocent question, would give too much away. The result was they said nothing. One subject explained his long period of muteness during an experiment with lysergic acid in these terms. At the time he felt that anything he said, even giving the colour of a test object, would reveal his innermost secrets. So silence followed. Only much later, he told us, did he regain the ability 'to go dumb selectively'. On another occasion we suspected that the subject was producing a similar ideas-of-reference refusal to speak, having requested her to carry out a task of naming adjectives. We were quite wrong. Much later she spoke, rather pathetically: 'I was trying to think what an adjective is.' In his therapy with subsequent patients my psychiatrist colleague, the late Dr Amor Ardis, told me how valuable it was in doing therapy to have undergone such experiences. He had learned about the range of subjective conditions which may underlie a single external happening: the inability or refusal to speak.

Retention of a sense of 'as if' has been discussed earlier as representing the kind of insight that distinguishes normality from psychosis. Frequently our subjects experienced a 'loss of the as if'. In one such experiment I experienced usual Category I effects:

loss of co-ordination and unsteadiness. This, I explained to myself and the experimenters, was due to new gravitational forces, including a levitational one on my body. It wasn't an 'as if' experience: to my clouded thinking such forces were definitely operating. Free floating certainty would often manifest itself, the subject seeming to be looking for something to be certain about. Often he or she would talk down to the experimenters in a pitying kind of way, as also seemed to happen in Aldous Huxley's case, when he claimed to Humphrey Osmond as experimenter that now he was able 'to see how things really are'. On another such occasion he was 'Seeing what Adam had seen on the day of creation'. It was not a question of 'as though', but a clear-cut assertion of 'it is so.' Some but not all of our subjects produced responses that were 'mystical' in this rather bad sense of the word: vague and dogmatic assertions about 'time', 'truth', or 'reality'. We also encountered the *presque vu* phenomenon, of seeming to be about to grasp – but not quite succeeding – some important and esoteric insight. Other subjects failed, however hard we prompted them, to produce anything remotely resembling a 'mystical' type of response. As regards the Category II-type effects, the upsurges of visual experiences, remarkably similar to hypnagogic imagery, may be extremely beautiful and impressive. The Sandoz chemist Hofmann, after taking 0.25 milligrams of LSD, reported 'a feeling of being at one with the world'. In 1986, years after having been subject in a BBC experiment with mescaline as a young man, Christopher Mayhew – now Lord Mayhew – described it in retrospect as 'the most interesting thing I've ever done'. A blend of dogmatism and enthusiasm often accompanies the judgements of subjects during and after hallucinogen experiences. With an over-inclusiveness we sometimes encounter with both alcohol and psychosis, one of our subjects looked for a long time at a plate of the Ishihara Colour Vision Test. Doubtless influenced by Blake's seeking 'a world in a grain of sand', he declared his ability to relate this to everything in the universe. When challenged, such utterances prove to be less impressive. We confronted one of our subjects with a grandiose and seemingly meaningless piece of philosophy – Hegel at his worst – and this impressed him greatly. It was so true that it was 'the only thing worth saying'. We asked him to put this profound truth into other words, but he declined, saying 'he has said it perfectly.' Our scepticism was naturally aroused. Sometimes, because of the imagery and general loosening of thought, subjects produce high-sounding statements of grandiose nonsense. At other times fresh insights of an intellectually interesting kind seem to occur. These, together with the form of the utterances themselves, may and do replicate some of the phenomena of psychotic thinking. Thus, in the tradition of Prentiss and Morgan's experiments (1895) and those of their successors, they may be of interest to psychological science.

PSYCHOSIS AND INDIVIDUAL PEOPLE

During the First World War two British soldiers escaped from a Turkish prisoner-of-war camp by pretending to be insane. Their simulated psychoses took them to a less secure hospital, from which escape was easier than from the camp itself. In his book, *The Road to Endor*, one of them reports their choice of two different types of psychosis (Jones 1919). One adopted a grandiose, dominating condition of a euphoric kind: his role was one he seemed to enjoy, not least because of what he was allowed to get away with through it. In this it reminds me strongly of patients diagnosed as manic, in clinical demonstrations before classes of medical or psychology students. Because of the euphoria, such patients give evidence of enjoying the experience; the atmosphere is relaxed and not, as often in such situations, embarrassing. Sometimes students find themselves laughing with the patient, as when he seems to be 'scoring points' off the interviewing psychiatrist. The second prisoner who escaped chose to act a simulated psychosis of a depressed and pathetic kind. His captors responded to him accordingly and he had a very miserable time, frequently being abused and ill-treated. The 'weep and you weep alone' dictum was well illustrated in his case. Although both men successfully escaped, the experiences they underwent in the process were very different: each invited very different kinds of response from others. In this – though the illnesses they chose were different – they might well have been respectively a paranoid schizophrenic, and a catatonic schizophrenic.

As individuals, schizophrenic patients resemble other people: some are colourful and likely to evoke interest, and some are not and do not. Among them are individuals who stand out, can communicate about the psychosis, and are likely to be frequently interviewed. Within a hospital they may play an important part in its social life, be well known to the staff, and have influence over other patients. In these respects they resemble the British prisoner who chose a grandiose, euphoric psychosis to simulate. By contrast, in a hospital are many others who resemble his less fortunate companion. It is their fate to be overlooked and they are, in their withdrawn depression, catatonic stupor, and apathy, unlikely to be sought out to take part in interviews for teaching purposes. In these respects we encounter the drab, grey 'ground', as opposed to the more colourful 'figure' of a psychiatric hospital population. On recovery such patients may show themselves to be intelligent, creative, and interesting personalities, but this does not show during their active or chronic psychosis. As Harry Stack Sullivan claims, conflicts of a 'cosmic' kind may be taking place in the mental life of the schizophrenic: there are some patients – often diagnosed paranoid schizophrenics – who can and do communicate about such internal happenings. But there are others in whom whatever is going on reveals itself only by apparent outward evidence of absence of any mental life at all, or silent acts of negative movements of withdrawal. There are psychiatrists like, for instance, R. D. Laing who seem to come close to suggesting that 'schizophrenia' is a synonym for unrecognized genius. Collections of psychotic art, paintings, and poetry may suggest this, but they are unrepresentative. The artistic productions of very many patients are, not surprisingly, of a different kind: average ability and mediocre talent are their main characteristics. In other words, the structure and content of many psychoses resembles, intellectually and emotionally, an entirely uninteresting conversation between neighbours over a garden fence.

The point I am making was well put to me by the medical superintendent of one psychiatric hospital. It was that the occupational therapy department of a good hospital should not, in any sense, be 'making a profit'. In his own he showed me emotionally withdrawn patients sorting out wools into colour categories. This, he argued, was better than leaving them to lie about in the exercise yard, a pathetic sight still to be seen in some hospitals, even in highly affluent countries. In occupational therapy, as in a school, it is too easy to focus attention on the high-quality products of dominant, bright, and 'interesting' individuals. Among the others are those who share with the non-psychotic the problem of having something to do to occupy the passage of time. In these respects the contribution of radio and television to psychiatric hospitals has been enormous. In their history of a period of 300 years, Hunter and MacAlpine (1963) deal with the various contributions of enlightened reformers who faced up to this issue.

TIME DISCONTINUITIES

Among the 'interesting' patients are cases of multiple personality. Miss Beauchamp and others invited numerous interviews, and books or articles about their subjective experiences. Prominent among these was a sense of loss of time, and of periods of amnesia. One such patient told me of being constantly blamed for things she simply 'didn't do': these proved to be things she had done, but didn't remember. In these much-studied patients the periods of amnesia can be penetrated by hypnotism, automatic writing, crystal-gazing, or other such techniques. Thus Sally was able to provide information about Miss Beauchamp's time discontinuities, and Eve Black was able to throw much light on the other Eve's hallucinations. Continuity of cause and effect could be established by detailed study of such individual cases. This not only assisted therapy, but also provided information into mechanisms that might help in the understanding of other types of patient. Although multiple personality is a rarity – perhaps less rare than once supposed – amnesias, hallucinatory happenings, and time discontinuities frequently occur. In the multiple personality cases the strange and seemingly uncaused events that took place were found to be things arranged by dissociated, often hostile, other selves. About these information could be obtained, and introspectively.

Consider now the schizophrenias. During an interview one patient told me how he had been doing 'nothing at all' when men appeared and took him to the psychiatric hospital where he now was. That was how he had perceived events and what he believed had happened. The realities were different. In fact he had been acting in an uncontrolled and violent way, though he still remained unaware of this. As in other such cases we encounter a Kafkaesque situation, which also resembles closely what we learn about in the time losses of multiple personalities. Consider what Kafka reports of his Joseph K in *The Trial*. 'Without having done anything wrong he was arrested one fine morning' (Kafka, edition 1983: 1). The experience of the patient was very similiar. In his story Kafka continues to tell how men came into the house and two of them 'tried to take K by the arms', and later he found them 'holding his hands in a methodical, practised, irresistible grip'. And so the wretched K 'realized the futility of resistance' (op. cit.: 166–7). Outside the areas of unexplained arrest, multiple personality, and schizophrenia, similarly experienced happenings can occur. We find an additional source of information in model psychoses experiments. In a much more minor way I experienced them myself. There was one game of chess I played which I will not forget, and it happened when I was subject in one mescaline experiment (McKellar 1957). During play my major pieces would simply disappear from the board. I would emerge from drug-induced introversion to glance at it, to discover loss of a rook, then a queen, and then some other major misfortune. Obviously, as always in a game of chess, my opponent was behaving in a threatening way. But surely he was also cheating? Yet knowing I had taken the hallucinogen that day I had insight into an alternative explanation. It was mescaline, not cheating, that was responsible for the apparent persecution. In this and in other of the experiments, I or other subjects experienced many alarming discontinuities, as when people would appear, disappear, and reappear in different parts of the room.

Such experiments, like multiple personality cases, permit study of the time discontinuity mechanism. Here are raw materials for persecutory or other types of delusion. In the experiments our subjects would try to make sense of these often alarming happenings. Mostly, though not always, they were successful. Paranoid schizophrenic patients may have similar insights, but often and very understandably they don't. There is all the difference in the world between being a subject in a hallucinogen experiment with colleagues one trusts, and being a patient in a bleak hospital ward. 'Voices, may be abusive, nagging, or otherwise provoking: the patient responds to such environmental happenings as mis-perceived, and may respond with aggression. The experimentally produced hallucinations of mescaline, though usually visual, can help understanding of such occurrences.

If things appear to happen without apparent cause we can find subject matter for other kinds of delusory development. The supernatural, popular science, or some other category may be drawn on by a paranoid schizophrenic seeking an explanation. As Julian Jaynes (1976) has reminded us, there have been many times in history when unexplained events or voices have been attributed to supernatural forces. The same continues to happen in our own society in certain patients, while for others superstitious attitudes to science provide the subject matter. In his study following the famous Orson Welles Hallowe'en broadcast of *War of the Worlds*, Cantril (1940) attributed readiness of many people to accept the notion of a real Martian invasion to scientific superstitions. Science fiction is one thing, but along with it has come a deluge of books of another kind, making such claims as colonization of Earth from outer space. Misinformation of this type is available for the delusions of patients, no less than for the fantasy beliefs of other people. It seems strange that one of the uses to which literacy is put is the reading of horoscopes in popular magazines and daily tabloid newspapers. Raw materials for other fantasies, and superstitions about science, as about religion, are readily available to non-psychotic people. Cervantes makes Don Quixote a victim of his reading, this providing subject matter for his delusions. Something similar may happen with actual patients.

BIOLOGY OF THE SCHIZOPHRENIAS

There are many known hallucinogens, of which mescaline, lysergic acid diethylamide, harmine, and psylocybin are illustrative instances. Their dramatic effects on mental life are a reminder that in psychology we are dealing with a body–mind. Similarly the naturally occurring psychoses, like the schizophrenias, give their evidence that mind is a biological phenomenon: interest in subjective experiences should not let us neglect this important principle. A leading article in the London *Times* (2 July 1986) assessed schizophrenia as probably a result of disturbed biochemistry. It seems highly probable that body chemistry is an important factor in at least some of the schizophrenias. Disturbance of adrenal metabolism has been postulated, and there are a variety of theories of this kind. Some investigators, like Woolley and Shaw (1954), and after Dr Woolley's death their successors, have paid particular attention to serotonin. There was some interest in histamine on the basis, explored by Lea (1955), of an alleged low incidence of allergies in schizophrenic patients. There is much interest in dopamine, and Warner (1985) has dealt in detail with available evidence for and against the 'dopamine hypothesis' (op. cit.: 242 ff.).

Some investigators like Crow (1980), in recognizing the diversity of the schizophrenias, do not exclude biochemical abnormality as sometimes involved. But in other of the schizophrenias they suggest an alternative pathology. I mention again the point made by Hunter and MacAlpine (1963) that in the schizophrenias 'identical symptoms by no means imply identical pathology.' As illustration, note how persecutory and 'paranoid reactions' can result from a variety of causal factors, including known brain lesions, as well as in patients with 'true paranoia' and no detectable brain changes. We have also seen with a hallucinogen like mescaline it is possible to simulate many phenomena of psychosis. Doses of alcohol and/or nitrous oxide may produce some of these. There is good reason to believe that the amphetamines, when misused, are particularly dangerous. Continued use of benzedrine may result in long-term, probably irreversible brain damage, reminiscent of chronic deteriorated schizophrenia. Evidence from Boston Medical School and elsewhere supports the view that there can be brain changes in from 20 to 35 per cent of patients diagnosed schizophrenic. But such impairment tends to be non-specific, and of the kind that 'can result from a variety of causes, (Seidman 1983: 195). The possibility of a slow virus as a causal factor – one encountered in other psychiatric conditions like the kuru of New Guinea – has been advanced (e.g. Fisman 1975; Torry and Peterson 1976). Since the time of Kraepelin and his 'dementia praecox', which overlaps with Bleuler's concept of 'schizophrenia', the notion of a physical pathology of such psychoses has been widely held. Another leading investigator of the past, Sullivan (1953), postulated two different things among the schizophrenias. One involved neurological degeneration with a physical pathology; the other he suggested was a complex disturbance of inter-personal relations. Finally there is a genetic approach, postulating heredity as an at least contributory factor, though clearly there is no evidence of a dominant gene of the kind that operates in the case of Huntington's chorea.

Overall the schizophrenias remain a mystery still to be unravelled, and one of central importance to psychiatry. Here, as elsewhere in nature, causality is, almost certainly, complex. Moreover, and it is worth saying it again, a diagnostic label may mask a wide variety of different things. And, if the schizophrenias remain the most important problem for psychiatry to solve, they may also be a model for the understanding of other problems for medical science. The perspective of history may help. In the past the dreaded word 'leprosy' also embraced other things now treated by dermatologists but then often cured by other means. There was also a residue, and today 'leprosy' has come to be known as 'Hanson's disease', named appropriately after the scientist who discovered the relevant bacteriological organism. With this additional biological knowledge cures have become possible. Recognition of similar diversity within a single diagnostic label may in the future help to solve the diagnostic and prognostic issues which surround 'the schizophrenias'.

SUMMARY

1 The first important thing about 'the schizophrenias' is this plural use of the word. The second is related: because the label covers a diversity of things, unpredictability of prognosis is characteristic and understandable. Bleuler, who introduced the term, used it in the plural.

2 Diversity and unpredictability also characterize the phenomena of the schizophrenias, but concepts that have survived from the past are of some use in classifying these: hebephrenic, catatonic, and paranoid. The phenomena themselves are discussed, together with the many analogies that have been used in attempts to explain them.

3 So far as the notion of 'splitting' is relevant, it is important to distinguish its 'molar' forms in multiple personality, from its 'molecular' schizophrenic kinds. Nevertheless detailed study of the rarer, but often very interesting, cases of multiple personality may be of help in understanding the schizophrenic psychoses

and their mechanisms. 'Time discontinuities' comprise one such mechanism that may help to explain development of delusions.

4   In the 'model psychosis' type of experiment we may learn about phenomena and mechanisms of interest to achieving empathy with some of the subjective experiences of the schizophrenias. Imagery interferences, oddities of association, blockages, and paranoid misinterpretations are considered.

5   As in abnormal psychology more generally, we need to take account of physical and bodily factors in their relation to mental life. The biology of the schizophrenias is considered with reference to biochemistry, physical pathology in some of the psychoses, and the need to take account of such biology in understanding the problems of diagnosis and outcome.

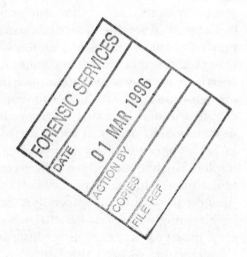

Chapter Eleven

THE PSYCHOPATHOLOGY OF THINKING

The schizophrenic – when he thinks in a typically schizophrenic way – accepts identity based on identical predicates.

Silvano Arieti

Thinking in relation to psychosis is difficult to discuss. There are several reasons. One is that much of the time psychotic thinking can closely resemble that of 'normal' people. In everyday life much – perhaps most – human thinking falls short of valid logical inference and careful assessment of relevant evidence. Introspectively we may sometimes notice how, even when we believe we are reasoning, we are in fact moving from one stereotyped concept to another, or taking reference in well-established prejudices or fashionable jargon. It is not surprising that patients diagnosed as 'schizophrenic' often do likewise. Moreover, as Silvano Arieti implies, such patients are not necessarily schizophrenic all the time. Indeed during a conversation their transitions from ordinary thought to oddities of association, or intrusion of delusions may be alarmingly sudden. Patients who communicate in interviews may, much of the time, differ little from their interviewer in the characteristics of their thinking.

To simplify this complex issue I suggest a distinction between three things. First is thinking in its ideal form, with the valid inferences that characterize logic and mathematics and the evaluations of evidence that distinguish science. Second is 'pathological' thinking: this includes what Arieti calls 'paleologic', that we associate with neurosis, psychopathy, and psychosis. Third is thinking in its everyday life forms, and this overlaps with the other two categories. Emotions and emotional habits like sentiments, minor phobias, superstitions, and prejudices may activate the less rational processes of normal, everyday thinking. Moreover, the intellectual level of thought of a given individual varies at different times and with different subject matter. Another feature of the thought processes of non-psychotic people is the influence of what might be called 'emotional clouds' that impede concern with logic and evidence. These take many forms: words like 'enthusiasm', 'sentimentality', 'romanticism', and 'bitterness' point to their variety. By contrast, when what I have called realistic or R-thinking is dominant, as Hervey de Saint Denys puts it, 'people guide their ideas along a chosen path, without allowing the mind to wander off in other directions' (Saint Denys 1867, reprinted 1982: 35). For Bleuler the schizophrenias are characterized instead by oddities of association: 'patients may lose themselves in the most irrelevant side associations' (Bleuler 1911). As I have argued, under the influence of mescaline something very similar may happen. The sub-vocal flight of ideas that occurred to one of our subjects explained the blockage that followed when we asked her to describe in what ways a dog and a lion are similar. Instead of responding in terms of such concepts as 'mammal' or perhaps 'carnivore', she became lost in other issues. Did we mean 'dog' in a generic sense, or 'dog' in the masculine sense as opposed to 'bitch', and did 'lion' include or exclude 'lioness'? The malfunctioning that occurred seemed to involve weakening of the ability to inhibit side associations. Upon such ability much normal reasoning greatly depends (McKellar 1963b: 13). Inhibition seems to be a distinctive characteristic of realism, or as I have called it R-thinking, with restraint upon intrusions of A-thinking and its upsurges of fantasy, imagery and side associations.

THINKING AND COMMUNICATION

In wakefulness and sane interactions we tend to be remarkably alert to what other speakers mean. What they mean often differs somewhat from what they say. Some internal vigilant system of control enables us to comprehend correctly, and somehow we inhibit what might seem to a foreign-language-speaking psychologist a 'reasonable' response to the actual words spoken. Image for a moment what we don't do when a person declares 'I can't see,' or 'I'm totally in the dark.' We don't offer sympathy for blindness, or offer to turn on the light! Mistakes of comprehension are also often avoided because we know the context. Thus statements like 'he went out for a duck', 'did a hat trick', or 'bowled a maiden over' are understood in the context of a game of cricket. At other times the words have very different meanings. An actor friend will understand, knowing the context – a play he is going to act in – though others may not when we tell him to 'go and break a leg'. A wish of 'good luck' would be counterproductive in the idiom of the superstitions of the theatre. But outside the context of games and plays people certainly say some very strange things to one another, in for example a statement like 'my lips are sealed.' Time and place seem to influence statements about loss of employment. Sometimes we hear an employee is 'given the sack', though in America it is the practice to 'fire them'. More recently there has emerged an alternative, a misuse of information theory, and now the 'sacked' or 'fired' person is 'made redundant'. Everyday communication seems to involve internal vigilance operating in the service of comprehension. Somehow it inhibits amusing images that might otherwise accompany statements carrying words like 'he has a chip on the shoulder' or 'she was born with a silver spoon in her mouth.' But we can, if we like, tune into such imagery, as cartoonists often do when they draw visual jokes. There are other situations when such visualizations can intrude, like model psychoses experiments. They also occurred in the experiments of Silberer with the cartoon-like hypnagogic images that intruded to illustrate or replace more abstract thought.

Among those who have exploited the humour of visual–verbal ambiguity have been the Marx brothers. A rather obvious example was when Harpo produced a pair of scissors when asked to 'cut the cards'. More subtle was an occasion in *Horse Feathers* when the kidnapped brothers are locked in a room where they see a coil of rope. Harpo is instructed to 'throw rope out the window and tie to the bed.' He responds with an insane kind of logic. Out the window goes the coil of rope, and on to the bed he tosses his tie. In normal life we just don't do such things: we are aware of what is meant despite what is said. But in dreamlife and hypnagogia, as sometimes in humour, the distinction is blurred. Even in everyday life we can find ourselves making some strange admissions. I recall once being asked, 'Are you the Scarborough Wuff and the Rainbow Trout?' I assented, thus confirming our order in the restaurant, but a psychiatrist from Mars might well have diagnosed delusions of bodily changes. But even earthly cross-cultural differences can be confusing sources of anxiety. Thus visitors to New Zealand have sometimes been alarmed when their host in a pub says, 'I'll go up to the bar and shout.' No public disturbance is implied, only his intention to buy a round of drinks. An American psychologist colleague, Louis Leland, drew my attention to very real possibilities of confusion when making a phone call from differences between the British and American uses of the English language. In London or Edinburgh the phone operator may ask the caller, 'Are you through?' The caller replies 'yes', meaning he is now in communication with the person he is phoning. The same reply of 'yes' in the United States results in the operator cutting him off, assuming he is 'through' or finished with his phone call. Mistakes arising from misunderstandings over words, and humour resulting from exploiting imagery accompanying words, provide an empathy bridge to some kinds of psychotic thinking. Consider again the unreasonably concrete response of Harpo Marx when, in *Horse Feathers*, he is forced by the kidnappers to remove his outer clothing. He crosses the room and, with modesty however inappropriate, first turns a picture of a woman with its face to the wall. A picture is not the person portrayed on it. But to a child, a patient, or Harpo Marx it may be.

In accord with the Economy Principle a disturbed patient may use available sense data as a framework for hallucination. In one such instance the patient – a man suffering from delirium tremens – hallucinated bushes and plants in his garden as friends and acquaintances. He talked with them. A photograph or picture is even better subject matter, sometimes even used in witchcraft to represent the actual person. One schizophrenic became distressed by a photograph of a friend that was hanging on the wall. He called for assistance: 'Help, they are hanging my friend.' A nurse with empathic understanding of the confusions over the alternative meanings of 'hanging' responded promptly with the words 'I'll get him down.' She gently took the picture from the wall and placed it in an armchair. Then followed conversation between the patient and the 'friend' she had rescued. Esquirol (1845) describes a patient who refused to drink saying 'Would you have me swallow my brother?' The problem was resolved by removing the bottle carrying his own reflection. By contrast, R-thinking was embraced by the surrealist René Magritte when, under his painting of a briar pipe, he wrote, 'this is not a pipe.' It was a picture of a pipe.

PALEOLOGICAL THINKING

The work of Arieti represents a sustained and important attempt to understand the principles underlying psychotic thinking. His statement of one basic idea, the Von Domarus Principle, heads this chapter. Paleologic accepts 'identity based on identical predicates' (Arieti 1966: 726). This can result in 'an orgy of identifications'. He instances as illustration a schizophrenic patient who identified herself with the Virgin Mary, because she also was a virgin. With such paleologic we may contrast logic itself, as understood by Aristotle and his successors. Take an example which is logically valid.

All Greeks have beards.
Aristotle was a Greek.
Therefore Aristotle had a beard.

As far as we know the conclusion happens to be true. Aristotle was bearded. But this – and the fact that not all Greeks have beards – is irrelevant to logic: the important thing is that the inference is logically valid. But consider a different piece of reasoning.

All Greeks have beards.
Freud had a beard.
Therefore Freud was a Greek.

As it happens, he wasn't. But the point is we are making an invalid inference. In accord with a predicate in common, via the Von Domarus Principle, we are asserting an identification. With this principle we begin to have some understanding of inferences that appeal in schizophrenia, dreamlife, hypnagogia, and the thought processes that occur with hallucinogens. As I don't happen to be particularly worried about voodoo witchcraft – though there are many people in the West Indies and Africa today who are – let me take an example from it.

> All voodoo goddesses are to be feared.
> Ezulie is to be feared.
> Therefore Ezulie is a voodoo goddess.

Though we may suspect that Ezulie belongs to the 'null class', along with other non-existent creatures of superstitious belief, in folklore at least Ezulie does happen to be a voodoo goddess. Yet the proposition that asserts this to be the case is invalid: it is based on merely a predicate in common.

While still exploring the very interesting category of the null class, let's try vampires.

> All vampires have sharp teeth.
> Dracula had sharp teeth.
> Therefore Dracula was a vampire.

Dracula, as portrayed by Bram Stoker, was a vampire, but this does not follow from the reasoning which is logically invalid. Instead it is an instance of paleologic we might encounter in psychosis or dreamlife. A visit to the dentist on the day before sleep might evoke imagery about teeth, their sharpness, and thus a nightmare about vampires. I admit to using an imaginary example, but in considering the associative thinking embodied in paleologic, let's continue with a real one. Many such instances were reported by Hervey de Saint Denys (1867) in his lifelong study of dreams. On one such occasion he dreamed of having lunch at a café. On the table was a metal spoon. This immediately became a metal key, the key to his house. The idea of returning home from the café had transformed itself in this concrete way into an image. 'It is only a moment before I find myself outside my door. My key turns the lock. I have been instantly transported from the café to my home' (Saint Denys, edition 1982: 141). In analysing the principles underlying magic also in *The Golden Bough*, Frazer (1911) placed emphasis on the part played by such association by similarity. Saint Denys himself deals with such association in terms of a process he calls 'abstraction', as when we abstract the different attributes of a whole. Each such attribute permits associative linkages. An example of this involved a dream in which he was coming down a winding staircase from a friend's apartment. The dark stairway reminded him of a well, and thus in the dream he found himself descending into a well. At the bottom he saw water, and immediately afterwards his dream was of himself in a swimming pool.

As Arieti puts it, in paleologic 'a class is a collection of objects which have a predicate or part in common ... which therefore become identical or equivalent.' He adds that these members of the class are 'freely exchanged' (Arieti 1966: 727). Another of his examples was the patient who believed that the two men in her life were in fact the same person. Attributes they had in common were two: both loved her, and both played the guitar. The composite people who appear in dreamlife previously discussed, and the half-belief confusion of the analyst in transference with other people, seem to involve a similar mechanism of identification. In the case of schizophrenic thinking it may be added that the attribute which links two things together may itself be highly imaginative, and bizarre. We find many instances of it also in hypnagogic imagery. And earlier mention has been made of other identifications in the phenomenon I have labelled 'hypnopompic speech', the schizophrenic-like utterances people sometimes produce in their drowsy waking-up state.

In his studies of imagery in states adjacent to sleep, Alfred Maury was impressed by resemblances between hypnagogic, psychotic, and absent-minded thinking. On occasion he found himself responding with incoherent speech resulting from 'the idea or the image that was in front of my eyes' at the time a questioner intruded (Quoted in Mavromatis 1987: 173). Maury provided his examples. I will contribute one of my own relating to absent-mindedness rather than to hypnagogia. While thinking about something else, in fact this book, I was asked 'What do you want for lunch?' My reply was 'Half-past one.' The reply, reluctantly dragged out of me, involved no image. Associative linkage was of similarity to previous situations when, while thinking about something else, I was asked the time. Although both Maury and some other investigators (e.g. Craik 1966; Singer 1966) explain hypnopompic speech in terms of accompanying imagery, it seems this is not always so. As in the example taken there may be other reasons. In our experiments with mescaline, sometimes subjects replied irrelevantly with answers determined by their imagery at the time. But often their response was to another question than the one asked, but associatively linked to it. As regards psychosis, on one occasion I asked a schizophrenic patient in interview to define 'a table'. His response was first to list a number of different kinds of table, and then to free associate about the objects he saw on the table in front of him. The mechanisms of control that usually restricts an answer to the question asked were fragile. As they began to fail him, the key word 'table' merely became a stimulus. To this, rather than any question about it, he responded. Here we have another instance in which, as Silberer puts it, consciousness 'switches to a simpler mode of mental functioning'. Outside hypnagogia, dreamlife and psychosis, resort to easier forms of thought is commonplace. When some tragic or otherwise emotionally charged event occurs it is often easier to find a scapegoat, someone to blame for it, than to attempt study of cause and effect. A general law of psychology still waiting to be formulated might perhaps be called the 'Culpability Principle'. We might state it as, 'For any event that occurs it is possible to find somebody to blame for it.'

Errors of thinking are common outside the psychoses in everyday life. The method of formulating counter-examples can be used in their detection. Take an example from a report in the *Daily Telegraph* (Tuesday 1 September 1987). This referred to a claim that stones from the sky 'may have fallen more than 50 million miles from Mars'. One geologist was quoted as allegedly arguing this 'because the gases trapped inside these meteorites are the same as that we find on the Martian surface'; it was further claimed 'that is conclusive evidence that they must have come from Mars itself.' But it isn't. A counter-example brings out the form of such an inference. On this basis I could argue that the liquid 'trapped' in the radiator of my car (H_2O) is 'the same' as the liquid in the Amazon River (also H_2O), this being conclusive evidence that it came from the Amazon. I happen to know it didn't. But there is no valid reason to think on this inference that it did. Two things may be similar, but similarity does not guarantee identity.

In psychosis, hypnagogia, and dreamlife we have seen how the intrusion of a visual image can disrupt association. An incident from my own experience illustrates similar happenings in everyday life. One day I learned that there was a man outside my office who wanted to see me. My colleague who passed on this message gave me the man's name. After talking with my visitor I had occasion to introduce him to the same colleague. I did so by name, 'This is Mr Lamb.' The poor man murmured to me with some embarrassment 'Er, the name is Gamble.' Inquiry revealed that the colleague to whom I had been introducing the visitor – who was both a practical joker and had a good visual image – was responsible. Sometimes imagery itself rather than the meaning of words results in such happenings. This can happen with memory when mnemonic techniques can increase capacity to recall a list of items. The technique involves associating each item with a 'mnemonic locus', an image of a place. Subsequently the person recalling the items mentally moves from one such locus to another – a mnemonic walk – retrieving at each the appropriate item. Errors can occur if the imaged place and item to be remembered 'blend' in some way. Thus if preparing a shopping list that includes a bottle of red wine it is better not to image it against the green of a laurel bush in the shade. In imagery one may simply fail to 'see' it there. The scholarly study by Frances Yates (1966) deals with the numerous mnemonic techniques that may be used in such ways, and their history from Greek and Roman times. Since the famous study by Luria (1968) there have been many investigations of remarkable and seemingly 'abnormal' powers of memory. Luria's subject used imagery, sometimes of the synaesthesia kind. And on occasion imagery would intrude and impede rather than help his feats of memory. Sometimes synaesthesia may play a part in associative linkages, as in the case of one person who regularly refers to lukewarm water as 'off white', a somewhat neologistic way of putting it. As regards such neologistic ways of thinking it will be noted how both history and fiction have provided us with reference points in certain names. Thus 'a Judas', 'a Jezebel', 'a Peter Pan', 'a Scrooge', 'a Quisling' and 'a Robin Hood' have agreed meanings: we may also refer 'a Marathon', 'a Utopia' or someone's 'Road to Damascus', and be understood. Within an in-group, as in 'family jokes', similar allusions are regularly comprehended. If the equivalent 'in-group' of a psychotic person includes only himself we may refer to the word he chooses – sometimes a proper noun – as a 'neologism'.

ANANKASTIC THINKING

Superstitious thinking provides close parallels to the emotionally charged thought of obsessions, compulsions, and phobic avoidances. There seems no good reason nowadays for not passing other people on the stairs, nor for the upsurge of anxiety that may occur when this proves unavoidable. Yet normal people often think and feel in this way. Specific occupational groups have their superstitions. Thus the crew of a ship may be disturbed by having to carry with them clergymen, missionaries, or other 'sky pilots'. One told me of the misfortunes that had dogged the whole passage of the ship after it had taken on a group of nuns. He added retrospectively, 'There were thirteen of them.' Outsiders may be surprised at the response of actor friends when the dreaded name, *Macbeth*, the unlucky play, is mentioned in a theatre. As with the fantasies that intrude in the life of a psychotic patient, the Koffka Principle again applies to superstitions, even if they are merely half-believed.

As regards actual phobias we have earlier considered fear of heights of an exaggerated kind. With 'acrophobia', and numerous other such words specifying irrational fears for a wide range of objects and situations, of interest is the history of this terminology. Hunter and MacAlpine (1963) uncovered this during their scholarly studies. It appears that Benjamin Rush 'in a half humorous vein' was tempted to parody current enthusiasm for invention of long words and diagnostic categories. Thus in 1798 he contributed an essay which provided new words for eighteen species as defined by the fear object. This has since been taken seriously and thus 'claustrophobia', 'agoraphobia', and many more now survive in numerous text-books. I will resist the temptation to invent an additional word for it, but of interest is one variant of fear of heights that has been reported.

A newspaper records this variant, a phobia for driving across bridges. It involved an incident with an unnamed woman motorist (*Daily Mail*, 3 October 1987). With her phobic fear guiding her route she had planned her 100-mile journey from Suffolk to

London. But while driving outside Ipswich she realized her mistake after taking a wrong turning. She found herself, in rush-hour traffic, confronted by a bridge, nearly 1 mile long and over 100 feet above the river. Despite angry sounding of horns from behind her, she was unable to proceed. Eventually a police officer arrived in a patrol car, and drove her over the bridge while she lay terrified in the back seat. Although her emotionally charged thinking and resulting actions – or non-actions – were excessive, empathy is possible. Among the things people often prefer to not do is drive over certain bridges that are high and long. Such bridges are interesting. If psychiatrists are equipped with vocabularies of words specifying phobias, psychologists also have theirs. We seem prone to use 'interesting' for things that arouse emotion, including, as in this case, the emotionally disturbing. Florida also possesses its memorable bridges. They extend from Key Largo out into the Gulf of Mexico, miles and miles across the sea towards Cuba. Length rather than height is their characteristic. But driving a car for miles out into the sea, perhaps towards the setting sun over distant Key West, is certainly another 'interesting' experience. A characteristic of words is their ability to lock up emotion in them, emotion that is released during therapy. This is one of the problems of technical terms, for phobias or other things, that can become ego defences against recognition of such stored emotion. The ego defence, named 'isolation' – compartmentalization – is the mechanism involved. And it plays an important part in personality and thinking in the 'anankastic' neuroses.

Criterion problems become formidable when we consider delusion-determined thinking and seek to distinguish it from thinking of other kinds. To illustrate: in one court case in southern New Mexico such issues arose. The court deliberated over whether the man accused of murder was deluded, or merely influenced by superstitions common within his culture. The defence, for which I was called, was much concerned as the death penalty – which was avoided – was a definite possibility. Earlier in New Mexico there had been another kind of case again involving a homicide. The defendant claimed that the man he had shot had appeared to him as a deer. Was this hallucination fed by delusion or merely the result of a culturally sanctioned belief, widespread in many parts of the world, that people can change themselves into animals? Anyway, the New Mexican court acquitted the accused. The tragic accident case, to be discussed in Chapter 14, tried in New Zealand also involved a man who was shot, having been confused with a deer. In this instance the court was concerned with an accidental misperception. The belief system differed and there was no question of animal metamorphosis. Again in some cultures, including southern Ireland, there are strong beliefs about 'little people', and I have talked with some who claim to have actually 'seen' them. Hallucination? Are leprechauns and similar things products of hallucination or perhaps merely of dreamlife and associated states? As Galton emphasized with visionary activities, when social norms are of a matter-of-fact kind the seers of visions keep quiet. But where supernaturalism prevails, 'then the seers of visions come to the front.' He adds that the 'faintly perceived fantasies of ordinary persons' become invested with authority, and may also become more vivid 'by being dwelt upon' (Galton 1883: 128). Moreover individual people may move from one area of culture to another and thus create additional criterion problems in labelling a given alleged subjective experience. The multi-racial society which England has become is already having to face such issues, and sometimes court cases involve them.

THE PSYCHOPATHOLOGY OF EVERYDAY LIFE

Psychologists as different as Freud and Skinner remind us that everyday life, in thinking as elsewhere, has its psycho-pathology. Cross-cultural, abnormal, and developmental psychology all provide some useful reference points. Earlier I discussed the apparent 'conversations' that occur with schizophrenic patients: both are talking but neither is listening. Such non-communicative thinking may sometimes be noticed even in older children. I take as an example an incident involving a child, myself, and a radio. The girl expressed her wish, which was to talk; and I expressed mine, to listen to the radio programme that interested me. It was the child who produced the solution. She would go on talking to me, but she didn't really mind if I went on listening to the radio and not to her! Piaget (1926) is on occasion disturbing to the adult ego when he suggests that a number of developmentally early forms of thinking can persist into adult life. One he mentions is 'proving' something by loud and repeated statements of conviction, 'I know', not of course necessarily evidence for anything. People are often dead certain, and dead wrong.

Very important in everyday life is the way people think – and feel – about other categories of people. As subject matter, human beings can be classified in numerous different ways. Among them are nationality, occupation, ethnic origin, occupation, sex, and religion. When there is a high degree of group consciousness and group loyalty for some category of people they may become, for others, objects of strong positive or negative sentiments. As regards nationality, of interest are the pages of *Punch* which reveal in their cartoons of the past such stereotypes as 'The unspeakable Turk', or 'The Prussian Bully', and more positively 'Brave little Belgium' of the First World War, defying the tyrant invader of the day. In more recent times journalists sometimes admit to making their contribution to hostile prejudice. One of them in the late 1980s has cynically described his work as often spending the first part of a week informing his readers of the existence of a country, and the second part inducing them to hate its inhabitants. Although influential, the press, radio, and television are not the only determinants of stereotyped hostile sentiments that interfere with accurate thinking in everyday life. Traumatic experiences of representatives of some group of people and over-generalization may be another recipe for the development of such sub-systems. Earlier I distinguished between primary prejudices, based on personal acquaintance, and secondary prejudices that are learned more indirectly. Both types may contribute to a kind of 'internal society' within a person: his repertoire of inaccurate stereotypes about other categories of people. In the case of nationality we have the classic study by Rosemary Gordon (1962) of relations of these introjected fictions to rigidity of imagery and ego defences. Later she, now an experienced Jungian analyst, has discussed what she describes as 'a very private world', this internal society of images she encounters in her patients. Very important in her work is this 'private film show', and the process of making a person 'aware that he has an inner world' of this type (Gordon 1984: 8). Moreover, patients are not unique, and as Gordon is prepared to admit, psychologists like herself also have stereotyped influences in their ways of categorizing members of national or other groups.

Parallel insights into irrational influences on thinking in everyday life were expressed to me by one informant. This man, a lawyer by profession, was aware from his introspections that personal acquaintance with a group does not necessarily lead to increased tolerance. He told me how before travelling abroad he had been virtually an internationalist, possessed of but a few learned secondhand prejudices. But having in his travels encountered many nationalities, he now possessed a fairly extensive repertoire of nationalistic antipathies. In his case a few minor secondary prejudices had been replaced by primary ones. These persisted despite his being prepared to admit that his experiences with individuals might have led him to unjustified over-generalization. Personality sub-systems of the emotional habit kind do not depart simply because we are aware of them, as we know also in the case of the minor superstitions of everyday life. Nor is nationality the only basis of prejudice in categorizing other people who are, or seem to be, in some way 'different'. Practical problems arise over what a person can do about the more emotionally charged irra-tionalities of his own internal society when he is aware of them. In everyday life we frequently encounter – through observation or introspection – occasions when a person has knowledge of expres-sing prejudice. Such a discharge of emotion in speech may be accompanied at the time, or at least afterwards, with insight into indulging a prejudice. Since such insight tends to be fragile Nietzsche suggests a principle: 'beware of those in whom the urge towards punishment is strong.' The Nietzsche Principle is perhaps of use as guiding restraint on how to think about prejudice and what not to do in relation to it, whether it is observationally or introspectively observed. Fortunately habit also contributes its restraints. Yet, as thinkers from Schopenhauer, to Hebb in psychology, and William Golding in literature, have shown, there are circumstances in which such restraints fail. People who are in some way 'different' then become vulnerable as scapegoats or targets of witch-hunting in one of its many forms. Even when aware that a prejudice is operating the personality still faces the task of what to do with it, and insight is not necessarily a guarantee of control, in relation to thought and judgement. As regards overt expression in action, perhaps the Nietzsche Principle is of some guidance in resisting the punitiveness towards 'others' that so readily accompanies hostile emotional sub-systems.

243

As Gordon suggests, we are equipped with an internal society of often inaccurate stereotypes of other individuals and groups. More generally the human personality is, like a coral reef, a structure that has resulted from past experience. I take as illustration a short period of time when, one evening, emotional habits of various degrees of importance were reactivated in myself. Casual conversation involved mention of four cities which, in two cases, aroused my awareness of dislike, and in two the emotional warmth of liking very much. Secondary perception contributed: appearance on the television of two politicians for whom I have strong distaste, followed more happily by an approved-of person, and then an advertisement involving a comedian whom I find irritating. I glanced at the newspaper which referred to a social group that has my support, and also to a country for which I have a well-developed positive sentiment. Much of everyday life is like this. Even in relaxed circumstances the personality is bombarded with primary and secondary perceptual information, and stimuli that arouse emotional responses to it. Nor is the personality itself an exception as an object of such emotion. Personality has a temporal dimension, a past, a present, and an anticipated future. In his autobiographical writings, Arthur Koestler (1954) has discussed in detail his antipathy to his own former self. This extended not only to his former beliefs and sentiments, but even to his own earlier body image. But he viewed in retrospect his later self with more approval, in for example recalling with satisfaction cartoons which showed his *Darkness at Noon* being burned by figures representing both Hitler and Stalin. He respected this former self, not its predecessor. Koestler's introspections involve one aspect of the phenomenon of intolerance of the convert. Any reminder of a former, but now abandoned, system of belief is uncomfortable, and we reserve a particular hostility for those who recall it. The Freudian mechanism of repression is much concerned with keeping out of consciousness memories of the rejected activities of the former self. Moreover, there is also a mental mechanism on which La Rochefoucauld placed emphasis: a tendency to strong hostility to those that remind a personality of some aspect of itself which it is motivated to deny. Koestler's analysis suggests that this same mechanism may apply retrospectively.

In considering depressive states of consciousness we encounter

244

a variety of manifestations of self-directed hate and punitiveness. Along with the guilt feeling that accompanies these there is often evidence of residual aggression and hostility to others also.

SUMMARY

1   Human thinking is variable in both 'normal' and 'abnormal' people. In an interview between a patient and another person, the thinking of the two concerned may be remarkably similar. Psychotic patients do not necessarily think psychotically all the time. There are some variants of normal association of considerable interest to abnormal psychology.

2   Arieti's 'paleologic' concept provides one basis for study of schizophrenic thinking, when a schizophrenic thinks schizophrenically. Central to this is the Von Domarus Principle. There are also occasions when – as is less usual in everyday life – a patient will respond in an unreasonably literal way to the words spoken.

3   Studies with model psychoses experiments, and of hypnagogia and dreamlife may provide additional information about processes resembling psychotic thinking. Interferences of imagery with association are considered.

4   Superstitious and anankastic thinking have close resemblances, and seem sometimes to be virtually indistinguishable. An atypical phobia is considered, and along with it the history of the long words sometimes used to specify different forms of phobia.

5   Emotional sub-systems are re-considered with particular reference to the influences of prejudices and the presence or absence of lucidity and co-consciousness. Sometimes these result in violence to others, or alternatively self-hostility and associated guilt feeling, next to be discussed in consideration of grief and the depressions.

Chapter Twelve

DEPRESSION, AGGRESSION, AND GUILT FEELING

Laugh and the world laughs with you;
Weep and you weep alone;
For the sad old earth must borrow its mirth;
But has troubles enough of its own.

Ella Wheeler Wilcox

The emotion of sorrow is complex. While the unpredictablity and the strange logic of schizophrenia is absent from depression, there are paradoxes. Darwin noted one of these in relation to weeping. The giving of sympathy evokes tears: by contrast the advice 'to have a good cry' may result in their cessation. Lund (1930) takes up this point. In considering what we might call 'Darwin's paradox' he points out that the relation of weeping to sorrow does not parallel that of laughter to amusement. He finds support in a study of psychiatric patients: weeping is a frequent accompaniment of transition from depressed to elated states. The condition most favourable to it is mixed emotion, not unrelieved depression. In everyday life this recognition may be acted on by people who have to deal with grief, bereavement, or depression. They may deliberately seek to reduce bottled-up emotional tension by offering sympathy, alleviating grief, and thus provoking weeping. Of her period of imprisonment Benazir Bhutto comments, 'if anybody had been sweet or kind to me, perhaps I would have broken down.' She adds, 'but I was treated harshly, which brought out all my individual defiance' (Interview, *Sunday Times Magazine*,

246

4 January 1987: 58). Lund refers also to the way people respond to the sufferings of others. Even in identifying with fictional hardships – watching a play or a film – something similar happens. While observing unrelieved misery the audience experiences no inclination to weep. But when alleviation or help comes there is a moisture of the eyes, even actual flow of tears.

Freud underlined resemblances between depression and bereavement. His *On Mourning and Melancholia* notes presence in both of exaggerated guilt feeling along with sadness. There is a search through one's past actions and omissions in pursuit of self-blame over things that an impartial observer might assess as innocent or trivial. Many depressed patients claim to have committed 'the unpardonable sin': if we are able to track down this focus of guilt feeling this proves, on scrutiny, almost to define the trivial. Here we encounter a further paradox. As Freud observes, the superego of the saint becomes more exacting than that of the sinner whose conscience is under-developed. Despite the superficial impression of insight in melancholic patients, and their otherwise unimpaired thinking, Yellowlees (1932) uses the term 'delusion'. 'Delusions of guilt' is, he argues, not too inappropriate a term for their ways of remembering, feeling, and thinking. Observations of what we may see and hear of guilt feelings before, during, or after a funeral support the Freudian emphasis on resemblances between bereavement and melancholia. One neglected aspect of bereavement may be mentioned. A lost object may not be a person. People develop emotional dependence not only on other people but also on animals. Indeed in discussing sentiments McDougall takes as illustration the development by a man of love for an animal. If death occurs the accompanying depression may have an additional component in the bleak lack of sympathy on the part of others: 'it was only an animal.' Professional vets who may have to kill an injured much-loved animal are often aware that they lack any specific training in coping with this kind of bereavement. The issue is discussed by Alan Bestie (*Independent*, 30 December 1986), who refers to a recent survey revealing that such loss can be 'akin in many ways to the death of a human'. He adds 'the elderly often suffer because they have lost their only friend' and also notes how to childless couples 'the pet has become the focus of their attention.' Anna Freud (1936) has discussed this loss of a loved object of a non-human kind in relation to the equivalent

247

problems of the child, and its often pathetic attempts to adjust to this.

Shand has much to say about what he calls 'this great clinging impulse' of grief: its unwillingness to give up the lost object. Drawing on a kind of symposium of thoughtful predecessors he points out that sorrow is an emotion 'which strives to maintain all that remains of the former union' (Shand 1920: 323). He refers to what Tennyson calls 'the cruel fellowship' of sorrow and the comment of Seneca 'all grief is obstinate' (Quoted in Shand: 321). There is additional obstinacy of resistance to being comforted: as most of us have discovered in efforts to cheer up a depressed person, this can be exceedingly hard work. Not surprisingly, as the poem cited at the head of this chapter implies, many people either shy off or soon give up the task. Granted obstinate resistance to mere words of comfort it is fortunate that pharmacology has provided chemical assistance to human sympathy. The seemingly trivial should not be overlooked. A medical colleague recently told me of the crucial part which the humble cup of tea plays in his daily work. Moreover, it is always 'tea', never coffee in his experience. His observation is supported – indeed quantified – by the estimate that in the United Kingdom approximately 196,000,000 cups of tea are consumed daily. In supplying this statistic, *The Times* (5 February 1987) adds, 'It was tea that got us through the Blitz, and it is keeping us going still.' Songs that survive from its predecessor, the First World War, remind us of the similar consolations, in, for example, the mud of trench warfare, of still having 'a lucifer to light your fag'. This also helped with fear, grief, and depression.

For Shand it is also paradoxical that despite its resistance to consolation sorrow nevertheless somehow seeks it and manages 'to obtain from others the strength or assistance it needs' (op. cit.: 314). Sorrow is 'the emotion of weakness'. Yet it betrays its characteristic obstinacy. It resembles the lovers' quarrel and its aftermath: overtures are at first rejected, but after two or more rebuffs begin to evoke some reward. Depression, sorrow, and grief may put great strain on persistent efforts to offer consolation first with initial refusal to accept it and later with unwillingness to depart until the would-be helper is similarly depressed. In the less familiar part of the quotation cited above the poetess provides a warning: elsewhere she adds 'the world is sad enough without *your* woe.' She provides a typology as between the people who lift, and the people who lean, that parallels two of Henry Murray's needs, *n*. nurturance, and *n*. succorance. On the press side Shand sees the sorrow emotions as 'the cry for help or assistance'.

There is an obvious overlap between states of depression and normal behaviour. Sentiments and other systems provide internal sources of painful emotions. On the other hand there are obviously many forms of environmental press that provoke them. Diagnostic systems place their emphasis upon severe stress or long-persisting suffering. As we move along the continuum we pass from states in which precipitating factors are important to those involving personalities constitutionally liable to depression. Various investigators like Warner (1985) have pointed out how changes in diagnostic criteria complicate what is assessed at a given place or time as psychotic depression. Warner points out that in the past in both the United States and Soviet Russia many patients diagnosed as schizophrenic would in other parts of the world have been diagnosed as manic-depressive. The American DSM III in this third revised form has both codified and influenced the trend towards a much narrower conception of the schizophrenias. One earlier attempt to re-examine the basis of diagnostic systems was made by I. D. Suttie (1935; reprinted 1945). This psychiatrist distinguished two major categories. In the first of these, the Wish or Aim Syndromes, the patient gives evidence of having, through delusion or in some other way, established a system of equilibrium. The schizophrenias and paranoia exemplify this. By contrast are the Self-Frustration Syndromes: through depression, anxiety, and general unhappiness they reveal clear absence of such internal equilibrium. Depressed and anxious patients may leave this unstable state by suicide or by getting better. But unlike the other group they do not 'drift complacently out of touch with social life into dementia, invalidism or a world of suspicion and grandeur' (op. cit.: 19). While it may be objected that there are many signs of disequilibrium in the panic and anxiety of early schizophrenia, Suttie's dichotomy is of interest. It fits the experience and behaviour of depression, also patients' suicide rates and otherwise better prognosis. But time has passed since Suttie's contribution, and with it have come both changes in diagnostic criteria, and advances of treatment including, for example, lithium and other therapies.

GUILT AND AGGRESSION

In his later writings Freud introduced the notion of an instinctual reservoir of destructive and self-destructive energy. A leading American theorist, Karl Menninger, accepted this formulation, and in *Man Against Himself* (1942) examined a range of phenomena. These included suicide often in a variety of symbolic forms, self-mutilation, chronic invalidism, recurrent resort to unnecessary surgery, and other manifestations. By contrast a major British theorist, J. C. Flugel (1945), rejected the instinct theory. His explanation of self-destructive aggression he found – as did Schopenhauer before him – in the thwartings, frustrations, and sufferings of the individual's life history. As the counterpart of Freudian narcissism, being in love with oneself, Flugel introduced the concept of nemesism. Martyrdom, asceticism in a variety of forms, and moral masochism were for Flugel some of the manifestations of nemesistic self-hatred. As Freud saw it, the superego may become a gathering place for the self-destructiveness of the death instincts, expressing themselves in moralized ways. By contrast Flugel made a distinction between the more primitive aspects of the superego, and its reality-adjusted, rationally defensible side which he calls the ego ideal. Analytic therapy seeks to strengthen the ego idea against the harsh dictates of moralized aggression and self-punitiveness. So far as this is successful man becomes less of a pain-seeking animal. In his detailed examination of the psychology of morality liberated by insight Flugel throws considerable light on the influence of nemesism as often a powerful motivational force. In depression there may be a part of oneself which observes, even enjoys, the misery of the person concerned. It wouldn't miss the show for worlds.

The part of hostility in depression is emphasized by many who have concerned themselves with this area of psychology. Freud refers to the strangeness of the behaviour of the melancholic who loudly proclaims his own wickedness to others rather than endure it in silence. Quiet shame seems more appropriate. The explanation is that the self-accusations do not really relate to the self. They express hostility against somebody else. There is ambivalence towards the other person who has been introjected, or taken into, one's own ego. Because, as Freud puts it, 'the shadow of the object' has fallen on the ego there is self-hatred and the need for punishment. The lost object is there to become a focus of exaggerated guilt feeling. As we have seen, Shand with his emphasis on the 'clinging impulse' of sorrow makes a similar point. There is reluctance to give up the rejecting or otherwise lost object, and there is also much hostility to other people, as well as oneself, in depression. Shand is very critical of the notion that people are necessarily ennobled by suffering and grief. Sometimes this happens, and sometimes it doesn't. As one of the proverbs, which Shand doesn't quote, puts it, 'the fire that melts the butter hardens the egg.' Beckfort portrays in *Vathek* an Islamic hell in which the sufferers in their agony glare at each other with hate. Shand makes the point that, 'though it shocks us to recognise it, what we suffer we think others ought to suffer' (Shand 1920: 338). As he also points out, depressed emotion may elicit anger, and thus become the source of envy and misanthropy. 'Envy is one solution to the problem.' Along with the self-directed hostility of depression may be a surplus of hostility which ensures that others will also suffer. Thus in Alan Ayckbourn's play *Absent Friends* the author portrays his character Colin as overwhelmed with grief. In the end a more cheerful Colin ensures everyone else is utterly miserable.

Aggression turned upon the self by suicide is a frequent sequel to an act of murder: there is a sufficient fund of aggression for both. Murder and suicide are forms of behaviour fortunately often a matter of fantasy. There is a sense in which very many normal people have 'committed' – in their imagery – a huge repertoire of crimes, including murder. Guilt feeling arising from such fantasy may play an important role in depression. The relations between fantasied aggression and guilt feeling, and their impact upon psychiatric breakdown, form the theme of Dostoevsky's last great novel. *The Brothers Karamazov* deals with the murder of a hated parent and the reactions to it of the four sons. One of these is causally guilty and though he escapes the law he inflicts upon himself the traditional penalty in suicide by hanging. A second son, Dmetri, is tried for the crime: though causally innocent he is judged legally guilty. Consumed with depression, remorse, and guilt feeling, he accepts – indeed welcomes – the punishment of exile to Siberia. The third brother, Alyosha, is portrayed by Dostoevsky as both emotionally robust and the kind of 'saint' that children look up to and admire. Yet when asked if he has 'killed' his father – a thoroughly unpleasant human being – he gives his assent. In his fantasy even this 'normal' man, one of Dostoevsky's most humane characters, has imaged himself in the act of murder. The fourth brother, Ivan Karamazov, exhibits what the author calls 'brain fever'. His psychosis involves delusion supported by visual and auditory hallucination. In this what he has thought is a contributory factor to dissociation that results from severe internal conflict. In these four reactions Dostoevsky uncovers the complexities of motivation relating to actions thought but not overtly performed. In the novel Dostoevsky exhibits his sure grasp of continuity between fantasy and imagery on the one hand, and overt action on the other.

Destruction of the lives of other people is very much an affair of fact, as well as fantasy, often with people who know each other well. Whether classified as homicide or in some other way it may be an accompaniment of actual or attempted suicide. The killing of a child by a depressed parent may be illustrated by a case discussed by Tuke (1892), an intentionally historically remote example. Becoming aware that the depression she had previously experienced was returning, the woman concerned took her three children to a canal, having left a suicide note for her husband, drowned them, but was prevented from carrying out her intention to drown herself also. The case came before a law lord, Lord Blackburn, who instructed the jury to find her 'not guilty on the grounds of insanity'. In the suicide note the mother expressed her gratitude to 'a good, hard-working husband'. It said that the children would be better off dead than if she left them 'in this world of trouble', and in expressing her affection for the husband and children she sought God's blessing and comfort. The judge in this case seemed satisfied about taking these expressions of affection at their face value. To others they may appear different: evidence that strong ambivalence may be an aspect of 'love', and that self-destructiveness may carry a surplus of destructiveness towards others. In this respect then, as is also true today, depression may clash with the law in the areas of homicide and infanticide. English law takes account of depression that occurs post-natally in distinguishing the offence of infanticide from murder. The introduction of the defence of diminished responsibility in 1957 can likewise have relevance to this and other forms of depression which may have overtones of motivation to kill other human beings. Such acts may on occasion occur under the label of 'love' in one or other of the strange usages of this highly ambiguous word.

THE VULNERABILITY OF THE CHILD

The most obvious source of silent misery of childhood cannot be sidestepped. It is being the victim of pain or humiliation intentionally inflicted. As Adler (1932) emphasized, every human being is first a child in an adult world. Those who are larger, stronger, and in authority over any child have numerous ways of producing for it misery, happiness, or something in between. Events in England during 1986–7 focused attention on sexual abuse of children. Parallel are the grim issues of physical aggression, sometimes rationalized under 'punishment'. Sir Cyril Burt's treatment of delinquency under the headings of the 'over-punished' as well as the 'under-punished' and 'inconsistently-punished' child is a reminder of differences to be considered in any given case of avoidable childhood misery (Burt 1937). The problems, whether they involve aggression as such or sexual assault, are simpler if the child's home is not involved. Bullying at school, for example, may not be easy to deal with if the child fears retaliation, but there are ways of coping with it with the aid of intelligence and imagination. A wise and empathic lawyer, the late Allan J. Nixon (1977), placed emphasis on the very positive emergence in history of the school and with it teachers who could become emotionally significant individuals, outside the home, in the life of a child. Tensions sometimes arise between school and home. But under ideal, perhaps usual conditions, there exists a potentially supportive triad: the home, the school, and other agencies concerned with the medical welfare of a child. With these acting in collaboration, with co-operation and good communication, the vulnerability of a child is reduced. Murray's supportive press, like '*p*. counteraction', '*p*. support', or sometimes '*p*. aggression' in defence of a child, may come from several different sources. Checks and balances exist, though sometimes they may fail, as retrospective accounts by adults testify.

Much more difficult is when the home itself is allegedly or

actually involved in child abuse. Various authorities like the law, medicine, social workers, and others may be involved. As emerged in the judicial inquiry over diagnosis of alleged sexual abuse of numerous children in Cleveland during 1987, communication and good co-ordination between competent professionals is all-important. Good intentions are not enough, and mistakes can be guaranteed to contribute to human misery. Mistakes may be of two kinds: overlooking cases of actual cruelty or other abuse, and errors of inclusion, like unjustified accusations against innocent adults. Issues may also arise over natural parents. I take as illustration the sense of powerlessness strongly expressed to me by two humane adults who were fostering a child, knowing what it would be forced to endure when it had to be returned to its 'natural' mother. Fortunately it later came back to them. They put to me their emphatic conviction that there are people, whether 'natural parents' or not, who should never be permitted custody of a child. As regards other vulnerable people, whether mentally ill, young, or aged, Hunter and MacAlpine (1963) have recorded a history of great variability of institutions, including 'private asylums', within Europe. Today, in Britain, inspection of such institutions and also lists of people who are not permitted to run them are two safeguards, in the case of, for example, 'homes' for the aged. In the case of the child in its own home, its vulnerability may nevertheless be overlooked, even by another parent living in it. Thus in the well-known Sybil multiple personality case, the father emerged as ignorant of the sadistic cruelty of the mother to the child (Schreiber 1975).

Allan Nixon (1977) draws on his own experience as a barrister in making references to the 'dark area' of statistics, cases which do not become known. Referring to a 'recent year', the date unstated, he cites 500 instances of prosecutions for assaults on police officers, but only 21 for cruelty to children. His reference is to New Zealand figures, and he refers to a similar disproportion in an Australian study. When a given case of alleged child abuse is encountered, he suggests three things. His first suggestion is to 'decriminalise' such offences. He believed this would help penetrate the 'dark area'. There is no controversy about his other two suggestions. They comprise 'an assurance that the wrong will be put right, as far as human ingenuity can achieve it'. His third comment is 'ensuring that matters of a like kind will not occur again'. Nixon adds that under such conditions 'you might indeed hear from the offender *himself* with a frequency which would surprise you' (Nixon 1977: 139, italics his). What should be done, in a given proven case, may include humane injections into court proceedings, some of which are already in use, like video-tapes which remove a child's evidence from the presence of an alleged offender. Dangers of conviction of the innocent, and of the influence of leading questions on childhood testimony are matters for imagination, skilled professionals, and legal vigilance.

In the grim issues involved, powers of empathy with an actual offender may be strained. Two points may be made. First is the well-established fact that such offenders have often themselves been victims in their own childhood. Second is the emotional response of 'normal' people in terms of what they would 'like to do' to such an offender. Revenge may echo, even surpass what it condemns. On these issues we may again turn to Ivan Karamazov and Dostoevsky. In *The Brothers Karamazov* Ivan confronts the intelligent and robust virtue of his brother Alyosha with his own religious scepticism about cruelty to children. Ivan declares that in this there is evidence that 'If the devil doesn't exist, but man has created him, he has created him in his own image and likeness' (Garnett 1968 edition: 244). Asked whether the whole of creation is worth what children have had to endure through history, or even the suffering of a single child, Alyosha – a young man prepared to take up religious orders – agrees that it is not. Forced to respond even he mutters 'No'. This powerful novel, with the insights of Dostoevsky's mature genius, ends with the words 'Hurrah for Karamazov!' The Karamazov in question is Alyosha. In the words of the boy who speaks them perhaps the author meant to convey the message that – in people like Alyosha who actually like children – there are exceptions to Ivan's grim overstatement about the human species and what individuals sometimes do. But in persistence of his intellectual honesty, Ivan is not yet finished. This emerges not least in the powerful reply Ivan makes to Alyosha in his story of the confrontation between 'Christ and the Grand Inquisitor'. The issues raised apply outside the realm of the vulnerability of the child. Dostoevsky is fully aware of other kinds of violence, aggression, and cruelty without pity to be considered.

Vulnerable like children are animals. On this, speaking of

civilized Britain of the 1980s, one RSPCA inspector declared 'The course taken during training can't even prepare you for some of the cruelty inflicted by people on animals' (*Independent*, 16 February 1988). In an earlier period such happenings led Hogarth (1697–1764), whose work influenced Dickens, to portray in his engravings transition from cruelty to animals to acts of violence against human beings. On this issue, the author of *Lord of the Flies* – which deals with cruelty without pity to both – makes the comment on the many things done during his lifetime 'from which I have to avert my mind lest I should be physically sick'. William Golding adds, 'anyone who moved through these years without understanding that man produces evil as a bee produces honey, must have been blind' (Golding 1962: 228). Fortunately, here as elsewhere human beings differ. The some–all antidote to this grim judgement has application, but as Golding implies this should not obscure the fact that within a whole society apparently 'normal' people may perform acts which strain our powers of empathy.

Among the major novels of modern times some have reflected the realities of political aggression against individuals and minorities. The writings of George Orwell and of Arthur Koestler are prominent examples. Dominance of psychopathology in a whole society, and the postulated abnormality of individuals who participated in genocide, torture, and murder has resulted in experimental studies as well as major works of literature. Experimental findings testify to the frightening conclusion that apparently normal human beings can do terrible things to one another. Two of these experiments are well known but must be mentioned.

AUTHORITY, OBEDIENCE, AND AGGRESSION

The experiments of the late Stanley Milgram (e.g. Milgram 1974) involved setting up situations in which subjects apparently – to the best of their knowledge – administered electric shocks of increasing severity. No shocks were in fact given, and the apparent 'victims' were confederates of the experimenter. The subjects administered the shocks to the victims under the influence of the experimenters, seemingly as punishment for errors in a verbal-learning task. The 'shock generator' carried a label of 'output 15 –

450 volts', and the victims were strapped into a device resembling a torture chair. After receiving shocks of apparently 135 volts the victims cried out in pain, and at 285 volts they responded with screams of agony. At earlier levels of shock the victims – as pre-arranged – told of suffering from a medical heart condition. Milgram reports no evidence that any of his forty subjects detected the deception involved. Despite this, twenty-seven continued to administer shocks of increasing severity – because the experimenter told them to – after the victims had cried out, complained of heart conditions, and demanded to be released. Seven of the subjects continued to obey authority and administer shocks up to the limit of 450 volts. Not surprisingly, the well-known Milgram experiments evoked much criticism from several ethical points of view of an obvious kind. But having been conducted, and repeated with a number of variations like physical proximity of the shock-administrator to the apparent victim, their conclusions are disturbing. Highly relevant is the fact that the subjects who took part were apparently 'normal' people: some of them were highly distressed by what seemed to be happening, but nevertheless continued with ever-increasing shocks. The notion that there are limits on what normal people, under obedience to authority, are prepared to do to others was shattered.

Another experiment was conducted at Stanford University by Zimbardo (1972). If possible this was even more disturbing in related findings. This again well-known experiment involved a simulated prison situation. Of seventy volunteers who had been screened as 'normal' people, half were assigned by lot to the role of prisoners, the other half to prison guards. Physical ill-treatment of the 'prisoners' was forbidden, but the 'guards' soon developed harsh standards of their own in treatment of their victims. They exhibited aggression, abuse, and bullying behaviour towards the prisoners. Outside the experimental situation they often exhibited guilt feelings and surprise at the reserves of aggression that welled up inside them. The guards did what they could to dehumanize their victims who, for their part, became passive, dependent, and frightened by the treatment they received. Some differences between the guards were noted by Zimbardo, and some were less tyrannical in their abuses of power. But these 'good' guards did not interfere with the commands of the 'bad' guards; did not intervene on behalf of the prisoners; and made no efforts to complain to the experimenter. After only six days the experiment had to be terminated, seemingly on the grounds of common humanity and a measure of fear on the part of the experimenters because of what they saw happening. Again the apparent normality of those who took part as guards may be emphasized.

One aftermath of the Second World War was a series of trials of war criminals. Foremost of these was the trial of Goering, Hess, and other principal Nazi leaders at Nuremberg.

THE NUREMBERG TRIAL

The mass extermination of human life in Nazi Germany represents crime in its most horrible form. Some among those causally responsible were tried by an international court at Nuremberg. Some, such as Col. A. Hoess and Adolf Eichmann, were tried and in these two cases executed at other times. Among the Nuremberg accused, Hess alone remained in Spandau Prison, from which others having served their sentences had been released. Albert Speer wrote about his own life and contributions to the Nazi state, and his account has much relevance to any attempt at understanding these terrible happenings. Speer in particular provided a good deal of still more relevant material at the time of the Nuremberg Trial, giving much indication of his own emotional rejection and guilt reactions. This information came to the American prison psychologist, G. M. Gilbert, who at the time of the trial interviewed again and again the various accused. With Speer Gilbert seems to have achieved a good rapport. Another of the leading Nazis was Frank, the Gauleiter of Poland who, having been converted to Christianity, claimed remorse, but was nevertheless hanged after the trial for crimes against humanity. The point emerges that a number of different kinds of people were involved and among them were some who gave indication of hatred towards one another. The relations between the Nazi financier Schacht and Goering were those of strong mutual antipathy, as emerged not least from the intelligence tests which Gilbert, as court psychologist, administered. Goering was for a time very enthusiastic about psychology and psychologists until two events occurred. The first was when Gilbert told him that

Schacht's intelligence test score was higher than Goering's; the second was when Gilbert administered and interpreted to Goering the Nazi's Rorschach Test. Rapport remained good with Speer who, Gilbert records, did his best to assist by telling to the best of his ability 'the whole wretched truth'.

Abnormal psychology certainly enters into the evidence accumulated by Gilbert and others as in, for example, Gilbert's book *Nuremberg Diary* (1948a). But the abnormalties that occur are of different kinds. Kaltenbrunner, for example, was by all standards a sadist of an unpleasant kind, and moreover a man of limited intelligence. Most intellectually limited of all, on test results, was Streicher with his violent anti-Semitism, who also exhibited an atypical form of compulsive-obsessional neurosis. Of Goering Gilbert also wrote a paper which assessed him as a 'psychopath', and in one interview Goering defended himself by making a distinction between 'cruelty' and 'brutality'. He admitted to being 'brutal' but not cruel, and Gilbert assesses the distinction as being to a certain extent valid (Gilbert 1948b). If the concept of 'normality' can be applied, it might refer to individuals like Speer; also perhaps to some of the military and naval men tried at Nuremberg. Among these were some who clearly disliked the politicians; shared in the general contempt for Streicher and Frank; and knowing they were to be executed, sought a firing squad rather than the ignoble form of death by hanging. Although the court had clearly communicated that such a plea would be invalid, these men mostly adhered to the defence of 'obedience to orders'.

The concept of 'normality' is not one which I am tempted strongly to defend in the case of the principal Nazi leaders. Perhaps we find it in such a person as the propagandist Fritzsche. Many accept him as a more minor figure and a stand-in for Goebbels who had by suicide escaped capture. When Gilbert visited him after a film of one of the concentration camps had been shown, Fritzsche burst into tears: 'No power in heaven or earth will erase this shame from my country, not in generations – not in centuries' (Gilbert 1948a: 30). During the film, Gilbert records, 'Doenitz has head bowed, no longer watching', and General Keitel resembled the admiral, 'averting his eyes' in apparent shame. In considering the mass destruction of human life, Jewish people, Poles, gypsies, and others, the question of causal explanation arises. First is our reaction that all the people responsible for such things must be 'abnormal'. But this explanation has to be rejected. A very large number of people were involved in such mass destruction, and the abnormality of all as opposed to some is improbable. The commandant of Auschwitz explained in evidence and interviews that the exterminations that killed people, as happened, at the rate of 10,000 a day involved complex organization. Hoess was in fact, on occasion, ordered to do more than was physically possible: this suggests a remoteness of those who issued the orders from those who carried them out. The beginnings at least of an explanation may lie in the conclusion that the things which made such actions physically possible also made them psychologically possible (McKellar 1950). We may distinguish those who prepared the way, with pseudo-biology that extolled the notions of 'Nordic' race superiority, to preserve such peoples from inferior and foreign elements. This culminated in the ideas of the Nazi philosopher Rosenberg. Then came the propagandists who popularized such thought: the ideas of *Mein Kampf* itself, the activities of Streicher with his anti-Semitic paper *Der Stürmer*, and the influences of the Propaganda Ministry of Goebbels, represented at the trial by Fritzsche. Next came the politicians, among whom Hitler and Himmler seem to have been most directly responsible for issuing extermination orders, but the assistance of many at this level was also necessary. Some, like Goering, could and did claim that the details of mass killings were remote from their own activities, and a by-product of other policies. Goering had been 'hard', but others like Himmler, Heydrich, and Kaltenbrunner had pursued cruelty for its own sake. Next were those who organized the executions, men like Colonel Hoess, who delegated the actual carrying out to subordinates. In an interview he told Gilbert, 'Don't you see we S.S. men were not supposed to think about these things; it never occurred to us. And besides it was something already taken for granted that the Jews were to blame for everything' (Gilbert 1948a: 156). Finally at the bottom of the hierarchy were the actual executioners.

In his final speech for the prosecution, Sir Hartley Shawcross quoted an eye-witness account of a mass shooting. The executioner was an S.S. Action Commando who sat with a cigarette in his mouth and his tommy gun on his knees. This man had already killed an estimated 1,000 people. The picture is of a low-ranking member of a hierarchy, obeying orders and carrying out duties for the day. Thus among the various members of this hierarchy we find some who were remote from the actual events, and the possibilities of self-deception at every level. At the top were those who 'didn't know' what was happening, at the bottom those who merely obeyed orders. One very unpleasant high-ranking person was Frank who, before the trial, had sought to appease guilt by an alleged religious conversion. But in the past he had, as governer of Poland, had much to do with what happened, and had vigorously advocated extermination of the Jews. The thing which had produced the religious conversion was, he explained to Gilbert, the discovery that a Dr J., an old Jewish lawyer who had been a close friend of Frank's father, had been an individual who had died at Auschwitz. Killing of two-and-a-half million people in this extermination camp became real to him through his memory of one 'upright, kindly old man'. An individual had died there.

An early paper by Maslow carried the title 'Cognition of the particular and the generic' (1948). The title summarizes this psychologist's argument and is highly relevant. Any category of people includes individuals. The earlier Frank, others like the pseudo-philosopher Rosenberg, the politician Ribbentrop, and the radio propagandist Fritzsche understood a phrase like 'extermination of the Poles' in a generic way. Admiral Doenitz, in expressing his contempt for Rosenberg, declared that he was a man who would not hurt a fly. Yet, Doenitz added, he had 'paved the way' for the 'terrible anti-Semitic acts'. There are many areas in which, in Maslow's terminology, mere 'cognition of the generic' insulates people from noticing the particular. We meet adjustments made by normal behaviour: something similar happens when a medical student, in dissecting the human body, focuses his attention on the generalities of anatomy not an individual body. As regards the Nuremberg Trial, I have met and talked with two of those who professionally took part in the proceedings. One was an American lawyer who helped prepare part of the prosecution's case against Goering and Streicher. An opinion strongly expressed was that, despite any actual or alleged conversion, by all standards one of the most unpleasant people of those who stood in the dock was Frank. Another of those who was present at the trial was the cartoonist, David Low. His written recollections are of interest in that he had, in his work, regularly drawn Goering,

Ribbentrop, and others of the accused. In his autobiography Low (1956) records that he recognized the men in the dock instantly. But he reports his surprise at the men he saw. 'Very ordinary-looking in fact. If you saw them sitting opposite you in a train you would think all were normal' (op. cit.: 358). Ribbentrop, once German Ambassador to Britain, he describes as 'a meek person like a family solicitor, with disordered hair, pursed lips and large spectacles, fussing shakily with a sheaf of papers' (op. cit.: 360). He adds the general comment that, as a whole, the accused were 'much too small'. The nondescript and apparent normality of these men recalls the experiments of both Milgram and Zimbardo, and their subjects selected for everyday normality. I understand what Low had in mind. On one occasion I attended an extended inquest taking the form of a public inquiry into a murder, discussed in detail elsewhere (McKellar 1979b). As the case involved an exorcism and the allegedly supernatural this inquest in Wakefield attracted the British press: reporters were present in large numbers. Before the inquest various witnesses had appeared in photographs in most of the daily papers. When I saw them in the coroner's court they were 'much too small', nondescript, and very ordinary-looking. Publicity, photographs, and the cartoonist's work may greatly 'blow up' political and other characters. Low refers to the experiences of a cartoonist who saw for the first time a statesman he had been drawing for years. He asked, 'Who's that?' Court proceedings or perhaps a visit to Madame Tussaud's – in the Hall of Fame or elsewhere – may well provide a better sense of perspective. So also may self-examining introspection in this area of human aggression, crime, punishment, and revenge.

ANGER, AGGRESSION, AND HATE

Psychologists sometimes have resorted to keeping a diary about one or other of the emotions: what provokes them, and how they find expression. Like many I once kept an anger diary. My findings on myself accorded closely with those of a group of normal people I subsequently studied by questionnaire and interview. Two types of situation tended to evoke anger: what I called need-situations, involving thwarting or frustration of some motive; and personality-situations involving threat, humiliation, or pain to the personality and its emotional involvements. The need situations tended to produce hot, short-lived anger directed to the removal of the frustration. Very different was the cold, resentful anger evoked by the personality-situations. This tended to be long-enduring and aimed at revengeful humiliation of the targets of the anger. On occasion such cold anger shaded into enduring emotional systems such as dislike, or, in extreme cases, hate. On no occasion, either in myself or the group of normal people later studied, did mere need-provocation lead to such sentiments: a personality-situation component was always present. The distinction between N–provocation and P–provocation, and the impulses which followed from them, seems of some importance (McKellar 1950; 1977b). Sometimes of course moral sentiments of the forgiveness kind operate, though regularly – indeed usually – the subjects who had developed the sentiment would attribute ethical inferiority to the object of that sentiment. The principle of Relative Ethics of Sentiments tends to operate (see Chapter 3). In this area we are confronted sometimes with breakdown of even the Mosaic restraint of an 'eye for an eye'. What my subjects were prepared to do in fantasy, and sometimes apparently in fact, to the targets of their moralized hatred seemed to be unrestrained. On some occasions it was restricted in terms of fantasies of inflicting no more, and no less, hurt and humiliation on the hated person than the subject had earlier experienced. I refer to the results of my later investigation of P–situation revengefulness in others. Introspectively I admit also to finding it in myself. As lighter relief on this subject I can recall how, at school, my fellow pupils and I would sometimes engage in the fantasy of being the dentist of one particularly unpleasant teacher. Cruelty provokes cruelty, fortunately sometimes only in imagery.

As regards the sentiment of hate it seems psychologically incorrect to argue that it is concerned to bring about the death of the hate object. In fantasy at least – and often in reality as history shows – its purpose is more malevolent: inflicting pain and humiliation before and even after death. In their emphasis on eternal punishment during an afterlife some theologians have been assessed as among mankind's greatest haters. The Christian epic of Dante elaborated in detail on such punishments. The correspondence columns of newspapers, and sometimes also their editorials when discussing certain types of crime as represented at Nuremberg, or in individual sadistic murders, have relevance to this depressing theme. There are many areas in which history and politics on the one hand and psychology on the other make contact with courts of law. This is one of them.

SUMMARY

1   The thought processes we encounter in the depressions may be less colourful than those of the schizophrenias. But the emotions of sorrow and grief are more complex than they may appear, as also can be the thinking that emerges from them. Darwin's paradox and certain other phenomena are considered.

2   In depression, as in reactions to bereavement, guilt feeling may be excessive in terms of anything the guilt-obsessed person has actually done. As Freud and his predecessor Dostoevsky showed, guiltiness may be the result of fantasy rather than of fact. A considerable amount of aggression against others, as well as against oneself, may play its part in depression.

3   Experimental studies have revealed the often frightening absence of restraints on human aggression. Moreover, we again encounter the Relative Ethics Principle, when anger becomes indignation, and hostility to some person or group becomes moralized.

4   The Nuremberg Trial was not only historically but also psychologically an important event. It uncovered the diversity of personalities among the principal Nazis accused. Partly through the court's psychologist it provided considerable information of value to forensic psychology about bureaucratic insensitivity and social remoteness, as well as guilt, depression, and aggression.

PARANOIA AND PARANOID REACTIONS

There is no loss of intellectual efficiency ... the person is quite capable of functioning adequately in all areas except those involving his delusional system.

George W. Kisker (1972)

It is time for the lecture on abnormal psychology in one New Zealand university. The audience of second-year students await their lecturer, but he does not appear. Instead another member of the psychology department comes in, and begins the lecture by referring to an interesting case he has recently encountered. The man concerned has agreed to come and be interviewed in front of the class. After these preliminaries this person enters. He is dressed in an anorak, wears climbing boots, and he trails an ice axe. By now a somewhat bewildered class of students recognize the new arrival. He is their usual lecturer on abnormal psychology, their professor, namely myself. In the interview which follows, I claim to be a guide on the Routeburn Track. This is a several-days walk through the mountains which is less well-known than the famous Milford Track: it crosses a higher pass, the Harris Saddle, from which descent can be dangerous, and there have been some tragic accidents. Sometimes guided parties are taken through these mountains. The pseudo-guide responds in the interview to questions in a reserved and somewhat guarded way. He admits that he does not always get on well with some of his clients on these guided trips: often they seem to resent his efforts to ensure their safety and welfare. In the evenings at the mountain huts —

there are three of them – he is glad to get away to sit by a small stream and listen to its sounds. Not only the rippling waters, but also the birds of the area, the keas or mountain parrots with their loud calls, and the wekas will comfort him. Without them he would feel very alone. Nature rather than people appeals to him. The interviewer presses him on this point: does he dislike any person in particular? A brief outburst of resentment against Stewart Islanders follows: people from this small island to the south of New Zealand who often think they know everything about the New Zealand bush. Sometimes they try to take over leadership of the party from him. Suddenly there follows a torrent of abuse against one of the other guides who is a Stewart Islander. This wretched man should never have been employed, certainly not promoted to be chief guide. He's irresponsible; he's insensitive to the care of his charges, even to their safety. He also plots against 'his betters': like the one who should have been made chief guide. Pressed for evidence and instances the man reports a series of innocent-sounding events. Despite considerable emotion accompanying the outburst, the hatred expressed appears to have shaky foundations in fact.

With the aid of the colleague who conducted the interview, in some years I would insert this demonstration into one of my lecture periods. It occurred during a series of lectures on the psychoses. Subsequent requests to the class for a diagnosis of the pseudo-patient produced the response 'paranoia', or sometimes 'paranoid schizophrenia'. In diagnostic terms the presence or absence of hallucination is a distinguishing criterion, as is also – in true paranoia – relatively systematized persecutory delusions. References to the sound of the birds and the river were deliberately inserted, with the implications of being 'spoken to', leaving this issue open. Was it merely a question of metaphor about nature of the kind a poet might use, an 'as if' experience, or was 'hearing' in the hallucinatory sense involved? Such difficulties of diagnosis are a feature of the realities of the external world as opposed to laboratory or lecture-room demonstrations. Moreover, much of what a paranoid individual has to say can seem very reasonable, granted his premise. Presence of delusions may not at first be obvious. What is at fault is the disturbed nature of such a premise, presenting what was called – at the trial of Daniel McNaghten – 'a monomania'. His whole mental life was re-organized around a

266

series of fancied grievances. The logic of a well-developed persecutory delusional system is difficult to fault and, as Kisker points
out, a paranoid individual may sometimes 'convince others of the
reasonableness of his ideas' (Kisker 1972: 341).

PARANOIA AND THE SCHIZOPHRENIAS

A distinction between paranoia and the schizophrenias – including paranoid schizophrenia – is widely accepted. We find it in
the writings of leading psychiatrists in both Britain and America,
and in diagnostic systems such as the DSM III. Yellowlees (1932)
postulated a continuum of delusions ranging, at the schizophrenia
end, from the unsystematized and often bizarre, to the well-
systematized at the paranoia end. As we move up this scale away
from paranoid schizophrenia, hallucination becomes less important until in true paranoia it is absent. Let us look at what is
actually going on in the mental life of the individual to distinguish
these two rather different manifestations of psychosis. In its early
and active states the schizophrenic may experience acute anxiety
and panic. Processes which frighten and baffle him are going on
inside, and he is unable either to predict or control the A-thinking
fantasy and autonomous imagery. In the catatonic manifestations
of schizophrenia these overwhelm the personality: absorbed as he
is in them he overlooks and ignores external events. A very great
deal is happening inside. But to external observation the mute
and seemingly stuporous state of the patient gives the appearance
of an apparent absence of mind. In paranoid schizophrenia the
residual self struggles to make sense of these Kafkaesque internal
events. They are attributed to some external agency. I have
known the Jodrell Bank telescope to be blamed. Wireless waves,
supernatural forces, and extra-terrestrial beings may be invoked.
Very often with the paranoid schizophrenic it is 'enemies' who are
held responsible for 'putting these ideas' into the patient's mind.
A struggle takes place between residual R-thinking seeking an
explanation, and A-thinking upsurges. The result of this is the
characteristic delusions of paranoid schizophrenia. Since the
upsurges are variable and unpredictable, efforts to rationalize
and make sense of them tend to result in bizarre delusions.
Contrast the true paranoiac, well described by Menninger (1946)

267

as a 'wistful outsider'. His preoccupation is not with hallucination but rather with the gap that divides him from other people. He feels deeply isolated, alienated, and, in some way he can not fully understand, different. Freud placed emphasis on homosexual inclinations or 'repressed homosexuality' as the basis for this sense of difference. Others from the standpoint of Gestalt psychology argue that there are many sources of this sense of unbearable isolation including, for example, language barriers. It may be added that immigrants from other areas of culture, coming from an environment of real persecution as they often do, may feel unrealistically persecuted in their new surroundings. Whatever the basis of the feelings of isolation, an attempt is made to close the gap by explaining it in some way. It is here that fantasy comes into it: 'they' are against me. Innocent actions by other people are misinterpreted within the frame of reference of this subjective re-orientation to inter-personal relationships. The social environment is perceived as hostile. Much of this hostility is a projection on to others of the paranoid personality's own substantial reservoir of resentful emotion. But in addition other people are indeed liable to be irritated and their genuine hostility to the paranoid individual may also feed his paranoia. For his part the patient – though he is often to be found not only in psychiatric hospitals but elsewhere – further reacts. Compensatory ideas of self-importance, of unrecognized greatness, and of being a prophet without honour develop. These delusory ideas, along with delusions of persecution, form the characteristics of true paranoia. If a continuum is involved it is not so much in the direction of paranoid schizophrenia with its efforts to make sense of upsurges of A-thinking fantasy. It is rather with human crankiness, often of a harmless kind, though it must always be remembered that – once he has identified his believed persecutors – paranoia can motivate homicide. Daniel McNaghten, with the 'brace of pistols' acquired for self-defence, was a very dangerous person.

The biological basis of paranoia is to be found in the learning history of the individual, in whatever ways this has been registered upon the organism, and perhaps also in genetic factors. Apart from this it has no known organic basis. The point is important because we also encounter paranoid reactions from brain injury, the process of ageing, or from drugs and cerebral infection. If this distinction is not observed and communicated confusions can arise, for example in courts of law. Elsewhere I discussed one such instance involving a trial held in Jamaica (McKellar 1968: 372–3). In the examination-in-chief the expert witness, a woman psychiatrist, referred to the accused as having 'a paranoid reaction resulting from brain damage'. She described it as 'the punch drunk reaction'. Later she was asked in cross-examination to confirm that her diagnosis was 'paranoia'. Fortunately the witness was allowed to explain what she meant: persecutory delusions following evidence – which was advanced – of brain injury. Because of the debate character of court proceedings, the expert witness is often at a disadvantage. The expert may be asked a question, seemingly simple to others present in the court, but to which nobody who is truly expert could reasonably answer 'yes' or 'no'. Paranoid schizophrenia, true paranoia, and paranoid reactions represent one such area for possible confusions.

Certain circumstances which have a clear biological basis merit mention in connection with quasi-paranoid behaviour. Among them are sensory defects about which the individual concerned may be highly sensitive. I have noted this on occasion, even with colour blindness. But most obvious is the case of deafness. An individual who, perhaps under the influence of the ageing process, develops a degree of deafness may develop a defensive hostility to other people who 'mumble' or 'do not speak clearly'. Others may also contribute their impatience, with loudness of speech that expresses not merely attempted better communication but also resentful anger. In everyday life quarrels ensue, fed also by the accusation of hearing-people that the deaf individual is selective in what he does and does not 'want to hear'. Other people present may also 'talk about him', in front of him and inaudibly: this he perceives sometimes correctly, along with the resentful hostility that may also be present. Everyday life has its psychopathology, not least in these inter-personal relations between the deaf and their relatives.

The paranoid personality of Rousseau, in terms of his intense suspiciousness and disastrous relations with others, including numerous benefactors, merits mention. Literature has also produced some strange personalities in writers who have to an often large extent documented their own case history. One such example may be taken.

269

FREDERICK ROLFE, BARON CORVO

In *Hadrian the Seventh* we have a story of an unsuccessful priest whose long unrecognized abilities eventually triumph. He is elected pope. The writer of the novel – himself an unsuccessful priest – was Frederick Rolfe, who later assumed the title of 'Baron Corvo'. He would also sometimes use the abbreviation 'Fr.', exploiting the ambiguities of Frederick. The hero of the novel mentioned – and all Rolfe's central characters are relatively transparent versions of himself – eventually triumphs over his critics and his persecutors. They acknowledge their mistakes, obey his demands, and eventually accept his infallibility. In *The Desire and Pursuit of the Whole*, Rolfe's hero is a man called Crabbe; the author mentions 'all his enemies' and adds 'by that I mean all the people with whom he had ever had some intimacy.' Although a novelist of some calibre, Rolfe emerges as an impossible man, and his words accurately describe his own personal relationships. Like Rousseau, whom he seems to have resembled, he had many benefactors. In the course of time all became objects of his hatred, his persecutors as he saw them.

In Frederick Rolfe we encounter a good illustration of how considerable ability may exist in a basically paranoid type of personality. He was not only a novelist but among other things a talented inventor, and his artistic skills, notably in calligraphy, were considerable. His gifts seemed to him to merit more recognition than they received, and he was consumed with resentment that they were under-valued or ignored. A reason for this lack of recognition may be present either prominently in the mind of such a person, or at the margin of his conscious awareness. In the case of Rolfe, as in that of Judge Schreiber with whom Freud supported his theory of 'repressed homosexuality', we encounter a secretive difference from other people. To a very considerable extent Rolfe was, particularly when resident in Venice, secretly engaged in homosexual activities. The experience of being rejected for the Catholic priesthood also undoubtedly played an important part in Rolfe's sense of isolation. Whatever the reasons, we again encounter Menninger's 'wistful outsider', lacking the ability to maintain stable relations with other people. Fantasy-attempts to bridge this gap are well documented in the novels, most notably in the 'I'll become Pope and then I'll show them' theme.

270

Hostility of other people towards oneself plays an important part – whether imaginary, real, or a little of both – in the consciousness of the paranoid personality. This itself increases the sense of isolation. Like the autocratic ruler described by Plato in *The Republic*, the paranoid individual distances himself from people likely to criticize his actions. Both types of people – and sometimes the two are the same – see themselves as 'right' and those who intervene on the side of reality as wrongheaded. If they continue in attempts to intervene they are no longer listened to, and relations with them are terminated. Unhappily the paranoid personality is more than averagely in need of such influences and interventions. His thinking and actions are testimony to the absence of critical 'press' from people emotionally close with such sensible comments as 'Isn't it ever your fault, not somebody else's'?, or even a robust 'Don't be silly.' Plato's excursion into early social psychology 2,000 years ago showed how paranoid suspiciousness may result in an absolutist ruler surrounding himself with yea-saying courtiers. There have been many examples of such close association between political tyranny and paranoid excess.

Outside the political scene and the psychiatric hospital, we often encounter grandiose and quasi-paranoid forms of human crankiness. In one of his books, the behaviourist J. B. Watson (1919) advised interviewers and potential employers to look out for such qualities. But, he added, 'such people lose little time in announcing themselves.' Indeed by holding us 'with glittering eye' they may well remind their reluctant hearers of Coleridge's Ancient Mariner. Something rather different occurs with a true paranoiac, who is a longstanding patient of a psychiatric hospital. As in the case of Lionel Terry, discussed earlier, he may be an important figure in the social life of the institution. He is well-informed, his thinking outside his system of delusions is unimpaired, he is often widely respected with much to say worth listening to. Having lost regularly at chess in frequent games with one such patient, I happily underline this point. Professor John Clark, a former colleague who is himself an unusually able chess player, makes the interesting point that a paranoid attitude is the best one to adopt when playing chess. Your opponent through his various chess moves is certainly 'plotting against you', making efforts to achieve your downfall. In such a game of skill empathy with the thought processes of the other player is involved, and we do well to be highly suspicious of every move he makes.

DEPTH PSYCHOLOGY AND PARANOIA

For Freud, the paranoid individual 'sees more clearly' than do others. His reference is to sensitivity to the complexities of unconscious factors in motivation. Various researches by social psychologists have shown that people with hostility towards some social group tend to be more able to recognize members of that group than are the non-prejudiced. Most of us are at times aware of being sensitive to the less reputable motivation of, for example, politicians we dislike. As La Rochefoucauld would remind us, their motivation, like other people's, is likely to be mixed. Freud's term is 'over-determined', and in practice psychoanalysis has tended to stress the irrational, self-interested, and less ethical aspects. One thing that is characteristic of paranoia is the huge reservoir of hostility towards others it involves. Thus the Freudian thesis has considerable plausibility. Theodore Reik (1949) makes a related point in a principle: we can assess the unconscious aspects of the motivation of an act from the effects this has on other people. The principle is often a good guideline. When some people are being helpful it has been well said that 'you can tell those being helped by their hunted expression.' Knowing that the most worthy professed motives may carry with them others less worthy, it is not surprising that the helped often react with resentment to unconsciously expressed hostility. This of course tends to be assessed as ingratitude. In this respect also the paranoid individual may again 'see more clearly'.

In *The Psychopathology of Everyday Life* Freud develops the notion of determinism in relation to behaviour. Phrased differently, this is an application of the notion that cause and effect operate in mental life no less than elsewhere. Mental events don't 'just happen'. There is a causal explanation of why they are so and not otherwise. Consider a case of paranoia reported by Yellowlees (1932). He explains how the results of a great deal of therapy were lost; when the patient concerned received at his meal an unbuttered slice of bread! Attempts to explain, including resort to 'chance', were of no avail. Why him, and not somebody else?

272

Yellowlees, with justification, assessed this interpretation as paranoid. But let us return to Freud's book. In this he reports an
incident in which, while on holiday, he established friendly
relations with another guest of the inn. The two men would go
for walks, and have meals together. One day his acquaintance
mentioned that his wife would be joining him 'tomorrow'. At the
meal table the next day, there were three chairs, the newly arrived
wife now occupying one of them. On the third chair an overcoat
had been placed. Despite the spoken invitation to come and sit
here as usual, Freud assessed the presence of the coat to mean
'you are now superfluous,' and his companionship was no longer
needed. I mention the incident from Freud's writings not to imply
paranoid traits in the psychoanalyst, but rather to underline
something else. How close the orientation of psychoanalysis on
the one hand and of paranoia on the other seem to be. Freud
interpreted the action in terms of unconscious motivation: a
paranoid individual might well regard it as a slight to himself.
Both might be right, though possibly placing a coat on a chair is a
way of reserving it for somebody, rather than of signalling to him
he is unwelcome. Let us return to the Yellowlees case and the
unbuttered slice of bread. Here psychoanalysis, like paranoia,
would reject the category of chance. Perhaps there is some
justification for doing so. As I have argued, paranoid behaviour
can provoke irritation in other people, and failure to provide
buttered bread could have been an expression of such irritation?
Obviously in the case of neither the slice of bread, nor the coat on
the chair will we ever know. The depth psychologist would argue
that such happenings do not occur through mere chance: there is
sufficient reason why such events are so and not otherwise. For his
part the psychotic's assessment of the significance of such actions
is very similar. Perhaps, as Freud would argue, of the unconscious
motives of other people he 'sees more clearly'.

Men and women of 'one idea' – often harmless eccentrics – are
represented on one continuum that radiates out from the central
axis of true paranoia. One elderly lady would, without any
exception, walk along the streets outside the gutter and never
along the pavements. She was a well-known character in one
English city. Police officers from this area told me that a responsibility they willingly accepted was preventing members of the
public from interfering with her eccentric but harmless one-idea

behaviour. The pagan saint of antiquity, Socrates, was not only eccentric as a person but also – standing still for hours at a time, listening to the internal voice of his daemon – the kind of eccentric who might well have been molested by unthinking bystanders. Socrates had other qualities, and was single-minded in his mode of life. As Robinson (1976: 50) points out in his history of psychology, Socrates questioned well-established assumptions, doubted the obvious, ridiculed cant – hypocritical speech – and lived a simple and virtuous life. Robinson adds, 'In short he could not have been more offensive.' To many people his virtue as well as his sceptical attitudes and his eccentricity must have been disturbing. Throughout history we encounter many such people. Consider for example Nietzsche, his grandiose and persecutory ideas, and deep insights into the less reputable aspects of human motivation. In his madness – paranoid reaction to bacteriological infection rather than true paranoia – he must have been also very objectionable to those near to him. One rather hopes he was to his devoted but otherwise distasteful sister – friend of Mussolini and acquaintance of Hitler – and her husband, whose violent anti-Semitism Nietzsche seems to have heartily despised. Apart from the matter of personal relations, in Nietzsche as in Rousseau, we come squarely up against one issue. It is that of evaluating ideas on their merits despite the apparent gross abnormality of the authors of those ideas.

'Folie à deux' refers to a system of delusions shared by two people. On this further continuum we meet 'folie à trois', etc., up to and including 'folie à N'. Cults as well as individuals may give evidence of the paranoid type of temperament: this may be the result of the influence of the members on one another, or perhaps of the kind of individual attracted to such groups. The content of the beliefs that distinguish smaller groups or whole areas of culture have varied greatly throughout history. Both the Copernican notion of a solar system with the sun at its centre, and Darwinian evolution have been in their time viewed as eccentricities. Nowadays it is a manifestation of eccentric and pathologically stable beliefs, akin to delusion, not to accept them. To cite Robinson's history again: he assesses Aristotle as having had a more 'enduring effect on more departments of scholarship than any other central figure' (op. cit.: 74). But elsewhere he points out that Aristotle's conception of the soul was not necessarily that of the general public of his own day and age. The average Athenian probably seldom thought about it, and if he encountered Aristotle's ideas 'would probably have found the philosopher's treatment bizarre' (op. cit.: 6). In individual delusions we may have beliefs that are greatly out of accord with the belief norms of a given area of culture, but not all such beliefs are necessarily delusory. The thoroughgoing materialism of another great thinker, Thomas Hobbes – with his total rejection of the accepted category of the supernatural – was assessed by some as the cause of both the plague and the Great Fire of London. It wasn't.

Two of the less usual variants of paranoid delusion may be noted. On the one hand is the condition sometimes called 'eroto-mania', in which the patient concerned believes himself or herself the target, not of persecution, but of the sentiment of love of somebody else. This belief proves on investigation to be grossly out of touch with reality. The second variant is the 'zoanthropic' form of paranoia, in which the sufferer accepts the delusion that he has been transformed into a wild animal. The werewolf tradition – and other societies have a variety of feared 'were' animals – represents one manifestation of similar beliefs widely accepted by a whole society. As regards seventeenth-century Europe, Hunter and MacAlpine reproduce the writings on the subject by Robert Bayfield, a physician of the time, on 'wolf madness'. As regards lycanthropy their own interpretation is naturalistic: in addition to superstition they suggest that hydro-phobia may have been linked to the widely accepted beliefs concerned (Hunter and MacAlpine 1963: 168).

SUMMARY

1   The systematized delusional psychosis, paranoia, is illustrated, though it is noted that paranoid reactions may accompany other conditions. True paranoia is distinguished from the schizophrenias.

2   One paranoid individual, who in his writings documented the characteristics of his own personality, is considered. Although insight may seem to be absent in paranoid behaviour, Freud has something to contribute from another standpoint.

3   The psychoanalytic view that the paranoid 'sees more clearly' into the mental life of others is examined. As regards unconscious motivation, there seem to be some similarities between the orientation of psychoanalytic psychology itself and that of paranoid thinking.

4.   There are a number of atypical kinds of paranoid psychosis which are considered. There may be *'folie à deux'*, when two people share a system of delusions, and just as there are eccentric individuals there are groups that subscribe to deviant but harmless eccentricities. On the other hand there are other groups whose social norms include hatreds and paranoid suspiciousness. These, like individual paranoiacs – some of whom have attempted or achieved assassinations – can be dangerous. Problems of forensic psychology will next concern us.

Chapter Fourteen

FORENSIC PSYCHOLOGY

The application of the findings and methods of psychology to the procedures of courts of law, police investigations, and related matters.

Connolly and McKellar

Psychology and the law have many points of contact. Three will be given emphasis. First are the personalities of the people concerned, including – in criminal cases – the accused, and the others who take part in court proceedings. Second are issues relating to the alleged offence and testimony of witnesses as to what actually happened. Third is the interesting and complex issue of evidence in court and the problems of communication that arise from it. My concern will be primarily with criminal cases rather than with those of civil law and related disputes. Systems of law distinguish different categories of offence: larceny, assault, arson, forgery, homicide, and those relating to drugs and sexual behaviour. Two points may be made. First, these legal categories may provide some clues as to the type of person likely to engage in a given type of offence. Second, criminals also do other things.

An important classic study appeared in 1937: this was E. H. Sutherland's book *The Professional Thief*. This investigation, though of a specialized criminal group, brings out some important points. Sutherland's professionals gave evidence of group consciousness – awareness of their group and membership of it – of group loyalty, and definite group norms. Such individuals, though violators of the law, like law-abiding citizens also had values, including moral sentiments. They would, for example, reject with contempt those who did not follow the correct rules of stealing. One value of importance to the professional thief was loyalty. Another was punctuality in keeping appointments: it is important to arrive on time as having to wait increases possibilities of arrest. This study, which I have considered in fuller detail elsewhere, brings out in a clear and interesting way human aspects of such members of 'the underworld'. Such people do not live underground – as our imagery might suggest – but are in many respects 'normal'. Moreover, they spend a great deal of the time with non-criminals (McKellar 1968: 341ff.). They travel in buses or motor cars, use post offices, read their newspapers, and buy their milk at corner shops or supermarkets. The students in classes of police officers and magistrates I have taught have repeatedly reminded me, here we encounter 'the normal criminal'. Mental abnormality and criminality may of course overlap, as when psychosis is involved, or when some intellectually dull person drifts into crime. On the personality side psychology's interest in forensic matters is broader and clearly not restricted to abnormality of mental life. Of fundamental importance are the areas in which psychological concepts overlap, or seem to overlap, with those of systems of law. Here arise questions of interpretation and with it translation of the languages of two disciplines. This task may seem at times to resemble discussing colours with another person whose concept of 'red' includes scarlet and pink, but whose concept of 'blue' includes crimson. Concepts may overlap, but only partially. Illustrations will be taken mainly from English law. Scottish, Commonwealth, and other law systems may differ.

A fight between two people may result in the death of one of them. Here we encounter 'intention', 'justification', and 'provocation'. An accused may in such a case claim that to kill was not his intention, and moreover he was provoked. To cite a well-known, standard authority on criminal pleading, the law is clear on this point. 'No provocation whatever can render homicide justifiable, or even excusable.' But, it is added, 'provocation may reduce the offence to manslaughter' (Archbold, Butler, and Mitchell edition 1973: para. 2501, p. 927). There are a number of legally different kinds of homicide, and in this case of killing by fighting the alleged offence may be murder, manslaughter, or killing in self-defence. The concepts of 'irresistible impulse' plays no part in English law, though it does have a place in the law of some American states. The notion of 'justifiable homicide' is something which can vary greatly between different systems of law. But here as elsewhere it is the law, not the offender, that defines the offence. On one occasion I took part as an expert witness in a trial held in the American state of New Mexico. The accused, who admitted to the killing, wanted to plead justifiable homicide, but in the end under legal advice did not. Had he been tried only 20 miles away across the border in Texas – where this plea is very broadly interpreted – it would probably have been successful. Very similar actions may be judged very differently in geographically adjacent places. Consider the application of the McNaghten Rules. Particularly up till the time of the Homicide Act of 1957 which introduced the concept of 'diminished responsibility', these have played an important part in English law. Under the McNaghten Rules – which have also applied in some other countries and some American states – the defence may claim that the accused 'did not know he was doing what was wrong'. In some of the famous cases that have involved this defence on the grounds of insanity, people in court including even expert witnesses have been unclear about how the word 'wrong' is legally interpreted. In the *Rex* v. *Windle* case of 1952 the Court of Appeal settled the issue: 'wrong' legally means 'contrary to the law'. Witnesses have appeared in court acting on the assumption that their own or the accused's moral sentiments were relevant. They were not. Several experts suffered for this mistake under vigorous cross-examination. The law is clear on this point that wrong 'does not have a further meaning of morally wrong'. Thus in law it is no justification to claim that, while knowing the act was contrary to the law, the accused 'believed that in his own view, or in the view of a number of persons, large or small, the act might be justified' (Archbold op. cit.: para. 34, p. 17).

The McNaghten Rules comprise the answers given by a panel of senior judges to questions put to them after the original trial. Judgement of the Court of Appeal, mentioned above, agrees with their original answers. When this question was put to them the reply was that the accused 'is nevertheless punishable ... if he knew, at the time of committing such crime, that he was acting contrary to law'. Hunter and MacAlpine (1963: 921) provide in their history a fuller account of the trial and all the answers of the authorities of the day which now comprise the basis of the McNaghten Rules. Whether these rules, or other legal principles, are involved it emerges that the complexities of communication in court are of fundamental interest and importance.

PROCEEDINGS IN COURT

In a court of law two types of people are present: the professionals and others. Many of the professionals in an English High Court are distinguished by wigs, gowns, and other external evidence of authority. These are largely absent in the Magistrate's Court, as in courts of law in the United States. Professionals include judges and magistrates, solicitors and barristers, court officials, and experienced expert witnesses. For them the courtroom is familiar territory. The other people present are very likely to find court proceedings both impressive and also anxiety-provoking: they include the accused, witnesses, and members of the public. The assumptions they bring with them into court may mislead them about what is happening, and the rules which apply. A trial is not a scientific experiment to discover the truth. On the contrary it is a proceeding which resembles in many respects a debate between prosecution and defence. Its purpose is to test whether, on the evidence presented to the court, the prosecution is, or is not, able to prove its case. The accused is innocent until proved guilty, and the burden of proof rests with the prosecution. If this fails he or she is judged not guilty.

A variety of options are open to the defence. On occasion a plea relating to mental abnormality at the time of the act may be made. Since it is a defence the burden of proof rests not with the prosecution but with the defence lawyers. In a major trial expert witnesses may be called who, unlike other witnesses, are permitted – indeed required – to give their opinion. Cases of homicide, of which murder is but one instance, may involve pathologists as important expert witnesses. Their testimony is often well received by the professionals of the courtroom as they have important information to provide on cause and time of death, and other very relevant matters. For its expert witnesses a court may draw on a wide variety of disciplines. One case I attended, as a member of the general public – it was an extended inquest rather than a trial – involved a witness who was an accepted expert on possession and exorcism. In his book on forensic science, Dr John Thompson (1980), trained as a chemist, stresses the importance of paint in such forensic matters. This has many identifiable qualities that tell a great deal about the history of a court exhibit. Thus, for example, he points out that clues involving paint were extremely important in 1979 in the trial that followed the murder of Earl Mountbatten. After the bombing the traces of paint on the clothes of the accused were found to be identical with the paint of the hull of Mountbatten's boat. Psychiatrist and psychologist expert witnesses are often less than popular in courts of law, and are wise to learn from experienced and more accepted professionals of other disciplines about what to do, and still more important, what not to do in court. The inability to say 'I don't know' when this is true was one of the most dangerous errors of the psychologist expert witnesses discussed by Jeffery (1964). Cross-examination about opinions or test results relating to intelligence is one area of danger, as when the prosecution resorts to the technique of 'selective demolition'. This is reading out individual test items with the scornful implication, 'Isn't that a silly question to ask?' One psychiatrist witness also suffered in this area when he unwisely tried to communicate about intelligence quotients as 'percentages of normal intelligence'.

In the debate-like proceedings of court, a barrister or advocate who asks a seemingly simple question, which isn't in fact simple, may well be fully aware of what he is doing. Take an example. In the text of the McNaghten Rules the term 'defect of mind' occurs, and a question like 'Was the accused suffering from a defect of mind?' is not a simple one. It may be perceived as simple by others present in the court: surely any expert should know? But the question is ambiguous. Does it mean that the accused person's thinking was influenced by delusion like the original Daniel McNaghten? Or does it mean intellectually retarded? McNaghten was not, but many defendants tried under the rules have undoubtedly been. The Homicide Act of 1952 did much to clarify communication about this, and many other matters relating to trials in English law of personalities who differed markedly from McNaghten.

In American law very important was a court case in the District of Columbia which gave rise to an alternative rule known as the

'Durham Decision'. This held that an accused 'was not criminally responsible if his unlawful act was the product of mental disease or mental defect'. This rule, for which Judge David Bazelon was responsible, has been repeatedly commended, being as one forensic psychiatrist expert has put it both 'sound psychologically and legally' (Overholser 1959). Few people are likely to make the same assessment of either the clarity or psychological validity of the McNaghten Rules. Virtually every word of these rules has been debated in English courts, or courts of appeal. The crucial words may be quoted, and relate to a defence claiming insanity as defined by them.

> It must be clearly proved that, at the time of the committing of the act, the party accused was labouring under such a defect of reason, from disease of the mind, as not to know the nature and quality of the act he was doing, or, if he did know it, that he did not know he was doing what was wrong.

It will be noted that the rules refer to 'disease of mind', in itself another huge area for rival interpretations. Such ambiguities have contributed to the widespread distrust of experts and the notion that either party can hire an expert and that experts are bound to disagree. In the case of 'disease of mind', as Connolly and I (1966) have pointed out, one such expert may interpret this concept to mean 'psychosis'. Another such witness interprets this category of legal as opposed to psychiatric thinking in some other way. There may be no difference between the two expert witnesses in the opinion of the actual state of mind of the accused which they hold, and wish to communicate to the court. Under the McNaghten Rules it will be noted that this state of mind relates to the time of the offence, not the time of the trial. In this there is another area of potential confusion if the witness is not clear on this point. But state of mind later on also has another type of relevance to the time of court proceedings. Is the accused 'fit to plead' or not? Fitness to plead, to understand court proceedings and to be able to instruct the defence, was the issue before the court in the well-known Podola case. In English law if the accused is found 'unable to communicate with his legal advisors', as in the 1957 case of *R. v. Sharp*, he is found 'unfit to plead' (Archbold op. cit.: para. 393). This issue may arise when, for instance, a defendant remains mute in the dock, over whether he is 'mute of malice or mute by visitation of God' (Archbold op. cit.: para. 390). Courts of law have to debate such issues. Too often the legal categories relating to state of mind are matters of confusion to a layman jury who are 'lay' as regards both psychiatry and the law.

DIMINISHED RESPONSIBILITY

The concept of diminished responsibility has been important in English law since 1957. This allows that an accused should not be convicted of the offence of murder 'if he was suffering from such abnormality of mind ... as substantially impaired his mental responsibility for his acts and omissions'. With diminished responsibility, if this is upheld, it permits him to be 'liable instead to be convicted of manslaughter' (Archbold, para. 2470, p. 911). Such a defence is psychologically more appropriate in, for example, cases of intellectually dull people who differ markedly from the original, paranoid deluded McNaghten. The concept of 'psychopathy' is also very likely to come up in the context of court proceedings. If found guilty of murder the convicted person may be sent to a psychiatric special security hospital, or as in the 1986 *Regina* v. *Bamber* case, to life imprisonment. Despite the clarification for communication in court achieved with the concept of 'diminished responsibility' many problems remain. Murder in some of its more usual forms is often a sordid but unspectacular matter of little legal, popular, or psychological interest. But murder that involves abnormal offenders can be a particularly horrible form of crime. With less responsible journalism to highlight it, strong emotionalism may be aroused within the community. Such an offender is very likely to go to a special psychiatric institution where in their daily work it is the task of dedicated professionals to look after him, and ensure his continued confinement. At one such institution, before interviewing a number of such abnormal murderers, I made the mistake of first reading in their case-notes details of the offences. The experience was sufficient to – in a minor way – highlight the problems of adjustment of those who have to work day after day in such institutions. Emotion may be very much involved. Because of it some important issues arise in relation to such trials.

First, it is necessary to remind oneself that it is the accused, and only the accused, who is on trial. Other people are involved as witnesses, or perhaps expert witnesses. They are there as responsible people to help the court, and despite strong emotion – whether inside or outside that court – it is not they who are the accused. Much depends on what a judge is, or is not, prepared to permit in his court and – unhappily – standards maintained have sometimes been less than admirable. In this we encounter a principle needing re-statement. 'Cross examination becomes indefensible when it is conducted without restraint and without the courtesy and consideration which a witness is entitled to expect in a court of law.' In citing this principle Archbold (para. 527a) makes reference to a 1935 case (not involving homicide). Some of the famous murder trials, particularly those involving interpretation of the McNaghten Rules, might well have been also cited.

Second, there arises the point that in law an accused is innocent until proved guilty. It is the task of the prosecution to prove that he or she was causally responsible. Despite emotion that the offence itself arouses, merely to come up for trial is not to be proved guilty. Before, during, or after such a trial, lynch law has no place in any civilized system of justice. Newspapers do not always help. Enforceable rules about what is *sub judice* apply during the trial itself, though there are loopholes. One might classify the British press of the 1980s as comprising: the press; the tabloid press; and – to put it very mildly – the less-than-responsible press. Not only do innocent people sometimes find themselves in court but back in the 1930s investigators like E. M. Borchard were able to establish that as many as sixty-five individuals were in England or America convicted, but later found to be innocent. Since that date similar claims have been made, from time to time, over individual cases. Among the safeguards of English law to protect a person accused of a crime are those which formally came into existence in 1964 and are known as 'Judges' Rules'. The principles involved have a much longer history, including among them the rule that any confession or statement made by an accused must be voluntary. Moreover, after being cautioned, under these Rules it is required that 'a record shall be kept of the time and place at which any such questioning or statement began and ended, and of the persons present' (Archbold: para. 1389, p. 687). Needless to add, any such persons present may be called as witnesses into court, and are subject to cross-examination by the defence. Reasons for these and many other such safeguards will be obvious. Violation of Judges' Rules and other such principles is likely to result in information so obtained being ruled 'inadmissible evidence'. The very existence of an organization like Amnesty International and its work on imprisonment without trial, and worse, testifies to the importance of all such safeguards.

ACCIDENTAL DEATH

Forensic psychology largely begins in the year 1907, when Hugo Münsterberg, at Harvard, published his book *On the Witness Stand*. This dealt mainly with the problems for both civil and criminal law of establishing what actually happened with a past event. Next the psychologist Karl Marbe took part in a civil case involving a railway accident. From laboratory experiments with reaction time he was able to establish that it was not possible for the driver of the train to have responded more rapidly than, in fact, he had done (Haward 1961). The role of the psychologist in such cases is illustrated by an accident which came before the New Zealand courts. It involved perception and imagery, and myself as an expert witness. There had been an accident resulting in the death of a man while deer-shooting on a bush-clad hillside. The man who had fired the rifle, whom I will call 'Mr C. D.', was charged with negligence. The police seemed to me reluctant about bringing the charge in these tragic circumstances but felt obliged to under the law. It emerged that C. D. was highly experienced with firearms, and well known to be careful in taking all necessary precautions. The first thing I did was request Mr C. D. to show me the scene of the accident. As we climbed over the thickly bushed hillside he reiterated that he had with certainty identified the target, when he had fired, as a deer. We also spent a lot of time in a deer park just looking at the kind of animal he believed he had seen. Afterwards the case was tried before a judge. Photographs of the area were shown but it was of advantage to be able to say that I had actually been there. In evidence it emerged that a second member of the party, E. F., had been with C. D. when he had fired. This witness swore under oath that he had not himself actually seen the deer. The rule of positively identifying a target before firing was involved, and on this the judge placed emphasis. The witness E. F. had been further down the hill, and the target, man or deer, was thus out of his vision. The crucial point which emerged was: failure of the witness to see the target as testified on oath was irrelevant. In firing the rifle C. D., who was sure that what he saw was a deer, believed his companion, who encouraged him to fire, had also seen and identified the target as a deer. What I have called the Koffka Principle was involved. The action took place within the auditory-perceived environment. The relevant thing in this case was the mistaken belief that the encouragement by E. F. was an indication that he had also seen and identified a deer. The judge regarded this believed confirmation of the target as crucial, and C. D. was discharged of the offence. It happened that Mr Justice Ross had in his earlier years attended lectures and laboratory classes on the psychology of perception. He was thus receptive to the points the expert witness – myself on this occasion – had been able to make about expectancy, illusions in dim light, and misperceived apparent confirmation.

Another New Zealand tragedy involved a passenger plane in Antarctica crashing into the slopes of the 12,450-foot volcano, Mount Erebus. Illusions involving discrepancy between the geographical environment and the perceived environment seem often to be involved in tragic accidents. Antarctica and polar regions may involve additional factors. Robert Holt (1964) mentions polar travel during 'whiteouts', and points out, in this area, that a few terms, notably 'hallucination', came in for 'a great deal of overuse and misuse'. Consider also a common situation like driving a car in fog, in which imagery as such may intrude and mislead. The driver images the road as going straight ahead when the geographical realities of the actual situation are a sharp bend and a cliff. Danger which is not perceived does not give rise either to fear or appropriate avoidance. Gestalt psychology – and Koffka in particular – have much to teach in this area.

THE FACTS OF PAST EVENTS

Perception and memory are two of the central topics of psychology. Both are relevant to establishing – in a court of law or elsewhere –

the 'facts' about a past event. Both are highly unreliable, and most unreliable in the areas of information most relevant to court proceedings. Every fact is a perceived fact and, as testimony, something that has been remembered. As the early psychologist Wilhelm Stern once put it, 'remembrance becomes personal mythology'. After Stern's pioneer experiments in this area came Sir Frederick Bartlett's book on *Remembering* (1932) and the further book by Professor I. M. L. Hunter (1957) on *Memory*. All draw attention not merely to forgetting but also to how actual 'remembering' is often creative in its errors. Bartlett introduced the concept of 'unstable items' for those most likely to be forgotten or misremembered. These include proper names, sequence of events, and assessments of time and distance. Imagination imagery regularly intrudes on what we come to believe happened in the past. Certainty of belief is no guarantee of accuracy: it is possible to be very certain and completely wrong. Finally people exhibit intentional and unintentional bias, and sometimes engage in plain lying even under oath. A witness as to the facts is required to tell the truth, and the whole truth. In discussions with numerous former witnesses I have found few who were satisfied about this: though they had told the truth to the best of their ability, after their ordeal in the witness box they rarely felt that they had managed to communicate 'the whole truth'. Like lawyers and historians, psychologists remain greatly interested in this important issue: how to establish the facts of a past event.

A lawyer friend of mine has commented on his daily work with clients. He tells me that it is necessary to prepare them for what they will hear from witnesses in court. They will not be lying. They will be telling about the events as they believe they happened: what they think they saw and heard. We have seen how, with the allegedly supernatural, it is a formidable task to establish past happenings. Even in the more prosaic area of committee behaviour it is not for nothing that minutes are kept, and later confirmed for their accuracy. In a court case involving, for instance, a driving accident, oaths and affirmations to tell the whole truth may help witnesses to be careful. Gross bias may be filtered out, but despite all this the single most important thing we know about the testimony of normal people of good-will is its unreliability. If information is passed from person to person we encounter what Bartlett called 'serial reproduction' and courts know as 'hearsay'. The serial reproduction effect amplifies errors. History as we know it rests on such hearsay evidence: indeed it is composed of it. To use legal terminology: in history we are dealing with 'alleged events' and often indeed with 'alleged people', namely unreal stereotypes. The first Duke of Marlborough once admitted that 'all the history he knew came from Shakespeare.' This included what Potter (1983) and others have since shown to be a very biassed and unreal account of the personality and actions of King Richard III. Rivalry in politics flourished then as it does now. What Potter has to say about history – in his defence of the reputation of Richard III – has more general relevance. He questions the view that history is 'made' either by social and economic forces, or by great men and women. 'It is made by historians who select, interpret and speculate' (Potter op. cit.: 1). So also do witnesses in court while doing their best to report faithfully on what people have done, and events that have taken place. To illustrate with one undoubted happening that concerns both history and law, the assassination of President Kennedy still remains in dispute despite careful and extended scrutiny.

There may be a considerable lapse of time between the occurrence of an offence and its coming before a court. Moreover, details that are relevant may not have greatly aroused the attention of a witness when they were observed. Yet a witness may be asked to give a highly detailed, near-scientific, account and at a much later date. In one murder trial involving shooting I heard a witness being asked to make a comparative assessment of the relative strength of the gunpowder smell as between two rooms of a house. This was months later than any actual, or imagined, smelling. In a school classroom or university lecture it takes an experienced and confident teacher to respond to a question with the words 'I don't know'. Few people are confident in the witness box. Under the pressure of cross-examination there is often the tendency to allow imagination to fill in gaps of memory on points of detail. Even experienced expert witnesses can make this usually disastrous mistake. There are numerous other sources of error. Not only are there problems relating to attempts to understand what legal or medical technicalities actually mean. There are also differences between people in concepts that relate to everyday life. What is a distance of '20 feet'? How much do two people differ in their assessment of 'half an hour'? Not only do we find differences in such estimates, but there may also be generation variations which divide those who think about lengths and distances in decimal terms from those who don't. There is also the intrusion of irrational certainty into judgements – however inaccurate – a witness may make. Here the debate character of court proceedings may again be emphasized. Professional lawyers are, like psychologists, aware of irrational confidence in spurious accuracy. Thus it is possible – and it has happened – to place a witness on his own testimony on a precisely defined spot. Then follows the bombshell that from where he was at this time he could not possibly have seen what he declares he did see. Recovery after such demolitions in the witness box is difficult to achieve. In an earlier chapter we noted how Freud was impressed with the sheer stupidity that highly intelligent people sometimes exhibit. Anxiety, fluster, and anger experienced by a witness under cross-examination can be provoked in a variety of ways. Much depends on what a given judge or magistrate is, and is not, prepared to permit in his court. Unfortunately in this matter we also encounter human variability.

Psychology and the law exhibit similarities and differences. The differences are obvious, but there are also underlying similarities, some of which are less so. Both are aware of the inadequacies of observation and memory that contribute to testimony. And both, whether they call it 'hearsay' or 'serial reproduction', have a sophisticated understanding of how passage of information from one person to another increases errors. There is also little difference of opinion about which types of information – Bartlett's 'unstable items' – are most liable to misperception and misremembering. In courses I have taken part in for both magistrates and police officers we have found in these areas a solid core of agreement. Often both those concerned with the law and psychologists have to deal with what is incomplete information. The data are inadequate but they are all that is available. A court may decide that the case is not proved and the accused is discharged as not guilty. There are many parallels in research as we have seen, for example as regards what can and cannot be produced in hypnosis. Thus there is either suspended judgement, or a provisional decision at the level of low probability. In either case judgement is involved under the constraint of impartiality and exclusion of the influences of emotions and sentiments. As one thoughtful historian of psychology has pointed out, there are many human activities that 'strive for impartiality, attempt to uncover relevant facts ... and are based upon more or less well-defined procedures'. In these respects Daniel Robinson likens scientific inquiry to 'the weighing of evidence by a properly instructed jury' (Robinson 1976: 11). Science is not unique but has things in common with courts of law.

Legal systems make distinctions between different kinds of offence. Such distinctions may be of interest as providing information about the kinds of people likely or unlikely to perform such actions. There may also be clues in the legally defined categories as to motivation. Much work of detection depends on the fact that offenders are often recidivists: they repeat their offences and sometimes psychologically as well as physically 'leave their finger prints'. Modern computing techniques have replaced old card-index methods in such areas. Such detection work may be approached from the side of the offence itself, as opposed to a suspected offender. Thus psychologists can in their researches provide useful information from studies in prisons or security psychiatric hospitals of the characteristics of groups of known offenders. In his pioneer studies Sir Cyril Burt (1937) suggested, for example, that the nature of the offence often permits us to place the probable offender somewhere on a scale of measurable intelligence. Later work by Tong (1958) measured the personality characteristics of convicted larceny and sexual offenders. MacDonald (1961), in his study of homicide, found evidence not only of the characteristics of potential murderers, but also of the fact that certain types of people tend to become victims.

MacDonald's study also dealt with murder and attempted murder with bombs in aircraft at a time when this was a relatively rare form of crime. It is no longer the case and the growth of terrorism results in murder of other than quasi-domestic kinds. A disturbing study has been reported by a Dr H. A. Lyons who, as a psychiatrist, has investigated over a hundred people who have killed. He compared 59 'ordinary' murderers with another 47 'political' murderers, and reports differences. The non-political criminals came from lower socio-economic groups; alcohol played a part in the case of half of them; many had a prior history of crime and 'very often the victim was well known to the person who carried out the killing.' By contrast the 'political' offenders lacked evidence of psychiatric problems, were mostly of average intelligence, and they committed the act 'while sober' (*Independent*, 29 November 1986). The report provides further evidence of the lethal potential of strong sentiments, including hate between opposing groups, in this case studied in Northern Ireland. Causal guilt tended in these cases to be unaccompanied by feelings of guilt or remorse. In other parts of the world political or religious sentiments of particular kinds accompanied by the 'relative ethics' of such sentiments continue in their destruction of human lives. In aircraft bombings and other such terrorist offences, the many victims are now often total strangers to the criminals concerned. As regards such criminals, a distinction must be drawn between those who organize such happenings and the mere 'trigger-people' who, like the action commandoes of Himmler we learned about at the Nuremberg Trial, actually carry them out. As in Nazi Germany, different kinds of people – some socially and geographically remote – are likely to be involved in the contemporary murder hierarchy. A similar component of distance from the victims and from the actual consequences of one's actions may emerge in warfare. This was expressed by an Argentine bomber pilot who declared, 'I didn't want to kill anybody: I just wanted to put the ship out of action.' This isolation mechanism plays a different and indeed necessary part in proceedings in a court of law. It is the task of the jury members to come to a judgement on the basis of the evidence presented to them. And it is the function of the judge to guide them towards an impartial decision within the constraints of existing law and relevant principles, including Judges' Rules, that define admissible evidence.

Like other sciences, psychology seeks to formulate principles which assist understanding of natural phenomena. It is less confidently concerned than once with penetrating the 'laws of nature'. In this psychology faces many difficulties, though I suspect by now it has gone some way towards formulating a few important principles of some generality. It is time it did, as efforts to achieve this have been going on for at least 2,000 years.

SUMMARY

1 The law and psychology have many interests in common, however much their concepts may differ. Communication in a

court of law despite such differences – whether about mental abnormality or other things – comprises one fascinating area of psychology.

2   Establishing the facts about a past event interests both, as it does historians and those concerned with explanation of an apparently supernatural happening. Psychologists may play a practical part in proceedings of courts of law themselves as expert witnesses. They may also have contributions to make to the study and evaluation of the testimony of other witnesses.

3   Court proceedings in a criminal case are more like a debate than a scientific experiment: their concern is to establish whether on the evidence presented the prosecution has proved its case. As regards factual guilt, the burden of proof rests with the prosecution; when a defence of mental abnormality is offered it is the responsibility of the defence to prove this. The law has its own concepts in such areas as provocation, diminished responsibility, and 'defects' or 'disorders' of mind. There are many opportunities for misunderstanding.

4   Some illustrations are considered in relation to communication, testimony, diminished responsibility, accidental killing, and problems that have arisen from the McNaghten Rules. The types of violation of the law that occur may, on occasion, give an indication of the type of person likely to have committed the alleged offence.

5   A different kind of 'law' will next be considered. The question arises of the achievement by psychology itself of principles or laws on which we can depend.

Chapter Fifteen

THE MAGIC NUMBER SEVEN: PRINCIPLES OF PSYCHOLOGY

Seven is a good handy figure in its way, picturesque, with a savor of the mythical ... more filling to the spirit than a dull academic half-dozen.

Thomas Mann

A century ago William James described psychology as 'the hope of a science'. In terms of this optimistic emotion he called his book *Principles of Psychology*. A hundred years later we face the question 'Are there any?' In other words, are there some generalizations – laws or principles – which are fundamental and of help in understanding experience and behaviour? A further question arises: 'If so, how many?' A large number of principles, some of them called laws, have in fact been formulated over the last 2,000 years of psychology's history of disciplined thinking. They relate to subjects like learning, perception, motivation, personality, and social interactions. Some do and some do not seem fundamental. In being selective we may perhaps make use of a longstanding human tradition. This highlights one very interesting number. It is, of course, seven.

In a brilliant and much-cited contribution to experimental psychology George Miller (1956) entitled his paper 'The magic number seven'. Psychology belongs with science, not magic, and in this tradition Miller wrote: but he also referred to earlier traditions and the mysterious recurrence of seven. His theme within psychology was a fundamental issue: what are the ordinary limits of the human capacity to absorb, retain and process information? In numerous experiments he found that seven, plus or minus two, kept recurring. He became alerted to seven and describes himself as being 'persecuted by an integer'. He records, 'for seven years this number has followed me around, has intruded in my most private data, and has assaulted me from the pages of our most public journals' (Miller op. cit.: 14). Miller discusses span of immediate memory, limits of judgement, and the human restriction that applies to what 'we are able to receive, process, and remember' (op. cit.: 41). Undoubtedly by the use of mnemonic devices we can do better than merely seven items. Miller distinguishes in this respect between mere 'bits', and 'chunks' of information, and much of his own work concerns the use of mnemonic systems. Yet seven remains a very interesting number. Outside the experimental laboratory it has played a prominent part in many longstanding human traditions.

THE MAGIC NUMBER SEVEN

Tradition repeatedly invokes the number. In terms of 'chunks of information' it embraces the Seven Seas, colours, heavenly bodies, vices, virtues, and wonders of the world. Jacob had to work seven years for the hand of Leah, and another seven for Rachel's. From these unions, and the surrogate motherhood of the handmaidens of the two wives, came offspring: founders of the twelve tribes of Israel. There were seven years of famine in Egypt, and after seven marches of Joshua's army on the seventh day the walls of Jericho fell. When Christianity developed it had, at first, seven churches. And there is much mystical reference to the magic number in the Book of Revelation with its trumpets, vials, and ultimate seventh seal. The history of human affairs – as well as George Miller's data – exhibits this mysterious recurrence. Miller speculates 'perhaps there is something deep and profound behind all these sevens?' (op. cit.: 43). It seems to me – as it did to him – that convenience in remembering chunks of information, and the limits of memory, had something to do with it. In any pre-literate society such limits would be important. Moreover, even as literacy spread, this spread was uneven. Limits of ability to remember remained important in areas like morality and religion: hence the seven deadly sins and virtues. These, like Shakespeare's seven stages of human development, were earlier excursions into a pre-scientific psychology. Among the chunks of information summarized by the tradition of seven have been primitive beginnings of science, but also superstitions and some culturally condoned errors. We will put to use this hardworking number on three problems that repeatedly concern psychology.

First is this issue of traditional error. As physical science had to establish, there are more than seven bodies in the solar system. Galileo had to struggle against the widely held false beliefs of his age. Numerous such difficulties have impeded progress within abnormal psychology: an example was the repeated recurrence of the idea that, because of its name, hysteria is related to female anatomy. Again and again the 'wandering uterus' theory had to be refuted by, for example, demonstration from actual cases that this neurosis also occurs in men.

Second, through the traditional seven we learn about the importance of criterion problems. Rome claimed seven hills: so also did many other cities. This raises the question of what is, and what is not, 'a hill' or indeed anything else. Within psychology an example is 'hallucination'. Galton (1883) found 'visionary experiences' in some very unexpected people. He was led to postulate a continuum ranging from inability to image at all to hallucination. Criterion problems arise in relation to eidetic imaging, hypnagogia, and false waking experiences: we have encountered a whole family of subjective phenomena that exhibit some interesting similarities. Cross-cultural psychology reminds us of the influence of different social norms. As one leading investigator has put it, on a world-wide basis 'hallucination is one of the most widely distributed modes of human behaviour' (Ward 1985: 118–19). There are also cultural influences on categories of diagnosis. Moreover, as Warner (1985) shows, as regards schizo-phrenias these vary not only between places, but also have changed at different periods of time. When does a rigid, strongly held belief become 'a delusion'? And it is likewise often difficult to distinguish between an irrational phobia and a fear of an unjusti-fied but understandable kind. As with differentiating between mere bumps on a landscape and 'hills', psychology is constantly concerned with problems of criteria and definition.

Third is the limited perspective of a culture or period of time. By any criteria there are more than 'Seven Seas'. The 'Wonders of the World' – excluding, for instance, the Great Wall of China – illustrate earlier restriction of thinking by available information. George Miller refers to the Pleiades, the 'seven sisters': with the aid of the telescope we find not seven, but a multitude of stars in this area. Observation within science with this, the microscope, and removal of taboos on anatomical dissection have enlarged horizons. As in science itself the newer knowledge of an individual is built on earlier learning of more primitive kinds. Within abnormal psychology we seek to build up a frame of reference to the neuroses and psychoses. It is likely that many people first encountered its subject matter under such crude and emotionally charged labels as 'madness', 'idiocy', 'perversions', and the 'ravings' of 'lunacy'. A more adequate frame of reference has been helped by those, including Freud, who have sought to build bridges that link the psychopathology of abnormal and normal mental life. Other contributions to a broader perspective have come through those who, like Wigoder (1987), have contributed information about subjective accompaniments of depression, and of suicidal and even homicidal impulses. Individually as well as collectively through science, newer learning is built on, and provides re-orientations to older learning.

In primitive physical science, history and geography, even in psychology itself, with 'chunks of information' seven has served many purposes. It has certainly been a hardworking number in human traditions. Let me employ it again, with the constraints it imposes and the mnemonic advantages it provides to our subject matter.

SEVEN AREAS OF PSYCHOLOGY

With it I return to my original question. Surely by now we should be able to find some agreed basic principles of psychology? Today we no longer set out to 'discover' the 'laws of nature'. A given science seeks to formulate principles which may prove helpful as a means of understanding some category of natural phenomena. In psychology concern is with *homo sapiens* – and other animals – both as an organism and as an individual personality. Seven areas of its subject matter will be considered.

First, the individual organism concerned is alive, and belongs to a specific biological species: it is not a disembodied mind. Second, it exhibits motivation to act in certain ways. Third, such actions occur within a framework of perception and beliefs. Fourth, unlike inanimate matter it exhibits learning from events of its life history. Fifth, in interaction with other individuals and groups it evaluates them and makes judgements. Sixth, it has characteristics as an individual personality with sub-systems. Seventh and finally, it exhibits imagination and thinking.

These seven areas will be considered with reference to principles of a basic kind which seem to emerge within them.

The biology of mental life

'Mind' has its relations to the bones and muscles that encase it within an organism. Behaviour, and also subjective experience, have reference to biological structure, and the physiology and pathology of that organism. In recognition of this, abnormal psychology represents the same kind of enterprise as other sciences. This does not mean that mental life is 'nothing but' atomic structure, chemical changes, and basic physiology. But it does mean that psychology and other sciences seek compatibility with one another. There are different levels of analysis. The 'molar' level of experience and behaviour largely concerns psychologists, but there is also the 'molecular' level that deals with physiological processes within the organism. Some psychologists have been concerned with both. Soviet psychology provides an example in the work of the late Professor A. R. Luria (1968; 1979). His predecessor Pavlov had sought to keep subjective experience and mental life out of his laboratory. Like Pavlov, Luria was also concerned with the molecular. An estimated 20 million Russians died in the Second World War. Luria was much concerned with brain injuries, and their effects on memory and thinking of wounded survivors. But he also devoted decades of intensive study, that included introspection, to a very remarkable mnemonist who also exhibited several of the rarer types of synaesthesia.

Many theories of the body–mind relationship have been advanced. In a major classic of philosophical psychology C. D. Broad (1925) dealt with evidence for and against seventeen of them. That there is a relationship may be obvious in the case of brain injuries, though less so when we are dealing with phenomena like synaesthesia and imagery. Often the language of psychology doesn't help. From time to time we need to remind ourselves that biochemical changes are presumably implied in the stored emotion of a 'complex' following emotional trauma of the kind that interested Freud. Trained as he was in neurology, Freud himself certainly recognized this, despite his choice of models from mythology in psychoanalysis. As regards psychopathology some of the conditions that occur have a known basis in brain lesions, virus or bacteriological infection, and drug misuse. General paralysis and delirium tremens are obvious examples. Earlier we considered 'model psychoses'. As experiments with the hallucinogens show, chemical effects on the body by such agents have dramatic effects on subjective experience. It seems almost certain that future advances in biochemistry will have much to contribute to the understanding of the schizophrenias. Some conditions like periodic catatonia have a known biochemistry that already permits rational forms of treatment in accord with such knowledge.

During its lifetime a human individual as an organism stores information and modifies its responses, and in many such ways exhibits learning. This is – in some not yet understood ways – recorded on that organism, in biochemical and structural ways. As we have seen, William James postulated such bodily changes as accompaniments (James 1890, vol. 1: 5). In his detailed study of James, Bird (1986: 207) underlines 'the importance attached to brain-states in explaining mental phenomena' to be found in James. What I have called the William James Principle – a reminder not to forget the bodily aspect – seems an appropriate name. It is fundamental to the very notion of psychology as a branch of science, seeking compatibility with other sciences.

Multiple motivation

Also fundamental are issues concerning causality in general, and motivation in particular. Everyday thinking seeks 'the cause' of an event. Science attempts something better, causal explanation. Within psychology any attempt at an adequate causal explanation of a neurosis or a psychosis involves recognition of complexity. We want to know why it is so, and not otherwise. Its aetiology may include 'constitutional factors': the combination of genetics and early learning that contributed to it. Environmental stresses of one or many kinds will figure as precipitating factors, and other types of 'press' (in Murray's sense) may be relevant to symptomatology. Recent or earlier learning, as prior sensory input, may have helped to shape the delusions, hallucinations, anankastic processes or thought disorders that form part of the condition. Some of these factors may be necessary causes though not in themselves sufficient, while others are merely contributory causal factors. Inter-personal and intra-psychic conflict are both likely to be important, with their by-products of anxiety or guilt feeling. Finally the beliefs of the patient, and the social norms of his or her area of culture, will all exert their influence. While not identifying motivation with causality I turn to this aspect of psychological explanation.

In its tendency to look for 'the motive' of an action, everyday thinking provides a parallel over-simplification. It becomes easy to assess the motives of political or other opponents, and of representatives of groups we dislike. Long before Freud gave his own robust support to a more satisfactory view on such issues, the Principle of Multiple Motivation was spelt out by La Rochefoucauld (1747–1827). As a study by Moore (1961) reveals, the famous *Maxims* have been much misunderstood. Court-life interested La Rochefoucauld, along with its self-deceptions and often discrepancies between the stated intentions of people and the obvious consequences of their actions. Ambivalences of 'friend-ship' and 'love' revealed their complexities. He believed (a) self-interest is likely to be present; but (b) it is not the whole story. Many thinkers have given their support to the notion of competing or co-operating motives. Joseph Butler (1729) provided his detailed analysis of a very complex internal motivational system that included conscience, prudent self-love, and benevolence, along with appetites and passions or emotions. Bishop Butler may not be of much help to our understanding of fanatics, psychopaths, or the self-destructiveness Nietzsche (1886) uncovered. But he is a good guide on normals.

Psychoanalysis, in its recognition of the Principle of Multiple Motivation, accepted along with it another fundamental concept.

This is the Principle of Over-determination: recognition that there can sometimes be a surplus of motivation. As with causes combining to produce a given effect, so motivation may be more than sufficient to produce a given action. The over-determination principle has important applications. Once we have ascertained the more obvious motives we should go on looking for others. These 'others' may not be prominent or available to ordinary introspection. Earlier I explored the idea that the figure-ground concept has applications to motivation – of the kind that psycho-analysis emphasized – as well as to perception (McKellar 1968). The 'ground' aspect of motivation is less noticeable, or may pass unnoticed altogether by contrast with the 'figure' aspects that are prominent to observation and introspection.

In an alternative language Freudian psychology – despite the myth that Freud 'reduces everything to sex' – firmly embraces the concept of multiple motivation. On the one hand is the influence of the pleasure principle – Freud's modified acceptance of the hedonism theory – interacting with the reality principle. Powerful motivational forces, viewed by Freud himself as instincts, pursue self-preservation. They are opposed by destructive and self-destructive urges, that play a prominent part in depression and melancholia. The ego, id, and superego were brought in as a way of conceptualizing the place of conflict, and with it guilt feeling and anxiety, in this struggle between motivational forces. Despite its 'rationality' the ego concept has reference to various defensive mechanisms like projection, reaction formation, and denial. These perform the function of keeping anxiety out of consciousness. Basic to the understanding of motivation is recognition of its complex, multiple character, and that there may be a surplus of motivation more than sufficient to determine a given action.

Perception and the Koffka Principle

In considering the fundamentals of perception we are wise to look to Gestalt psychology. Its concept of 'figure and ground' may, as has been argued, be applied also to motivation. Experiments by Akhter Ahsen (1987) on waking imagery invite applications to imagery. In addition to the focus of their imaging his subjects reported a periphery of other images, 'a sideshow in the form of a running commentary', there to be seen, 'not repressed but ignored'. As Gestalt psychology has acknowledged – though it uses other language – there are many situations in which imagery can intrude upon perception. This is one of the manifestations of what I have called the Koffka Principle. This major Gestalt psychologist was led to differentiate between the perceived or 'behavioural environment', and the realities of the actual 'geographical environment'. Within abnormal psychology we encounter numerous instances in which the individual responds to the surroundings as he perceives and believes them to be. In the schizophrenias hallucinatory imagery may largely replace perception; in paranoid reactions neutral happenings are wrongly interpreted as threatening. Unpredictable acts of aggression may follow. The reasons for them may become apparent once we have achieved understanding of how delusion and hallucination distort perceived reality.

The anankastic reactions provide other applications of the principle when objects and situations of a neutral kind become stimuli to phobias, obsessive preoccupations, or compulsive avoidance rituals. In the psychopathology of everyday life we encounter many strikingly similar forms of behaviour, though we classify them differently as products of superstition rather than of neurosis. Again under the Koffka Principle, behaviour within the perceived environment may result in the reverse situation. People are unaware of actual danger. The famous case studied by Rivers concerned claustrophobia, resulting from a childhood experience with a dog perceived as fierce. Even more potentially dangerous than a neighbourhood garden may be a parked car with a dog in it. To the animal this may be territory to be defended, something not appreciated by a child intruder: tragedy may follow, and sometimes does. How an animal perceives its surroundings has sometimes been misunderstood. Anthropomorphism gets in the way, as when an animal that has been reared in captivity is seen as 'a prisoner' needing to be released.

Perception and belief about the intentions of other people are examined by Martin Orne (1973). His context is psychological experiments themselves. Orne points out how essential it is for an investigator 'to understand how a particular experimental situation is perceived by the subject, in order to draw sensible inferences from the subject's responses' (Orne op. cit.: 158). He is particularly concerned with experiments involving hypnotism. In these – as in therapy – a hypnotist may unwittingly, as well as intentionally, communicate his expectations. In this Orne considers the experiments we have earlier mentioned by Rowland (1939), when hypnotized subjects carried out self-destructive and anti-social actions. There were confirmatory experiments by Young (1952). Tasks involved picking up a poisonous snake, removing a coin from fuming nitric acid, and throwing acid in an experimenter's face. Orne and Evans (1965) replicated these experiments, and found five out of six hypnotized subjects prepared to carry out such actions. In addition they found that all six of a group of non-hypnotized subjects would do likewise. This accords with what Orne concludes on the basis of a great deal of experimental evidence: 'the range of behaviour which an individual will carry out if requested to do is vastly greater than is generally believed' (Orne 1977: 15–16). As regards seemingly anti-social or self-destructive acts, very important is how the subject perceives the situation: he may believe 'the behaviour is in fact harmless despite appearances.' Later discussion with the subjects in the experiments mentioned revealed that 'the demand to carry out actions apparently dangerous to the self or others *communicated* that it must be safe to comply' (Orne 1973: 159, italics mine). In such cases it was what the individual perceived and believed to be the case that determined his action.

The Koffka Principle holds that experience and behaviour occur in the environment as the person concerned perceives it, and believes it to be. It has many important applications for abnormal psychology, and within psychology more generally.

Principles of learning

Living organisms, unlike inanimate matter, learn. Events during their life history register their effects in accord with the William James Principle on that organism, and modify subsequent experience and behaviour. The physiological mechanisms involved are little understood, though Hebb's theory (1949) of their neurology in terms of 'phase sequences' and 'cell assemblies' has generated much research. At the molar level this included pioneer experiments on the effects of sensory deprivation (Bexton *et al.* 1954).

This work by Canadian psychologists stresses the extent to which new learning is based on, and modifies, older learning. The personality itself, and the sentiments, motives and other sub-systems that comprise it, is largely a product of learning. One of the things it may learn is neurotic signs and symptoms. And the delusory beliefs and other features of a psychosis are shaped by the learning process. Although its language is different, many of the basic concepts of psychoanalysis may be translated as affairs of learning. New forms of experience and behaviour are built up from, or replace, older maladjusted learning. Within clinical psychology and psychiatry an alternative approach has been developed, and has proved influential. Psychologists like Eysenck, and psychiatrists like Wolpe have rejected psychoanalytic thinking in favour of therapies based on the experimental study of learning and Pavlovian conditioning (e.g. Eysenck 1953; Wolpe 1958). One such technique is 'desensitization', in which therapy involves moving progressively through imagery from less frightening to more frightening situations relating to a phobia. Through this eventually the patient becomes 'able to visualise all phobic situations comfortably in his imagination' (I. Marks 1976: 388). In such treatment techniques, we see the fundamental importance of conditioning and associative learning.

The principles of association have a long history. 'Association by Contiguity' has seemed to many the essential basis of learning: 'If A and B have been experienced together in space or in time, the recurrence of A tends to result in the recurrence of B.'

Thus in Morton Prince's case with the bell-tower phobia, the sound or sight stimuli evoked the emotions that had accompanied for the patient the operation and death of the mother. Various factors affect the strength of associative linkage between two items. The Scottish philosopher Thomas Brown introduced some 'secondary' laws of association to specify these. Brown wrote of 'suggestion' rather than association, in the sense that A when it occurs tends to suggest B. He provided a general statement which summarizes these principles: 'When two associate feelings have both (together or in close succession) been of long continuance, very lively, very frequently renewed, and that recently, the tendency to suggest each other is more powerful' (Brown 1820: 240). Brown's Recency has reference to one advantage in ordinary associative learning and remembering, though there are some interesting exceptions. One involves the 'Dallenbach Phenomenon', the value of an intervening period of sleep, allowing associations to age without interference. A related paradox fascinated James, who suggested that we 'learn' to skate in summer and to swim in winter.

In addition to the secondary principles, another primary association law is sometimes stated. This is 'Association by Similarity': 'If A and B resemble each other, the occurrence of A tends to result in the occurrence of B.' Thus in the Albert B case it will be remembered that Albert's phobia for the white rat generalized to other furry objects, and to a degree that was proportionate to the extent of the resemblance. In *The Golden Bough* Sir James Frazer (1911) used both the Contiguity and Similarity principles as a basis of explaining human thinking about the seemingly supernatural. On Frazer's analysis there are two kinds of magic. One involves misapplication of the notion of Association by Contiguity: the mistaken notion that if A and B have once been together it is later possible to affect A by doing something to B. The other kind involves misapplying the Similarity Principle, as when malevolent magic uses a wax image or a photograph to injure the person concerned. Many magical rituals and taboos make sense in terms of this analysis of 'contagious' and 'imitative' magic. Survivals include treatment by 'the hair of the dog that bit you', and fear of breaking a mirror with its reflection of oneself. The principles concerned have application to anankastic fears and taboos, as well as to magic and superstition.

Within the now well-developed and complex area of learning theory, another principle has been influential. First it emerged as Thorndike's Law of Effect, which Mowrer (1950) assessed as perhaps the most important of all principles so far formulated in psychology: 'Actions which lead to a satisfying state of affairs tend to be repeated.' This linking of reward, and – in some versions of the principle – of 'reduction of drive' to learning may seem obvious. But things can be 'obvious' without being true. Much research followed this law, or its later modified statement, under the label of 'reinforcement'. One of the interesting things that emerged was that the second part of the 'law', which linked unsatisfying states of affairs with tendencies not to be repeated, had to be withdrawn. As Hilgard (1948) once put it, in his survey of learning theories, 'punishment and reward are *not* equal and opposite.' Thorndike himself 'truncated' his law of effect. Mowrer (1950) has devoted much study to 'the neurotic paradox', the persistence of maladaptive behaviour in the apparent absence of satisfaction or reward. Apparent punishment may mask a hidden reward. Clinical studies have revealed many manifestations of self-punitive behaviour. Menninger (1942) and Flugel (1945) have dealt with some of these. Reinforcement has been studied by Skinner, though he interpreted it differently. 'Schedules of re-inforcement' have been used with success in treatments that have been used with handicapped and autistic children. This work has, like learning itself, an extensive literature. As regards learning principles, three seem to emerge. First, the association principle; second, the reinforcement concept; and third, the relatively high predictability of positive reinforcement and relatively low predict-ability of its negative counterpart.

Social interactions: principle of relative ethics

Among the relevant 'facts' are the moral judgements people make about one another, and the groups they identify with or reject. There are some paradoxes. One of them is that moral judgement is sometimes associated with motives and actions that seem to impartial observation to be aggressive or otherwise anti-social. The sombre comments of Schopenhauer (1897) on the moralized cruelty of the in-group against the outsider preceded many later repeated instances of it. Nietzsche (1886) described the influences of the harsh morality of conscience bereft of restraint by any other principles of conduct as 'dangerous to life'.

From Genghis Khan onwards to Hitler and Stalin, as from Torquemada to evidence of the mid-1980s at the trial of Klaus Barbie, we encounter the excesses of the 'tribal' morality of the in-grouper against others outside it. In *Mein Kampf* Hitler declared that 'in protecting' himself against the Jews he was 'doing the Lord's work'; in his act of murder Daniel McNaghten regarded this as a legitimate self-defence against the 'Catholics and Jesuits' he associated with the Tory party; and Lionel Terry behaved with moral righteousness when 'executing' a Chinese. One patient whom I interviewed had gone out with a gun in response to a hallucinated 'divine command' to kill; another man also interviewed was in psychiatric care following remorse at the atrocity he had committed (which I won't specify) in revenge for something similar that had been done in a war by the enemy to one of his own men. University teachers learn to stop talking about 'the last war', and if they don't are brought up to date by their students. As regards war it has been estimated that not a month has passed since 1945 without a war being fought somewhere. Loyalty to the in-group and limited restraint on actions to the out-group enemy are very probable accompaniments of such physical conflicts. Moralization is regularly invoked by those concerned to excuse violence in action.

The Principle of Relative Ethics, formulated by Shand (1920) in connection with his concept of the sentiment, seems fundamental. Some other individuals and social groups are of little emotional concern to a given person. They are strangers. Social norms tend to dictate politeness to them, and non-interference with their doings. There are others with whom strong affection, or strong negative feelings including hatred and contempt, plays its part. Loves and hates, lesser emotional habits of the liking–disliking kind, together with group loyalties and aversions, form the personality's repertoire of sentiments. In physical science, as Spinoza pointed out, 'nature abhors a vacuum.' Something similar seems to happen with 'human nature' and its motivation: moralization tends to seep in. As regards positive sentiments, the objects of these are protected by relative ethics. Publicly we defend them and may even physically fight for them and seek revenge for their hurt or humiliation. The intellect mobilizes its ego defences like rationalization, projection, denial, and repression, though sometimes introspection may reveal to us what we are doing. The same applies to groups or institutions we identify with.

Objects of negative sentiments, whether people or social groups, are the main victims of the Relative Ethics of Sentiments. Though love is – in accord with its relative ethics – proverbially 'blind', we also speak of 'blind hatred'. Shand admits that our general ethical standards of conscience may intervene but stresses that hate tends to exclude sympathy and 'tends to destroy all virtues, ideals and duties that restrain it from its ends' (Shand 1920: 119). Exceptions are made against the people and institutions that are its objects. As an earlier unpublished study of my own indicated, we tend to evaluate people and things we hate as morally 'evil'. Because of this we feel released from ethical restraints in dealing with them, and thus the end justifies the means in our efforts for their downfall. Such people are 'less than human' and deserve to be swept aside or punished. As with the relative ethics of positive sentiments our defence mechanisms may be penetrated by moments of insight. There is a flash of recognition that such sweeping aside resembles what we would elsewhere assess as brutality; and perhaps there is an affinity of such 'punishment' to cruelty. We may notice the personal convenience of our 'less than human' labelling, or perhaps recall our hurt or humiliation that gave rise to the original hatred. But such co-conscious insight into noticing thoughts and feelings seems to be a rarity, even in the solitary individual. In crowd situations of the mob kind the analogy is closer to somnambulism than to co-conscious insight.

Shand's Relative Ethics of Sentiments concept may be re-formulated in terms of several facets. Cognitively there is an alertness to notice the morally less reputable aspects of motivation of those we dislike, together with a tendency to overlook these in objects of our positive sentiments; emotionally a sense of righteousness about our own motivation; and in action a tendency to make moral exceptions for and against in accord with our pro and con sentiments.

Personality: systems and integration

Since the personality is itself non-spatial – except so far as it is based in a biological organism – some model for it must be sought. The most obvious model is from biology, that organism itself with its various functioning sub-systems. Like a living organism the personality has characteristics of a Gestalt: it is an integrated whole with component parts that interact. There are occasions when these develop a degree of autonomy and may inflict hallucinations, delusions, or anankastic compulsions on the personality. Using the traditional distinction, in neurosis the individual concerned rejects these as part of himself, while in psychosis he fails to notice that they are. There are also occasions in everyday life when we do not merely introspect but also stand back from ourselves and 'watch' our own doings. We thus notice our own irrationality, prejudices, or superstitions, and observe with interest their expression in speech or action.

307

Introspection reveals that the personality, like other systems, has its functioning component parts. A speaker uses words like 'I' and 'me' to refer sometimes to only one aspect of the personality. Sometimes 'the committee of the personality' is firmly chaired, but there occur at other times rebellions and conflicts. In discussing these issues McDougall provides his own introspections. 'I who consciously address you am only one among several selves or Egos which my organism, my person, comprises. I am only the dominant member of a society, an association of similar members' (McDougall 1926: 547–8). Special techniques, including free association, projective testing, and hypnotism, may be used to extend awareness of sub-systems outside focal consciousness. In sleep and adjacent states they emerge of their own accord.

The major and lesser forms of dissociation that have been discussed suggest not one 'unconscious', but a number of such sub-systems. In many phenomena of psychopathology they seem to play an important part. To return to the analogy. Sometimes a personality resembles a firmly chaired committee, high in integration and unified in pursuit of its purposes. In other instances conflict prevails; there is an oligarchy of warring sub-systems and limited control by any kind of chairmanship. Such situations occur in major and minor maladjustments, and characterize the neuroses. By contrast there is an alternative: not oligarchy but anarchy. In terms of Mowrer's (1950) alternative analogy for this, psychosis, the 'walled city', has been taken over, and central control overcome. There has been a 'return of the repressed' and with it chaos and unpredictability. For the personality it is no longer a matter of warring sub-systems, but of disintegration. Conjunctivity, or degree of personality integration, seems to be an important variable. We become much aware of it in study of the problems of abnormal psychology.

Sixth, a general principle emerges. For certain purposes it is useful to conceptualize the personality as a system, with component sub-systems, varying in their degree of integration with the personality as a whole.

Imagination and thinking

To external observation very little may seem to be going on. But internally a great deal is happening: the person observed is thinking. This may involve a chain of reasoning through a problem, engaging in a waking fantasy, or perhaps recalling through imagery a recent holiday. Thinking embraces this wide variety of mental activities. On the one hand is autism and fantasy or A-thinking; on the other is realistic or R-thinking. Both seem to play an important part in valued human thought-products like works of literature, paintings, inventions, and scientific theories (McKellar 1957; 1963a; 1968). I have likened the A-thinking and R-thinking interaction to the respective functions of creative authorship and critically evaluative editorship. Yet thinking, however creative, and its thought-products are subject to certain constraints: to what is available to the person concerned from sense perception. This limitation is obvious in the case of recall of a past event, like the holiday in terms of a series of images: an internal display of scenes resembling a lantern-slide lecture. Such imagery is never wholly reproductive, but like all imagery composite and thus creative. A distinction between memory and imagination imagery is relative not absolute, diversity of sensory origins seems to be the most relevant variable.

In the case of dreams, and sometimes with hypnagogic, eidetic, or hallucinatory imaging, origins can – through introspection – sometimes be located. The notion of the origin of the form and content of mental life in sense perception has had much influence on the development of modern psychology. In terms of one of his important predecessors I will label the basic concept involved as the 'Hobbes Principle': 'There is no conception in a man's mind which hath not at first, totally or by parts, been begotten upon the organs of sense' (Thomas Hobbes 1651). As a working principle we make use of this a great deal, as when we seek to interpret a dream with reference to past events in the life of the dreamer. Applications within abnormal psychology are many, as when we pursue a delusion or a phobia into a life history, though repression may impede the immediate recall. Other principles that have emerged in our consideration of six areas of psychology may have reference to the Hobbes concept. Consider for instance motivation. Freud and earlier dream theorists drew attention to the way motives – Freud called them 'wishes' – select from past memories those relevant to the motive's expression. The psychoanalyst Ella Sharpe (1937) draws an analogy with a magnet being passed over a hundred small objects. The magnet, alias the motive, will gather together those of ferrous metal from among the others. Such a selection – whether for a dream or some other thought-product – will not necessarily be confined to the 'figure' of past perception. Largely unnoticed perceptual 'ground' may also be drawn upon. In the case of Relative Ethics, or other moral principles, learning from models provided by emotionally important adults, and from introjecting elements of an area of culture, are obviously involved. Such learning, like learning in general, begins with sensory input. Perception that is going on at the time may also play its part. An example is a thought-product like a speech, in which the speaker observes some feature of his environment, comments on an interjection, or otherwise draws on immediate sense data.

The fundamental biology of the individual concerned may make its contribution to immediate perception. Thus the functioning of the retina of the eye contributes sensations of shape and colour even in darkness. Ladd (1892) suggested these may contribute content and structure to dreams. Leaning (1925) claimed their relevance to hypnagogic imagery also. And William James (1890) earlier postulated that hallucinations of sight may be influenced by these sensations which he called 'idio-retinal light'. When a person is thinking or imagining, much is going on internally: important in it is immediate sensory input, together with re-activated past perception. The relationship of a thinker to his own immediate mental life is not to a blank screen or, though eyes are closed, to a wall of darkness. It is more like a process of interpreting Rorschach ink blots or TAT pictures: images and sensory experiences contribute to the thought process itself. In sleep these emerge as dreams. External cues may also contribute to creativity. Thus Boorstin (1984) suggests that the threads of the silk on which early Chinese maps were printed may well have suggested the use of grids, prominent in later Chinese geography and now universally used.

Thought-products exhibit structure as well as content. Again the Hobbes Principle may be applied. In analysing creative thinking, Spearman (1930) emphasized the importance of analogy.

He described it as perceiving a system of relations, abstracting it, and applying it to a new subject matter. The standard example is Darwin's reading of Malthus, and from this his arriving at the notion of natural selection applied to biology as a whole. Less well known is the fact that Alfred Wallace was influenced in a similar way by the system of relations he found in the *Principles of Population*. Wallace had reached an impasse in his thinking. He recalled the Malthus study he had read twelve years earlier. Now it occurred to him that, with animals also, 'the inferior would inevitably be killed off ... the fittest would survive.' Wallace then spent two evenings writing his paper, which he then posted to Darwin (Boorstin 1984: 474). Not only did Darwin and Wallace arrive independently at the same idea. Both drew on relationships in another subject matter, and chose the same guidance. Obviously much more was involved in their scientific thought-product than Malthus. Both men were experienced biologists, knowing other systems of relations – in Darwin's case from observations of coral reefs – to be drawn on. In major thought-products we would expect to find complex interactions of both primary and secondary perception. Yet with both, Malthus played a causally necessary part.

Re-organizations of previous sensory experience obviously do not always take place at this conscious level. The products of waking and sleeping fantasy are often surprising in their originality. Yet, as in the case of the 'impersonal' and seemingly 'archetypal' kinds of hypnagogia, in some less conscious way they may operate. To these also the Hobbes Principle may have its useful applications.

Despite the formidable problems of differences between individuals I have attempted in seven areas of the subject to find generalizations. They are contributions to a sketch map rather than to a finished atlas. In summary the list is:

1 Biological foundations of psychology: the William James Principle
2 Motivation: the Principles of Multiple Motivation and of Over-determination
3 Perception: the Koffka Principle
4 Learning: the Association and Reinforcement Principles

5 Judgement: Principle of Relative Ethics
6 Personality: Integration and sub-systems
7 Imagination and thinking: the Hobbes Principle

There are, of course, many alternative possibilities. Some that might have been selected may be mentioned.

SOME OTHER PRINCIPLES

With some regret I left out what might be called the Economy Principle: 'Available sense data tends to be used.' This has numerous applications, as when hallucinatory imaging is in effect a highly personalized misinterpretation of visual or other stimuli actually present. Thus in one case mentioned, a delirium tremens patient hallucinated friends and acquaintances in the shapes of trees and shrubs of the garden. From actual projection I have distinguished what I have called 'projective distortion', as when for example a person perceives in an exaggerated way hostility that is, in fact, genuinely present in others. Thus both projection and projective distortion may contribute to paranoid reactions.

The History–Geography Principle is a statement to the effect that by travel within the geography of the modern world we can still encounter happenings and attitudes that do – and perhaps should – belong to the past. In many parts of the world insensitivity and worse still characterize institutional or other treatment of the mentally ill. Closer to home we often find that supernaturalism, even demonology, remain not far from the surface in the thinking of even 'civilized' people. The individual superstitions many of us retain are a reminder that such things can be studied intro-spectively as well as observationally. More positively, as social anthropology reveals, many 'other' areas of culture have evolved different ways of treating both physical and mental illness. Among them may be some which are therapeutically as good as our own.

Let us consider what may be termed the 'Some and All Principle'. Reference has been made to the logician's concept of the Square of Opposition: four types of proposition that may be stated. Over-generalizations attract interest and attention. Take an illustration. A colleague once made a study of how a sample of housewives spent money of the family income in housekeeping. She found that a small number of her informants did not have accurate knowledge of the amount of money that was earned by their husband. Then followed a press report headlined 'Wives do not know husband's income!' Very true in the sense of a relatively small 'some' but much more interesting as a headline-catching 'all'. Consider our Bouvet Islanders, in terms of the claim 'Bouvet Islanders are red-headed'. This would be much more interesting than the more prosaic finding that 'some' of the islanders have red hair. With real national groups, as opposed to this imaginary population, such assertions are often made. By contrast science has to content itself with the more modest study of the incidence of red hair, paranoia, psychopathy, or other such traits in the national group concerned. It is much less exciting.

The Von Domarus Principle has been used as a basis of understanding how psychotic patients – when they think in a psychotic way – behave in their thinking. It has also been applied to the study of dreamlife. Prejudiced thinking of the kind discussed above about national groups may also exhibit it. The principle is a good example of one which may be put to effective use in one specific area of psychology to which it has applications.

My concluding reference is to a concept deriving from logic rather than a principle: the category of the Null Class, of non-existing things. With the abnormal, the paranormal, and indeed the normal, psychology is much concerned with the products of human imagining. Jung attributed to people in a primitive society, fears which were present not in the head of such people but 'projected into the jungle'. Similarly the ghosts and other imaginary things 'present' in the darkness to a frightened child may be very real. Fear is but one kind of response. Thus my colleague was merely interested when during his pre-lucid dream he 'perceived' a purely non-existent dog by his bedside. But with hypnagogic imagery or body image changes sometimes reassurance is needed. For the robust materialism of Thomas Hobbes, null class phenomena had no terrors, and moreover he provided an explanation that others have since often used. He argued that it was 'from ignorance of how to distinguish dreams and other strong fancies from vision' that there arose the notions of ghosts, fairies, and goblins, and the fear of witches. Along with imagined inhabitants of the null class are imaginary events. In dreams all things are possible. People may fly like a bird, or change in shape or size; characters from history may appear and talk. The constraints of physics and biology no longer apply. The implications for abnormal psychology and in the study of the seemingly supernatural are considerable.

Seven areas have been considered, and some principles have emerged. If some or all of these principles are rejected at least they have provided a challenge for others to do better. Psychologists should certainly be getting on with the task of formulating perhaps better equivalents. If science seeks general laws, literature is often concerned with the individuality of people. Some illustrations will next be considered from imaginative writings. In works of art the Hobbes Principle may be applied. Imaginative thought products are built on the earlier imagining of predecessors. Writers have read works of their predecessors, just as painters have seen and responded to earlier paintings. Observations and imagination about the individual person will next concern us.

SUMMARY

1   Like other sciences, psychology is concerned with classifying phenomena in the hope of explaining them. Pre-scientific thinking in a huge number of areas resorted to classifying chunks of information by making reference to a number. The number seven has recurred in many traditions of such information-processing. Limitations of memory may have something to do with this.

2   Three ways in which such ways of dealing with 'chunks' of information of interest to psychology are considered. It is concluded that seven is a useful number with mnemonic advantages, and we may put it to use again in considering seven areas of psychology. Perhaps within these areas we may be able to find some fundamental principles of agreed importance and generality.

3   The seven areas are considered, together with some of the generalizations we have already encountered. These relate to the biology of mental life, motivation, the perceived environment, learning and association, ethical and social factors, the personality, and the limitations of imagination and thinking.

4   Other principles claim our attention in psychology, and some of those that might have been included are more briefly discussed.

5   If science is concerned with basic principles, literature has often sought vivid portrayal of individuality within both subjective experience and overt behaviour. This will next concern us.

Chapter Sixteen

THE ABNORMAL PERSONALITY IN LITERATURE

Fiction should use life merely as raw material which it arranges in ingenious patterns.

W. Somerset Maugham

In creating imaginary characters writers draw on their observations of real people. Such perceptual sources may be composite and through secondary perception imagining may build on the previous imaginings of others. All this accords with what I have called the Hobbes Principle and the sensory sources of even highly creative thought. In his comment cited above, Somerset Maugham provides his personal confirmation of this, presumably with reference to his own characters and plots. Within the body of literature we encounter a wide variety of characters, including many we may assess as abnormal. Since perceptual observations of real people have made their contribution it is not surprising that some of these imaginary characters are of considerable interest to psychology. In illustrations I shall confine myself largely to well-known literature, though readers will be able to add to these from less familiar writings of their own preference.

The works of Shakespeare are a text-book of abnormal psychology. In the plays we encounter psychosis in its schizophrenic, depressed, and paranoid form. We find hallucinations, obsessions, and automatisms, as in the frequently noted nocturnal somnambulisms of Lady Macbeth. Earlier we considered how lack of empathy characterized many of the leading participants in *King*

316

Lear. Measure for Measure uncovers the fragility of the puritanism of Angelo in his reaction formations against sexuality; we may also find a parallel in those of his female counterpart, Isabella. The famous speech by Mark Antony over the dead body of the murdered Julius Caesar, with his readiness to reject pity, reveals that Shakespeare well understood the principle of Relative Ethics of Sentiments.

In Coleridge we have not only a great poet but also a thinker who was deeply interested in psychology as such. These interests embraced the laws of association and repeated excursions into the psychology of superstition and the allegedly supernatural. *Christabel, The Rime of the Ancient Mariner*, and *The Three Graves* all explore this, and Coleridge is careful to leave undefined just where naturalistic explanation ends and the supernatural begins. *The Three Graves* is introduced by him with a preface dealing with his interest in Caribbean witchcraft and the effects of a curse on its victim. The poem explores this, and with it human suggestibility, in three people living in the 'western' world. Livingstone Lowes (1927) explores similar themes in *The Ancient Mariner*, whose model may well have been Fletcher Christian. The year 1789 was that of not only the French Revolution but also the Mutiny on the *Bounty*, but it was not until twenty-five years later that it became known what had happened to Christian. As Lowes points out (op. cit.: 28), Coleridge and his contemporaries 'could only guess', the poet having recorded his intention to write a poem on 'adventures of Christian, the mutineer'. It is curious that Wordsworth was himself remarkably insensitive in his evaluation of Coleridge's poem. When the second edition of *Lyrical Ballads* appeared, Wordsworth's accompanying critical comments on the poem's alleged defects included the charge that the principal person had no distinct character, either in his profession of mariner, or 'as a human being' (Quoted in Lowes op. cit.: 197). In this Wordsworth seems greatly to have under-estimated Coleridge as a psychologist.

THE ANCIENT MARINER AS A PERSON

On the contrary the 'principal person' is of considerable interest to psychology. He represents the epitome of a man in an altered mental state. Many of us can recall having played 'wedding guest' to such a character type. A stranger intrudes upon us, often when – like the wedding guest – we have something else to do. He has a long story to tell, and he demands our attention. We don't know what to make of this intrusion, or of the person concerned, and many disturbing thoughts pass through our mind. Is the man dangerous? Certainly the way he is acting is not normal. Perhaps he is insane? Or perhaps he is drunk or drugged? Of course he may merely be a harmless eccentric? But we wish he would leave us alone. With great skill Coleridge, the 'subtle-souled psychologist', portrays such a situation and the difficulties of dealing with it. Most of all our motive is to escape. Sometimes, as in the poem, the intrusion involves a physical act. To this the wedding guest responds with anger: 'Hold off! unhand me, grey-beard loon!' The mariner drops his hand, resorts to the use of his 'glittering eye' and his victim resigns himself. 'The mariner hath his will.' There were 'magnetizers' and 'mesmerists' whom Coleridge probably encountered in Bristol or London. But I suspect the poet was referring not to hypnotism, but to something else. If there are different kinds of 'ancient mariners' they seem to have something in common. They are very familiar with efforts to escape on the part of their unwilling audiences. From past experience they have developed a range of techniques to prevent this happening. It is not that they are socially insensitive. On the contrary they are, in these respects, often highly skilled. The poet explores the subtle features of such inter-personal relations.

It may seem hard-hearted to refer to the Ancient Mariner as a 'type' or person. Also it is an over-simplification of variability of behaviour. What the same person does may vary greatly on different occasions. We may all sometimes be 'ancient mariners', sometimes 'wedding guests'. Often we have more to tell an unwilling captive audience than they want to hear; likewise there are other occasions when we suffer similarly from the long stories others come to tell us. A depressed or bereaved person may perseverate at length about his own misery in ways that lead his hearer to seek escape. As the poetess reminds us, people are often left to 'weep alone' (see page 246). Consider again the Rosenhan study in which normal people pretended to be psychotic in a psychiatric hospital. As we have seen, even enlightened professionals resorted to responding to what they sought to communicate with a 'yes, yes' that was very deaf. In courts of law, as in hospitals, there is abundant evidence that time spent on *not* listening to what other people have to say is highly valued. Even in psychotherapy the sessions are usually limited chunks of time: between them the therapist goes off and does something else. On the telephone, as elsewhere, we encounter ancient mariners to whom we become wedding guests.

We may thus view such inter-personal relationships from the two alternative standpoints. With empathy towards the Mariner we may take account of a variety of different kinds of people, and loneliness, depression, and even drunkenness may invoke sympathy. In an appropriate setting, and when we are not urgently concerned about doing something else, we may listen for a long time to such a person. On the other hand, viewed from outside, the intrusion of a stranger who behaves in seemingly abnormal ways can be not merely tiresome, but frightening. Fear of assault, and sometimes superstitious fear of the unknown, may be aroused. In many societies 'madness' or 'insanity' is itself subject matter for superstitious ignorance and fear. And in some there may also be dread of spirit possession and witchcraft. Coleridge's poem takes account of this. As the story unfolds about the crime, the curse, and the death of the crew of the ship, the Mariner himself has to give reassurance. He is not himself a ghostly embodied spirit, but a real living person.

> Fear not, fear not, thou Wedding Guest!
> This body dropt not down.

This theme of the supernatural recurs later. The Mariner takes the oars, the hermit prays, and the pilot's boy is tempted to express his fear that the man is possessed. What follows afterwards, by the intervention of the holy man, is perhaps psychotherapy. Or perhaps it is an exorcism?

Coleridge's great poem suffered parody on several occasions. An offender was W. S. Gilbert in one of his *Bab Ballads*, the same Gilbert who, in *Rosenkrantz and Guildenstern*, parodied *Hamlet*. Gilbert also had his blind spot of a kind that resembles ancient mariner behaviour, recurrent enthusiasm to write a comic opera about a 'magic lozenge' which had the property of conferring invisibility. (Another of the *Bab Ballads* deals in fact with this plot.)

319

But Sullivan was totally unimpressed and no Gilbert and Sullivan opera about such a lozenge emerged. Gilbert, it seems, was persistent and would 'go on' about his magic lozenge, while Sullivan, like Coleridge's wedding guest, would seek to escape if he saw his partner coming ready to suggest yet again writing such an opera.

These happenings are the more interesting because they concerned, in Gilbert, a man who possessed considerable wit and a developed sense of humour, qualities allegedly closely related to insight. A neglected aspect of the psychopathology of everyday life may be noted. It is not merely behaving like an ancient mariner, or trying yet again to sell the idea of some favoured 'magic lozenge'. It is that while doing so the person concerned is seemingly aware of the sufferings of his victim, efforts to escape, and reluctance to listen. There are resemblances to what Piaget called 'egocentric speech', utterances which are engaged in for their own sake, irrespective of whether anybody is listening or not. In such a situation the audience must not be allowed to escape, and a whole repertoire of skills is likely to be exercised by the speaker to prevent this. He has a fund of relevant experiences with past listeners to draw on, and uses this to prevent either escape or being 'switched off'.

Related issues are discussed by Miles Kington (1982) in an essay 'In praise of useless information'. He writes with his usual wit, but in the style of the 'true word spoken in jest' about a common phenomenon. And he prefers 'useless', rather than allegedly 'useful' information. Much of the time we are being overwhelmed by 'useful' information far in excess of what we need to know. Tables of statistics, 'back-up data', and 'in-depth breakdowns' provide many instances of details far in excess of anything we really want. We may encounter this while being guided round a factory or some other such institution, listen politely, and nod in a way that has the advantage of not having to make eye contact with the hard-working guide. Kington refers to other situations and 'our almost religious belief in useful information', as when something goes wrong and 'a commission' is set up to look into it. This collects a lot of statistics and data, most or all of which is irrelevant to anything in fact being done. There are of course exceptions. Apart from individual ancient mariners, and others with their 'magic lozenges', society itself inflicts on us much 'useful/useless' information.

THE PEOPLE IN DICKENS

In creating his characters, memorable in their diversity, Charles Dickens has much to say of interest to psychology. He makes considerable use of the notion of internal reservoirs of emotional and motivational energy. Consider *A Tale of Two Cities*. Thérèse Defarge is guided by her long-festering sentiment of hate towards the name 'St Evremonde' and all who bear it, despite their personal innocence. Love for Lucie arouses Sydney Carton from his aboulia and cynical apathy to his act of self-sacrifice. Protective concern for the same girl energizes the maiden lady, Miss Potts, to physical action, leading to her actually killing the fanatical Defarge. In the same novel is an account of somnambulistic automatism in Dr Manette after his imprisonment in the Bastille. This recurs under stress and he exhibits amnesia and an inability to recognize even his own daughter. Dickens is known to have had an interest in altered mental states, including hypnotism which he himself practised. Dr Manette's diurnal somnambulisms exhibit similarities and differences to the drug-induced somnambulistic behaviour that is central to the plot of *The Moonstone* written by Dickens' friend, Wilkie Collins. It is likely that the two authors often discussed these and other altered states.

Abnormal mental life often involves exaggerations of the normal. Focus on some detail of personality and exaggeration of it is central to caricature and in this respect Dickens was fortunate in his illustrators, who amplified his written words about people. One critic, John Drinkwater (1940), assesses as characteristic of Dickens his remarkable talent for originality in detail, revealing his 'little touches of genius'. There have been many criminal and shady characters in literature, but exaggerations of detail give reality in Dickens to Fagin, Bill Sikes, and the Artful Dodger. Drinkwater suggests that people should try reading some other good novel, noting how other writers leave a vacuum where Dickens puts in 'the colour of character ... the colour of caricature' (op. cit.: 686). In one of his most remarkable exaggerations, Mr Pickwick, Dickens produces a man who describes himself as 'An observer of human nature, Sir'. With or without Mr Pickwick's famous note book, Dickens himself observed. He records, 'I don't invent, but see it and write it down.' Observation of details about actual people is obviously implied. But commenting on this

321

remark, Enid Blyton put to me the opinion that 'seeing' in the visual imagery sense was also involved. She suggested that Dickens probably had a capacity for what I have called 'cinemato-graphic eidetic imagery' for characters he could 'see' and 'hear' similar to that she used in her own creative writing. Some authors obviously became strongly emotionally involved because of the realism of their created characters. Conan Doyle even tried to kill off his fictional detective, and Agatha Christie, who came to detest Poirot, succeeded in doing so. Dickens liked and disliked his own people. The hypocritical Uriah Heep and the hate-driven Quilp, though imaginary, have become objects of hostile sentiments for generations of readers. By contrast, despite their eccentricity Pickwick and Micawber are portrayed as likeable, while Nicholas Nickleby was obviously a man with robust and admirable moral sentiments. Charles Dickens, despite having himself created the imaginary murder of the warm-hearted Nancy, was much upset by this event, reacted to it as a real tragedy, and could not rest until he had imposed retribution on Bill Sikes.

In accord with his own moral sentiments, Dickens ensured that his created characters received their deserts. Uriah Heep is given a life sentence in prison; the sadistic Squeers of *Nicholas Nickleby* is transported; the villainous Carker of *Dombey and Son* falls in front of a train and is killed; and Steerforth is drowned. On the more positive side, Mr Micawber, relieved of debt, becomes a respected colonial magistrate. Mr Pickwick is released from prison, and together with his associates goes on to take part in further amiable adventures. All this is satisfying to the reader as to the author. Real life is only sometimes like this.

HYPNOTISM AND TRILBY

George Du Maurier published *Trilby* in 1894. The stereotype of a sinister hypnotist – Svengali in the novel – with power over a beautiful young girl has clouded much popular thinking about hypnotism. To begin with, as Du Maurier makes explicit, Trilby isn't particularly beautiful. And the author also knew a great deal more about hypnotic states than is widely believed. The complete and unexpurgated version of the book appeared only in 1983 (ed. Alexander). The story concerns the young artist's model,

Trilby O'Farrell, who is tone deaf. There is only one song she can sing, 'Ben Bolt', and that out of tune. But when hypnotized by Svengali, her latent powers emerged, guided by specific musical gifts he possessed. Thus Trilby becomes a famous singer by hypnotic rapport. Towards the end of the book there is a climax: Trilby stands before a large audience about to sing. But she seems bewildered, and has awakened from her hypnotic trance. The restive audience loudly demand a performance from her. She does the only thing she can do, and pathetically sings 'Ben Bolt' out of tune. Rapport has been broken. Svengali, sitting there in the theatre, has had a heart attack.

The author was very familiar with the Paris in which the story is set. He had lived in this part of the city as a struggling young artist. As narrator of the story and through his characters, he reveals that he was also well informed about hypnotism. Svengali is a composite character. He is modelled to some extent on Du Maurier's friend, the hypnotist Felix Moscheles. Alexander (1983), in his edition of *Trilby*, includes a sketch by the artist-author, who wrote on it 'Moscheles or Mephistopheles', a sketch for Svengali. If Du Maurier had personal acquaintance with an experienced hypnotist there is also a factual aspect to his plot. Alexander points to a further model for Svengali in a man called Charles Boscha. He was a strange and eccentric musical conductor who had 'influenced' a girl, Anna Bishop, and transformed her into a prima donna. This 'influencing' included a course of hypnotic training during the music lessons she received from him. Along with further clues to the sources of the imaginaive character Svengali, we encounter the germ of the plot. It had reference to real events. Gecko, Svengali's close associate, is Du Maurier's 'psychologist in literature' character. In the novel Gecko explains, 'I will tell you a secret.' He goes on to say, *'There were two Trilbys'* (Alexander 1983: 304, italics Du Maurier's). Then follows, 'there was the Trilby you knew who could not sing one single note in tune,' but also the other personality: 'Svengali could turn her into the other Trilby, his Trilby, and make her do whatever he liked' (ibid.). The words Du Maurier speaks through his psychologist character use the language of dissociation. This other Trilby becomes, through Svengali's skill, 'an organ to play upon'. The fuller explanation is interesting. Now it is the narrator who becomes his own psychologist. He explains how the uneducated

Trilby is given books to read. Through Dickens, Thackeray, and Scott she develops a good knowledge of the English language. Her speech is sophisticated, the narrator explains, and has no 'ungainliness' like dropping an 'H' or broadening an 'O' or an 'A'. By contrast Trilby's French remains that of the poorer quarters of Paris, full of slang and picturesque phrases. 'Trilby speaking English, and Trilby speaking French were two different things' (op. cit.: 94). The marked social and economic differences reflected in the personalities of the two Trilbys are underlined. They were part of her instruction and preparation for her feats of singing in hypnotic trances.

The hypnotic training given to Trilby and her instruction in another language closely parallel a later actual event. Elsewhere (McKellar 1979b) I have discussed a multiple personality of the 1930s, G. E. Morselli's case of Elena. There were two sub-personalities, one which spoke French and the other Italian. The therapist decided that the Italian one was the most normal and proceeded to reinforce it. His method closely parallels that of Svengali's with Trilby: 'he sought to strengthen the Italian personality system by getting his patient to read aloud long passages from Dante in Italian' (McKellar op. cit.: 162). As regards hypnosis the psychologist Sutcliffe (1961) has distinguished between those who take a 'sceptical', and those who take a 'credulous' view of the actual and alleged phenomena. From the sceptical standpoint we might take the view that Du Maurier was merely writing science fiction, placing impossible happenings in the Latin Quarter of Paris which he knew very well. But there is good and bad science fiction. Indeed certain rules about it have since been laid down: we are told they shouldn't be broken. Science should be there as well as fiction. From the alternative, so-called 'credulous' standpoint it might be argued that Du Maurier not only knew Paris but was better informed about hypnotism than is often supposed. Consider both subject and hypnotist. Trilby was a trained hypnotic subject. Her hypnotic rapport with Svengali was optimal: she is portrayed as being highly motivated to perform hypnotically as required by her teacher. Martin Orne, as a leading researcher on the psychology of hypnotism, expresses the view – based on knowledge of many experiments – that 'the range of behaviour which an individual will carry out if requested to do is vastly greater than is generally believed' (Orne 1977: 15–16).

Consider now the hypnotist. Svengali lacks the ability to sing overtly. 'He was absolutely without voice, his sounds being "harsh" and "hoarse".' But in fact he does engage in a great deal of 'singing' in his sub-vocal auditory imagery. We learn in the story that 'in his head he went forever singing' (Alexander 1983: 73). But with a musical instrument, Svengali is different, and with an instrument he betrays his qualities of musical genius. Some readers may be able, like myself, to enter empathically into Svengali's situation. They may lack voice like Svengali – and me – but sub-vocally may 'sing' a great deal. On occasion they may demonstrate to their musical friends that they know the words to an extent that may even impress such friends: but they are words that they would not attempt to sing in public. Moreover, when they are sure they are alone they may even sing overtly, loud and clear. Notice what Du Maurier's psychologist character Gecko has to tell us. Gecko reports that Trilby has become for Svengali 'an organ to play upon – an instrument of music – a Stradivarius' (op. cit.: 304). For the musically frustrated man she is potentially a 'flesh and blood' musical instrument. Moreover, musically and hypnotically Svengali possesses the abilities and skills with which to train her. The music she produces is vocal not instrumental. Not irrelevant are the physique and bodily structure of Trilby. In the story she is described as 'a Burne-Jones' type of woman, with a latent voice and the vocal structure of a powerful singer. Some scepticism is perhaps appropriate about terms like 'tone deaf', absence of a 'sense of pitch', and 'a latent voice'. A good teacher with relevant skills can do much with a seemingly untalented pupil. Svengali's motivation was strong, Trilby is co-operative, and much time goes into the preparation. This combination of factors, subtly introduced into the story, make the Trilby per-formances in the hands of Svengali not merely meaningful, but plausible. Science fiction perhaps? But Du Maurier had considerable understanding of relevant scientific realities: the psychology of hypnosis, dissociative phenomena, potential and actual abilities, and motivation to succeed.

In evaluating the alternative 'credulous' and 'sceptical' views of the *Trilby* novel we encounter the question that pervades hypnotic research. Could it be done in fact? Many of the alleged 'limitations' of hypnosis, so often asserted, come back to this same issue: whether under ideal conditions it can be done at all. Inspired by the Trilby story there were several who tried it out at the time. The French hypnotist, Albert de Rochas, tried it with a model called Lina. He claimed success, thus supporting the idea that Du Maurier's story was not mere fiction. In 1902 in San Francisco the hypnotist Leon Silvani claimed another success, this time with a tone-deaf girl, Viola West, who when hypnotized performed as a talented singer (Alexander 1983). It is also reported that on one occasion the post-Trilby emerged from her trance on the stage, like her fictional predecessor, unable to sing. Obviously such claims of success need scrutiny and further experimental studies. But in many areas of actual experiments on hypnosis it has often seemed that the notion of 'the impossible' has been too often claimed, and in too cavalier a fashion.

CONSCIENCE AND ITS PATHOLOGY

The three psychiatric adjectives of 'hypo' or too little, 'hyper' or excess, and 'para' or distorted, may be related to conscience and moral motivation. Many instances have been explored by literature. Apparent absence or minimal functioning of conscience, and aggressive, malevolent, or irresponsible conduct without guilt feeling is traditionally associated with 'psychopathy', personality disorders of an anti-social kind. In his classic study of this type of abnormality, Cleckley (1955) defines it in terms of what he calls 'the mask of sanity'. Smooth talk, plausibility, and outward charm mask a seriously deviant, potentially criminal, and sometimes even dangerous personality. (See also Cleckley in Arieti 1959.) Cleckley himself finds many examples of the conscience-bereft character in literature. One of Cleckley's examples is Mildred in Somerset Maugham's *Of Human Bondage*, with her characteristic emotional shallowness, insensitivity to others, and almost incredible depths of ingratitude. Did Somerset Maugham have, as his autobiography suggests he often had, a model for his Mildred? 'Psychopathy' is a controversial category, but one to which the Mental Health Act of 1959 gave legal recognition. Elsewhere (1968) I have discussed the concept in fuller detail. Alcohol has been neatly defined as a 'superego solvent', and sometimes we encounter people – in life as in literature – through whose bloodstream alcohol, or something like it, seems perpetually to flow.

Excess of conscience appears in literature in many superego-driven characters. An outstanding example is to be found in Ibsen's *Brand*. Ibsen's puritanical Pastor Brand, with his 'nought or all' morality, because of this dominant sub-system inflicts widespread suffering. Those emotionally near to him are his first victims. As Nietzsche observes, sometimes 'the categorical imperative is dangerous to life.' The same conclusion is advanced in the drama by a 'psychologist in literature' character whom Ibsen brings in to unmask the alliance in Brand's motivation of morality on the one hand, with both destructiveness and self-destructiveness on the other. What Brand regards as 'right', others in the play are provoked to assess as misguided and morally 'wrong'. This issue is examined in a different way by Mark Twain in *The Adventures of Huckleberry Finn* (1884) and concerns slavery. Perhaps we need to remind ourselves that in the mid-1980s slavery still exists in parts of the world. An anti-slavery society survives and still has to function. As in the Russia portrayed in Gogol's *Dead Souls*, ownership of people was an accepted part of the society of the Mississippi area about which Mark Twain wrote. He himself had factual information to draw on, and used it in his famous story. During the events reported, Huckleberry helps his slave friend Jim to escape from Jim's 'owner', a Miss Watson. In the course of this escape his conscience begins to trouble him greatly but not about slavery. Huckleberry asks himself, what has poor Miss Watson ever done to him that he should 'treat her so mean'? He is so miserable with his sense of guilt in depriving the 'rightful owner' of her legitimate property that he wishes he were dead. Things are made worse when his friend Jim declares that now he is free he will be able to save money, go back, and buy his wife and two children: if their owner won't sell he'll arrange to steal them. The conscience-stricken Huckleberry goes through acute conflict at what seems to him this additionally monstrous possibility. For a while he is tempted to give Jim up, though in the end he lies to protect Jim's escape. It is his friendship that determines a courageous decision in that religious sentiments intrude and he believes he 'will go to hell' for his acts of wickedness. Today we would view things very differently and in terms of our own moral sentiments assess Huckleberry's conscience as distorted. Yet in terms of his area of culture and period of time, there is little that is 'abnormal' about this moral struggle: it is just that civilization has progressed a little.

Intervention of the Relative Ethics of Sentiments may be noted: both those that stem from loyalty to a friend, and others from a hell-fire variant of religion. On the whole 'evil be thou my good' represents, happily, a rare form of moral motivation. Perhaps in literature we find it portrayed in Stevenson's Mr Hyde. Even in *Dracula* and in *Frankenstein* injected by their authors are elements of pathos, and some sympathy for the wretchedness of the two creatures involved. In reality as opposed to literary fiction there are some grim exceptions, as in the Manson murders, and the reminders during 1987 of the Brady–Hindley crimes. Some of the things human beings do to others strain empathy with actions and their motivation. Quasi-pathological justifications of 'obedience to orders' were resorted to at Nuremberg and elsewhere, and yet again in 1987 during the trial of Klaus Barbie. Relative ethics in support of political, religious, or other sentiments have throughout history continued to serve often grim purposes. Indignation also produces its excuses.

From within literature two instances may be taken. Both are in Shakespeare's *Julius Caesar*. First, in the famous quarrel scene between Brutus and Cassius (IV. iii.) we have the relative ethics of positive sentiments between the two playing a part. Brutus accuses Cassius of having 'an itching palm', a readiness to give way to being bribed. Cassius responds, 'you know that you are Brutus that speak thus, or by the gods this speech were else your last.' A moral exception is made, and with it restraint. Second, no such restraint is imposed by the relative ethics that accompany the sentiment of hate, when Antony views the dead body of Caesar (III, i). In the speech beginning 'O, pardon me, thou bleeding piece of earth ...' Caesar's friend declares the revenge he will achieve. But more than this, nothing will stand in its way. There will be 'fierce civil strife ... all pity choked' to lay waste the land. Revenge for a wrong done to a friend will know no restraint. Earlier in discussing these issues I referred to the defence of the Alamo in 1836 and its finale; the advance of the 6,000-strong Mexican army playing the 'Deguello', the Mexican war song signifying 'no quarter' (McKellar 1977b). The massacre of 150 Texans followed. There was the aftermath when Sam Houston's Texan forces fought and defeated the Mexican army that had been responsible. The Texans did not play the 'Deguello' but, in the massacre of the Mexicans that followed, they advanced with the war-cry 'Remember the Alamo'. As in the portrayal of warfare in literature, relative ethics played its part in the killing that followed. Powerful reserves of motivation are stored in sentiments, with relative ethics as their accompaniment.

HUMAN NATURE AND TROPICAL ISLANDS

The psychology of Rousseau differed from that of Aristotle. Rousseau lacked the notion of ethical neutrality – of raw materials for virtue and viciousness – that Aristotle provided as a basis for subsequent development of psychology. In the state of nature people are naturally good, but 'society depraves them'. Had Rousseau lived to see the French Revolution and the forces released by the breakdown of social norms, the great Frenchman might have been less optimistic. The reforms which Rousseau sought are reflected in his view of education of the child, expounded by him in his own novel *Emile*. Skinner has argued that Rousseau's view in *Emile* of 'man's original goodness' and his attempt to show 'vice and error foreign to his nature' is incorrect. The book in fact shows how human beings can be changed (Skinner 1972: 124). As regards the raw materials, consider fictional accounts of life on exotic tropical islands. Thus R. M. Ballantyne's *Coral Island* may seem to some of us misleading in its Rousseau-like optimism. When it is read today this book seems less objectionable than its sequel, *The Gorilla Hunters*, the myths it provided and its savagery towards one of the harmless primates. On Ballantyne's island the central characters, Ralph, Jack, and Peterkin, enjoy themselves, as vicariously does the reader, in their tropical paradise. By contrast with this is another book, *Lord of the Flies*.

There are strong parallels between William Golding's novel and its predecessor. Again we meet a Ralph and a Jack. In Simon – who in the Bible is also called 'Peter' – it is not difficult to find the third of Ballantyne's characters Peterkin. If there are similarities there are also startling differences. What happens in *Lord of the Flies* is a rejection of the norms of civilization. There emerges a replacement of them in stark and frightening savagery. Around Jack there develops a group of 'hunters'. First is their assault – reminiscent of the onslaught in Ballantyne's second book on gorillas – on animals, the wild pigs of the island. Ralph and his friend the fat boy – unhappily nicknamed 'Piggy' – both stand against Jack's tribe but with only limited success. It is the visionary Simon, possessed with both psychological insight and a kind of mystical wisdom, who becomes the sacrificial victim. The other two are saved only by the arrival of a ship. This brings with it re-statement of the norms of civilization. In their absence what has happened is something very different from events on Ballantyne's coral island. Golding's novel states the novelist's own pessimism about violence and ability of civilization to restrain it. His novel reflects knowledge gained during the period of his own lifetime of what, in certain circumstances, human beings will do to one another. Referring to Nazi Germany and mass murder he points out that these things were 'not done by the headhunters of New Guinea, or by some primitive tribe in the Amazon'. On the contrary 'they were done skilfully, coldly, by educated men, doctors, lawyers, by men with a tradition of civilization behind them' (Golding 1962, in ed. Meek, Warlow, and Barton 1977: 228). His stated conscious intention as author of *Lord of the Flies* was to underline this theme of civilization, its breakdown, and restraints on human cruelty. In Golding's lifetime, as emerged at the principal Nuremberg Trial, there is abundant justification for the statement that apparently normal people may engage in barely credible acts of sustained cruelty. In doing so they do not become 'wild beasts' or 'animals': they disgrace our own species. A major theorist who was himself well informed about animal psychology, the late Professor D. O. Hebb, has commented, 'Man is not a tame animal, but inherently dangerous, to be domesti-cated only with great pains' (McKellar 1977b: 15). Hebb's con-clusion is that the human being is the most emotional of all animals, but the norms of civilization are basically devices to hide this fact, and to limit occasions for such arousal (Hebb and Thompson 1954).

When *Lord of the Flies* was made into a film, something happened. Fiction and fact came together. I am indebted to the encyclopaedic knowledge of Mr Richard Weatherley about the history of the film. His information to me is that during the filming on a tropical island problems arose: the young actors did more than act. They needed restraint because often they tended to actions more reminiscent of Golding's than of Ballantyne's novel. As regards abnormalities of behaviour the film itself merits notice along with other human thought-products.

LITERATURE AND THE FILM

Films like books can be preserved, and the development of video-tapes now makes major films readily available. It is thus meaningful to consider some of the enduring portrayals of mental abnormality acted by talented men and women. Such performances have sometimes amplified the text of the written word. An example can be found in the Olivier version of *Hamlet*. This was the interpretation by Jean Simmons of the madness of Ophelia: a very convincing portrayal of schizophrenia in its hebephrenic form. Shakespeare may have had the intention of presenting this syndrome but, whether or not he meant to do so, the actress concerned exhibited its characteristics to a remarkable extent. Both *The Three Faces of Eve* and *Sybil* have been filmed. In the first of these, Joanne Woodward acted the patient, and in the second the psychiatrist: multiple personality was portrayed with empathy and insight in both. As a director Alfred Hitchcock was no less interested in abnormal psychology than Coleridge among poets, or Dostoevsky among novelists. Through him and his actors we encounter the psychopathic murderer, acrophobic fears of heights, obsessional thinking and many excursions into terror. Dame Edith Evans in one of her films portrayed late paraphrenia and the delusory suspiciousness of old age. Through the distorting mirror of her thinking we are shown how paranoid interpretations can be further supported by exaggerated perception of actual hostility in others. This mechanism I have labelled 'paranoid distortion'.

Somnambulisms, fugues, and amnesia have figured in many films, and a sequence of major actors has portrayed the Jekyll–Hyde syndrome. Delirium tremens, with its visual hallucinations and panic reactions in Ray Milland's *Lost Weekend*, must certainly be mentioned. As regards altered states induced by alcohol it has been suggested there are three main forms of being 'drunk'. There is fighting drunk, maudlin drunk, and under-the-table drunk. Often we see one or other of these in the film. Very challenging is a role which requires an intelligent actor or actress

331

to portray intellectual retardation. Sir John Mills received an award for such an interpretation of 'Michael' in *Ryan's Daughter*. When I first saw this film my companion was incredulous at its portrayal of bigotry and moralized hate, believing it to be a fictional exaggeration. It wasn't. In another film a performance resembling that by Mills also received an award. When invited to take a main part in *Murder on the Orient Express*, the late Ingrid Bergman refused. A major actress chose instead the minor role of an intellectually limited woman who, in a memorable performance, she played in a 'low-profile' way. If great acting can achieve remarkable authenticity it may also contribute to fictional stereotypes. Captain Bligh certainly, and perhaps also Mr Barrett of Wimpole Street gained little in their historical reputations from their brilliant portrayals by Charles Laughton. As we have seen, through the written word, King Richard III has suffered similarly. Despite all the Tudor propaganda he may well have been, like Captain Bligh, a relatively normal person and not a monster. But perhaps Sir Laurence Olivier redressed the balance somewhat, making him – possibly without intention – rather likeable. In literature we have seen that authors sometimes come to develop strong sentiments, including intense dislike, about their own imaginative creations. Dickens is unlikely to have had much enthusiasm for what a musical version of *Oliver Twist* did for Fagin. Acting skill produced in the film an amusing character – at worst an amiable psychopath – quite unlike the target of Dickens' own hatred and determination to punish after the murder of Nancy. Bill Sikes at least still comes through as thoroughly hateful.

The invented characters of fiction and the perhaps often equally fictional stereotyped characters of history have appeared in film and on television. Here human imagination has built on previous imagination, and the skills of actors and actresses have often contributed a portrayal of credible abnormality. Readers may be provoked into looking for other examples.

WITHIN THE PERCEIVED ENVIRONMENT

In a variety of ways writers have employed the Koffka Principle. Their characters have exhibited experience and behaviour within the environment as they perceived or misperceived it to be. In literature Shakespeare provides many instances in which one character, falsely believing that another character has died, acts on this misperception of the realities. In another major work of literature Cervantes builds his story on the fantasy and illusions of Don Quixote.

Cervantes rivals Shakespeare in the numerous phrases, now proverbs or clichés, he contributed to human language. Shand might well have explored these. 'Tilting at windmills' is but one of very many. For the gallant don they are not windmills but giants. His horse Rocinante, perceived by others as a wretched creature and a figure of fun, for Don Quixote is a magnificent charger. The loyal devotion of Sancho Panza – one of the great psychologist characters in literature – reinforces his fantasies, delusions, and even hallucinations. Constantly the don projects qualities that are not there on to the Lady Dulcinea in his romantic imaging 'between his lucid intervals'. For him 'faint heart n'er won fair lady' and he is at all times courteous to 'the fair sex'. But as Sancho Panza observes, 'he preaches well that lives well,' and it is perhaps because of this that many such often-quoted sayings have accumulated around the don. He represents a type of personality that has interested other authors. In his short story *Salvatore* later, Somerset Maugham sought to hold his readers' attention for a few pages to portray in a courteous, gentle, but poor fisherman the simple quality of 'goodness, just goodness'. In Cervantes we have a greater-length portrayal of 'the holy fool'. The other outstanding example is Dostoevsky's Prince Myshkin in *The Idiot*. This novel – which incidentally also brings out the resemblances that sometimes occur between epileptic and mystical altered mental states – deals at length with one view of the world in terms of simple-minded virtue in Myshkin as in Don Quixote. By contrast it is noticeable that another of Dostoevsky's characters, Alyosha of *The Brothers Karamazov*, while sharing a robust kind of saintliness is not a holy fool. As a Karamazov he possesses acute insight into the darker human qualities about which he has the disturbing self-knowledge that characterized Dostoevsky himself.

The relation of illusions about the self to ultimate self-knowledge is explored by Karel Čapek – author of the concept of the robot – in his story *The Cheat*. In this the central character Fulton is presented as perceived by a succession of different people. Finally the man is portrayed, stripped of every one of his ego defences, now forced to face his own personality. This same theme, in the finale of the wretched Fulton's self-loathing, occurs in a better-known work of literature. The monster in Mary Shelley's *Frankenstein* was not a robot. Viktor Frankenstein had somehow endowed it with self-consciousness. In the final part of the book we again encounter self-hatred, with focus on the creature's body image as well as actions. Pathos replaces the horror and fear that stemmed from the original nightmare that inspired the story. These two imaginative stories deal with a fundamental problem of insight, along with perhaps a measure of co-conscious awareness in facing the self, and reality as opposed to illusory fantasy about events relating to it. At an important stage of his work Freud came to terms with this problem in a confrontation that might have overwhelmed a lesser man. It was the discovery that reports about traumatic events, especially sexual assaults during childhood, that patients were bringing to him were often fantasy. These things had never happened. Freud's decision on the matter, that on such occasions 'fantasy equals fact', is well known. Was he right?

Henry Murray (1938), in his theory of personality, takes account of this issue. There are both alpha and beta types of press: the one, the person's autobiographical account of what has happened to him; the other, the realities of the life history when an independent check on the facts is possible. This is one application of the Koffka Principle. As regards literature, in Murray's work we also find an invitation to create imaginative literature of one's own. His TAT involves making up stories in response to twenty standardized pictures, saying what is happening, what led up to it, and what is the outcome. Analysis of these twenty thought-products suggests a link between literature and the personality, whether of a well-known author or of oneself. As we have seen, writers have sometimes helped psychologists by themselves providing introspection.

If psychologists like Murray invite their subjects with the TAT to compose literature, literature itself has sometimes imaginatively created its own psychologists. To look for such characters is itself a kind of projective test, and I believe a rewarding one. I return to the concept of the psychologist in literature with illustrations from some choices of my own.

THE PSYCHOLOGIST IN LITERATURE

The concept does not merely relate to the contribution writers have made to psychology. It refers to something more specific. The notion of a psychologist character relates specifically to bringing in a person whose psychological awareness becomes a device for revealing the author's own. An example considered earlier was Poe's character Auguste Dupin, through whom the author revealed his clear understanding of the psychology of empathy on the one hand, and of association of ideas on the other. Again it is noticeable how Ibsen used his psychologist in literature characters, and through them unmasked the unconscious motivation of other characters in the plays. Through the insight, however cynical, of such characters, Ibsen confronts us with the issue: are such people as the fanatical Pastor Brand 'entitled to their opinions', being righteous but not right? His decision as a profound psychologist on the moral aspect of human motivation is on the side of insight: no, they are not.

Without apology I turn again from Ibsen to a still more profound psychologist of the past, though he didn't happen to be a professional. Even Freud acknowledged Dostoevsky's power as introspectionist, and indeed seems to have found it very disturbing. Both directly and through his psychologists in literature, Dostoevsky provided a remarkable series of studies in personality and motivation. *Crime and Punishment* reveals through Raskolnikoff the continuity of mental life between wakefulness and sleep. As elsewhere in Dostoevsky the relation of guilt feeling to actions which belong only to imagery and ideation are explored. Forensic psychology and the courtroom situation are vividly presented here, and also in the prosecutor Ippolit Kirillovitch, with his logic and penetrating persistence, in *The Brothers Karamazov*. And in different ways the Karamazov brothers are all psychologists in literature, but Ivan with his story of 'Christ and the Grand Inquisitor' is the most disturbing. Despite his apparent simple-mindedness, Prince Myshkin of *The Idiot* is a character who uses his sheer goodness as a very powerful device of insight. In *Letters from the Underworld* there is a portrayal of anguished thinking; *The Gambler* takes us into the mental life of compulsive anankastic neurosis; and *The House of the Dead* portrays human experience and behaviour under the conditions of acute suffering. In Dostoevsky we encounter, along with his saints and sinners, the nihilism of Kirilov and the thoughtful suicidal mind. Also in *The Possessed* is a study of the psychology of fanaticism, and in Pytor Verkhovensky, of the icy ruthlessness of the Robespierres and the Stalins still to be born. Our powers of empathy may be strained in attempting to understand the strange, though convincing, portrayal of inconsistencies in characters like Stavrogan or Grushenka. The people in the pages of Dostoevsky differ from those of Dickens. Like Gogol, Dickens achieves his realism through detail defining and exaggerating individuality. By contrast Dostoevsky uses not only actions but also dreams and inner thought as a means of penetrating deeper into processes at the margin of consciousness. The notion of unconscious mental life is not, as such, present in the novels, yet it is appropriate to regard Dostoevsky as one of the major forerunners of modern depth psychology. We learn from his characters about the complexities of multiple motivation, both conscious and unconscious.

SUMMARY

1   If science seeks to formulate general principles, the arts often have a contribution to make about individuality. In literature we encounter numerous attempts to provide a better understanding of normal and abnormal individual personalities.

2   It is not surprising if literature sometimes has information of value to scientific psychology. Creative writers, in designing their fictional characters, draw on observations of real people and introspections from their own mental life. Sometimes they are explicit that this is what they do. The greater the imagining, the more likely is a diversity of perceptual sources of such creative thinking.

3   Readers will have their own preferred literature, but I have selected illustrations of insight into personality and abnormality from mine. Shakespeare, Coleridge, Dickens, Du Maurier, and Golding are among these choices.

4   The pathology of conscience is considered in terms of both psychopathic deficit and superego-ridden excess, and I have given attention to another area of it in the writings of Mark Twain.

5   On stage and screen able professionals have sometimes amplified, in their acting, the psychological insights of writers and dramatists.

6   A concluding reference is made to the notion of the 'psychologist character in literature', in the hope that readers will pursue this concept in novels, poetry, and dramas of their own choice.

Chapter Seventeen

UNCONSCIOUS MENTAL LIFE

We make to ourselves pictures of facts. The picture is a model of reality.

Wittgenstein

Various constructs have been used in attempts to understand experience and behaviour better. Influential among them has been the notion of an unconscious. This has a long history. Freud himself claimed that in philosophy, literature, and science he had many predecessors in 'discovery' of the unconscious. Yet it was not a place or a thing to be discovered: it is a way of talking about certain complex phenomena in such areas as memory, personality, and motivation. Moreover, it has many variants. Points of emphasis on unconscious mental life have differed among those who have used it as their 'picture of facts'. In the terminology of Gestalt psychology, what has been an important 'figure' for one thinker has been passed over as less significant 'ground' by others. In recognizing these different psychologies of the unconscious let me develop an analysis I attempted elsewhere (McKellar 1986).

SEVEN PSYCHOLOGIES OF THE UNCONSCIOUS

Freud's own early formulation was a *dipsychic model*, a division between conscious and unconscious which he regarded as 'the fundamental premise of psychoanalysis'. I illustrate from the

338

most famous case history of this tradition, Breuer's 'Anna O' (Breuer and Freud 1893–5). In one period, during a hot summer in Vienna, the patient developed a phobic aversion to drinking water. She suffered greatly from thirst. Under Breuer's hypnotic treatment this was cured by inducing her to recall an incident from childhood. This emotionally traumatic experience involved seeing her governess feed water to a dog from a glass tumbler. The forgotten incident – seemingly not available to consciousness – was recalled with intense disgust. Breuer reports bringing her out of hypnosis with a glass of water at her lips, and following this the drinking phobia vanished. As psychoanalysis developed hypnotism was abandoned, and repression came to be regarded as but one of a number of defence mechanisms, one closely associated with the hysterical neuroses. The dipsychic theory was also modified with the addition of a pre-conscious, from which memories could be recovered by simple acts of recall. In the alternative frame of reference which Jung brought to depth psychology, a still more elaborate polypsychic rather than dipsychic system emerged. For Jung there were in his archetypes numerous unconscious sub-systems.

The notion of *the unconscious as a reservoir* of motivational forces has a long history. In *Die Welt als Wille und Vorstellung*, Schopenhauer's 'will' has much in common with Freud's unconscious, viewed as the source of dynamic energy. As later translations of this book as *The World as Will and Representation* imply, Schopenhauer was very much concerned with unconscious mental life in terms of constructs. His own interpretation, like Freud's libido, also placed emphasis on the sexual aspect of such motivational energy. Jung's 'libido', like Groddeck's unknown self or 'It' – in common with the later Freudian emphasis on destructive forces – is more neutral in this respect. Jungian complexes, Freudian object cathexes, and the introjected objects of Melanie Klein all have resemblance to Shand's sentiments, as constructs that deal with the attachments of such energy to specific objects and situations. Within inter-personal relations Jung places emphasis on the mechanism of projection and the ambivalence it may carry with it: 'there can be no indifference to the carrier of a projection.' Here we encounter the 'Doctor Fell' phenomenon, as in Thomas Brown's

> I do not love thee, Doctor Fell,
> The reason why I cannot tell. . . .

Strange aversions, loves, hates, and ambivalences to people we have only just met occur, which may, as Jung would argue, result from projections of anima, shadow, or other sub-system on to them. The Freudian construct of the parent imago being carried by such a person, prominent in the transference of a psycho-analysis, conveys a similar idea. On occasion in everyday life, like Ivan Karamazov, we may encounter our own projected alter ego, but in a real and not hallucinated other person.

In Harry Stack Sullivaŋ (1953; 1954) there is emphasis on this idea, with less interest in 'an unconscious' than in 'unconscious factors in *inter-personal relationships*'. Mechanisms resembling those of transference and counter-transference may, for Sullivan, pervade everyday life. Thus in an interview, though geographically only two people are there, others are in a sense 'present'. The interviewer may be responding 'as if' to his own ambivalence to a younger sibling, while his would-be employee is irrationally re-acting as though to a harsh teacher, or perhaps to his imago of the school bully. Sullivan (1954) argues both may be unaware of these emotional intrusions from the past. The basic idea was recognized in the psychoanalyst Edward Glover's comment that if the Battle of Waterloo was won on the playing fields of Eton, perhaps it was lost in a nursery in Corsica! For many of the depth psychologists the first five years of life – that because of limited linguistic development, are unverbalized and thus unconscious – are of fundamental importance.

Among others it was Erik Erikson who has given the *process of development* 'figure' in his system of psychology. For some the elaborate formulations about childhood of Melanie Klein have had a strong appeal. Others have found in the ego psychology of Anna Freud's view of development much common ground with more orthodox areas of psychology. The notion of extension of the ego beyond the bodily self to include possessions, valued social groups, and introjection – Cantril would call it 'introception' – of the norms and values of one's culture into an enlarged self, has had greater appeal (Cantril 1940; 1941). Much of this process of assimilation, which leads to notions of what is 'common sense', 'right' or 'obvious', is in a sense unconscious. The limitations of such cherished assumptions may sometimes come home to us when we recognize language differences between peoples as an index of cultural diversity. To illustrate, the Cardinal of Manila has commented on the frequently reported seeing of visions of the Virgin Mary in the Philippines, and attributed them to food deprivation (*Independent*, 5 February 1988). In doing so he probably spoke in English. But in which of the eleven languages of the islands did those who reported such experiences speak and think? As regards elsewhere, the languages of the Soviet Union have been numbered as 130, those of India over 150, American Indian languages comprise more than 1,000 and the single island of New Guinea contributes 'some 700 more' languages (Katzner 1986). In their 'picture of the facts' of the estimated 3,000 – 4,000 spoken languages of the world and the influences on thinking these provide, specialist linguists – like psychologists – face criterion problems. When, for example, is the concept of 'a dialect', rather than 'a language', more appropriate? When, within this present chapter I claimed that the concept of 'the unconscious' has a long history, I was writing within the European tradition. Schopenhauer, though writing in German, was one of those who injected a broader perspective in this area and took account of Hindu and Buddhist tradition. Thought-products, and the constructs that guide them, depend on the norms of a given place and time, and on the language in which they are thought.

In relation to the unconscious, one influential thinker, Nietzsche – himself by profession a linguist – emphasized its role in *human self-deception*. This we also encounter in the formulations of La Rochefoucauld, Ibsen, and Dostoevsky; and it is prominent in Freud, even more so in Anna Freud (1936). In the history of the concept of the unconscious, Ellenberger (1970) places emphasis on this 'great unmasking tradition' of depth psychology. The mechanisms of ego defence named by the psychoanalysts are many: along with repression and projection are denial, isolation, undoing, ego restriction, introjection, and identification with the aggressor. These are defences against anxiety, conflict, and stress, and may perform self-deceptive functions. Unrecognized ambivalence, masquerading as sentiments of love or friendship, greatly interested La Rochefoucauld, and we may find a specific La Rochefoucauld mechanism in the hostility a person may feel to another who reminds him of his own shortcomings. Despite his admiration for Dostoevsky, Nietzsche deals harshly with the notion of salvation, or even self-improvement through suffering. Instead he suggests we should be vigilant in relation to the disguised revenge those who have suffered deeply may be strongly motivated to take on others. The 'some–all' dichotomy may seem an appropriate antidote to the motivational unmaskings of Nietzsche, for whom traditional respectability was no barrier. Thus for him Kant's categorical imperative morality 'smelt of cruelty', and Socrates was viewed not as a pagan saint but a man determined to self-destruction and talented in his capacity for finding rationalizations to ensure it.

A sixth tradition relates to *unconscious motivation*. This is related to the view that we do not seek the motive of an act, but rather multiple motivation in its full complexity. Rational and ethically respectable motives that are prominent to introspection are not the only ones, nor necessarily the most influential. Pursuit of others leads to a notion of unconscious mental life, to motives at the threshold of consciousness or beyond it. I have argued that La Rochefoucauld's view was not of pervasive self-interest, but a recognition of multiple motivation. Freud was to accept pursuit of pleasure as but one, but not the only motivational factor. Simplified theories of egoism and hedonism were killed so effectively, and buried so deeply by Joseph Butler in his analysis of the complexities of motivation that it is a wonder that they so continually resurrect themselves. But they do. Of course people who differ from our cherished beliefs are motivated by stupidity; our more vigorous enemies by viciousness; and politicians we dislike by both. When in moments of insight we question such assumptions we are on the way to understanding how exponents of psychoanalysis and other systems of depth psychology think about motivation.

A seventh way of looking at 'the unconscious' questions the concept itself. Instead its emphasis is on *re-establishing unconscious connections* within mental life. Within psychoanalysis we find this standpoint in Ernest Kris who argues that self-observation leading to insight proceeds 'by re-establishing links that have been lost' (Kris 1951: 480). A near-synonym phrase for having insight is thinking intelligently about oneself. The psychologist Spearman (1922) has laid down a series of principles for distinguishing more intelligent from less intelligent ways of thinking. These include

342

apprehension of experience: knowing that we feel, knowing that we strive, and knowing what we know. Spearman's second principle involves the ability to grasp relationships. In practice there seems to be much in common between what is achieved in successful therapy, and Spearman's criteria of intelligent thinking. In acquiring therapeutic insight the person concerned gains in apprehension of his or her own mental life. Moreover, linkages are established, or re-established, between memories or other items of experience. Re-orientation results from such linkages. Much of what takes place during a psychoanalysis or other such therapy seems to be grasping relationships. What has been unconscious or repressed has been these connections, between perhaps a remembered childhood happening and present ways of thinking, feeling, or striving. The block repression of a whole incident, as in the case of Anna O, is less common than such improvements in relational thinking, and overcoming barriers to it. Freud speaks of 'resistances', and others like Bernard Hart write of 'logic tight compartments' in mental life. My contention is that much of the therapy process resembles learning to think straight, and feel straight, about oneself and dealings with other people. It is less a matter of 'excavating' wholly unconscious memories from areas of depth and darkness, and more a matter of linkage between ideas, and between sub-systems of the personality. As I expressed this idea in an earlier discussion of this issue, despite traditional differences of terminology, can we view psychoanalysis as a technique for ridding the personality of some of the undesirable aspects of 'dissociation' (McKellar 1986)? A more general issue arises, well expressed in a question asked by the poet who wrote *The Kasidah*: 'When doctors differ, who decides ...?' As I suggested earlier, an answer is perhaps to be found in a case conference in which the participants sort out not differences of diagnosis, but mere differences in their preferred choices of words and concepts. As will be apparent I believe it is timely for a re-examination of some of the territory explored by psychoanalysis in terms of other constructs, like those of a modified dissociationist theory. In this I suspect much common ground may be discovered between the two, and perhaps also with those who view neurosis in terms of learning theory and behaviour therapy.

PERSONALITY, ITS RESOURCES, AND ADJUSTMENT

In our consideration of abnormal psychology, 'the normal personality' may have eluded us. But perhaps not altogether. A sketchy outline of this difficult concept may have emerged. And not least, I hope, in our consideration of the numerous innocent variants of mental life, however 'abnormal' some of these may seem. These are wholly compatible with good mental health, and many are statistically common though often overlooked. A variety of upsurges of A-thinking from systems outside consciousness occur in wakefulness, sleep, and hypnagogia. These may frighten a child, be subject matter for superstition in adults, or in both be sources of anxiety about 'becoming insane'. There are very many reminders that self-knowledge involves coming to terms with unconscious as well as conscious mental life. Integration of the personality, Jung (1940) has emphasized, can be helped by 'messages' from outside consciousness, communicated for instance in dreams. A very different kind of psychologist, Thurstone (1952), makes essentially the same point. His emphasis is on receptivity of two kinds: to what emerges from *within* one's own mental life as well as perceptual information about the external world. As regards normality and adjustment, many people – perhaps most – resemble moderately efficiently run social organizations that on the whole get by without too many internal or external emotional crises. Like such organizations they are assisted in this by reasonable but not excessively efficient internal systems of communication. But there are also some darker areas in which uncomfortable and emotionally charged memories are 'locked away' as in untidy drawers, store-rooms, or ill-kept filing systems. A sympathetic listener or, in more extreme cases, a therapist, may sometimes be needed in occasional emotional spring-cleanings of these.

Personality and its mechanisms for achieving adjustment were the subjects of the presidential address to the American Psychological Association by Ernest Hilgard (1948). In more recent years Professor Hilgard has been much concerned with rehabilitating the constructs of integration, disintegration, and dissociation of the personality (e.g. 1973a; 1977). It is in this context that he has asked the question, 'Why does the personality not fall to pieces more often?' (Hilgard 1982). This question is none the less

344

interesting in that he has tossed it by implication in my own direction, and is seeking some comment from me. Any attempt to answer – whether in terms of an unconscious, or within the integration–dissociation framework – leads to recognition of the diversity of concepts psychology has used about this basic issue. We have noted a variety of psychologies of the unconscious. From this standpoint Freud would consider ego strength as all-important: seeing the task of psychoanalysis as strengthening the ego so as better to cope with external reality, forces from the unconscious, and demands of the superego. Freud and McDougall were 'irrationalists' only in the very specific sense of recognizing the power of often irrational emotional forces in mental life. Both stood for such rationality as could be achieved: in Freud's case control by the 'reality principle' which guides the ego system. From Plato onwards we find similar formulations and a parallel between the healthy society and the mentally healthy personality. Ideally, in the state the embodiment of rationality, Plato's philosopher-king, should rule, and the parallel rational system should maintain dominance in the individual.

McDougall's conception of a stable personality relates his master sentiment to the attribute of persistence we associate with 'will'. For him the self-regarding sentiment expresses itself in the formulation '*I* felt tempted but *I* resisted it.' Conversely blows to self-respect reduce morale and thus tend to weaken the capacity for sustained action. An application of this theory can be found in the system of 'active psychotherapy' evolved by Hertzberg (1945). This involves setting the patient a series of tasks, from the emotionally easy to the emotionally difficult, to perform. Successful completion of each early task builds up morale and self-confidence, thus greater powers of volition to attempt and succeed in the later, difficult ones. This technique is widely used in modern behaviour therapy of the kind associated with leaders in this field like Eysenck, Wolpe, and Isaac Marks. When things seem to be falling apart an individual, like a whole society, may be said to be 'demoralized'. As McDougall and Hertzberg in different ways suggest, what is needed is an injection of positive self-feeling, namely morale or self-respect. Something needs to be done to strengthen the Freudian ego, McDougall's sentiment of self-regard, or whatever else we choose to call it. With severe internal conflict, rival ego systems may struggle for control, and in extreme cases result in multiple personality or other phenomena of dissociation like fugues and somnambulisms. In the schizophrenias this ego system is so weakened that functionally it is virtually non-existent: the anarchy that ensues is characterized by the autonomous functioning of an indefinite number of personality sub-systems.

Thouless (1951, first printed 1935) has argued that integration of the personality under McDougall's sentiment of self-regard is one among several alternatives. He points to the similiar function strong religious convictions may play. In his study of personality G. W. Allport (1938) examines six of the different values which may operate as integrating factors in ways resembling McDougall's master sentiment of self-regard. Allport's view of what he calls 'the mature personality' – presumably resistent to disintegration – involves three attributes. These are a variety of autonomous interests, a capacity for self-objectification involving 'insight', and a basic philosophy of life or value system. Another psychologist, the pioneer behaviourist J. B. Watson, himself no stranger to stress and personal disappointment, emphasizes the morale-enhancing qualities of what he calls 'balancing factors'. Within the realm of the stresses of political life we encounter a whole catalogue of balancing factors as varied as oil painting and bricklaying in one famous case, to golf-playing, music, and yachting in two rather lesser people. In the alternative terminology of the psychoanalysts we encounter the preferences different personalities have for alternative ego defences against internal conflict or external stress. Indeed one approach to personality differences is in terms of these preferences. Thus confronted with threat from outside, one individual may respond by identification with the aggressor, adopting defensive aggression of his own; another may project or rationalize; a third may deny, repress, and refuse to accept the threat as a reality.

Within a personality, as in competing groups in a society, we encounter sub-systems. Important among these, along with sentiments, are beliefs. Rigidity of belief may be an important factor in resisting psychiatric disturbance, but alternatively may also contribute to disintegration of the personality, when undermined or destroyed. An early study by Thouless showed how certainty of conviction is often closely associated with beliefs for which there is least evidence. One of the beliefs he studied was belief about 'whether there are tigers in China'. To be right or wrong about such an issue is not a matter of major emotional involvement as tends to be the case with beliefs about religion, politics, or other such issues. Rokeach (1960) has been interested in rigidity of the personality's beliefs, and relatedly in 'opinionation': rejection of those who don't share our own beliefs as stupid, ignorant, or vicious. In later work Rokeach (1968) distinguished different kinds of belief. His A-type beliefs are of a fundamental kind relating to such things as the consistency and reliability of the physical environment. Changes of some kinds of belief, type B, are difficult to achieve by mere education and may need psychotherapy. There are authority-determined beliefs, type C, in which discrediting of previously relied upon authorities may be a serious danger to mental health. There are others again – like the 'tigers in China' case – which exhibit minimal degrees of ego involvement. In the phrase used by Hilgard, the personality is unlikely 'to go to pieces' if they are disturbed. Retaining or abandoning a very different kind of belief may be emotionally all-important. Thus Koestler (1954) has written introspectively about the attractiveness of entry into a 'closed system' of belief – Soviet Communism of the period – and the ego defences used in maintaining confidence in it. Koestler goes on to argue that psychoanalysis is another instance of such a closed system of thinking. Sometimes it appears to be as when Freud, or some over-diligent disciple, seeks relentlessly to find the Oedipus Complex in an unlikely place, or perseverates about sexual aspects of motivation when other things may also be involved. But even 'orthodox' psychoanalysis is not necessarily at fault in this way when successful attempts have been made to establish linkages with other areas of psychology. Recognition of unconscious mental life seems, to me at least, compatible with development of psychology as a whole within the eclectic framework of a natural science.

A parallel between a stable society and stability of the individual personality which impressed Plato has interested many of his successors, like McDougall, Freud, and Mowrer with his 'walled city' analogy. We find it also in Joseph Butler (1729), who likened his ideal personality to a well-run school. Since there is harmony between the various component sub-systems, conscience or Butler's 'headmaster' can withdraw vigilance and absent himself for a time with an awareness that chaos will not ensue. Parallel issues about whether such a society will or will not 'fall apart' have interested social – and educational – psychologists. Thus as a social psychologist Ng (1980) examines and classifies the disruptions of groups: turmoils, conspiracies, strikes, riots, and civil warfare. Mowrer's view of coping with 'repressed' and rebelling sub-systems is by rehabilitation of these a few at a time, resulting in return to the stability of lawfulness. In the case of the personality, very relevant is Hilgard's own clear recognition of how the various mechanisms of the ego play a part not only in repression and self-deception, but also in making realistic social adjustments (Hilgard 1948). Among such coping mechanisms of the personality are introjection, isolation, and restriction of the ego.

Here as elsewhere – in Wittgenstein's words – the 'picture of the facts' that different thinkers have provided varies greatly. They differ in their constructs about what holds a personality or a society together, and prevents either from 'falling apart'. To take another illustration, in the final chapter of his major book, Kurt Koffka (1935) conceived of both the personality and the social group as a Gestalt. Both are integrated wholes, the functioning of whose parts is dependent on the nature of that whole. Gestalten differ in strength, that is, the extent to which such part-functioning is dependent on the whole. Thus some personalities are strong Gestalten, while in others the components are relatively autonomous. Such functioning with a measure of independence is not necessarily undesirable. As I have argued, one of the manifestations of 'insight' may be co-conscious awareness of the irrational aspects of our own mental life. Hilgard argues, there are many forms of normal 'dissociation' in everyday living. Many people are aware of this in their own hypnagogic imagery or upsurges of creative ideas from some system outside consciousness, and some experience it in atypical lucid dreams. Receptivity to the processes of inner mental life has, we have seen, often been assessed as a positive feature of the normal and adjusted personality. In these respects Freud, and to a greater extent Jung, taught a measure of trust towards the unconscious, and both added a dimension to the Delphic oracle's admonition 'Know thyself.'

Within psychology itself an equivalent to self-knowledge is to be found in an awareness of the limitations of the models we use, and prefer, in dealing with its subject matter.

COMMUNICATION: EXPLAINING AND TRANSLATING CONCEPTS

Psychology is, as I said in Chapter 1, concerned with communication about mental life. When a person asks a speaker to explain a statement, this request is for something other than mere repetition of the same words. Different words and perhaps a new analogy are invited: thus many different ones have been used in attempts to communicate about the schizophrenias. Breuer and Freud (1893–5) likewise used many alternative similes and metaphors in their early attempt to explain the relation of hysteria to the unconscious. Some of these led to a persisting temptation to imagery of a psychological underworld of depth and darkness. Some psychologists resisted, by acts of translation aided by different words and other analogies. One alternative formulation, dissociation, involved a spatial metaphor of 'splitting', but of a different kind from the 'disintegration' of schizophrenia. Bernard Hart (1939) rebelled against this usage, and suggested an alternative functional construct about dissociation as 'an affair of gearing'. This, he argued, better fitted the actual clinical facts. Throughout normal, abnormal, social, and developmental psychology we encounter a variety of words for often rather similar instances of experience and behaviour. Different schools of thought have had their preferred terminology, words that have sometimes become a rallying point of loyalty to their in-group. As a result three things have happened: similarities have been overlooked; differences have been exaggerated; and psychological understanding of mechanisms and phenomena often suffered.

Of special interest has been the frontier that divides or seems to divide the normal from the abnormal. In one area, subjective experience, that concerns us are many phenomena and mechanisms that simply lack known or widely accepted names. And sometimes, in the neologisms of a psychosis a patient has provided his own. For their part psychologists and psychiatrists have continued to invent new technical terms, or have extended the usages of existing ones. As I have indicated earlier, in the cases of synaesthesia and *déjà vu*, sub-types within an existing category can be specified and labelled. Despite all these activities, subjective experiences in their variety provide a challenge and for many it is difficult to provide an appropriate label. Consider a common phenomenon encountered in the drowsy state before sleep. While lying in bed one person finds himself still, in a sense, 'driving his car'; a woman who has been doing this during the day finds herself still 'playing tennis'; and for others in the pre-sleep state their games of chess or golf persist. What do we call this experience? Is it a 'kinaesthetic hallucination'; an 'eidetic image'; a 'perseveration' of the day's activities; some kind of 'illusion'; or perhaps a 'hypnagogic' or 'hypnopompic' image? If we choose hallucination, then hallucinating is a commonplace occurrence in normal mental life. If eidetic imagery, then such imagery is much more frequent than traditionally assessed. And if it is a hypnagogic experience then it suggests that motor imagery of this kind may be commoner than the visual or auditory types. By contrast with phenomena, consider mechanisms as subject matter for an excursion into psychological natural history: describing, naming, and classifying. Many ego defence mechanisms have been labelled by the psychoanalysts. In earlier pages I have suggested two more that might be added to the list: 'projective distortion', and the 'La Rochefoucauld' mechanism. Many areas of the subject await the attention of those prepared to accept the mental set of the psychologist naturalist.

But sometimes more than one name exists, though they are sealed off from one another by different – often mutually hostile – schools of thought. As in the process of therapy, the notion of linkage of ideas is again relevant within psychology, and some-times between psychology and other disciplines like psychiatry and anthropology. Although Koestler (1954) assessed psycho-analysis as a closed system of thought, sometimes it isn't: the 'some–all' antidote to this generalization can be applied. Consider, for example, a major theorist like Flugel (1934; 1945; 1955) who, as a practising Freudian psychoanalyst, was also a historian of psychology (Flugel 1933), and well acquainted with other areas of the subject. Those like myself who attended the late Professor Flugel's lectures were well aware of the broad perspective of his approach to theory within psychology. To take a contemporary example on this theory side, for a long time a group in London has been actively engaged in studying relations between Freudian and Jungian concepts. As regards therapy, the Sybil case of multiple personality was treated by Dr Wilbur, a leading investigator of dissociation, by relatively orthodox psychoanalysis (Schreiber 1975). The dogma that therapy should only be administered by medically trained practitioners – strongly opposed by Freud himself – has been largely overcome. Moreover, there are today in the United Kingdom numerous psychologist therapists. Some of these clinical psychologists use techniques developed from the experimental study of learning and conditioning, but also, when appropriate, others that derive from the concept of the unconscious.

To understand something fully is difficult. I suggest a principle, that comprehension and understanding of psychological phenomena and mechanisms relate directly to the ability to formulate the issues in alternative language. It seems to be inversely related to slavish adherence to rigid concepts, without the ability to say what one wishes to communicate in a different terminology. Language plays an important part in psychological understanding and within psychology itself there are many languages. As B. F. Skinner puts it, to know is largely to be able to talk about. His behaviourist predecessor, Watson, made the suggestion that what others called 'the unconscious' might alternatively be named 'the unverbalised'. Consider some examples of alternative uses of words. The 'traumatic experiences' of early childhood are phenomena of early learning, and a subsequent working through a transference involves extinguishing responses and a process of re-learning. Across the cultural differences that divide parts of Africa and Asia from Europe we can recognize affinities between spirit possession and dissociative phenomena resembling multiple personality. Although there are some obvious differences, the time losses of such multiple personalities may, we have seen, have much in common with the time discontinuity mechanism prominent in the schizophrenias. At different times, in different cultures, and within the preferred terminology of ways of thinking even within psychology, there are a variety of ways of labelling such phenomena. If we know more than one of these we may be closer to the goal of scientific understanding.

Within the constructs of psychoanalysis and its derivative systems we have an account of how an individual acquires the moral and intellectual standards of his or her personality. The process is one of introjection, and identification with emotionally significant individuals, especially from within the family. Sexual

351

identity is built up by a similar process of introjection. Social psychology has its alternative language, as in Bandura (1977) with his emphasis on observation of others, and 'modelling' from the personalities thus observed. Again, there is little if any difference between the Freudian introjection, and in Cantril (1941) the concept of introception of the social norms of a culture or sub-culture. This same social psychologist has provided a name I have used in stating one purpose of this book: establishing a frame of reference to abnormal mental life. In Cantril's own work on social psychology we have seen how important were the alternative frames of reference of different individuals, in a situation involving fear and panic (Cantril 1940), and in study of a variety of social movements (Cantril 1941). He might have used alternative constructs, just as Freud chose to draw largely on analogies from classical mythology. Others today use the language of information theory, and more recently explore vigorously analogies from computing technology. There is also a healthy intellectual interest today in similes, metaphors, and analogies as such. Writing of this, Allan Paivio makes a vivid contribution, declaring that 'metaphor is a solar eclipse.' He adds, it 'may block out the central stuff so you can see the subtle stuff better' (Paivio 1979: 169). Analogies have played an important part in scientific thinking, including psychological theory. In seeking to communicate about psychological phenomena, mechanisms, and principles we may understand better by seeking to re-formulate; critically evaluate fashions in analogy; and perhaps look for new ones.

ENVOI

As it happened, I began this book in draft on board a ship bound for the West Indies. It was a French ship, and everybody else on board spoke and thought in this language, for me a constant reminder of cultural diversity and of at least one other of the estimated 3,000–4,000 languages spoken today. Ways of classifying people were put to me on an earlier occasion when, on another ship, a fellow passenger remarked to me, 'Irrespective of race, colour, or creed – I hate everybody.' Fortunately, being an amiable and in fact tolerant person, he was joking. But conversely in psychology, as elsewhere in science, we should – and sometimes do – try to use and evaluate ideas irrespective of their authorship. Science seeks to be open to flow of information, in Wittgenstein's terms to alternative 'models', irrespective of any ways of categorizing human thinkers. Science is eclectic. Yet in its history, hostility to a given thinker has too often sealed off valuable sources of information; and loyalty to a school of thought has certainly been a barrier to progress within psychology. Partisan uses of different words for similar phenomena and processes have flourished in the history of this science. Moreover, many terms that imply abnormality invite translation into others that are meaningful within normal mental life. If we take account of these similarities we may even wonder if any hard core of residual 'abnormality' remains. I conclude with a reminder of the aim of this analysis, to explore linkages between ideas and some of these resemblances.

SUMMARY

1   In abnormal psychology the concept of unconscious mental life has been influential. Freud had his predecessors and successors. In relation to him, and them, a number of different psychologies of the unconscious are considered.

2   What often seems to be 'unconscious' is linkages between individual items of memory, or between sub-systems of the personality. Self-knowledge involves re-establishing such lost connections, and encouraging better intra-psychic communication. Moreover, instead of a single 'unconscious' perhaps we should consider the functioning of a number of different dissociated sub-systems.

3   Dissociation, in the tradition of Pierre Janet, William James, and Morton Prince, represents a view of mental life which differs in emphasis from psychoanalysis. Its re-consideration seems timely in view of current developments in both psychiatry – appearance of numerous cases of diagnosed multiple personality – and also in psychology, notably in the important work of Hilgard. Resistance to personality disintegration is considered in this context.

4   Emphasis has been given to the constructs of dissociation and personality sub-systems. There are many alternative ways of conceptualizing the problems of abnormal psychology. A stand is

taken in support of 'translation' between the concepts of different traditions of psychology. It is argued that comprehension of a problem is related to our being able to consider it in more than one language. Differences between rival schools are often verbal rather than real.

5   Many of the phenomena and mechanisms we have encountered are only seemingly 'abnormal'. Close equivalents are often to be found in well-adjusted human beings. There may be a residue, but a much smaller one than we often acknowledge. Thus the principles of psychology as a whole have much to teach us about 'abnormal psychology'.

BIBLIOGRAPHY

Where it has seemed historically important I cite below original date of publication; also to avoid, here or in the text, such citations as 'Freud 1984' or 'Hobbes 1987'.

Adler, A. (1932) *The Practice and Theory of Individual Psychology*, London: Kegan Paul.

Ahsen, A. (1965) *Eidetic Psychotherapy: a Short Introduction*, Lahore: NAI Matbooat.

Ahsen, A. (1968) *Basic Concepts in Eidetic Psychotherapy*, New York: Brandon House.

Ahsen, A. (1977) 'Eidetics: an overview', *Journal of Mental Imagery*, 1:1, 5–38.

Ahsen, A. (1984) *Rhea Complex: a Detour around Oedipus Complex*, New York: Brandon House.

Ahsen, A. (1986) 'New surrealist manifesto: interlocking sanity and insanity', *Journal of Mental Imagery*, 10:2, 1–32.

Ahsen, A. (1987) 'Principles of unvivid experience: the girdle of Aphrodite', *Journal of Mental Imagery*, 11:2, 1–52.

Alexander, P. (1983) *Svengali: George du Maurier's Trilby* (1894), first complete and unexpurgated edition, London: W. H. Allen

Allport, G. W. (1938) *Personality: a Psychological Interpretation*, London: Constable.

American Psychiatric Association (1980) *Diagnostic and Statistical Manual of Mental Disorders* (DSM III), Washington D.C.: American Psychiatric Association.

Anon. (1889) 'Recent experiments in crystal-vision', *Proceedings of the Society for Psychical Research*, 5, 486–521.

Archbold: *Criminal Pleading, Evidence and Practice in Criminal Cases*, 38th edition, Butler, T. R. F. and Mitchell, S. (eds) (1973) London: Sweet & Maxwell.

Ardis, J. A. and McKellar, P. (1956) 'Hypnagogic imagery and mescaline', *Journal of Mental Science*, 102, 22–9.

Arieti, S. (1951) 'Special logic of schizophrenia and other types of autistic thought'. In Hartley, E. L. (ed.) *Outside Readings in Psychology*, New York: Crowell.

Arieti, S. (ed.) (1959) *American Handbook of Psychiatry*, vols I–II, New York: Basic Books.

Arieti, S. (1966) 'Creativity and its cultivation', Ch. 44 in Arieti, S. (ed.) *American Handbook of Psychiatry*, vol. III, New York: Basic Books.

Arnold-Foster, M. (1921) *Studies in Dreams*, London: Allen & Unwin.

Aserinsky, E. and Kleitman, N. (1953) 'Regularly occurring periods of eye motility and concomitant phenomena during sleep', *Science*, 118, 273–4.

Bandura, A. (1977) 'Self-efficacy: towards a unifying theory of behavioural change', *Psychological Review*, 84, 191–215.

Bannister, D. (1966) 'Psychology as an exercise in paradox', *Bulletin of the British Psychological Society*, 19, 63.

Barber, T. X. (1970) *LSD, Marijuana, Yoga, and Hypnosis*, Chicago: Aldine Publishing Co.

Barber, T. X. (1984) 'A new look at hypnosis, cognitions, imagery, and the body–mind problem', Ch. 4, 69–127 in Sheikh, A. A. (ed.) *Imagination and Healing*, New York: Baywood.

Barber, T. X. and Wilson, S. C. (1978) 'The Barber suggestibility scale and the creative imagination scale: experimental and clinical applications', *American Journal of Clinical Hypnosis*, 21, 84–108.

Bartlett, F. C. (1932) *Remembering*, Cambridge: Cambridge University Press.

Bennett-Levy, J. and Marteau, T. (1980) 'Fear of animals', *British Journal of Psychology*, 75, 37–42.

Bernheim, H. (1900) 'Suggestive therapeutics: a treatise on the nature and uses of hypnosis', reprinted in Goshen, C. E. (ed.) (1967) *Documentary History of Psychiatry*, London: Vision Press.

Bettelheim, B. (1943) 'Individual and mass behaviour in extreme situations', *Journal of Abnormal and Social Psychology*, 38, 417–52.

Bexton. W. G., Heron, W., and Scott, T. H. (1954) 'Effects of decreased variation in the sensory environment', *Canadian Journal of Psychology*, 8, 70–6.

Binet, A. (1896) *Alterations of Personality*, translated by Galdwin, H., London: Chapman & Hall.

Bird, G. (1986) *William James*, London: Routledge & Kegan Paul.

Bleuler, E. (1911) *Dementia Praecox or the Group of Schizophrenias*, New York: International Universities Press, 1950.

Bliss, E. L. (1980) 'Multiple personality: a report of 14 cases with implications for schizophrenia and hysteria', *Archives of General Psychiatry*, 37, 1388–97.

Bliss, , E. L. (1984) 'Spontaneous self-hypnosis in multiple personality disorders', *Psychiatric Clinics of North America*, 7:1, 135–48.

Bliss, E. L. (1986) *Multiple Personality, Allied Disorders, and Hypnosis*, New York: Oxford University Press.

Boorstin, D. J. (1984) *The Discoverers: a History of Man's Search to Know his World and Himself*, London: Dent.

Boring, E. G. (1953) 'A history of introspection', *Psychological Bulletin*, 50, 169–89.

Bourguignon, E. (1973) *Religion, Altered States of Consciousness and Social Change*, Columbus, Ohio: Ohio State University Press.

Bradshaw, P. W. and McKellar, P. (1978) 'Exorcising the neurocracy, with garlic and the control group', paper presented at New Zealand Psychological Society Conference.

Braid, J. (1843) 'The rationale of nervous sleep', reprinted in Goshen, C. E. (ed.) (1967) *Documentary History of Psychiatry*, London: Vision Press.

Braun, B. G. (1984) Foreword to Symposium on Multiple Personality, *Psychiatric Clinics of North America*, 7:1, 1–2.

Breuer, J. and Freud, S. (1893–5) *Studies on Hysteria*, (1962) *Standard Edition of Complete Psychological Works of Sigmund Freud*, vol. 2, London: Hogarth.

Bridgman, P. W. (1927) *The Logic of Modern Physics*, London: Macmillan.

Broad, C. D. (1925) *The Mind and its Place in Nature*, London: Routledge & Kegan Paul.

Brosin, H. W. (1959) 'Psychiatric conditions following head injury', Ch. 57, 1175–1202 in Arieti, S. (ed.) *American Handbook of Psychiatry*, vol. II, New York: Basic Books.

Brown, K. M. (1976) 'The vèvè in Haitian voudou', unpub. doctoral thesis, Temple University, Philadelphia.

Brown, T. (1820) *Lectures on the Philosophy of the Human Mind*, London: Longmans.

Buchman, J. (1976) 'Hallucinogens', in Kraus, S. (ed.) *Encyclopaedic Handbook of Medical Psychology*, pp. 218–20, London: Butterworth.

Bugelski, B. R. with open peer commentary by 17 others (1982) 'Learning and imagery', *Journal of Mental Imagery*, 6:2, 1–22; 23–92.

Burt, C. (1937) *The Young Delinquent*, London: University of London Press.

Butler, J. (1729) *Sermons on human nature*, Gladstone, W. E. (ed.) (1897), Oxford: Clarenden Press.

Butler, T. R. F. and Mitchell, S. (eds) (1973) *Archbold: Criminal Pleading, Evidence and Practice in Criminal Cases*, 38th edition, London: Sweet & Maxwell.

Cantril, H. (1940) *The Invasion from Mars*, Princeton: Princeton University Press.

Cantril, H. (1941) *The Psychology of Social Movements*, New York: Wiley.

Cholden, L. (ed.) (1956) *Lysergic Acid Diethylamide and Mescaline in Experimental Psychiatry*, New York: Grune & Stratton.

Clark, J. R. (1976) 'Superstition, magic and ritual', in Kraus, S. (ed.) *Encyclopaedic Handbook of Medical Psychology*, London: Butterworth.

Clary, W. F., Burstin, K. J., and Carpenter, J. S. (1984) 'Multiple personality and borderline personality disorders', *Psychiatric Clinics of North America*, 7:1, 89–100.

357

Cleckley, H. (1955) *The Mask of Sanity*, St Louis: Mosby.

Cohen, J. (1964) *Behaviour in Uncertainty*, London: Allen & Unwin.

Collins, W. (1868) *The Moonstone*, London: Collins edition 1971.

Connolly, K. and McKellar, P. (1966) 'Forensic psychology', *Bulletin of the British Psychological Society*, 16: 51, 1–8.

Coons, P. M. (1984) 'The differential diagnosis of multiple personality', *Psychiatric Clinics of North America*, 7:1, 51–67.

Courmelles, F. (1891) *Hypnotism*, translated by Ensor, L., London: Routledge.

Craik, K. (1966) *The Nature of Psychology: a Selection of Papers, Essays and Other Writings by the late Kenneth J. W. Craik*, Sherwood, S. (ed.) Cambridge: Cambridge University Press.

Crow, T. J. (1980) 'Molecular pathology of schizophrenia. More than one disease process?' *British Medical Journal*, 280, 66–8.

Darwin, C. (1871) *The Expression of Emotion in Man and Animals*, 2nd edition, London: Murray.

Dostoevsky, F. M. (1880) *The Brothers Karamazov*, translated by Magarshack, D. (1982), Harmondsworth: Penguin; and by Garnett, C. (1912; reprinted 1968) London: Heinemann.

Dostoevsky, F. M. *The Notebooks for The Brothers Karamazov*, edited and translated by Wasiolek, E. (1971), Chicago and London: University of Chicago Press.

Drinkwater, J. (ed.) (1940) *The Outline of Literature*, London: Newnes.

Dubois, P. (1904) 'The psychic treatment of nervous disorders', translated by Jelliffe, S. E. and White, W. A., in Goshen, C. E. (ed.) (1967) *Documentary History of Psychiatry*, London: Vision Press.

Eban, M. (1974) *Exorcism, Past and Present*, London: Cassell.

Efran, E. H. (ed.) (1967) *Ethnopharmacologic Search for Psychoactive Drugs*, Washington D.C.: National Institute for Mental Health.

Ellenberger, H. F. (1970) *The Discovery of the Unconscious*, New York: Basic Books.

Ellis, H. (1897) 'A note on the phenomenon of mescal intoxication', *Lancet*, 1, 1540.

Esquirol, J. E. (1845) 'A treatise on insanity'. In Goshen, C. E. (ed.) (1967) *Documentary History of Psychiatry*, London: Vision Press.

Eysenck, H. J. (1947) *Dimensions of Personality*, London: Kegan Paul.

Eysenck, H. J. (1952) *The Scientific Study of Personality*, London: Routledge & Kegan Paul.

Eysenck, H. J. (1953) *Uses and Abuses of Psychology*, Harmondsworth: Penguin Books.

Eysenck, H. J. (1961) *Handbook of Abnormal Psychology*, New York: Basic Books.

Eysenck, H. J. (1983) 'Behaviourism, imagery and imagery therapy', *International Imagery Bulletin*, 1:1, 30–1.

Eysenck, H. J. and Furneaux, W. D. (1945) 'Primary and secondary suggestibility: an experimental and statistical study', *Journal of Experimental Psychology*, 35.

Fisman, M. (1975) 'The brain stem in psychosis', *British Journal of Psychiatry*, 126, 1414–22.

Flugel, J. C. (1933) *A Hundred Years of Psychology*, London: Macmillan.

Flugel, J. C. (1934) *Men and their Motives*, London: Kegan Paul.

Flugel, J. C. (1945) *Man, Morals and Society*, London: Duckworth.

Flugel, J. C. (1955) *Studies in Feeling and Desire*, London: Duckworth.

Frazer, J. (1911) *The Golden Bough: a Study in Magic and Religion*, 3rd edition, London: Macmillan.

Freud, A. (1936) *The Ego and the Mechanisms of Defence*, London: Hogarth.

Freud, S. (1894) *The Neuro-psychoses of Defence*, in Strachey, J. (ed.) (1962) *Standard Edition of Complete Psychological Works of Sigmund Freud*, vol. 3, London: Hogarth.

Freud, S. (1900) *The Interpretation of Dreams*, in Strachey, J. (ed.) (1953) *Standard Edition of Complete Psychological Works of Sigmund Freud*, vol. 4, London: Hogarth.

Freud, S. (1904) *The Psychopathology of Everyday Life*, in Strachey, J. (ed.) (1960) *Standard Edition of Complete Psychological Works of Sigmund Freud*, vol. 6, London: Hogarth.

Freud, S. (1907) *Delusions and Dreams in Jenson's 'Gradiva'*, in Strachey, J. (ed.) (1959) *Standard Edition of Complete Psychological Works of Sigmund Freud*, vol. 9, London: Hogarth.

Freud, S. (1923) *The Ego and the Id*, in Strachey, J. (ed.) (1955) *Standard Edition of Complete Psychological Works of Sigmund Freud*, vol. 19, London: Hogarth.

Fromm, E. (1947) *Man for Himself*, New York: Holt.

Galton, F. (1855) *The Art of Travel*, 6th edition, London: Murray, 1876.

Galton, F. (1883) *Inquiries into Human Faculty and its Development*, London: Macmillan.

Garwood, K. (1961) 'A psychological study of human fear', unpub. Ph.D. thesis, University of Sheffield.

Ghiselin, B. (ed.) (1955) *The Creative Process: a Symposium*, New York: New American Library.

Gilbert, G. M. (1948a) *Nuremberg Diary*, London: Eyre & Spottiswoode.

Gilbert, G. M. (1948b) 'Herman Goering, amiable psychopath', *Journal of Abnormal and Social Psychology*, 43, 211–29.

Gjessing, R. L. and Jenner, F. A. (1976) *Contributions to the Somatology of Periodic Catatonia*, Oxford: Pergamon Press.

Goffman, E. (1961) *Asylums*, New York: Doubleday.

Golding, W. (1962), in Meek, M., Warlow, A., and Barton, G. (eds) (1977) *The Cool Web: the Pattern of Children's Reading*, 226–40, London: Bodley Head.

Gombrich, E. H. (1954) 'Psychoanalysis and the history of art', *International Journal of Psychoanalysis*, 35:4, 401–11.

Gordon, R. (1962) *Stereotypy of Imagery and Belief as an Ego Defence*, London: Cambridge University Press.

Gordon, R. (1972) 'A very private world', in Sheehan, P. (ed.) *The Function and Nature of Imagery*, New York: Academic Press.

Gordon, R. (1984) 'Imagination as a mediator between inner and outer reality', *International Imagery Bulletin*, 2:1, 3–9.

Goshen, C. E. (ed.) (1967) *Documentary History of Psychiatry: a Source Book on Historical Principles*, London: Vision Press.

Granit, R. (1955) *Receptors and Sensory Perception*, New York: Hale University Press.

Green, C. (1968a) *Out of the Body Experiences*, Oxford: Institute of Psychophysical Research.

Green, C. (1968b) *Lucid Dreams*, Oxford: Institute of Psychophysical Research, edition 1982.

Green, C. and Leslie, W. (1987) 'The imagery of totally hallucinatory or "Metachoric" experiences', *Journal of Mental Imagery*, 11:2, 67–74.

Green, C. and McCreery, C. A. S. (1975) *Apparitions*, London: Hamish Hamilton.

Grinspoon, L. (1971) *Marijuana Reconsidered*, Cambridge, Mass.: Harvard University Press.

Groddeck, G. (1923) *The Book of the It*, London: Vision Press, 1949.

Grossmann, L. (1962) *Dostoevsky, a Biography* translated by Mackier, M., London: Allen Lane, 1974.

Harris, B. (1979) 'Whatever happened to little Albert?' *American Psychologist*, 34, 151–60.

Hart, B. (1936) *The Psychology of Insanity*, London: Cambridge University Press.

Hart, B. (1939) *Psychopathology*, London: Cambridge University Press.

Haward, L. R. C. (1961) 'Psychological evidence', *Journal of Forensic Science*, 2:1.

Hearne, K. M. T. (1981) 'A light switch phenomenon in lucid dreams', *Journal of Mental Imagery*, 5:2, 97–9.

Hearnshaw, L. S. (1987) *The Shaping of Modern Psychology*, London: Routledge & Kegan Paul.

Hebb, D. O. (1949) *The Organisation of Behaviour*, New York: Wiley.

Hebb, D. O. (1953) 'On human thought', *Canadian Journal of Psychology*, 7:3, 99–110.

Hebb, D. O. and Thompson, W. R. (1954) 'The social significance of animal studies', Ch. 15 in Lindzey, G. (ed.) *Handbook of Social Psychology*, Cambridge, Mass: Addison Wesley.

Hertzberg, A. (1945) *Active Psychotherapy*, London: Heinemann.

Highwater, J. (1976) *Indian America*, New York: Hodder & Stoughton.

Hilgard, E. R. (1940) 'Human motives and the concept of the self', *American Psychologist*, 4.

Hilgard, E. R. (1948) *Theories of Learning*, New York: Appleton Century.

Hilgard, E. R. (1973a) 'A neodissociation interpretation of pain reduction in hypnosis', *Psychological Review*, 80, 396–411.

Hilgard, E. R. (1973b) 'Dissociation revisited', in Henle, M., Jayner, J., and Sullivan, J. (eds) *Contributions to the History of Psychology*, New York: Springer.

Hilgard, E. R. (1977) *Divided Consciousness*, New York: Wiley.

Hilgard, E. R. (1982) Review of McKellar, P. 'Mindsplit: the psychology of multiple personality and the dissociated self', *Journal of Mental Imagery*, 6, 187–90.

Hilgard, E. R. and Hilgard, J. R. (1975) *Hypnosis and the Relief of Pain*, Los Altos: Kaufmann.

Hobbes, T. (1651) *Leviathan*, London: Bohn, 1836.

Hoffer, A., Osmond, H. and Smythies, J. (1954) 'Schizophrenia – a new approach: results of a year's research', *Journal of Mental Science*, 100:14, 29–45.

Holt, E. B. (1931) *Animal Drive and the Learning Process*, New York: Holt.

Holt, R. R. (1964) 'Imagery: the return of the ostracized', *American Psychologist*, 19, 254–64.

Horney, K. (1950) *Neurosis and Human Growth*, New York: Norton.

Horowitz, M. J. (1934) *Image Formation and Psychotherapy*, revised edition. New York and London: Aronson, 1983.

Howells, J. G. (1965) *Modern Perspectives in Child Psychiatry*, Edinburgh: Oliver & Boyd.

Hull, C. L. (1933) *Hypnosis and Suggestibility*, New York and London: Appleton.

Hunter, I. M. L. (1957) *Memory*, Harmondsworth: Penguin Books, edition 1964.

Hunter, R. and MacAlpine, I. (1963) *Three Hundred Years of Psychiatry, 1535–1860*, London: Oxford University Press.

Hurlock, R. and Burnstein, A. (1932) 'The imaginary playmate', *Journal of Genetic Psychology*, 41.

Jaffe, J. H. (1965) 'Drug addiction and drug abuse', in Goodman, L. S. and Gilman, A. (eds) *The Pharmacological Basis of Therapeutics*, London: Macmillan.

James, W. (1890) *Principles of Psychology*, London: Macmillan.

Janet, P. (1899). 'Treatise on applied therapeutics: psychological treatment of hysteria', reprinted in (1967) Goschen, C. E. (ed.) *Documentary History of Psychiatry*, London: Vision Press.

Janet, P. (1901) *The Mental State of Hysterics*, vol. II in Robinson, D. N. (ed.) (1977) *Significant Contributions to the History of Psychology, 1750–1920*, Washington D.C.: University Publishers of America.

Jaynes, J. (1976) *The Origin of Consciousness in the Breakdown of the Bicameral Mind*, Harmondsworth: Penguin Books, 1982.

Jeffery, R. (1964) 'The psychologist as an expert witness on the issue of insanity', *American Psychologist*, 19.

Jenner, F. A. (1970) 'Biological rhythms in psychiatry', *Clinical Trials Journal*, 7, 1–13.

Jenner, F. A. and Damas-Mora, J. (to appear 1989) 'Philosophical reflections and neurobiological studies of some periodic psychoses', in *Festschrift in Honour of Professor Hatotani*.

Jones, E. (1961) *The Life and Work of Sigmund Freud*, New York: Basic Books.

Jones, E. H. (1919) *The Road to Endor*, London: Pan Books, 1955.

Jones, M. C. (1924) 'A laboratory study of fear: the case of Peter', *Pedagogical Seminar*, 31, 308–15.

Jung, C. G. (1940) *The Integration of the Personality*, translated by Dell, S., London: Kegan Paul.

Jung, C. G. (1953) *The Collected Works of C. G. Jung*, London: Routledge & Kegan Paul.

Jung, C. G. (1961) *Memories, Dreams, Reflections*, ed. Jaffé, A., London: Collins and Routledge & Kegan Paul, 1963.

Kafka, F. (1925) *The Trial*, translated by Muir, W. and E., London: Secker and Warburg, 1983.

Kalupahana, D. J. (1987) *The Principles of Buddhist Psychology*, Albany: State University of New York Press.

Katzner, K. (1986) *The Languages of the World*, London: Routledge & Kegan Paul.

Kelly, G. A. (1955) *The Psychology of Personal Constructs*, vols 1 and 2, New York: Norton.

Kelly, G. A. (1958) 'Man's construction of his alternatives', Ch. 2, 33–64, in Lindzay, G. (ed.) *Assessment of Human Motives*, New York: Rinehart.

Kington, M. (1982) 'In praise of useless information', 133–6, in Kington, M., *Miles and Miles*, London: Hamish Hamilton.

Kisker, G. W. (1972) *The Disorganised Personality*, 2nd edition, New York: McGraw-Hill.

Kleitman, N. (1939) *Sleep and Wakefulness*, enlarged edition, Chicago: Chicago University Press, 1963.

Kluft, R. P. (1984) 'Treatment of multiple personality disorder: a study of 33 cases', *Psychiatric Clinics of North America*, 7:1, 9–29.

Klüver, H. (1928) *Mescal: the Divine Plant and its Psychological Effects*, London: Kegan Paul.

Klüver, H. (1942) 'Mechanisms of hallucination', in Bernreuter. (ed.) *Studies in Personality in Honour of Lewis M. Terman*, New York: McGraw-Hill.

Koestler, A. (1954) *Arrow in the Blue: an Autobiography*, London: Collins and Hamilton.

Koffka, K. (1935) *Principles of Gestalt Psychology*, London: Kegan Paul.

Kris, E. (1951) 'On preconscious mental processes', in Rapaport, D. *Organisation and Pathology of Thought*, New York: Columbia University Press, pp. 474–93.

Ladd, G. T. (1892) 'Contributions to the psychology of visual dreams', *Mind*, new series, 1, 299–304.

Langfeldt, G. (1976) 'Schizophrenic states', pp. 495–6, in Kraus, S. (ed.) *Encyclopaedic Handbook of Medical Psychology*, London: Butterworth.

Laver, J. (1942) *Nostradamus*, Harmondsworth: Penguin Books.

Lea, A. J. (1955) 'Adrenochrome as the cause of schizophrenia: investigations of some deductions from this hypothesis', *Journal of Mental Science*, 101, 538–47.

Leaning, F. E. (1925) 'An introductory study of hypnagogic phenomena', *Proceedings of the Society for Psychical Research*, 35, 289–403.

Low, D. (1956) *Low's Autobiography*, London: Michael Joseph.

Lowes, J. L. (1927) *The Road to Xanadu: a Study in the Ways of the Imagination*, London: Constable.

Lund, F. H. (1930) 'Why do we weep?' *Journal of Social Psychology*, 1, 136–51.

Luria, A. R. (1968) *The Mind of a Mnemonist*, New York: Basic Books.

Luria, A. R. (1979) *The Making of a Mind: a Personal Account of Soviet Psychology*, Cambridge, Mass.: Harvard University Press.

McCreery, C. (1973) *Psychical Phenomena and the Physical World*, London: Hamish Hamilton.

MacDonald, J. M. (1961) *The Murderer and his Victim*, Springfield, Ill.: Thomas.

McDougall, W. (1923) *An Outline of Psychology*, London: Methuen.

McDougall, W. (1926) *An Outline of Abnormal Psychology*, London: Methuen.

McDougall, W. (1939) *The Group Mind*, Cambridge: Cambridge University Press.

McKellar, P. (1950) 'Provocation to anger in the development of attitudes of hostility', *British Journal of Psychology*, 40:3, 104–14.

McKellar, P. (1952) 'Responsibility for the Nazi policy of extermination', *Journal of Social Psychology*, 34, 153–63.

McKellar, P. (1957) *Imagination and Thinking: a Psychological Analysis*, London: Cohen & West; New York: Basic Books.

McKellar, P. (1962) 'The method of introspection', in Scher, J. (ed.) *Theories of the Mind*, 619–44, New York: The Free Press of Glencoe; London: Macmillan.

McKellar, P. (1963a) 'Three aspects of the psychology of originality in human thinking', *British Journal of Aesthetics*, 3:2, 129–47.

McKellar, P. (1963b) 'Mescaline and human thinking', *Proceedings of Quarterly Meeting of Royal Medico-Psychological Association, Feb. 1961*, 12–15, London: Lewis.

McKellar, P. (1965a) 'Thinking, remembering and imagining', Ch. 7, 170–91, in Howells, J. G. (ed.) *Modern Perspectives in Child Psychiatry*, Edinburgh: Oliver & Boyd.

McKellar, P. (1965b) 'The investigation of mental images', in Barnett, S. A. and McLaren, A. (eds) *Penguin Science Survey*, B (Biological Sciences), Harmondsworth: Penguin Books.

McKellar, P. (1968) *Experience and Behaviour*, Harmondsworth: Penguin Books.

McKellar, P. (1971) 'Emotion and the patient: a psychologist's view,' *New Zealand Dental Journal*, 66, 331–8.

McKellar, P. (1975) 'Twixt waking and sleeping', *Psychology Today*, European edition, 4, 20–24.

McKellar, P. (1977a) 'Autonomy, imagery and dissociation', *Journal of Mental Imagery*, 1:1, 93–108.

McKellar, P. (1977b) 'The origins of violence', Ch. 1, 14–27, in Kerr, M. G. (ed.) *Violence: the Community and the Administrator*, Wellington: New Zealand Institute of Public Administration.

McKellar, P. (1979a) 'Between wakefulness and sleep: hypnagogic fantasy', Ch. 12, 189–97, in Sheikh, A. A. and Shaffer, J. (eds) *The Potential of Fantasy and Imagination*, New York: Brandon House.

McKellar, P. (1979b) *Mindsplit: the Psychology of Multiple Personality and the Dissociated Self*, London: Dent.

McKellar, P. (1986) 'Imagery and the unconscious', Ch. 2, 47–71, in Marks, D. (ed.) *Theories of Image Formation*, New York: Brandon House.

McKellar, P. (1987a) 'Coleridge, the imaged albatross, and others', *Journal of Mental Imagery*, 11, 113–24.

McKellar, P. (1987b) 'Co-conscious reflection: dissociation and imagery psychology', *Journal of Mental Imagery*, 11:3.

McKellar, P. (1988) 'Surrealism, co-consciousness, and imagery', *Journal of Mental Imagery*.

McKellar, P. and Simpson, L. (1954) 'Between wakefulness and sleep: hypnagogic imagery', *British Journal of Psychology*, 45:4, 266–76.

McKellar, P. and Tonn, H. (1967) 'Negative hallucination, dissociation and the five stamps experiment', *British Journal of Social Psychiatry*, 1:4, 260–70.

MacLaine, S. (1986) *Dancing in the Light*, London: Bantam Books.

Mace, C. A. (1950) 'Introspection and analysis', in Black, M. (ed.) *Philosophical Analysis*, New York: Cornell University Press.

Marks, D. (1972) 'Individual differences in the vividness of visual imagery and their effect on function', in Sheehan, P. W. (ed.) *The Function and Nature of Imagery*, New York: Academic Press.

Marks, D. (1973) 'Visual imagery differences and the recall of pictures', *British Journal of Psychology*, 64, 17–24.

Marks, D. (1986a) 'The neuropsychology of imagery', Ch. 9, 225–41, in Marks, D. (ed.) *Theories of Image Formations*, New York: Brandon House.

Marks, D. (1986b) 'Imagery, consciousness and the brain', pp. 152–7, in Russell, D. G., Marks, D., and Richardson, J. (eds) *Proceedings of Second International Imagery Conference, Swansea, Wales*, Dunedin, N. Z.: Human Performance Associates.

Marks, D. (1986c) *Theories of Image Formation*, New York: Brandon House.

Marks, D. and Kammann, R. (1977) 'The non-psychic powers of Uri Geller', *Zetetic*, 1:2, 9–17.

Marks, D. and Kammann, R. (1980) *The Psychology of the Psychic*, Buffalo, N.Y.: Prometheus Books.

Marks, D. and McKellar, P. (1982) 'The nature and function of eidetic imagery', *Journal of Mental Imagery*, 6:1, 1–28; 100–24.

Marks, I. (1976) 'Phobic states, treatment of', 386–95, in Krauss, S. (ed.) *Encyclopaedic Handbook of Medical Psychology*, London: Butterworth.

Maslow, A. H. (1948) 'Cognition of the particular and the generic', *Psychological Review*, 55, 22–40.

Mason, H. (1986) 'A crushing blow to friendship'. *Observer*, 17 August: 41.

Mavromatis, A. (1987) *Hypnagogia: the Unique State of Consciousness between Wakefulness and Sleep*, London: Routledge & Kegan Paul.

Mayer-Gross, W. (1951) 'Experimental psychoses and other mental abnormalities provided by drugs', *British Medical Journal*, 11 August.

Mayer-Gross, W., Slater, E., and Roth, M. (1954) *Clinical Psychiatry*, London: Cassell.

Meek, M., Warlow, A., and Barton, G. (eds) *The Cobweb: The Pattern of Children's Reading*, London: The Bodley Head.

Menninger, K. (1942) *Man Against Himself*, New York: Harcourt Brace.

Menninger, K. (1946) *The Human Mind*, New York: Knopf.

Métraux, A. (1972) *Voodoo in Haiti*, London: Deutsch.

Milgram, S. (1974) *Obedience to Authority*, New York: Harper & Row.

Miller, G. (1956) 'The magic number seven, plus or minus two: some limits on our capacity for processing information', *Psychological Review*, 63, 81–97.

Mintz, A. (1948) 'Schizophrenic speech and sleepy speech', *Journal of Abnormal and Social Psychology*, 43, 548–9.

Mitchell, S. W. (1896) 'Remarks on the effects of anhalonium lewinii (the mescal button)', *British Medical Journal*, 2, 1625–8.

Moody, R. (1975) *Life after Life*, Atlanta, Georgia: Mockingbird Press.

Moore, W. G. (1961) *La Rochefoucauld, his Mind and Art*, London: Oxford University Press.

Morgan, W. P. (1978) 'The mind of the marathon runner', *Psychology Today*, European edition, 4:6, 26–30.

Mowrer, O. H. (1950) *Learning Theory and Personality Dynamics*, New York: Ronald Press.

Mullan, B. (1987) *The Enid Blyton Story*, London: Boxtree.

Müller, J. (1848) *The Physiology of the Senses*, London: Taylor, Walton & Maberly.

Murray, H. A. (1938) *Explorations in Personality*, London: Oxford University Press.

Murray, H. A. (1943) *Thematic Apperception Test and Instruction Manual*, Cambridge, Mass.: Harvard University Press.

Muslin, H. L. (1981) 'King Lear: images of the self in old age', *Journal of Mental Imagery*, 5:1, 143–56.

Myers, F. W. H. (1904) *Human Personality and its Survival after Death*, London: Longmans Green.

Myers, O. H. (1957) 'Images in the mind', *Journal of the American Society for Psychical Research*, 51, 62–73.

Naranjo, C. (1987) 'Ayahuasca imagery and the therapeutic properties of the harmala alkaloids', *Journal of Mental Imagery*, 11:2, 131–6.

Nemiah, J. C. (1975) 'Hysterical neurosis, dissociation type', in Freeman, H. J., Kaplin, H. I., and Sadock, B. J. (eds) *Comprehensive Textbook of Psychiatry*, 2nd edition, Baltimore: Williams & Wilkins.

Neppe, V. M. (1983) *The Psychology of Déjà Vu*, Johannesburg: Witwatersrand University Press.

Ng, S. H. (1980) *The Social Psychology of Power*, London: Academic Press.

Nietzsche, F. (1886) *Beyond Good and Evil*, translated by Kaufmann, W., New York: Vintage Books, 1966.

Nixon, A. J. (1977) 'Whose violence?' Ch. 7, 133–45, in Kerr, M. G. (ed.) *Violence: the Community and the Administrator*, Wellington: New Zealand Institute of Public Administration.

Orne, M. (1959) 'The nature of hypnosis: artefact and essence', *Journal of Abnormal and Social Psychology*, 58, 277–99.

Orne, M. (1962) 'On the social psychology of the psychological experiment: with particular reference to demand characteristics and their implications', *American Psychologist*, 17, 776–83.

Orne, M. T. (1973) 'Communication by the total experimental situation: why it is important, how it is evaluated, and its significance for the ecological validity of findings', in Pliner, P., Krams, I., and Alloway, T. (eds) *Communication and Affect*, New York: Academic Press.

Orne, M. T. (1977) 'Construct of hypnosis: implications of the definition for research and practice', *Annals of the New York Academy of Science*, 296, 14–33.

Orne, M. T. and Evans, F. J. (1965) 'Social control in the psychological experiment: anti-social behaviour and hypnosis', *Journal of Personality and Social Psychology*, 1, 189–200.

Osmond, H. and Smythies, J. (1952) 'Schizophrenia: a new approach', *Journal of Mental Science*, 98, 411–20.

Overend, K. (1977) *Tiger on a String*, St Ives, Cornwall: United Writers.

Overholser, W. (1959). 'Major principles of forensic psychiatry', Ch. 95 in Arieti, S. (ed.) *American Handbook of Psychiatry*, vol. 2, 1888–1901, New York: Basic Books.

Owens, A. C. (1963) 'A study of mental imagery', unpublished Ph.D. thesis, University of Liverpool.

Paivio, A. (1979) 'Psychological procession: the comprehension of metaphor' in Ortony, A. (ed.) *Metaphor and Thought*, London: Cambridge University Press.

Parry, M. H. (1968) *Aggression on the Road*, London: Tavistock.

Pear, T. H. (1922) 'Contribution to Symposium on "The relations of complex and sentiment", Manchester', *British Journal of Psychology*, 1.

Piaget, J. (1926) *Language and Thought of the Child*, London: Kegan Paul.

Pines, M. (1978) 'Invisible playmates', *Psychology Today*, 12: 4, 28–38.

Potter, J. (1983) *Good King Richard? An Account of Richard III and his Reputation, 1483–1983*, London: Constable.

Prentiss, D. W. and Morgan, F. P. (1895) 'Anhalonium lewinii (mescal buttons). A study of the drug with especial reference to its physiological actions upon man, with report of experiments', *Therapeutic Gazette*, 11, 9.

Prince, H. M. (1901) 'The development and genealogy of the Misses Beauchamp', in N. G. Hale and Morton Prince (eds) (1975) *Psychotherapy and Multiple Personality: Selected Essays*, Cambridge, Mass.: Harvard University Press.

Prince, H. M. (1905) *The Dissociation of a Personality*, Rycroft, C. (ed.) London: Oxford University Press, 1978.

Prince, H. M. (1929) *The Unconscious*, New York: Macmillan.

Rapaport, D. (1951) *Organisation and Pathology of Thought*, New York: Columbia University Press.

Rawcliffe, D. H. (1959) *Illusions and Delusions of the Supernatural and the Occult*, New York: Dover.

Read, G. D. (1948) *Revelation of Childbirth*, London: Heinemann.

Reed, G. (1972) *The Psychology of Anomalous Experience*, London: Hutchinson.

Reik, T. (1949) *The Inner Experience of a Psychoanalyst*, London: Allen & Unwin.

Richardson, A. (1977) 'Verbalizer-visualizer: a cognitive style dimension', *Journal of Mental Imagery*, 1:1, 109–26.

Richardson, J., Mavromatis, S. A., Mindel, T., and Owens, A. C. (1981) 'Individual differences in hypnagogic and hypnopompic imagery', *Journal of Mental Imagery*, 5, 91–6.

Rivers, W. H. R. (1920) *Instinct and the Unconscious*, Cambridge: Cambridge University Press.

Rivers, W. H. R. (1923) *Conflict and Dream*, London: Kegan Paul.

Robinson, D. N. (1976) *An Intellectual History of Psychology*, London: Macmillan.

Rochefoucauld, F., Duc de la, *Maxims of La Rochefoucauld*, posthumous text and translation, Pratt, K. (ed.) (1931), London: Haworth.

Rokeach, M. (1960) *The Open and Closed Mind*, New York: Basic Books.

Rokeach, M. (1968) *Beliefs, Attitudes and Values*. San Francisco: Jossey-Bass.

Rosenhan, D. L. (1973) 'On being sane in insane places', *Science*, 179, 250–8.

Rosenzweig, S. S. (1944) 'The picture association method and its applications in the study of reactions to frustration', in Hunt, J. McV. (ed.) *Personality and the Behaviour Disorders*, New York: Ronald.

Ross, W. D. (1930) *The Right and the Good*, Oxford: Viking Press.

Rossman, M. L. (1984) 'Imagine health: imagery in medical self care', Ch. 10, 231–58, in Sheikh, A. A. (ed.) *Imagination and Healing*, Framington, N.Y.: Baywood.

Rothenberg, A. (1979) *The Emerging Goddess: the Creative Process in Art, Science and Other Fields*, Chicago: Chicago University Press.

Rowland, L. W. (1939) 'Will hypnotized persons try to harm themselves or others?' *Journal of Abnormal and Social Psychology*, 34, 114–17.

Russell, D. G., Marks, D., and Richardson, J. (eds) (1986) *Proceedings of the Second International Imagery Conference, Swansea, Wales*, Dunedin, N.Z.: Human Performance Associates.

Saint Denys, Hervey de (1867) *Dreams and How to Guide Them*, translated and edited by Schatzman, M., London: Duckworth, 1982.

Savage, C. (1952) 'Lysergic acid diethylamide (LSD–25): a clinical psychological study', *American Journal of Psychology*, 108:2.

Schacter, D. L. (1976) 'The hypnagogic state: a critical review of the literature', *Psychological Bulletin*, 83:3, 452–81.

Schopenhauer, A. (1897) *Essays on Human Nature*, posthumous, London: Sonnenschen.

Schreiber, F. R. (1975) *Sybil*, Harmondsworth: Penguin Books.

Schultes, R. E. (1966) 'The search for new natural hallucinogens', *Lloydia*, 29, 293–308.

Seidman, L. J. (1983) 'Schizophrenia and brain disfunction: an integration of recent neurodiagnostic findings, *Psychological Bulletin*, 94:2, 195–238.

Serpell, J. (1986) *In the Company of Animals*, London: Blackwell.

Shand, A. F. (1920) *The Foundations of Character*, London: Macmillan.

Shand, A. F. (1922) 'Contribution to Symposium on "The relations of complex and sentiment", Manchester', *British Journal of Psychology*, 1.

Sharpe, E. F. (1937) *Dream Analysis*, London: Hogarth.

Sheehan, P. W. (ed.) (1972) *The Function and Nature of Imagery*, New York: Academic Press.

Sheikh, A. A. (ed.) (1984) *Imagination and Healing*, Farmingdale, N.Y.: Baywood Publishing Co.

Sherif, M. and Cantril, H. (1947) *The Psychology of Ego Involvements*, New York: Wiley.

Sidgwick, H. (1894) 'Report on the census of hallucinations', *Proceedings of the Society for Psychical Research*, 10, 25–422.

Sidis, B. and Goodhart, S. P. (1905) *Multiple Personality*, New York: Appleton.

Silberer, H. (1909) 'Report on a method of eliciting and observing certain symbolic hallucination phenomena', in Rapaport, D. (ed.) (1951) *Organisation and Pathology of Thought*, New York: Columbia University Press.

Simpson, L. and McKellar, P. (1955) 'Types of synaesthesia', *Journal of Mental Science*, 100:422, 141–7.

Singer, J. (1966) *Daydreaming: an Introduction to the Experimental Study of Inner Experience*, New York: Random House.

Skinner, B. F. (1953) *Science and Human Behaviour*, New York: Macmillan.

Skinner, B. F. (1957) *Verbal Behaviour*, New York: Appleton Century.

Skinner, B. F. (1972) *Beyond Freedom and Dignity*, London: Jonathan Cape.

Spearman, C. (1922) *The Nature of Intelligence and the Principles of Cognition*, London: Macmillan.

Spearman, C. (1930) *Creative Mind*, London: Nisbet.

Spiegel, D. (1984) 'Multiple personality as a post-traumatic stress disorder', *Psychiatric Clinics of North America*, 7:1, 101–9.

Steinberg, H. (1956) 'Abnormal behaviour induced by nitrous oxide', *British Journal of Psychology*, 47:3, 183–94.

Stekel, W. (1951) 'The polyphony of thought', in Rapaport, D. (ed.) *Organisation and Pathology of Thought*, New York: Columbia University Press.

Stengel, E. (1951) 'Classification in mental disorders', *Bulletin of the World Health Organization*, 21.

Stoney, B. (1974) *Enid Blyton, a Biography*, London: Hodder & Stoughton.

Sullivan, H. S. (1953) *The Interpersonal Theory of Psychiatry*, London: Norton.

Sullivan, H. S. (1954) *The Psychiatric Interview*, New York: Norton.

Sutcliffe, J. P. (1961) '"Credulous" and "skeptical" views of hypnotic phenomena: experiments on anaesthesia, hallucination, and delusion', *Journal of Abnormal and Social Psychology*, 62, 189–200.

Sutherland, E. H. (1937) *The Professional Thief*, Chicago: Crowell.

Suttie, I. D. (1935) *The Origins of Love and Hate*, London: Kegan Paul, reprinted 1945.

Taylor, A. L. (1952) *The White Knight: a Study of C. L. Dodgson*, Edinburgh: Oliver & Boyd.

Taylor, W. S. and Martin, W. F. (1944) 'Multiple personality', *Journal of Abnormal and Social Psychology*, 39, 281–300.

Thigpen, C. H. and Cleckley, H. (1954) 'A case of multiple personality', *Journal of Abnormal and Social Psychology*, 49, 135–51.

Thompson, J. (1980) *Crime Scientist*, London: Harrap.

Thouless, R. H. (1935) *General and Social Psychology*, 3rd edition, London: University Tutorial Press, 1951.

Thurstone, L. L. (1952) *Applications of Psychology*, New York: Harper.

Tong, J. E. (1958) 'Stress reactivity and its relation to disordered behaviour in mental defective subjects', unpublished Ph.D. thesis, University of Sheffield.

Torry, E. F. and Peterson, M. R. (1976) 'The viral hypothesis of schizophrenia', *Schizophrenia Bulletin*, 2, 136–46.

Tuke, D. H. (1892) 'The McNaghten Rule', in Tuke, D. H. *Dictionary of Psychological Medicine*, reprinted in Goshen, C. E. (1967) *Documentary History of Psychiatry*, London: Vision Press.

Ullman, L. P. and Krasner, L. (1975) *A Psychological Approach to Abnormal Behaviour*, second edition, New Jersey: Prentice-Hall.

Van Eeden F. (1913) 'A study of dreams', reprinted in Tart, C. T. (ed.) (1969) *Altered States of Consciousness*, New York: Wiley.

Veith, I. (1965) *Hysteria: the History of a Disease*, Chicago: Chicago University Press.

Ward, C. (1983) 'Imagery, dissociation and mental health: a cross-cultural perspective', *International Imagery Bulletin*, 1:1, 19–20.

Ward, C. (1985) 'Scientific methodology and experiential approaches to the study of mental imagery', *Journal of Mental Imagery*, 9:2, 113–25.

Ward, R. H. (1957) *A Drug-taker's Notes*, London: Gollancz.

Warner, R. (1985) *Recovery from Schizophrenia*, London: Routledge & Kegan Paul.

Warren, H. C. (1934) *Dictionary of Psychology*, New York: Houghton Mifflin.

Watkins, J. G. and Watkins, H. H. (1984) 'Hazards to the therapist in the treatment of multiple personalities', *Psychiatric Clinics of North America*, 7:1, 111–19.

Watson, J. B. (1919) *Psychology from the Standpoint of a Behaviourist*, New York: Lippincott.

Watson, J. B. (1928) *The Ways of Behaviourism*, New York: Harper.

Watson, J. B. and Rayner, R. (1920) 'Conditioned emotional reactions', *Journal of Experimental Psychology*, 3, 1–14.

Wigoder, D. (1987) *Images of Destruction*, London: Routledge & Kegan Paul.

Wilbur, C. (1984) 'Multiple personality and child abuse', *Psychiatric Clinics of North America*, 7:1, 3–7.

Wilson, I. (1981) *Mind out of Time: Reincarnation Claims Investigated*, London: Gollancz.

Wolpe, J. (1958) *Psychotherapy by Reciprocal Inhibition*, Stanford: Stanford University Press.

Woolley, D. W. and Shaw, E. (1954) 'Some neurophysiological aspects of serotonin', *British Medical Journal*, 17 July, 122–6.

Yates, F. (1966) *The Art of Memory*, Chicago: University of Chicago Press.

Yellowlees, H. (1932) *Clinical Lectures on Psychological Medicine*, London: Churchill.

Young, P. C. (1952) 'Antisocial uses of hypnosis', in McCron, L. M. (ed.) *Experimental Hypnosis*, 376–409, New York: Macmillan.

Zimbardo, P. C. (1972) 'Pathology of prisons', *Society*, 9:4, 4–8.

Zusne, L. (1983) 'Imagery as magic, magic as natural science', *International Imagery Bulletin*, 1, 28–9.

Zusne, L. and Jones, H. W. (1982) *Anomalistic Psychology*, Hillsdale, N.J.: Lawrence Erlbaum.

INDEX